FRENCH DEPARTMENT
COLLEGE OF ST. MARY OF THE SPRINGS

THE MODERN LANGUAGE ASSOCIATION OF AMERICA

MONOGRAPH SERIES

ARTHURIAN LEGENDS IN MEDIEVAL ART

Approved for publication in the Monograph Series of the Modern Language Association of America.

CHRISTIAN GAUSS
JAMES H. HANFORD
E. C. ROEDDER
ROBERT K. ROOT
A. G. SOLALINDE

Committee of Award

Published in part under a grant awarded by the American Council of Learned Societies from a fund provided by the Carnegie Corporation of New York.

1. The First Kiss of Lancelot and Guinevere (vol. I, f. 67).

2. Lancelot at the Tomb of Galehaut (vol. II, f. 185).

PROSE LANCELOT MANUSCRIPT.

Formerly Yates Thompson and Cortlandt F. Bishop Collections.

Arthurian Legends in Medieval Art

ROGER SHERMAN LOOMIS

Columbia University

PART II IN COLLABORATION WITH

LAURA HIBBARD LOOMIS

Wellesley College

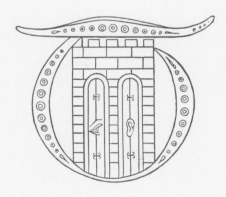

LONDON: OXFORD UNIVERSITY PRESS

MODERN LANGUAGE ASSOCIATION OF AMERICA

NEW YORK: MCMXXXVIII

• DESIGNED AND PRINTED BY
GEORGE BANTA PUBLISHING COMPANY, MENASHA, WISCONSIN, U. S. A.

Full-Tone Collotype Plates by Meriden Gravure Company
Meriden, Connecticut, U.S.A.
Colored Frontispiece by Walker Engraving Company, New York City, U. S. A.

Dedicated to

ARTHUR KINGSLEY PORTER

and

LUCY KINGSLEY PORTER

PREFACE

THIS study was first begun in 1911 when the author of Part I was a student at Oxford as a beneficiary of the Rhodes Trust. The further collection of materials has in recent years been facilitated by grants from Columbia University, the Frick Art Reference Library, and the American Council of Learned Societies. For all these benefactions the authors make grateful acknowledgment. They wish to thank also the many who have rendered assistance, often invaluable, in the prosecution of the study and the gathering of photographs: Professor Myrtilla Avery, Professor Adriaan Barnouw, Mr. Bernard Berenson, Professor Dino Bigongiari, Professor Louis Cons, Mr. Frederick Coykendall, Miss A. M. Draak, Mr. T. Fitzroy Fenwick, Miss Margaret Freeman, Professor Adolph Goldschmidt, Miss Belle Da Costa Green, Professor Jacob Hammer, Mr. R. L. Hobson, Dr. Edward Hodnett, Mr. William M. Ivins Jr., Mr. Mitchell Kennerley, Professor William W. Lawrence, Professor Ezio Levi, Dr. Millard Meiss, Dr. Jean Misrahi, Mrs. Cecilia Mackinnon Pearson, Dr. Bernard Rackham, Mr. James Rorimer, Dr. Marvin Ross, Miss Margaret Scherer, Dr. Eleanor P. Spencer, Fräulein Erna Suadicani, M. Emile-A. Van Moe. In addition to these the authors would also recall those who will not now see this belated acknowledgment of their help: the late Edmund G. Gardner, J. R. Holliday, Raimond Koechlin, W. R. Lethaby, and Raimond Van Marle.

The authors owe a special debt to Professor Walter W. S. Cook for generous counsel; to Professor Percy W. Long for his interest and practical assistance; to the American Council of Learned Societies and the Modern Language Association for financing publication; to the late Kingsley Porter and to Mrs. Lucy Porter for unfailing friendship, help, and inspiration.

We have not included a list of illustrations in the belief that the reader will find the index an easier method of reference than a list of 420 figures.

CONTENTS

ARTHURIAN LEGENDS IN MEDIEVAL ART

CHAPTER I

INTRODUCTION—THE STUDY OF ARTHURIAN ICONOGRAPHY

HEADING the page on which Richard de Fournival begins his fantastic work *Le Bestiaire d'Amour*, in a MS at the Bibliothèque Nationale (Fr. 412, f. 228), is a miniature representing a strange tower, here reproduced on the title-page. On one door is painted a human eye; on the other, a human ear.[1] The author explains at length that his book is concerned with the nature of beasts and birds, which are better realized when painted than when described. God has given to man the two doors of the eye and the ear, through which enters all the knowledge with which his memory is stored. "When one sees a picture either of Troy or some other thing, one sees the feats of the worthies who were of old even as if they were present... When one hears a romance read, one perceives the adventures as if they were in his presence." Thus does Richard urge the somewhat obvious but oft neglected truism that in the re-creation of the past, the imagination needs not only verbal but also visual assistance. It is not enough to hear a romance of Troy; one must see it illustrated. Our medieval ancestors, whenever they could afford it, had the pages of their books filled as it were with little windows through which the reader could behold "les fes [faits] des preudomes," as well as comprehend them through the written word.

We of the twentieth century who read the romances of the Middle Ages need some such help if we are to perceive imaginatively what the authors wished us to see, or at least what their contemporaries saw with the mind's eye. The Troy town or Caerleon or Constantinople envisaged by medieval poets are not to be reconstructed from Schliemann or Dr. Wheeler or Dr. Barnette Miller; they can be realized only from medieval miniatures and tapestries. The classical student has long recognized the intimate bond between the literary and the representative arts, and reproductions of painted vases and sculptured marbles have been almost as familiar to him as his myths, epics, and dramas. They have not only filled his imagination with something like a faithful vision of what literature narrated and described, but also taught him much concerning oral tradition. Classicists have learned that at least before the fourth century B.C. the artist was "never an illustrator of Homer or any other writer"; that he may have derived suggestions directly or indirectly from written sources, "but he did not therefore feel bound to adhere to his text."[2] In fact, myths and traditions unrecorded in literature have been preserved only on the painted clay or the carven marble. Classical literary scholarship has from its inception in the Renaissance found archeology a valuable ally.

THE NEGLECT OF MEDIEVAL SECULAR ART

Medieval literary scholarship has a much shorter history, and has been comparatively slow in understanding the illustrative and complementary value of art, especially of secular art. During the nineteenth century there were men who seemed familiar with both fields, such as Thomas Wright and Alwin Schultz; but they were the exceptions. Among connoisseurs of medieval art there was little knowledge of its secular side, and even less of the secular literature which it illustrated. Today, though things have changed immensely for the better, it is still possible for a standard English work on tapestries to go into a second edition containing a translation from a French inventory which is wrong on every possible word, and reveals that the author has not looked up the most obvious literary source for the tapestry in question. The Bayeux embroidery, which has received excellent treatment from historians,[3] still awaits a thorough treatment by a judicious art specialist, who can at the same time handle the highly significant linguistic and literary evidence.[4] Literary scholars since the beginning of this century have shown a steadily increasing acquaintance with medieval secular art and have produced in France, Germany, and Sweden good illustrated histories of medieval literature, but nothing satisfactory of this kind has come out of England or America.

What has been the reason for this comparative neglect of profane iconography by students both of medieval letters and medieval arts? In all likelihood the main reason is the rarity and, to be candid, the inferiority of secular art in this period as contrasted with the art of the Church. Even the most casual tourist in Europe sees in every church and almost every gallery and museum he visits the persons of

---

[1] R. de Fournival, *Bestiaire d'amour* (P., 1880), p. 1.

[2] H. B. Walters, *History of Ancient Pottery* (L., 1905), II, 3. Cf. Ernest Gardner, *Poet and Artist in Greece* (L., 1933); *Philologische Untersuchungen*, V (1881); Pausanias, *Description of Greece*, ed. J. G. Frazer (L., 1898), V, 365–395; *Neue Jahrbücher f. das Klassische Altertum*, VII (1901), 385.

[3] Freeman, *Norman Conquest* (1869), III, 563. *Monthly Review*, XVII (1904), Dec., 109. H. Prentout, *Études sur quelques points d'histoire de Normandie* (Caen, 1926), p. 51. *Revue des cours et conférences* (1922), 15 mai, p. 200; 31 mai, p. 310.

[4] E. du Méril, *Études sur quelques points d'archéologie et d'histoire littéraire* (P., 1862), 384–426. *Romania*, LX (1934), 1, 153.

the Trinity, the drama of salvation, patriarchs and prophets, devils and angels, saints and their martyrdoms, St. Peter at the gate of the Paradise, and the yawning mouth of Hell. From the period before 1500 he may likewise see in the way of secular art a few Flemish portraits and Italian battle-pieces and scenes from classical mythology. But the chances are, he would never glimpse the Bayeux embroidery or the frescoes at Runkelstein and La Manta, discover the misericords of English cathedrals or distinguish at Chartres the Charlemagne window. Medieval art illustrative of secular literature has to be searched for, and when found is rarely of the highest order.

The Church was throughout the Middle Ages the chief patron of the arts, and the subjects prescribed for the adornment of ecclesiastical buildings were for the most part sacred. To be sure, there were exceptions, such as the Bayeux embroidery (commissioned probably by Bishop Odo and his vassals for his cathedral), the misericords which lurk in the darkness of many choirs,[5] the tiles prepared for (and probably at) Chertsey Abbey, the costly mural paintings of the Trojan war which in the twelfth century, according to Hugues de Fouilloi,[6] adorned the palaces of bishops. But in general the vast wealth which the Church expended on the decorative arts went very properly to the illustration of sacred dogma and history. It is safe to say that until the thirteenth century the laity spent little on the arts. Figure sculpture, stained glass, and mosaics were rare in secular buildings. Not until the fourteenth century was well advanced did historiated books on strictly profane subjects vie in splendor with the finest service books. The conclusion is inevitable that the actual production of profane art in the Middle Ages ran far behind that of religious art in both quantity and quality.

More than that, secular art has been subjected far more drastically to the ravages of Time. Much of it was executed in such perishable media as fresco, embroidery, and tapestry, which require careful preservation; some of it was enameled or engraved on precious metals, which went promptly to the melting pot when the owner felt the need of cash. Moreover, churches and monastic buildings, despite the Reformation and the Puritan regime, the French Revolution and the onslaughts of our industrial civilization, have not been repeatedly and systematically destroyed on the same scale as medieval castles, nor have they changed hands so frequently. Few were the castles, palaces, manors, and town-houses of the nobility which between 1100 and 1700 were not pillaged or wrecked once in a century; many, of course, were completely and finally razed. Few, comparatively speaking, were the remaining movable ob-

jects which through change of ownership or through change in fashion did not find their way sooner or later to the scrap-heap. So the embroideries, paintings, enamels, and MSS of the laity vanished from their repositories or from the earth itself more rapidly than religious art, which found a securer shelter in churches and monasteries. Thus is to be explained the comparative scarcity of medieval art illustrative of secular literature. This scarcity in turn accounts for the comparative neglect which until recent times secular iconography has suffered at the hands of medievalists.

Of all the realms of secular art none is more alluring to research than the illustrations of the Round Table cycle. To see that adventurous fellowship with the eye of illuminator, ivory-carver, embroidress, or mural painter is no common delight. To be sure, when we survey what is left today of medieval iconography concerned with Arthur and his knights, we discover no work of supreme genius, and we have no historic record of any. That such existed, we may well believe. The twelfth and thirteenth centuries could not have passed away without leaving on the walls of some French, English, or Italian palace an artistic counterpart to the literary power of the *Mort Artu* or Gottfried's *Tristan*. Yet there is still much work of the second rank. The Modena archivolt, the Chertsey tile pavement, the tryst scene at S. Floret, the miniatures of the *Poire*, the Yates Thompson *Lancelot*, the *Estoire del S. Graal-Merlin* (Fr. 95) at the Bibliothèque Nationale, are minor masterpieces.

THE HISTORY OF ARTHURIAN ICONOGRAPHIC STUDY

The study of Arthurian iconography has an interesting history, which may be sketched in a few pages. Barring possible oversight, the first person to have an Arthurian miniature copied as a matter of antiquarian and artistic interest was one Claude du Moulinet, who in the seventeenth century compiled a catalog in MS of the library of the Abbey of Ste. Geneviève (now MS. 965, Bibl. de Ste. Geneviève, Paris).[7] On p. 16 he writes: "A volume of the history of the high deeds (*prouesses*) of the knights of the Table Round, and of the romance of King Arthur of England, who was chief thereof, adorned with many rather beautiful miniatures, of which I have had some drawn." Two outline drawings in ink follow, evidently based on miniatures of the mid-fifteenth century. On the next page another Arthurian MS is listed, with the note: "The miniatures are very Gothic and of little interest (*fort gothiques et peu considérables*)." Was this comment inspired simply by

---

[5] Francis Bond, *Woodcarvings in English Churches, Misericords* (L., 1910).

[6] *Romania*, XLII (1913), p. 84. *Mélanges Bémont* (P., 1913), p. 105. Migne, *Pat. Lat.*, CLXXVI, col. 1019.

[7] *Revue des bibliothèques*, XVIII (1908), 143–145.

the same spirit of neo-classic condescension which led Addison to write in 1694 of Chaucer, "In vain he jests in his unpolish'd strain/And tries to make his readers laugh in vain," or were the miniatures really botches? At all events, Moulinet was so little interested in even the better miniatures as related to literature that he gave no indication of subject.

In the year 1730 a new edition of Dugdale's *Warwickshire* mentioned briefly a late fresco in the hall of Tamworth Castle of Sir Lancelot de Lake and Sir Tarquin.[8] But so little value was attached to the painting, the only painting of Arthurian romance in England of which we have record, that it was whitewashed over in 1783.

In 1753 Levesque de la Ravalière published in the *Histoire de l'Académie des Inscriptions et Belles Lettres* a fourteenth-century ivory casket, but though he realized that the carved panels had some connection with chivalric literature, he metaphorically threw up his hands at the prospect of identifying the subjects. "Since these compositions are numerous and of fatiguing length, it would be assuming a task even more thankless than tedious, to read and compare them in order to discover the sculptor's source. Such a discovery would require almost the courage of a knight of old."[9] Considering that in Levesque's time most of Arthurian romance remained in MS or black letter only and that there was not a clue which might guide him to one book rather than another, one can sympathize with his difficulties and admire his candor. But rather than leave the reader completely in the lurch, he concocted a romance to fit the ivory reliefs. There was certainly no connected story to account for the scenes, and the one scene which surely had a literary source had been boldly modified by the carver's fancy.[10]

Another casket from the Parisian workshops in ivory, belonging to a group of which several have survived, was published by John Carter in 1787, but it was not till a hundred years later than Antoniewicz gave the correct identification of five Arthurian scenes,[11] and even he failed to identify Galahad receiving the key of the Castle of Maidens. In 1835 Michel published the Tristram casket now at Leningrad.[12]

The first engravings of Arthurian miniatures appeared in Willemin's *Monuments français inédits* in 1839. Lady Guest in 1849 illustrated *Peredur* with the reproduction of a miniature from Chrétien de Troyes's *Conte del Graal*.[13] In the same year appeared the first colored reproduction, when Mithoff illustrated Wienhausen embroidery I. Though the sculpture at Modena had been mentioned and the name "Artus de Britania" [sic] had been set down by Vedriani as early as 1662,[14] it was not until 1845 that Borghi made the plausible guess that Winlogee was Guinevere and Mardoc Mordred,[15] and not till 1898 that Foerster brought the matter to the general attention of scholars and pointed out that the subject of the sculpture was related to the story of Caradoc of the Dolorous Tower.[16]

Despite these sporadic publications up to the year 1850, there was very little understanding of the themes and no general comprehensive effort to collect material. Paulin Paris in 1868 expressed himself with Gallic pungency on the situation when he remarked apropos of the sculpture at Bourges of Tristram's rendezvous:[17]

If only the artist had reproduced a subject from Greek or Egyptian mythology, our antiquaries would long since have explained it; but since the medieval artist committed the crime of resorting to a French romance, to a scene from our ancient French poetry, everyone misunderstood it, because such things have become for us so much Hebrew, or worse than Hebrew.

This situation in French scholarship Paulin Paris and his son, Gaston, worked indefatigably and successfully to remedy. In 1870 E. Hucher in a provincial journal made the first attempt to list illustrations of the Tristram legend.[18] This was followed up by Professor Golther in 1907[19] and by the present writer in 1916 and 1919,[20] in an effort to which there seems to be no end.

In 1895 the first comprehensive survey of secular art in the later Middle Ages was made by that great scholar, Julius von Schlosser.[21] The twentieth century has not been lacking in feeble and inaccurate work in the general field, but it can boast, besides many excellent isolated studies, such as those of Panzer and Von der Leyen, fine comprehensive work such as that of Frau Betty Kurth on Ger-

[8] Vol. II, p. 1138. The painting was probably done between 1554 and 1576, and represented two knights of gigantic size jousting. Cf. *Birmingham and Midland Archaeological Institute* (1878–79), p. 60; C. F. Palmer, *History of the Town and Castle of Tamworth* (1845), pp. 368, 417; *Gentleman's Magazine*, LIV (1784), 501.

[9] *Histoire de l'Académie Royale des Inscriptions et Belles Lettres*, XVIII (1753), 323.

[10] Cf. infra p. 72, Fig. 142.

[11] *Romanische Forschungen*, V, 241.

[12] F. X. Michel, *Tristan* (P.), I, lxxii ff.

[13] C. Guest, *Mabinogion* (L., 1849), I, opp. p. 386.

[14] L. Vedriani, *Raccolta de' pittori, scultori, et architetti Modonesi* (Modena), p. 19.

[15] *Il duomo ossia cenni storici e descrittivi della cattedrale di Modena* (Modena), pp. 68–76.

[16] *Zeits. für Romanische Philologie*, XXII, 243, 526.

[17] *Mémoires de la Soc. des Antiquaires du Centre*, II, 14.

[18] *Bulletin de la Soc. d'Agriculture, Science, et Arts de la Sarthe*, Ser. 2, XX, 633.

[19] Golther, *Tristan u. Isolde in den Dichtungen des Mittelalters* (Leipzig), 408–412.

[20] *University of Illinois, Studies in Language and Literature*, 1916. "Illustrations of Medieval Romance," 9–13. *Romanic Review*, VIII (1919), 197, n. 6.

[21] *Jahrbuch der Kunsthist. Sammlungen des Allerhöchsten Kaiserhauses*, XVI (1895), 156 ff.

man tapestries, Kohlhausen on *Minnekästchen*, Koechlin on French Gothic ivories, and Van Marle's volumes on "l'iconographie profane."[22]

The growth of interest in medieval *objets d'art* not only added to our knowledge of the genuine article, but also added a few counterfeit specimens. Two illustrations of Tristram's Tryst beneath the Tree are strongly suspect,—one an ivory mirror-back formerly in the Spitzer collection and now in the Hamburg Museum,[23] the other a wooden comb in the British Museum, which is a replica of the Bamberg comb.[24] Koechlin was also suspicious of the lid of the Tristram casket and of the whole *Folie Tristan* casket, both at Leningrad,[25] though in the latter instance his doubts seem unjustified.[26] Besides these forgeries a considerable number of genuine works have been hastily and wrongly connected with the Arthurian cycle: a series of mural paintings at Bobberröhrsdorf in Silesia has been mistakenly connected with Ivain;[27] an ivory mirror-back at the Mayer Museum, Liverpool, though long accepted as depicting Lancelot's abduction of Guinevere, actually represents the departure from the Castle of Love;[28] the famous first kiss of these lovers is suggested, though without adequate grounds, as one of the subjects on a carved casket at Freiburg in Breisgau.[29] Lacroix, with his capacity for blundering, illustrates and describes what he calls a book-cover with a scene representing Merlin and Viviane, which as a matter of fact is part of an enameled casket and has no connection with the wizard or his love.[30] The miniatures reproduced in Enlart's *Manuel d'archéologie*, III, as coming from a *Lancelot* MS in the Arsenal Library, Paris, actually derive from a *Renaud de Montauban*. More than one eminent scholar has yielded to the temptation to add to the long list of mistaken Tristram identifications.[31] On the other hand, it is possible that the Bobber-

röhrsdorf murals just mentioned may depict some other Arthurian romance than *Ivain*, and there is in the Wessenbergsammlung at Constance a line-drawing from some lost painting which certainly suggests a scene from romance. At the left a squire with long hair holds up over his chest a tunic. Next stands a young knight with a sword girt at his side, wearing chausses and skirt of mail, but apparently without mail protection for trunk and arms. Next a knight completely armed rides a caparisoned horse toward a table at which a king, a queen, and a courtier are seated. A very odd feature is a cloth draped back from this knight's left shoulder and suspended as it were from a toy parachute! At the right of the picture we have the incomplete figure of a knight riding away. The period seems to be early fourteenth century, but the subject is mysterious.

THE SCOPE AND ARRANGEMENT
OF THIS BOOK

This book endeavors not only to exclude counterfeit and mistaken illustrations of Arthurian romance, but also to give a conspectus of Arthurian iconography up to the year 1500 as complete as it can reasonably be made. Since there is no agreement as to when the Middle Ages ended, the wholly arbitrary date when incunabula ceased to be incunabula and became just plain books seems as good as any, and the stroke of midnight, December 31, 1499, has been adopted as a terminus. The completeness of the survey has necessarily been limited in certain ways. Omniscience alone can determine how many illustrations of the Round Table legend remain to be discovered under a coat of whitewash or in some provincial museum or in an art-dealer's shop, and only Fortunatus' purse and at least a lifetime of patience

[22] Panzer, "Dichtung und Bildende Kunst des Deutschen Mittelalters in ihren Wechselbeziehungen," *Neue Jahrbücher für das Klassische Altertum*, XIII (1904), 135. F. von der Leyen, "Deutsche Dichtung und Bildende Kunst im Mittelalter," in *Abhandlungen zur Deutschen Literaturgeschichte Franz Muncker zum 60 Geburtstag Dargebracht* (Munich, 1916). B. Kurth, *Die Deutschen Bildteppiche des Mittelalters* (Vienna, 1926). H. Kohlhausen, *Minnekästchen des Mittelalters* (Berlin, 1928). R. Koechlin, *Ivoires gothiques* (P., 1924).

[23] E. Molinier, *Hist. gén. des arts appliquées*, I, pl. 29. Koechlin, *op. cit.*, II, 386.

[24] Cf. infra p. 68.

[25] Koechlin, *op. cit.*, I, 517, 518, n. 1.

[26] *Pantheon*, I (1928), 80.

[27] *Mitteilungen der Schlesischen Gesellschaft f. Volkskunde*, XX (1918), 72.

[28] Koechlin, *op. cit.*, II, No. 1105. *Amer. J. of Archaeology*, Ser. 2, XXIII (1919), 259.

[29] A. Goldschmidt, *Elfenbeinskulpturen aus der Romanischen Zeit*, IV (Berlin, 1926), 59.

[30] Lacroix, *Sciences et lettres au Moyen Age*, ed. 2 (P., 1877), p. 422.

[31] Murals, Palazzo Teri (destroyed), Florence, Gabrici and

Levi, *Lo Steri di Palermo* (Milan, Rome), p. 102; *Gaz. d. beaux arts*, Ser. 4, VI, 235. Photographs from copies in the Frick Art Reference Library, N. Y., show love scenes without distinctive features. Mirror, Bargello, Florence, Gabrici and Levi, *op. cit.*, fig. 64. Comb, Bargello, Florence, *ibid.*, fig. 62; Suchier and Birch-Hirschfeld, *Geschichte der Franz. Lit.*, ed. 1913, I, 117. Cf. Koechlin, *op. cit.*, II, No. 1148. Mural (destroyed), Haus zur Kunkel, Constance, *Mitteilungen der Antiquarischen Gesellschaft in Zürich*, XV, 228; cf. infra p. 74. Tapestry at Langensalza, A. Schultz, *Deutsches Leben im XIV u. XV Jahrhundert* (Vienna, 1892), I, 91. Misericord at Bristol, *Journal of Architectural, Archaeological, and Hist. Soc. for County and City of Chester*, N.S., V (1895), 52. Probably confused with that at Lincoln. Trivulzio saddle, R. Forrer, *Tristan et Yseult sur un coffret inédit* (extract from *Cahiers d'archéologie et d'histoire d'Alsace*, fasc. XXIV, XXV), fig. 47. Westminster tile, *Proceedings of Brit. Acad.*, XIII (1927), 149. Stained glass, Bourges Museum, C. Enlart, *Manuel d'archéologie, archit. civ.*, ed. 1, I, 144. Sculpture at S. Pierre, Caen, R. de Lasteyrie, *L'archit. rel. en France à l'époque gothique* (P., 1927), II, 288. Choir stall in Schnütgen Museum, Cologne, F. Witte, *Tausend Jahre Deutscher Kunst am Rhein* (Berlin, 1932), I, 96. All eleven have been investigated and can be pronounced wrongly identified.

would serve to discover and reproduce every minia-ture from an Arthurian MS, every woodcut from in-cunabula, and every illustration of Arthur among the Nine Worthies. Nor would such a vast and unwieldy library of illustrations be worth making. It is noto-rious that there is a certain sameness in the adven-tures of the companions of the Round Table, and the defect is even more noticeable in the MS illustration of their adventures. There are literally hundreds of insignificant combats of a Sagremor or an Espinogres, of battles with Saxon or other paynim chiefs, of ban-quets, Pentecostal or otherwise, represented often with charm, but with an inevitable monotony. Ob-viously selection has been both necessary and desir-able, and in Part II miniatures have been chosen for comment and reproduction for one or more of the following reasons: (1) artistic excellence; (2) rarity as illustrations of an important text, such as Geoffrey of Monmouth's *Historia*, Chrétien's *Erec*, or *Gawain and the Green Knight*; (3) importance of the scene il-lustrated; (4) interest as pictures of medieval life; (5) datability. There are twenty dated Arthurian MSS noted on pp. 87f.; in the chronological confusion found at times even in recent works *points d'appui* may be welcome. The MS material reproduced and discussed, though frankly selective, covers three cen-turies and represents at least five schools of illumina-tion and many different romances. Manuscripts iden-tified as having once belonged in medieval libraries are noted as a further means of tracing their geo-graphical distribution and possible influence.

Outside the illuminated MSS, selection has been neither necessary nor desirable, and in Part I every-thing known to the author has been recorded, and everything has been illustrated with a few exceptions: (1) cases of close imitation of the same pattern, such as we find in some French ivories and English miseri-cords; (2) Arthur among the Nine Worthies. Since within these groups we should find a monotony simi-lar to that sometimes prevailing among the minia-tures, the treatment is correspondingly cursory and selective. With these reservations, this book offers a corpus of Arthurian iconography in the Middle Ages.

The nature of the subject has made it impossible to find a single principle of classification. The art stu-dent would naturally like to see the material dis-cussed and classified according to the materials, forms, and schools of art. The student of letters would with equal justice prefer to find the material grouped according to the branches of the legend. A compromise has been adopted, based on the following fact. The illustrations outside the MSS are so scat-tered in time, provenance, and form that they do not fit into any ordered, coherent scheme of artistic de-velopment. They do not furnish enough material to make possible a study of sculpture or painting; and far less of ivory carving or tile design, since really

only two very limited groups of ivories and one set of tile designs exist for Arthurian iconography. These materials lend themselves most readily to arrange-ment by subject. On the other hand, the miniatures fall into schools, whose artistic development can in most cases be traced. That development would be completely lost if the MSS were to be arranged ac-cording to the heroes or branches of the cycle which they celebrated. A complete MS of that vast com-posite known as the Vulgate cycle would have to be treated in separate sections devoted to Arthur and Merlin, Lancelot, and the Grail respectively. The result would be dire confusion so far as the artistic side of the illuminated MSS was concerned. Clearly, then, the miniatures must be handled by schools.

The compromise adopted has been this. Part I, ex-cept for the first chapter, is divided into chapters con-cerned with one or several heroes. Within those chapters is found an account of all illustrations out-side of books connected with a central figure, arranged approximately in the order of their produc-tion. Thus in one chapter are brought together illus-trations of the person and the adventures of King Arthur; another chapter deals with illustrations of the earlier versions of the Tristram legend; another chapter with illustrations of the *Prose Tristan* and its redactions and continuations; the next with several knights, Lancelot, Gawain, and so on. In this part the illustrations which lie outside of books—sculp-tures, embroideries, wall-paintings, etc.—will be handled and what is known of their provenance and date, as well as their subject matter, will be set forth. Thus the reader primarily interested in the literary aspect will find all the adventures of a romance hero illustrated in the decorative arts grouped together; and the amateur of the arts, it is hoped, will not be wholly disappointed. Part II is devoted to book illus-tration (miniatures and woodcuts), and since here it is possible to make a study of the evolution of the art and since the problems of identification of subject are of minor importance, the material is classified by the chief schools of miniature painting represented in Arthurian MSS: French, Italian, Flemish, German. A few Spanish miniatures are treated in Chapter VIII; a few English miniatures in Chapter XII. The last chapter is devoted to the woodcut and painted incunabula. The chronological arrangement within the chapters renders feasible a tracing of the evolu-tion of secular miniature in various lands.

Thus it is hoped that the student of medieval ro-mance will find his major interests satisfied with Part I, and the student of the arts will find within Part I a treatment of such matters as concern him regard-ing paintings, ivories, enamels, and so forth, while in Part II he will be able to follow through the develop-ment of the one form of Arthurian illustration which survives in sufficient quantity to make possible an artistic study. In the reproductions the non-manuscript material comes first, arranged as in Part I according to the dominant figures of the cycle, and the miniatures follow, arranged according to schools, and finally the woodcuts. This classification doubtless has its defects, but no better way to satisfy the demands of two distinct classes of readers has suggested itself. The index and cross-references within the text should make it easy for every reader to find what he wants.

That these hundreds of examples of medieval secular illustration should have interest for the student of literature who is concerned with something more than mere words should be equally obvious. Here is evidence as to the spread of the legend, its fascination for lords and ladies from Palermo and Valencia to Chester and Lübeck. Lost forms of the legend are reflected in an archivolt at Modena, a mosaic at Otranto, and the Forrer casket at Strasbourg. The Chertsey tiles, the Wienhausen and Erfurt embroideries, the Sicilian quilts, the S. Floret painting of the Tryst beneath the Tree, and the Bamberg comb, all fill out our information about once current versions of the Tristram romance. It becomes pretty clear that though it is the fashion to pooh-pooh lost versions, that fashion must be reshaped to accord with the facts. Not that every variation from a text means a "lost version"; the miniatures too often depart from the very words which accompany them to render such an inference necessary. Sometimes designers must have read a book in substantially the form we have it but felt no obligation to adhere in all respects to its indications; as a result they produced at haphazard various novelties. But when a Sicilian quilt combines the indications of different surviving texts, then the existence of a lost source becomes a probability; when it introduces a scene essentially different from anything recited in the texts, then we must postulate, as classical archeologists have long readily granted in their own field, that the Arthurian traditions which have come down to us in writing do not tell the whole story.

The Development of the Arthurian Legend

What do we know about the early history of this tradition? Between 1174 and 1179 Alanus de Insulis in his *Prophetia Anglicana Merlini Ambrosii Britanni* wrote the following extraordinary statement:[32]

What place is there within the bounds of the empire of Christendom to which has not extended the winged praise of Arthur the Briton? Who is there, I ask, who does not speak of Arthur the Briton, since he is but little less known to the peoples of Asia than to the Britons, as we are informed by our palmers who return from the countries of the East? The Easterns speak of him, as do the Westerns, though separated by the breadth of the whole earth. Egypt speaks of him, and the Bosphorus is not silent. Rome, the queen of cities, sings his deeds, and his wars are not unknown to her former rival Carthage. Antioch, Armenia, and Palestine celebrate his acts.

There is certainly here some rhetorical exaggeration, for it is almost unthinkable that the fame of Arthur extended beyond the bounds of Christendom. But Alanus could not have imposed too far upon the credulity of his learned readers, and there are facts to prove that he did not. As we shall presently see, an Arthurian scene was carved at Modena in the Po valley early in the twelfth century, and in 1165 Arthur's figure was laid in mosaic at Otranto in the heel of Italy, along with such old-timers as Alexander the Great and Noah. Early in the thirteenth century is recorded the legend that the British king was still alive and held court in the mountain fastnesses of Etna.[33] In 1223 knights of the kingdom of Cyprus masqueraded as knights of the Round Table.[34] Though knowledge of the Arthurian legend in Sicily and Cyprus is not attested until the thirteenth century, we may well believe that it had been familiar long before. In the opposite corner of Europe the Icelandic monk Gunnlaug Leifsson translated Geoffrey of Monmouth's *Prophetia Merlini* probably before the year 1200.[35] Alanus' hyperbolic phrases about the geographic extent of Arthur's fame seem therefore to be not so remote from the truth. His glory had reached the bounds of Christendom, and was spoken of in the eastern and western extremities of Europe.

It is one of the marvels of literary history that an obscure British battle-leader of about the year 500 should suddenly have become during the twelfth century the central figure of a brilliant and fascinating legend, developed and spread largely through the agency of the French, who would not seem to have had the slightest motive for resurrecting and celebrating this alien hero. Though the origins of Arthurian romance are still the subject of vigorous debate, there are some points on which nearly all scholars agree.[36] Arthur is first mentioned in extant literature about 826 by a Welshman, Nennius, in his *Historia Britonum*. Referring vaguely to a period

[32] Alanus de Insulis, *Prophetia Anglicana* (Frankfort, 1608), p. 26; (Frankfort, 1603), pp. 22 f.

[33] E. G. Gardner, *Arthurian Legend in Italian Lit.* (L., 1930), pp. 12 f. P. S. Barto, *Tannhäuser and the Mountain of Venus* (N. Y., 1916), pp. 11–17.

[34] Phillippe de Novare, *Mémoires*, ed. C. Kohler (P., 1913), pp. 7, 134. Trans. La Monte (N. Y., 1936), p. 66.

[35] H. G. Leach, *Angevin Britain and Scandinavia* (Camb., Mass., 1921), pp. 137–139.

[36] J. D. Bruce, *Evolution of Arthurian Romance* (Baltimore, 1923), I, 1–36. E. K. Chambers, *Arthur of Britain* (L., 1927), pp. 1–52. E. Faral, *La légende arthurienne, Première Partie* (P., 1929). R. H. Fletcher, *Arthurian Material in the Chronicles* (Boston, 1906).

in the Anglo-Saxon conquest of Britain, probably early in the sixth century, Nennius tells us that Arthur fought against the Saxons, together with the kings of the Britons, but Arthur himself was a battle-leader (*dux bellorum.*) He won twelve victories at twelve sites, a few of which can be identified in northern England and southern Scotland. Gildas, who wrote about 545, though he does not mention Arthur, does mention one of these victories of the Britons and a resulting peace of forty years, during which the Anglo-Saxon drive was checked. It would seem that this feat eternized the memory of Arthur among the Britons even after they had been once more attacked and driven westward into the mountains of Wales, among the moors of Cornwall, and over the seas to Armorica, thenceforth to be known as Brittany or Little Britain.

From Wales we get a few brief references during the succeeding centuries which imply the existence of an Arthurian tradition, and then about the year 1100 we find the full-fledged tale of *Kilhwch and Olwen*, which also implies the existence of many antecedent stories of Arthur. But more startling is the discovery that before 1125 men of Padua and Modena were bearing the names of Artusius and Galvanus (Arthur and Gawain),[37] and that Arthur and his knights appear on a sculpture at Modena. In 1125 William of Malmesbury speaks of "the trivial tales of the Bretons" about him and of the belief that he was destined to return.[38] Between 1136 and 1138 an ingenious but unscrupulous Oxford canon, Geoffrey of Monmouth, declares that the deeds of Arthur and other British kings are rehearsed by word of mouth among many peoples, and proceeds to foist on the learned public a *History of the Kings of Britain*, compiled from multifarious sources, including Nennius and other Celtic traditions, with a liberal seasoning of his own imagination. This pretentious work, even though recognized here and there as a fabrication, established the prestige of Arthur in the learned world, for it represented him as the conqueror of nearly all western Europe and a victor over the legions of imperial Rome. Copies were multiplied, translations made; sober historians inserted Geoffrey's fabulous materials in their chronicles; poets like Wace (1155) and Layamon (1175–1205) charged them with poetic feeling and adapted them to French-speaking and English-speaking audiences. No one can doubt the prodigious influence of Geoffrey. He is the father of Arthurian pseudo-history.

Thus far scholarly opinion is united, but it divides over the issue whether Geoffrey of Monmouth was also the father of Arthurian romance. In the middle of the century Provençal troubadours speak familiarly of Tristram as a famous lover,[39] and by 1180 Chrétien de Troyes has written (besides a lost poem on the Tristram theme) five long poems—which represent Arthur as little more than a majestic figurehead, never mention his wars with the Saxons or with Lucius of Rome, but introduce us instead to new characters such as Erec, Lancelot, and Perceval, and to a new world of strange adventure and of love. We are transported in fact to that very world which was destined to give its magic coloring to the word *romance;* and a world more different from that of Geoffrey's *Historia* it would be difficult to conceive, except that both contain courts and giants. Nevertheless, certain eminent scholars—Foerster, M. Faral, and Sir Edmund Chambers—contend that Geoffrey begat Arthurian romance as well as Arthurian pseudo-history.[40] Bruce, realizing that Geoffrey was too different from his romantic successors to be a very plausible father, asserted the paternity of Chrétien de Troyes.[41] These scholars agree, however, in maintaining that Arthurian romance was an artificial literary product, to which oral traditions of Celtic derivation contributed little in the early stages but a few names, a half dozen narrative motifs, and the nucleus of the Tristram legend, and contributed nothing at all after 1200.

Against this position the advocates of a Celtic origin for Arthurian romance would urge these considerations. The argument that the rise of Arthurian romance followed the popularization of Geoffrey by Wace in 1155 simply illustrates the fallacy of *post hoc ergo propter hoc* unless specific signs of influence can be pointed out and marked divergences accounted for. Wace undoubtedly had some influence on Chrétien, Thomas, and others;[42] but the substance of these romances and their utter difference in character remain unaccounted for by this hypothesis. Moreover, if Geoffrey was responsible for the existence of Arthurian romance, how account for the names in Northern Italy, William of Malmesbury's reference to the trivial tales of the Bretons, the allusions to "tot l'or d'Avalon" in the *Couronnement Louis* about 1130[43]—all antedating Geoffrey? How account for the extraordinary fact that the earliest bits of romantic Arthurian tradition surviving in literature, Biket's *Lai du Cor*, Marie's *Lanval* and

---

[37] *Romania*, XVII (1888), 161, 355. *Regesta Chartarum Italiæ*, XVI (Rome, 1931), 295.

[38] *Speculum*, II (1927), 449.

[39] *Mod. Phil.*, XIX (1922), 287. *Zeits. f. Rom. Phil.*, XLI (1921), 219.

[40] Chrétien de Troyes, *Löwenritter*, ed. W. Foerster (Halle, 1887), p. xxx. W. Foerster, *Christian v. Troyes, Wörterbuch* (Halle, 1914), pp. 15* f. Faral, *op. cit.*, II, 398. Faral in Bédier and Hazard,

[*Hist. de la litt. franç. illustrée*, 19. Chambers, *op. cit.*, p. 232.]

[41] Bruce, *op. cit.*, I, 122: "The vast forest of medieval Arthurian romance sprang mainly from the seeds of his sowing."

[42] *Ibid.*, I, 37 n. M. Pelan, *L'influence du Brut de Wace sur les romanciers français* (P., 1931). Thomas, *Tristan*, ed. Bédier, II (1905), 99 ff.

[43] *Couronnement Louis*, ed. E. Langlois (1888), clxx, vv. 1796, 1827.

Chievrefoil, all probably antedating 1165, betray a complete ignorance of Geoffrey? The same may be said of the three earliest representations of Arthur in art, to be described in the next chapter—the Perros relief, the Modena archivolt, and the Otranto mosaic —all likewise executed by or before 1165 and equally ignorant of Geoffrey. As for Chrétien, Bruce greatly underestimated the Celtic element in *Erec*, the *Charrette*,[44] *Ivain*, and the *Conte del Graal*.[45] And even in romances written after 1200 there is an extraordinary number of Irish and Welsh parallels which cannot be derived from Chrétien.[46] On this showing neither Geoffrey nor Chrétien could have sired Arthurian romance, could have created the typical features of the genre. The most that Geoffrey could have done was to add directly, or indirectly through Wace, to the prestige of Arthur; the most that Chrétien could have done was to add to the literary vogue of the legend, to influence poets on matters of style or detail, to furnish a part of the material for such works as the *Vulgate Lancelot* and Wolfram's *Parzival*, and to be translated into Hartmann's *Iwein*, the English *Ywain and Gawain*, and so forth.

Since it seems impossible to fit the iconography of Arthur into the framework of a legend inspired wholly by Geoffrey or Chrétien the literary comment in this book has necessarily proceeded on other assumptions. They may be summarized as follows. There were, to be sure, artificial, spurious, non-traditional romances of Arthur, such as *Cliges*,[47] *Gliglois*, and *Garel*, in which the Celtic element is practically nil. There are other romances, such as the *Prose Tristan* and *Estoire del Saint Graal*,[48] in which a traditional element exists, overlaid by later accretions. Apart from such inevitable developments from the vogue of the *Matière de Bretagne*, there existed a genuine traditional legend, which may be found even in such late romances as *Gawain and the Green Knight* and Malory's book of Gareth.[49] The seeds of this genuine tradition lie in the mythology and heroic lore of Ireland and Wales.

Wales during the first centuries after Arthur's death seems to have been a melting pot for the traditions concerning his career, for the conviction of his immortality and his return, and for a considerable part of the fading mythology of the Irish and Welsh. With additions from Strathclyde and Cornwall, the stories passed on to the Bretons.[50] In the eleventh century apparently the Bretons adapted this mass of fiction to purposes of entertainment, first among themselves, and then (as they became fluent in

French) among their neighbors. A class of professional *conteurs* began to circulate wherever people understood French. Hence the names of Galvanus and Artusius in Northern Italy early in the twelfth century and the allusion of William of Malmesbury in 1125 to the "nugæ Britonum." The emotional power of these tales is attested by Ailred of Rievaulx in 1142 and by Peter of Blois nearly fifty years later.[51] It is the existence, the geographical range, and the charm of these *conteurs* which explain a multitude of facts, literary and iconographic, which would otherwise merely mystify us. It is these reciters who make comprehensible and plausible the extravagant remarks of Alanus quoted earlier in this chapter.

Chrétien was one of the earliest to rime the tales with felicity and to fill them with French manners and ideology. Thomas and Béroul and the French source of Eilhart von Oberg turned into verse the *contes* of Tristram and Ysolt, which were already famous by the middle of the century. The Burgundian, Robert de Boron, composed about 1200 an incoherent poem based on a fantastic attempt to connect old Welsh traditions with the Passion of Christ —an attempt, however fantastic, which had far reaching consequences for literature, art, and music.

By the middle of the thirteenth century the influence of Guillaume de Lorris had shifted the attention of French poets from romance to allegory, though a few Arthurian poems remained to be written. Meanwhile, beginning in the early thirteenth century, romances in prose—based in part on French poetic originals, in part on Breton traditions, in part on Wace, in part on the author's fertile fancy—came into great favor and achieved in some instances a prodigious length. In the first quarter of the thirteenth century was composed the huge Vulgate cycle, including the *Lancelot* and the *Queste del S. Graal*. About 1230 the *Prose Tristan* was done, and this together with its supplements, the *Palamedes* and the *Meliadus* of Rusticiano da Pisa, provided much of the favorite reading of the fourteenth and fifteenth centuries.

The adoption of Arthur and his knights into the other vernacular literatures of Europe is illustrated in Germany by the successive poems of Eilhart von Oberg, Gottfried von Strassburg and his continuators, and Wolfram von Eschenbach; in England by several poems in rime and alliterative verse, of which the greatest was *Gawain and the Green Knight*, and by Malory's prose epic, the *Morte d'Arthur*; in Italy by *cantari* and prose romances.

[44] Cf. new edition by Herbert K. Stone (1938).
[45] *Romania*, LIX (1933), 557.
[46] *PMLA*, XLV (1930), 432 ff.; XLVIII (1933), 1000 ff. *Revue Celt.*, XLVII (1930), 39.
[47] (New York) *Nation*, XLVI (1898), 150 f. *Romania*, XLIV (1915), 34.

[48] *Mod. Lang. Rev.*, XXIV (1929), 416.
[49] *PMLA*, XLVII (1932), 315; XLVIII (1933), 1021.
[50] *Mod. Phil.*, XXXIII (1936), 228 ff.
[51] Migne, *Pat. Lat.*, CXCV, col. 565; CCVII, col. 1088. *Bulletin of John Rylands Library*, VI (1921-2), 454 f., 478.

The Arthurian legend became all things to all men. It offered, thanks to Geoffrey of Monmouth, history to the historically curious; it offered love and mystery and chivalry to gallant knights and sentimental ladies; it offered to the religious new light on some of the most sacred relics of the Passion and on the conversion of the West. That its vogue, though waning, was still strong in the dawn of the Renaissance is demonstrated not only by its influence on Spanish romance and on Boiardo, and by the sumptuous MSS of the period, but also by the editions of prose romances that issued from the presses of Vérard, Caxton, and Wynkyn de Worde. Today among English-speaking peoples it is still the most living of legends: boys pore over the pages of Malory; scholars are tantalized by its problems; pilgrims make their way to Tintagel and Glastonbury, Cadbury Castle and Caerleon on Usk; music lovers never tire of Wagner's *Tristan* and *Parsifal*; and poets, even during the postwar reaction toward stark and cynical modernism, set out on voyages to the shores of old romance.

PART I

THE DECORATIVE ARTS

CHAPTER II

REFLECTIONS AND RECORDS OF A VANISHED ART

A HAPPY introduction to the pageant of Arthurian chivalry lies in certain passages in medieval prose and poetry and in a few ancient inventories and account books which mention illustrations of the Round Table cycle.[1] In other chapters in this book the actual survivals of Arthurian illustration will be enumerated and described, but those remains, it must be confessed, are in many cases but the broken and faded remnants of what once existed in brilliant color and lovely form. In the actual inventories and account books of the fourteenth and fifteenth centuries we possess, however, records and brief descriptions of these things when they were still the immensely valuable personal possessions of great lords and kings, and were still untouched by Time's long wreckful siege. Such records preserve the list of treasures now almost unknown, the huge and gorgeous tapestries, the golden cups, once decorated with Arthurian story. Supplementing these few lists are the numerous passages, many of much earlier date, preserved in Arthurian romance itself and elsewhere, in which appear allusions to Arthurian sculptures, wall paintings, embroideries, and other delightful things. Whether these descriptions are in any sense realistic or not, they bear witness to the medieval taste for beautiful handicrafts; they offer partial suggestions as to what were favored Arthurian subjects for pictorial representation, and they supplement, sometimes in surprising and revealing ways, the actual survivals which chance has left us of Arthurian decoration.

THE EARLIEST REFERENCES TO ARTHURIAN IMAGES

The earliest reference of this sort is to be found in the *Liber Floridus*, composed by Lambert, canon of St. Omer, in 1120.[2] He tells us: "There is in Britain, in the land of the Picts, a palace belonging to the warrior Arthur, built with marvelous art and skill, in which all his exploits and wars are seen sculptured." The author adds a list, obviously borrowed from Nennius, of Arthur's twelve victories over the Saxons. Though possibly there was some meagre nucleus of fact in Lambert's report, perhaps some crumbling reliefs of Roman triumphs which, like the Meigle sculpture,[3] came to be associated in the popular fancy with Arthurian personages, yet we can place as little reliance on Lambert's words as we can on the passage from the contemporary Pseudo-Turpin (chap. 30) to the effect that Charlemagne caused his victories to be painted on the walls of his palace at Aix-la-Chapelle. The most plausible explanation of Lambert's statement is that he elaborated on a gloss in his copy of Nennius, like the one, preserved in two MSS, which declares that Carausius built "a round house of polished stones on the bank of the River Carun, erecting an arch in memory of his victory." Since the Carun is in "the land of the Picts" and since this very structure was known in 1293 as "Furnum Arthuri" and later as Arthur's O'on (Oven), it is possible that an eleventh century gloss may have connected it with that hero instead of Carausius and thus stimulated Lambert's imagination to combine it with Nennius' list of the twelve battles.[4]

Only some sixty or seventy years separate the mention of these but dimly imaginable sculptures in the Pictish wilds from the description by the Anglo-Norman poet Thomas of some equally imaginary sculptures in Brittany, but it is a different world, a different art, to which we are introduced. We emerge from a Celtic twilight into the clear day of the twelfth-century Renaissance. The sculptures Thomas describes are stately figures, like those on the west front of Chartres. Their subject is not the historic wars of the British hero, but the new French religion of love embodied in the beauty of Queen Ysolt.

Thomas tells us[5] that Tristram, though formally married to Ysolt of the White Hands, Ysolt of Brittany, languishes with love for his lost Ysolt of Ireland, the wife of King Mark. To solace his grief, Tristram in a remote cavern in the woods fashions a fair hall, and within it places images of Queen Ysolt, of her gentlewoman, Bringvain, of Ysolt's little lapdog, of the giant from whom Tristram has won the cavern, of the dwarf and the Seneschal who are enemies of the lovers. For Tristram this Hall of Images becomes his temple of love, where he comes to worship, to suffer and rejoice in passionate remembrance. Thomas says:

So beautiful of stature and countenance was the image of Ysolt that no man beholding it might think otherwise than that life was in all the limbs... She was richly clad as beseemed the noblest queen. She had on her head a crown of

---

[1] The only collection of such references is that by O. Söhring, in *Romanische Forschungen*, XII (1900), 493.

[2] Migne, *Patrologia Lat.*, CLXIII, col. 1012. Cf. E. Faral, *La légende arthurienne, première partie*, I, 256 n.

[3] *Merlin*, ed. H. B. Wheatley, III (L., 1869), liii.

[4] *Ibid.* lviii; H. N. and N. K. Chadwick, *Growth of Literature*, I (Camb., 1932), 157 n. 2; Nennius, *Historia Brittonum*, ed. F. Lot (P., 1934), p. 166 n.

[5] Thomas, *Roman de Tristan*, ed. Bédier (P., 1902), I, 306–317. Trans. R. S. Loomis (N. Y., 1931), 215 ff. The Middle English *Sir Tristrem* condenses and modifies as follows: "At his dais in the hall sweet Ysonde was wrought; Hodain and Peticru at her call (?); how Brengwain brought the drink; Mark clad in white silk and Meriadok full of sorrow—so lifelike were they all, they did not seem images—and Tristram, how he fought with monstrous Beliagog." Ed. Kölbing (Heilbronn, 1882), p. 77.

pure gold wrought with all manner of skill and set with costliest jewels, . . . and in the leaf thereof, that was in front upon her forehead, stood a great emerald. . . . In the right hand of the image was a wand or sceptre; in the upper end it was carved in flowers by the subtlest smiths. . . . The image was clad in purple and white furs. . . . Near the image was wrought of fine gold a little plaything, her lap-dog, shaking his head and ringing his bell, wrought with great cunning.

For this vivid story of Thomas there was, perhaps, a Celtic kernel. It resembles a story told by Geoffrey of Monmouth concerning Locrine, father of Milton's "Sabrina fair."[6] Locrine loved a damsel Estrildis, whose skin surpassed in whiteness ivory, lilies, or the new fallen snow. Forced to marry another, Locrine nevertheless built a subterranean vault, placed poor Estrildis in it, and there for seven years continued to visit her and enjoy her caresses, giving out that he was paying secret sacrifice to the gods. Similarly in the Tristram romance the hero loves the fair Ysolt, whose name in Welsh was Essylt; persuaded to marry another, he refashions a subterranean cavern, sets up the image of Ysolt, visits and caresses it, giving out the report that he was hunting a boar in the wild woods.

Such correspondences as these point to a possible source in Welsh tradition, though that tradition has been ingeniously blended with the story of Elfildis in William of Malmesbury.[7] When the story was first attached to Tristram, it may have been the real Essylt whom he visited in the vault, just as it was the real Estrildis whom Locrine visited. But some ingenious redactor, perhaps Thomas himself, seeing practical difficulties in the idea of keeping the Queen in a dark cavern for some time, unknown to Mark or to Ysolt of the White Hands, realized that he could remove the difficulties by giving to Tristram, not Ysolt herself, but her image as the object of his caresses. Thomas himself seems to have been inspired by the magnificent achievements in his own day of Romanesque art. His details about woodcarvers, goldsmiths, stone workers, about color, ornament, grotesques, are all significant. "There was an arch," he tells us, "carved with leaves, birds, and beasts." Under Ysolt's feet was a pedestal, "in the likeness of the evil dwarf that had slandered them unto the king. The Queen's image stood upon his breast, seeming most as she trod him under her feet, and he lay under her feet crying as he were weeping." It is as if this image of the dwarf had come straight from under the feet of one of the stately queens of Char-

tres. From some great saint's figure with a reliquary in the breast Thomas may have drawn the idea for having Tristram put in the breast of Ysolt a little coffer "full of the sweetest herbs in the world, mingled with gold," so that even the breath of the image should seem fragrant. So too, there was realism in the guardians of the door:

On the other side of the chamber where one entered, Tristram had made a great image in likeness of the giant, as he were standing there himself, one-legged, and brandishing with both hands over his shoulder his club of iron, for to defend the other image. He was clad in a great goat-skin and he was naked below the navel and he gnashed with his teeth, and his eyes were wood as he would smite all those who came within. On the other side of the door stood a great lion. He stood on four feet and wound his tail about an image that was made after the Seneschal that slandered and accused Tristram.

The real practice in medieval times of posting warders with axes or cudgels at the gates of castles seems to have been supplemented, as M. Faral has shown,[8] by "images painted in gateways, which brandish an ax and yet smite no one," or by "knights depicted on walls and a churl who holds an ax at the gate." The lion standing over a prostrate human figure is, of course, a familiar image in Romanesque art.

FRENCH MURALS

It has been pointed out that Thomas' idea of the hero consoling himself for his absent lady by creating and caressing her image was the inspiration of an interesting episode in the most famous romance of all, the *Vulgate Lancelot*, composed early in the thirteenth century.[9] The artist is here Lancelot himself. In the thirteenth century it did not seem strange that the sinewy hand which braced a lance as with iron chains should be supple with a brush as a reed in the wind. The story tells[10] how Morgan le Fay enticed the hero to her castle, blew a powder into his nostrils through a silver tube while he was asleep, and then imprisoned him in a room overlooking a garden.

After Christmas when the cold was passed, it befell one day that he came to a window that was of iron to lean thereat and one might well look through that window into the palace. And he looked and saw there a man who painted an ancient history of Æneas, how he came from Troy. Then Lancelot bethought him that if the chamber where he lay were likewise portrayed with his deeds and sayings, it would much delight him to see the fair visage of his

[6] Geoffrey of Monmouth, *Historia Regum Britanniae*, ed. A. Griscom (N. Y., 1929), pp. 254 ff.

[7] *Speculum*, XI (1936), 121.

[8] E. Faral, *Recherches sur les sources latines des contes et romans courtois* (P., 1913), p. 333 n. These painted figures corresponded to the real practice of posting warders with axes or cudgels at

the gates of castles. Cf. Dillon and Hope, *Pageant of the Birth, Life, Death of Richard de Beauchamp* (L., 1914), p. 22.

[9] Cf. Thomas, *Tristan*, ed. Bédier, I, 309, n. 1.

[10] H. O. Sommer, *Vulgate Version of the Arthurian Romances*, V (Wash., 1912), pp. 216 ff.

lady and greatly assuage his woes. Then he prayed the good man who painted to give him of his colors to make a picture in the chamber where he lay. And he said he would do it gladly and gave him all the tools that belonged to that craft. Lancelot took them and then closed the shutter of his window so that no one should see what he would do. Then he began to paint first how [his foster-mother] the Lady of the Lake brought him to court to become a knight, how he came to Camelot, how he was abashed by the great beauty of his lady [Guinevere] when he saw her for the first time, and how he went to bring succor to the Lady of Nohaut. That was the first day's work of Lancelot. The images were as well and subtly wrought as if he had followed that craft all the days of his life.

Now Morgan entered the room at midnight, discovered her prisoner's activities, and exclaimed to her damsel:

'By my faith, you may see the marvel of this knight who is so skilled both in knighthood and in handicraft. Verily Love would give the hardest man of the world skill and wit. I tell thee this knight would never make these images so well if he were not destroyed with love which has brought him to this pass. But since he is set in this way, there is no man in the world who could attain to him.'

Then Morgan showed her the images which Lancelot had made and set forth the meaning of each and said, "Here is Lancelot and here is the Queen and here is King Arthur." Morgan then departed hoping that Lancelot would continue his autobiographic murals, and she was not disappointed.

In the morning when Lancelot was risen, and he had opened the window towards the garden, he looked into the room where the image of his lady was painted. He bowed and saluted it and approached it and kissed it on the mouth and had delight more than he had of any other woman save his lady. Then he began to paint how he came to the Dolorous Tower, which was called the Dolorous Garde, and how he won the castle by his prowess. The next day he portrayed all that he did until the tournament where he bore the vermeil arms the day that the King of the Hundred Knights wounded him. Thereafter he portrayed from day to day not only concerning himself but also concerning others, as the tale has already rehearsed. He busied himself therewith until Easter was passed.

The conclusion to this story of Lancelot's artistic activity comes long afterward in the *Mort Artu;* it occurs between the affair of the Maid of Astolat and the accusation brought by Mador de la Porte against Queen Guinevere.[11] King Arthur, being lost in a wood, comes by chance to the castle of Morgan le Fay. She entertains him richly and at last reveals that she is his half-sister. Presently, the sun shining in, Arthur begins to notice the paintings on the walls

of the chamber, and since he knows enough of letters (so the author informs us) to understand the writing, he begins to read the inscriptions. (Cf. Fig. 297) He perceives that these are the deeds of Lancelot when he was newly knighted, and recognizes their truth. But "when he came to the images which told the behavior of Galehaut he was greatly shamed and he said to himself: 'By my faith, if the interpretations of these images are true, then Lancelot has wronged me with my wife!'" Then Arthur swears Morgan to tell him the truth, and she relates how Lancelot has come to paint these scenes and shows how the various stages of his love, including the first famous kiss, were depicted. Arthur vows vengeance, if he can take them with the deed, on his return to Camelot. Though the suspicions bred by these paintings were subsequently somewhat allayed in Arthur's mind by Lancelot's conduct, they played at last an important part in bringing on his final disillusionment.

Though this story is close to Thomas' in thus representing a lover solacing himself by depicting the story of his love and by lavishing caresses on the image of his lady, it is lacking both in plausibility and in that vivid sense of art itself which give such vigor to the earlier account. The improbability of Lancelot's thus revealing, in the house of his enemy and Guinevere's, the dangerous secret of their love—or of leaving without a qualm, when he escapes from his prison, this record behind him—did not trouble the later story-teller. He was in fact using the artistic situation simply as one of his many summarizing devices. The passage, however, is not without its own charm and does suggest that secular mural paintings were far more familiar even in the earlier part of the thirteenth century than the actual remains would lead us to believe.[12]

The same thing might likewise be said concerning another set of Arthurian murals, though these are described as being in a chapel. The passage occurs in the romance of *Perlesvaus*,[13] which Professor Nitze dates between 1191 and 1212.[14] Here Arthur and Gawain are said to have ridden to a ruinous castle inhabited only by a priest and his clerk. In the charming translation of Sebastian Evans we read:[15]

The King and Messire Gawain lodged there that night, and on the morrow went into a right rich chapel that was therein to hear mass, and it was painted all around of right rich colors of gold and azure and other colors. The images were right fair that were there painted, and the figures of them for whom the images were made. The King and Messire Gawain looked at them gladly. When the mass was said, the priest cometh to them and saith, 'Lords, these images are right fair and he that had made them is full loyal, and dearly loved the lady and her son for whom he

[11] *Ibid.*, VI, 238. *Mort Artu*, ed. Frappier (P., 1936), p. 49.
[12] Cf. pp. 4, 35, n. 45.
[13] Ed. Nitze and Jenkins, I (Chicago, 1932), pp. 307 f.

[14] *Mod. Phil.*, XVII (1919–20), pp. 165, 611.
[15] *High History of the Holy Grail*, trans. Sebastian Evans, Branch XXIII, title 1.

had them made. Sir,' saith the priest, 'it is a true history.' 'Of whom is the history, fair sir?' saith King Arthur. 'Of a worshipful vavasour that owned this hold, and of Messire Gawain, King Arthur's nephew, and his mother. Sir,' saith the priest, 'Messire Gawain was born there within and held up and baptized, as you may see here imaged.'

Thereupon follows the story, told also in the *Enfances Gauvain* and the *De Ortu Walwanii*,[16] of Gawain's birth out of wedlock, of his nurture in a far country, and of his being brought to the Pope with the evidence of his royal birth. At this recital Gawain hangs his head for shame, but Arthur consoles him with the reflection that they are both marked with the same stigma, and the priest, when he learns that it is Gawain, the subject of the paintings, who stands before him, makes great cheer and charges him to take over the castle.

Two Goblets and a Platter of Gold

Surprising as is this account of secular scenes thus supposedly painted in a holy chapel, it is less startling than another instance of Arthurian illustration to which we may now turn. In the poem, *L'Escoufle* (*The Kite*), written by Jean Renart about 1200, a rich goblet is described; it consisted, as actual goblets of this type did, of base, stem, bowl, and cover. It was enameled with several of the least edifying scenes from the amours of Tristram and Ysolt, and this cup, so the poet astonishingly tells us, the Count of Montivilliers offered, on a pilgrimage to Jerusalem, at the high altar of the Holy Sepulchre and—supreme irony —as a receptacle for the Host!

Those who watched over the Sepulchre and relics and treasure, took the rich vessel of gold and looked at it long. Each crossed himself by reason of its beauty and workmanship. . . . The Count besought them that for God's sake the rich vessel might hang above the chief altar, and that He by whom the world was saved should be placed and worshiped therein. 'Sire,' said they, 'say nought thereof to evil end; all shall be at your pleasure. This very day it shall be placed there.'[17]

The cup so eagerly accepted by the guardians of the Holy Sepulchre is thus described.[18]

A cup of gold it was, worth ten marks. Inside was portrayed King Mark and how the swallow brought him through the window the yellow hair of Ysolt the Blonde; and how because of it Tristram was expected to be killed in Ireland, in his land. The ship in which he went to seek her was depicted in this vessel. Outside, around, upon the bowl there were represented in enamel Tristram, his master

Governal, Ysolt, and their hound Hudain, how he caught hinds and stags for them without noise or barking. On the cover was the bed, how they lay within the rock, and how the sword with all the breach was found lying quite naked between them, and how Mark saw them, and how he had pity on them, and how he waked neither him nor her, so mightily he loved them, and how there fell a sunbeam through a branch upon her face; there was naught in the world delighted him so; and how Mark put near Ysolt's ear his glove so gently that he might not wake her and in order that the sun might do her no harm. Now he no longer desired to hate Tristram. How he saw them under the branches. On the pommel was the dwarf, how he lay on the floor; and how he was outwitted, and how Ysolt espied him, and how Tristram deceived him who knew too much thereof by trickery and wit; and how Tristram slew him in spite of Mark.

Such a cup on the altar of the Holy Sepulchre must have presented something of the incongruity of the Bishop's tomb in St. Praxed's church as Browning describes it.

> Those Pans and Nymphs ye wot of, and perchance
> Some tripod, with a vase or so,
> The Saviour at His sermon on the mount,
> Saint Praxed in a glory, and one Pan
> Ready to twitch the nymph's last garment off,
> And Moses with the tables.

The account of the incidents does not agree, as Sudre long since noted,[19] with any one extant version of the romance. The episode of the swallow and the golden hair is found in Eilhart von Oberg's version and is depicted on several German embroideries to be treated in Chapter IV. The hunting of the hound Hudain follows the versions of Eilhart and Béroul. The third incident with its mention of the hollow rock suggests Thomas' account. The final series of references to the dwarf are obscure and do not seem to fit any known narrative of his spying. It is quite possible that the whole group of allusions was based on one of the many versions of the legend which we know once existed but are now lost,—versions by Breri, Le Chévre, Chrétien de Troyes, or one of the still more obscure texts alluded to by Thomas.

Still another imaginary cup is mentioned in the first half of the thirteenth century by the long-lived troubadour, Peire Cardinal. Born of a noble family at Le Puy, he was "much honored and cherished by my lord the good King James of Aragon,"[20] the same for whom the Arthurian romance of *Jaufré* was composed.[21] In a poem Peire tells of a cup of gold encrusted with rubies, sapphires, garnets, with a car-

[16] *Historia Meriadoci*, ed. J. D. Bruce (*Hesperia, Ergänzungsreihe*, Heft 2), pp. xxxvii–lv. R. S. Loomis, *Celtic Myth*, pp. 331 ff.
[17] Ed. H. Michelant, P. Meyer (P., 1894), v. 628 ff.
[18] *Ibid.*, vv. 579–616.
[19] *Romania*, XV (1886), 540. Thomas, *Tristan*, ed. Bédier, II,

58, 250. R. Lejeune-Dehousse, *L'œuvre de Jean Renart* (P., 1935), pp. 235 ff.
[20] I. Farnell, *Lives of the Troubadours* (L., 1896), 218. C. A. F. Mahn, *Biographien der Troubadours* (Berlin, 1878), p. 49.
[21] Ed. H. Breuer (Göttingen, 1925), I, 58 ff.

buncle set in the pommel.[22] Around the cover were pictured the Seven Arts of Love and certain fine lovers,—Pyramus and Thisbe, Flores and Blanchefleur, and "Tristram who never laughed and who loved Ysolt the Blonde."[23] This rich cup, Peire gravely remarks, was sent by the Sultan of Turkey as a present to the Franks.

In *Diu Krone*, composed by Heinrich von dem Türlin about 1220, there is an unusually romantic episode centering round an engraved golden platter.[24] A certain lord, Laniure, had the platter made to remind him of his humiliating defeat by Gawain. After Laniure's death, Gawain was enticed to his castle and given a potion which deprived him of his memory and rendered him the infatuated lover of Laniure's daughter, Amurfina. She summoned her vassals to a banquet to introduce Gawain as their new lord, and somewhat negligently ordered the golden platter brought in.

On the platter was carved the strife of the two knights, and the names of both were written on it. One knight was left wellnigh vanquished by the other till he saw as a refuge a piece of water, to which he withdrew whenever his strength departed. Around this was written: 'Laniure von der Serre was with difficulty saved from Gawain, when Gawain sought adventure at the stream.' . . . Closely Gawain beheld it and marked what the writing said, but he did not understand anything of the meaning, except that he marked the story of the pictures, how they covered themselves with shields and strove hard with the swords and dealt many blows.

Gawain was thus reminded of his old life and forsook the beguiling Amurfina.

EMBROIDERIES

The *Chevalier aux Deux Epées* (1200–50) informs us that the bridal gown of the heroine, Flore, was decorated with somewhat inappropriate subjects, and Miss Pelan has shown that the description was inspired by the text of Wace rather than by any embroidery.[25]

The mantle was wholly covered with designs portraying how Merlin changed the countenance of Uther, and how he seemed to be Count Gorlois in voice and feature; and in what manner Ygerne mistook him for her lord; and how good Arthur was begotten at Tintagel; and how Ygerne made dole by reason of the tidings which came that night, for they who escaped from the battle believed her lord to be slain; and how the barons of Britain were accorded that she should espouse Uther, and that he should crown her.

And the deeds of prowess which Arthur had wrought up to that day [the day of Flore's wedding] were portrayed on the mantle.

Later in the century, between 1250 and 1275, the romance of *Floriant et Florete* describes an elaborate set of curtains hung in the ebony bark in which Morgan le Fay sent the hero forth from her isle.[26] The curtains were covered in part with designs from the Trojan war and the adventures of Æneas. At the end "the God of Love was depicted, so joyous, so well wrought that never was a work better done. A barbed arrow and a bow he bore in his hand, with which he shot early and late those who were not in accord with him. The string of the bow was vermeil." To one side of Cupid's bow sat Tristram and Ysolt the Blonde; around them were "fresh roses, citoles, harps and other musical instruments, and ladies and maidens, well-shapen, fair, courteous." With these delightful curtains we may include, by anticipation, the account of a rich robe which occurs in the late fourteenth-century Middle English poem of *Emaré*,[27] that romanticized version of the famous Custance legend. On this robe for seven winters had labored "the amerayle dowghter of hethennes," fashioning it with gold and far-sought jewels, rubies, topazes; in one corner was set the son of the Sowdan of Babylon, a maid and a high-horned unicorn; in the others were famous pairs of lovers, Amadas and Ydoine, Floris and Blaunchefleur, and, set with stones, "as thykke as they may be, Tristram and Isowde so bright, That semely wer to se."[28]

STATUES AND PORTRAITS

It is already obvious on the basis merely of the allusions we have been noting that the romance of Tristram and Ysolt was by all odds the favorite in these imaginary works of art, as in so many other ways. In the thirteenth-century French *Prose Tristan* (c. 1230), so bulky, so confused, so changed from the passionate and (by comparison) swiftly-told story of the verse romances, there are numerous passages in which Arthurian paintings and sculptures are described, though not a word is said of Thomas' Hall of Images and though not a single passage has the vitality and beauty which Thomas gave to his account. The passages are not without a certain interest, however, as they do exemplify the interweaving of the various legends of Arthurian story, and also in individual manuscripts give us bits of surprising information.

---

[22] C. A. F. Mahn, *Gedichte der Troubadours* (Berlin, 1873), IV, 89. *Romanische Forschungen*, XII, 559 f.

[23] The correct reading must be "e Tristan canc non ris," imitated from Chrétien de Troyes, *Erec*, v. 1713, "Et Tristanz qui onques ne rist."

[24] Heinrich von dem Türlin, *Krone*, ed. Scholl, vv. 8845–944.

[25] Ed. W. Foerster (Halle, 1877), v. 12180 ff. Pelan, *Influence du Brut de Wace* (P., 1931), pp. 134 ff.

[26] Ed. F. X. Michel (Edinburgh, 1873), I, 871 ff.

[27] Ed. E. Rickert (L., 1908), v. 183 ff. Cf. L. A. Hibbard, *Mediaeval Romance in England* (N. Y., 1924), p. 28 n.

[28] V. 134.

One MS tells us that while Erec and other knights were seated at table there rode up on a white mule the ugliest damsel one could imagine and rebuked Erec for not accomplishing a certain adventure.[29] Robert de Boron, we are gravely informed, says he has seen at Oxford, in the treasury of the Abbey of St. Vincent, a silver image in the likeness of this damsel, which King Arthur had caused to be made and had left at Oxford, where it is still to be seen. She held in her hand a silver rod, which measured exactly the height of Erec. Needless to say, there never was any Abbey of St. Vincent at Oxford, and there is no trace of the Loathly Damsel in silver in our authentic records.

Another of these passages[30] tells of Perceval's visit to Lancelot's castle of Joyous Garde, wherein he was shown three portraits: Lancelot on the right, Tristram on the left, and in the middle the good knight who would accomplish the adventures of the realm of Logres. Perceval was informed that if one of the three heroes died, his portrait would fall. (Cf. Fig. 274) Later on,[31] when in his turn Tristram came to visit Joyous Garde, he too was shown the three portraits in the chapel, and was informed by Lancelot that though no letters yet appeared to reveal the name of the unknown knight, the time was fast approaching when he would come to Arthur's court, the Quest of the Grail would begin, and the Siege Perilous would be fulfilled. Tristram, who in this romance loses largely his great character as a lover, and alternates fits of piety with casual philanderings, at once assures Lancelot that he will not miss being present when that great day comes and that he will not fail to leave Ysolt in order to go on the quest!

In due course the story tells how Galahad, the original of the mysterious portrait, appears and becomes the hero of various miscellaneous adventures. After his victory over Claudin, according to one MS, he was so admired that his statue was set up in bronze.[32] The patriotic French writer goes on to add that one hundred and thirty years after Arthur's death Charlemagne conquered England, found there the statue and the inscriptions concerned with Galahad's feats of arms, and declared that Arthur must have been a king of little intelligence, for with such knights as Galahad, Tristram, Lancelot and Palamedes, he should have been able to subjugate the whole world. According to still another manuscript,[33] Charlemagne after conquering England, restored the great keep of the Chateau Felon, which Galahad had destroyed by his prayers, and caused to be made a statue bearing a shield and helm like those of Galahad, and he had the statue placed sitting in a golden chair beneath an arched canopy on the top of the great tower. The figure bore in its hand a golden apple to betoken that Galahad had been the best knight of the world. In the midst of his breast there was a stone so wondrous that when it was dark, one could see half a day's journey away, so marvelously did the stone shine. The statue is said thus to have remained on high for two centuries, but was then removed by the evil kings of the land.

Towards the close of the *Prose Tristan* there is mention of still another sculpture.[34] The story has been told how Mark, made in this version into a cowardly and brutal king, had murdered Tristram. Overcome with sudden remorse he ordered for Tristram and Ysolt, who had died beside her lover, a sumptuous tomb, the richest that had ever been seen in Cornwall and had it placed in the cathedral of Tintagel. At the foot of the tomb were two copper images of life size. (Cf. Fig. 321) Tristram placed his left hand close to his breast as if he were holding the cord of his mantle—a familiar attitude, of course, in thirteenth century art—and his right hand he extended toward the people; he held in this hand a sword all bare, and this was the very sword with which Morhaut was slain. The manuscripts differ as to the inscription on the sword; one has: "He in whose hand I am, once delivered the realm of Cornwall from servage to that of Ireland through a blow which he dealt with me upon Morhaut of Ireland." Another text reads: "With this sword Morhaut of Ireland was slain, and this knight who lies here, for whom these images were made, was called Tristram of Loenois, the son of the noble King Meliadus, and he delivered Cornwall from the great servage of Ireland." Still another says that the blade was inscribed with a lay made by Dinas the Seneschal, and the image of Ysolt with another lay. But the sentiments expressed in these lays are so antagonistic to Mark, that it is absurd to find them on monuments supposedly commissioned by Mark himself.

The *Prose Tristan*, despite its imaginative inferiority to the poetic versions, maintained its vogue and its influence for centuries. It inspired the curious *Meliadus*, composed in French by the Italian Rusticiano da Pisa between 1270 and 1273, when Prince Edward of England passed through Italy on his way to and from the Holy Land. Rusticiano relates a prodigious duel between Meliadus, Tristram's father, and the Saxon Ariohan. After Meliadus had won and had spared the life of his adversary, King Arthur caused a chapel to be built, and over the gateway statues of the two champions, with rimed inscriptions, to be carved.[35]

---

[29] Ed. E. Löseth (P., 1890), p. 216.
[30] *Ibid.*, p. 244.
[31] *Ibid.*, pp. 258 f.
[32] *Ibid.*, p. 302.

[33] *Ibid.*, p. 371.
[34] *Ibid.*, pp. 390–392.
[35] *Ibid.*, p. 446.

The *Huth Merlin* follows the same tradition.[36] Arthur after his victory over Loth and his allies

had made twelve kings of metal richly covered with silver and gold, and each had on his head a crown of gold, and each had his name written on his breast; and therewith he had made a king in the semblance of King Loth, as like as could be. After these kings he had made another king ten times richer than the others, and he was made in semblance of King Arthur. . . . The thirteen were made in such wise that each held in his hand a candlestick, but the other, which was made in semblance of King Arthur, held in his hand a sword all bare, in semblance that he menaced the folk. . . . The King had the images set on the chief fortress of the tower, high above the battlements so that all those of the city might see it openly, and each of the kings held a great lighted candle. In the midst of the twelve images, the image of King Arthur, somewhat higher than all the others, held his sword in his hand and made semblant that he threatened those who were about him; always they bowed to him as if they cried him mercy of some misdeed.

ITALIAN FANTASIES

The fanciful descriptions of sculpture, fresco, and embroidery on Arthurian themes which we have been tracing through the twelfth and thirteenth centuries have all, except the *Meliadus*, emanated from countries north of the Mediterranean. Rusticiano's French romance attests the popularity of the cycle in Italy, where during the fourteenth and fifteenth centuries several descriptions reflect, however faintly, the delight not only in "ambages pulcerrimae regis Arturi," but also in the arts of the Pisani and Giotto.

The *Tavola Ritonda*, a prose romance written between 1325 and 1350 and concerned mainly with the story of Tristram, contains three passages of iconographic interest. The first is a pale reflection of the Hall of Images in Thomas.[37] After his marriage to Ysolt of Brittany Tristram

had painted a statue of fair Ysolt the Blonde, for the great desire he had to behold her; and so a master of the city of Gippia depicted her, who had drawn her portrait erstwhile in the city of London in Ireland for Queen Lotta; and he had made her so natural and fair and true that indeed she seemed her very self. Sir Tristram kept her in his chamber. One day Kaherdin (Ghedino) looking into the chamber, Tristram for a jest said: 'The fair Queen Ysolt has come to me.' Kaherdin seeing her from the end of the chamber, weened that verily it was herself and at a distance he bowed and greeted her saying: 'My lady, you are right welcome a thousand times, for you are most gracious when you deign to come to see your Tristram, for so greatly did he desire to see you.'

Tristram and Governal broke into the greatest laughter in the world, and Kaherdin, seeing the jest,

urged setting out at once to Cornwall to look upon the original of so fair an image. With a true Italian's appreciation of art, the author goes on to relate that the hero knighted the artist and gave him the lordship of the city of Gippia for ten years. In the *Vulgate Lancelot*, it will be remembered, the French author attributed to a great lord like Lancelot supreme skill as an artist, but in this Italian text it is significant that the author rewards a supreme artist with a great lordship.

The second episode is obviously an elaboration of the account of Galahad's statue in the *Prose Tristan*.[38] After the tournament at Lonazep (Verzeppe) when the guests had departed, Arthur ordained in the meadow before the castle four metal statues of Tristram, Lancelot, Palamedes and Morhaut, bearing swords. Later the statue of Galahad was added, and each figure was of striking likeness to its original. The figure of Tristram held in its hand the standard of victory, and at its foot letters were cut which narrated his prowess at the tournament. After the destruction of the Round Table the five swords were united to the five images. Still later Charlemagne, riding in the realm of Logres, saw the five statues and, noting their form and height, gave judgment that Arthur was worthy of a dolorous death, since with five such barons he should have subjugated all Christendom and the lands of the Saracens.

The third passage concerns the tomb of Tristram and Ysolt.[39] It repeats with characteristic variations the account already found in the *Prose Tristan*. The monument is said to have stood before the portal of the cathedral; it was of silver-gilt and precious stones, and above it Mark had placed two most life-like golden images. The image of Ysolt held a flower in its hand to signify that she had been Ysolt, flower of all the ladies in the world; and the image of Tristram held in its hand a sword, to show how by his prowess he had once delivered the realm. (Cf. Fig. 321) At their feet were letters which told of their lives; how they had died in the year 368, how Tristram had been born in 333, and the fair Ysolt in 337. In the long account of the mourning for the lovers the author soberly informs us, though he will not himself vouch for the truth of the rumor, that Pope Dionido granted during Tristram's lifetime indulgence to all who prayed for his continuance in life and happiness, and that after his death Pope Agabito, learning that enchantment and not evil intent was responsible for the amour, granted indulgence to all who prayed for the souls of the lovers. Here is another exhibition of tolerance toward the erring lovers on the part of the clergy, to set beside the acceptance of the enameled cup by the guardians of

[36] *Merlin*, ed. Paris, Ulrich (P., 1886), I, 263. Cf. *Mod. Lang. Rev.*, XXVI (1931), 421.

[37] Ed. F. L. Polidori (Bologna, 1864), I, 205. Cf. E. G. Gardner, *Arthurian Legend in Italian Literature* (L., N. Y., 1930), pp. 152 ff.

[38] *Tavola Ritonda*, ed. Polidori, p. 391.

[39] *Ibid.*, p. 507.

the Holy Sepulchre. The attitude of the clergy cannot be wholly imaginary as we shall find the same romance of Tristram illustrated in the abbeys of Chertsey and Halesowen and worked into their embroideries by the nuns of Wienhausen.

The *Tavola Ritonda* or some kindred book seems to have afforded inspiration to the author of the *Sala di Malagigi* in the same century, for it would account for the mention of "the Old Table," an order of knighthood founded by Arthur's father, Uther, and of "Brunor del Bruno." From the *Sala di Malagigi*[40] we learn that the enchanter Malagigi, the French Maugis, presented himself before Lucrezia, a queen of the Orient, and offered to do whatever she wished, and she demanded that her hall be filled with a company of noble folk. The wizard summoned his spirits and over night they adorned the hall with the sculptures of thirteen hundred armed knights. Tristram, Lancelot, King Arthur were there, together with Saladin and Penthesilea. "Of the Round Table good Galahad was there, King 'Runcivallo' and good Sir Gawain, 'Brunor del Bruno,' who holds the pass; . . . and all stood with their swords in hand as if each were proving himself in arms. The Old Table was there, and the New." In the *Tavola Ritonda* there are three knights called Brunor lo Bruno; one, the Branor le Brun of the *Meliadus*, a gigantic knight of the Old Table, whose deeds of prowess, as we shall see, are still visible on the painted walls of S. Floret; the second, whom the author of the *Tavola* confuses with the first, is known to readers of Malory as Sir Breunor, lord of Castle Pluere, slain by Tristram;[41] the third also appears in Malory as Breunor le Noir, better known as La Cote Male Taillée.[42] But none of these three Brunors of the *Tavola* ever held a "passo." Perhaps the author merely needed a rime for "Galasso." He gives also a catalogue of the fair ladies who were represented in the hall, and there in strange companionship were Guinevere, Cassandra, Polyxena, Ysolt with the blond tresses, Mary, Martha, the Magdalen, Catherine, a damsel of the Orient, and Morgan le Fay with the lovely visage.

It is evident in the *Sala di Malagigi* that the list of romantic names is of more importance than the manner in which the figures were supposed to be represented. If we turn back to the beginning of the fourteenth century, we find in an allegorical poem of 2800 lines, the *Intelligenza* (ascribed rather doubtfully to the Florentine chronicler, Dino Compagni), another instance of exuberant cataloguing in connection with supposed Arthurian carvings and paintings. The catalogue is itself more enthusiastic

than accurate, and the art interest, though a shade more genuine than in the later poem, is palpably subordinate. The poet of the *Intelligenza* gives us an elaborate description of the palace of his love, the Lady Intelligenza.[43] In the midst of the vault of her hall of delights was the God of Love, a dart in his hand. Around him were victims of his power, most of them famous in antiquity. But among them too were "the fair Ysolt and good Tristram, as they were surprised by vain love, which has destroyed many kingdoms," the fair Queen Guinevere, and Sir Lancelot; Sir Erec and Enid; Alexander and "Rosenna d'Amore"; Analida and the good Ivain; Ysolt of the White Hands, "even as she died for fine love, so greatly did she love the peerless Lancelot"; and the noble Lady of the Lake; she of Malehaut with the yearning heart; and Palamedes, the pagan knight.

It will be observed that even in so short a list the poet has made several blunders, as Gardner and others have noted.[44] Alexander, the father of Cliges, Chrétien's hero, had for his love Soredamors, not Rosenna d'Amore; Laudine not Analida, was the love and the bride of Chrétien's Ivain; Ysolt of the White Hands, the neglected wife of Tristram, neither loved nor died for Lancelot; that was the fate of the Fair Maid of Astolat. The Lady of the Lake and the Lady of Malehaut, both from the *Vulgate Lancelot*, are placed in somewhat incongruous proximity to Palamedes, who belongs to the *Prose Tristan*.

The *Intelligenza* goes on to mention, between descriptions of Narcissus and Julius Caesar,

the forest of Arnante, where Merlin was imprisoned by great craft; here is the tomb made by enchantment, as he himself taught the charm to her who held him in her power. . . . On the other side of the rich palace the Table Round was sculptured, the jousts, the tournaments, the great disport. There was Arthur, the joyous Guinevere, for whom the puissant Lancelot went mad, Mark, Tristram, and Ysolt the Blonde. There were the pines, and there the fountains, the jousts and the sword-play; the rivers, forests, rocks, and [strange intruder!] the King of Trebizond. . . . All of fine gold are the figures, the hunts, the horns, the varlets, and the squires.

Similar in descriptive manner to the *Intelligenza* though far more poetic and significant in content is Boccaccio's tribute to the charm of Arthurian story. While he was recovering at Florence from his ill-starred intrigue with "Fiammetta," he wrote about 1342 in the *Amorosa Visione* an account of the triumph of Glory.[45] In the hall of the castle of Mundane Life he sees painted a long cavalcade of famous warriors. After the great captains of ancient Rome

[40] Ed. Pio Rajna (Imola, 1871), st. 12–21.
[41] Malory, *Morte d'Arthur*, Bk. VIII, ch. 24.
[42] *Ibid.*, Bk. IX, ch. 9.
[43] Ed. P. Gellrich (Breslau, 1883), st. 72–6; st. 287. Ed. also by

V. Mistruzzi (Bologna, 1928), and R. Piccoli (Lanciano, 1911).
[44] E. G. Gardner, *op. cit.*, p. 108.
[45] *Ibid.*, p. 228.

come the valorous knights of the Round Table:[46]

King Arthur was among the first there, riding in front upon a great destrier, armed at all points, fierce and proud. Bors followed spurring close after him, and with him Perceval and Galahad at a slow pace, talking together. Behind them came Lancelot armed and gracious of carriage, a lance in his hand, uttering no word, often striking his powerful horse in order to be near the sweet lady whom to touch seemed to him the end of desire. How beautiful and how excellent was she! At his side came Guinevere upon a palfrey, smiling in manner, full of grace, holding sweet converse with him in silent, sober words. She was with him for whose sake she had lived in joy, loving him long and without measure, even though afterward she wept therefor. Not far behind him there followed in great sorrow Galehaut, whose worth is shown beyond any of his companions. Kaherdin, Hector de Maris, and Ivain followed, each craving greater honor; Morhaut of Ireland, Palamedes, Lionel, Pellinor, Gawain, Modred, Dodinel. Close behind came good Tristram upon a mighty and swift horse; Ysolt the Blonde came beside him, his hand clasped in hers, often looking into his face. How anguished was her visage by the power of love, with which all the soul within her seemed to burn, so that it shed light through all her outward acts. Timidly she seemed by her aspect to say: 'Thou art he whom I desire. Turn hither a little, my love, I pray thee, that I may see the face to see which I entered upon such a way.' Behind them seated on a steed came Brunor, cruel and proud.

Later on,[47] in the pageant of lovers, the poet sees again, after Floris and Blanchefleur, "Lancelot depicted with her who was so long his glory, and behind him at his right was Tristram and she whom he loved above all others." Even in prose translation it is evident that in these passages poetry has taken the place of mere artifice; the list has ceased to be the catalogue, as it were, of an art gallery, and something of aching beauty has been communicated to the lines.

A variation from the monotony of painted walls is afforded by the brief descriptive poem, *Il Padiglione di Carlomagno*, written probably late in the fifteenth century. The unknown author calls humbly upon the Muses of Parnassus to give him the requisite power and knowledge to describe the pavilion of Charlemagne, and he cites Bishop Turpin as his authority. The pavilion was woven of silk and gold threads, was powdered with pearls and divided into eight parts. Among other subjects there were Nimrod and Nessus, Hector and Hannibal, Alexander's ascent into the air[48] and descent into the sea, Aristotle on all fours, bestridden by a woman,[49] and Virgil in the basket.[50] In the sixth division, between Cato and Hercules, came the inevitable Tristram.[51]

In that part was Morhaut (Amorotto), fighting on the island with Tristram, and how this wise man saw that he would die by his hand, and how Tristram gave him so great a stroke that he stretched him mortally wounded on the earth, and how he asked his name. Morhaut, seeing that he could not escape, shot him with a poisoned arrow, so that he could not boast of his death, and that wound gave him a deadly agony; and how Tristram set forth upon the sea, and how he was borne at random, and how he arrived soon in Ireland, where Morhaut's father was king. There was to be seen the gentle and fair Ysolt, healing good Sir Tristram of the poisoned wound so grievous, and how they fell in love. . . . In the seventh part of this pavilion were Queen Guinevere and Lancelot,—who was the wife of King Arthur,—who burns with love for a certain word. On the other side was that baron called Sir Galehaut (Galeotto) by name; he fought with Tristram of Loonois, and in the end Tristram slew him.

The writer's capacity for confusing his pronouns seems equaled only by his capacity for confusing his stories. The late Professor Gardner, consulted on the subject, was unable to tell of any text which states that Tristram told Morhaut his name on the battlefield, or that Morhaut's father was King of Ireland, or that Tristram slew Galehaut. If the clause, "who burns with love by reason of a certain word (ch'arde d'amor per si fatto motto)" was not concocted merely to furnish a rime with *Lancilotto* and *Galeotto*, and if it applies to Guinevere, the allusion, Gardner suggested, is to Galehaut's introduction of his friend to Guinevere with the words: "Lady, lo, here is the best knight of the world."

IMAGES OF ARAGON

Spanish literature offers some curious contributions to the imaginary illustration of the Arthurian cycle.[52] In the *Testament d'Amor*, written in Catalan prose about 1400, an imaginary lover, writing his will in the Castle of the Perilous Garde, includes among the provisions:

Item, I desire and furthermore command my executors that the monument where my body will lie be of a rich green jasper, . . . and in the said monument let there be

[46] Canto 11.

[47] Canto 29.

[48] For bibliography of this scene in art cf. *Gests of King Alexander of Macedon*, ed. F. P. Magoun (Cambridge, Mass., 1929), p. 41, n. 3. Add A. K. Porter, *Romanesque Sculpture of the Pilgrimage Roads* (Boston, 1923), IV, pl. 461; *Bulletin du Comité des Travaux Historiques*, 1902, pp. 297 ff., pl. XL.

[49] Henri d'Andeli, *Œuvres*, ed. A. Héron, xxxiii ff. *Abhandlungen der Königliche Bayerische Akademie der Wissenschaften*, I Kl., XIX, 55 f. A. Borgeld, *Aristoteles en Phyllis*, ch. 3. O. Ryd-beck, *Meteltida Kalkmålningar i Skånes Kyrkor*, pp. 59, 74, 146. D'Essling, Müntz, *Petrarque* (P., 1902), pp. 116 f., 141, 143, 146, 159, 170. P. Schübring, *Cassoni* (Leipzig, 1915), figs. 198, 199, 201, 202, 213.

[50] *Schauinsland*, XXXI (1904), 12 f. J. W. Spargo, *Virgil the Necromancer* (Camb., Mass., 1934), pp. 254 ff.

[51] *Il Vanto delli Paladini e del Padiglione di Carlo Magno* (Florence, Pistoia, n. d., Brit. Mus. catalog, 11426. c. 16).

[52] *Revista de Bibliografia Catalana*, III (1903), 16 f. *Boletin de la Sociedad Arqueologica Luliana*, III (Sep., 1890), 294.

carved divers figures, among which there shall be represented the courtesies of Tristram and the chivalrous deeds of Galehaut and the adventures of Perceval and the nobility of Lady Guinevere.

More conventional are the two references in the Catalan romance of Johannot Martorell, *Tirant lo Blanch*, composed about 1460;[53] one chamber of the palace at Constantinople was "right well adorned and storied all about with the following loves: of Flores, Blanchefleur, Thisbe, Pyramus, Æneas, Dido, Tristram, Ysolt, Queen Guinevere, Lancelot, and many others, so that all their loves were depicted with right subtle and skillful painting." Another chamber bore on its walls "divers histories of Bors, Perceval, and Galahad, how he achieved the adventures of the Siege Perilous and all the conquest of the Holy Grail,"—a patent allusion to the *Queste del Saint Graal*.

PAINTED WALLS OF AVALON

A poet of the nearby Balearic Isles, Guillem Torella, displays a bizarre and humorous fancy; at least the account of his adventures in *La Faula* (*The Tale*), composed between 1350 and 1381, has elements of absurdity as amazing as those of Chaucer's eagle flight in the *Hous of Fame*. According to *The Tale* Guillem,[54] riding down to port one summer morning, sees a beautiful parrot perched on a rounded rock. Dismounting, he goes toward the parrot, but no sooner do his spurs strike the rock than the rock begins to move rapidly out to sea; it is, in fact, a whale! Before midnight the whale has carried the poet five hundred miles to the east and sets him ashore on an island. A serpent, who to his astonishment speaks French, though with a Catalan twist, informs him that he is on the isle whither Morgan le Fay and Arthur have retired. In the morning a gorgeously caparisoned horse appears. The saddle, like that of Enide in Chrétien's *Erec*, was of carved ivory, but it set forth, not the story of Æneas, but many a story of love, all adorned in blue and gold,

> De Floris e de Blanchaflors,
> D'Isolda la blonda e Tristany.

The poet mounts his horse, rides to a palace in the midst of a marvelous garden, and Morgan le Fay herself informs him that there abides the wounded Arthur. All about are painted walls:[55]

There you may see painted the loves of Tristram, the fine lover, the feats of prowess for which he had in his time praise and fame. There you could see the proof of the puissant Lancelot du Lac, the wisdom, the strength, the ardor with which he maintained chivalry. There you could see the folly of Palamedes the Strong, who with his haughty heart accomplished many a noble task. There you may see the deeds of arms and courtesy of Ivain the courteous, and the chivalry of Erec and the adventures of Gawain and the mighty battles of Bors and Perceval, who in the quest of the Holy Grail were with Galahad, who never was wearied by his arms nor the travail that he suffered. There you might see how Galehaut, whom men call the son of the Fair Giantess, had great love toward Lancelot, for whose sake he died, because he had not seen him a long time and could learn no true tidings of him. Of Blio and of Lionel, how they were valiant and adventurous; of Kay (Quochs) and Dinadan, the foolish jests which they told. Moreover you can place there the feats of arms and the labors of Sivarlot (?), Brunor, Gaheris, Sagremor, and each of the fine lovers who suffered for love in vain without any other gain. And Hector de Mares was there and Dodinel le Sauvage, and the many noble exploits of Ivain, and there were the lives of others.

In the course of the story Guillem is ushered into the presence of the wounded Arthur lying on his couch of pain. Though the king has reigned for over ninety years, he still seems young, because, as the poet learns, he is fed each year by the Holy Grail. He gives Guillem a message of no great import for the world, and the whale conveys the poet back to Majorca.

In this extraordinary mélange the painted walls serve again only as a device for Guillem's enumeration of his favorite Arthurian stories. But it is especially interesting to note that his poem preserves, as do the tales of Gervase of Tilbury and Caesarius of Heisterbach and the romance of *Floriant et Florete*,[56] a tradition which identified the isle of Avalon with that of Sicily. Perhaps the tropic beauty of its orange groves, its Arabian gardens with their plashing fountains, and the Byzantine mosaics of its palaces, seemed so complete a realization of the enchanted isle of Celtic story, that inevitably there arose a newborn tradition that here Arthur still lived, and here in time there were folk who swore they had seen him in a mysterious palace in the wilds of Etna. In some such way probably was launched one of the most curious of medieval legends.

Both the *Prose Tristan* and the traditions regarding Morgan's palace in Avalon seem to have inspired certain passages in the *Myreur des Histors* of that prolific and amusing scamp, Jean d'Outre-

[53] *Tirant lo Blanch*, ed. M. Aguilo y Fuster, II (Barcelona, 1905), 13, 18. *Tirant lo Blanch* (N. Y., 1918), chap. 117–119.
[54] *Canconer dels Comtes d'Urgell*, ed. D. G. Llabres (Societat Catalana de Bibliofils, 1906), pp. 131 ff. M. Mila y Fontanals, *Poetes Catalans* (P., 1876), pp. 9–22. V. M. O. Denk, *Einführung in die Geschichte der Altcatalanischen Literatur* (Munich, 1893),

pp. 222–228. W. Entwistle, *Arthurian Legend in the Literature of the Spanish Peninsula* (L., 1925), pp. 81, 186.
[55] Mila y Fontanals, *op. cit.*, p. 16.
[56] A. Graf, *Miti, leggende, e superstizioni del medio evo* (Turin, 1892), II, 303 ff.

meuse.[57] This citizen of Liége wrote in the second half of the fourteenth century and, as is now known, fobbed off on the credulous world a guidebook to the Holy Land and an account of travels in the Orient as the work of a Sir John Mandeville, who actually lived and died in Liége in his time, whereas, as a matter of fact, the work was a barefaced concoction of Jean's own. In the *Myreur* we have a universal history in which fact was likewise seasoned with fancy. In the year 893 Charlemagne's paladin Ogier took a sightseeing tour in Britain, and of all the sights the relics of Arthur's time were the chief. At Tintagel Ogier and his companions were entertained and taken to the church. At the entrance they saw

two images on the walls, carved in the round; within the forehead of the man was written, 'Here is Tristram'; and on the forehead of the woman 'Here is Ysolt, who came by her death for Tristram's sake, and Tristram for hers.' A hawk was perched on her fist; with the other hand she pointed to Tristram. Tristram rested one hand on the tassel (?) of his mantle, and in the other hand a sword was grasped. Ogier had a person climb up to measure the figures; the lady was found to measure seven feet and Tristram ten feet three inches; and it was written there in the church that they were fashioned in their own size.

Some time later Ogier arrived at a mysterious island, and there fought first with a "capalus,"—the Cath Palug of Welsh tradition,—then with Arthur and Gawain, and decided that he must have arrived in "faerie," to which as all the world knew Arthur and Gawain had gone. He came to Morgan's palace of ivory and jewels. "The great hall was written and painted with all the history of King Uther and Arthur, and of all the knights of their time." When Ogier asked Arthur what seems to have been one of the burning questions in medieval chivalric circles, who was "le plus preux" of his knights, Arthur displayed a remarkable tact and could not answer.

Morgan sprang up, came to the wall, and bade that there the best knight of King Arthur's time should appear, in the name of God the Father, the Son and the Holy Spirit. At once Tristram appeared there first of all, then Lancelot, and afterwards Palamedes; and the image of Galahad appeared in a little corner; and each of the other three bowed and made reverence to him, and he laughed. Ogier saw it and smiled.

It is surely permitted to us to smile too.

Three English Descriptions

We now come to three descriptions in Middle English literature. We have seen already how firmly established in French and Italian literature was the

convention of describing the subjects of mural decoration, and Chaucer was conventional enough to adopt it, but apparently without enthusiasm. In the *Book of the Duchess* (1369) he dreamed of a chamber in which were painted in fine colors "bothe text and glose, of al the Romaunce of the Rose." Perhaps Chaucer should not be held to strict verisimilitude in the account of a dream; but a bedchamber would have to be fairly large to accommodate a complete series of illustrations of the *Roman de la Rose*, and it would be unique if it were to include a commentary on that lengthy poem, since none such exists even in MS. One suspects that the "glose" at least was injected for the simple reason that Chaucer needed a rime for "rose." After his *Italienische Reise* in 1372–73 he succumbed to the spell of Italian literature, if not of Italian art, and in his *Parlement of Foules*, composed probably in 1377, there are many signs of Italian influence. Among these is the luxuriously sensuous palace of Venus and its walls "peynted over al of many a story." Chaucer was certainly not interested in the details of the painting; he merely enumerates the lovers depicted there, Semiramis, Candace, Dido, Thisbe, Paris, Troilus, and so forth; and of course includes Tristram and Ysolt.[58]

> All these were peynted on that other syde,
> And al here love, and in what plyt they dyde.

Not even the list was Chaucer's own invention, for, as Professor Lowes has proved, it was compounded from a passage in Dante's *Inferno* and another in Boccaccio's *Teseide*.[59]

It was doubtless from this very passage in the *Parlement of Foules* that Chaucer's loyal disciple, John Lydgate, monk of Bury, took the hint for his painted series of lovers. Chaucer had given three descriptions of the Temple of Venus (in the *Parlement*, the *Hous of Fame*, and the *Knight's Tale* respectively), and Lydgate, when he wrote the *Temple of Glas* about 1403, made a composite of the three, and of course its walls had to be covered with "sundry lovers."

I saw some stand, and some kneel with scrolls in their hands, and some make woeful and piteous laments with doleful cheer to Venus, as she sat floating in the sea, that she might have pity upon their woe.

Among the lovers, chiefly classical or Chaucerian, he sees at least one famous figure of Arthurian story:[60]

> There was eke Isaude—and meni an othir mo—
> And al the turment and al the cruel wo
> That she hade for Tristram al hir live.

[57] Jean d'Outremeuse, *Myreur des Histors* (Brussels, 1877), IV, 36, 51 f., 57.
[58] L. 290. The statement of Miss Evans in *Rev. of Eng. Studies*, VI (1930), 412, about Chaucer's art interests seems exaggerated.
[59] *Mod. Phil.*, XIV (1917), 705.
[60] Lydgate, *Temple of Glass*, ed. J. Schick (L., 1891), v. 77.

More zestful, more individual is the description of a chamber in the romance of *Sir Degrevant*, composed early in the fifteenth century. In the room where the heroine entertains her lover with a feast and her own harping the roof is carved with gold "besauntes," or discs; it is painted with scenes from the Apocalypse, the Epistles, the "Parables of Solomon," and serves to remind us of the vogue, strong at this time in Norfolk, for painted ceilings and carved screens.[61] The walls are said to have been of black marble; the corbels were golden archangels; the four "gospellers" sat on four pillars, while Austin, Gregory, Jerome, and Ambrose listened to them. Probably sculptured under little canopies sat kings of many lands,—great Charles with his crown, Godfrey de Bouillon, and Arthur the Briton, all "with their bright brands."[62]

WARRIORS AND WARS

Germany contributes, besides the description of the golden dish in *Diu Krone*, a description of a fresco in *Der Kittel* (*The Kirtle*), written by the Alsatian poet Altswert about 1400. The poet enters the palace of Venus, but *mirabile dictu!* he sees painted on the walls not languishing lovers but combative knights.[63]

King Arthur stands as if he were living. King Gameret fights there even as he has done on earth. I name without any mistake Wigalois, the fearless man. Perceval also stands painted there, and William of Orleans beside him. Of Lancelot of Troy (!) the high renown and praise were not there forgotten.

We return to France for our last quotation, found in the fifteenth-century *La Mort de Tristram et d'Iseut*.[64] It describes a chamber, "curtained with a curtain the fairest and richest that ever was, for all the history of Arthur, how he conquered the lordship over the Britons, was there portrayed."

A review of all the foregoing passages of description engenders certain reflections. First, it appears that for the most part they were produced by men with literary rather than pictorial imaginations. They tell us little of technique, shape, color, or even the more obvious features of dress and gesture. Thomas alone, vitally inspired by Romanesque art, gives us enough detail to reconstruct and visualize the image of Queen Ysolt in her carved and colored splendor. Thomas, again, and Boccaccio are the only poets who infuse into the supposed picture or sculpture of great lovers, anything which really suggests the power of their passion. For the most part, poets were content, as was Chaucer himself, simply to take over

as a literary device the idea of a painted wall, to string together in a more or less melodious list, the names of such lovers as they had encountered in books; without any actual image in mind, they were careless whether their rather meagre details of description fitted such an image or not. On the other hand it is clear that this literary convention, of walls painted with famous lovers and scenes from romance, could never have come into being had there not been behind it a widespread reality. The taste for secular wall paintings, even in the first half of the thirteenth century, finds in these numerous literary passages important corroborative attestation. It is also to be noted that just as the greater number of these references concern the lovers Tristram and Ysolt, so too, as we shall presently see, do the actual remains of Arthurian art. In this detail also literature confirms the evidence of art that the story of Tristram and Ysolt was the best loved of all Arthurian stories.

SPANISH RECORDS

From the more or less imaginary descriptions which in greater or less degree suggest the decorative possibilities of Arthurian story, we may turn to the various account books and inventories which beyond all question preserve the record of its actual uses. They are of particular value because they establish the former existence of Arthurian tapestries and enameled cups, though the ruthlessness of Time and Man have left to the world today but one of these cups and no tapestries except those in which Arthur appears as one of the Nine Worthies. The documents in question are, however, rather late in date and limited in scope since they cover a period of only seventy years and touch on but three countries.

The earliest is the order sent in 1352 from Barcelona by the Machiavellian Pedro IV of Aragon to his counselor Johan Ximenez of Huesca at Saragossa concerning the tiling and roofing of the Moorish chamber in the Aljaferia, "on the walls of which is painted the history of Jaufré."[65] This Arthurian romance, composed in Provençal between 1222 and 1232, has as its hero Jaufré, the son of Dovan, who is to be identified with the French Giflet son of Do, and the Welsh Gilfaethwy, son of Don. It was composed for the great great grandfather of King Pedro, Jaime or James I, who won back the Balearic Isles from the Moors in 1229 and Valencia in 1238. The anonymous author speaks in hyperbolic strain of the loyalty, piety, and justice of his patron, and of (what probably touched him more nearly) his generosity to jongleurs.[66] It was no coincidence, then, that his ro-

[61] Cf. L. A. Hibbard, *Mediæval Romance in England*, p. 308.
[62] J. O. Halliwell, *Thornton Romances* (L., 1844), p. 238, v. 1467.
[63] Meister Altswert, *Der Kittel*, ed. W. Holland, A. Keller (Stuttgart, 1850), p. 37.

[64] H. Göbel, *Wandteppiche* (Leipzig, 1923), Teil 1, Band I, 58.
[65] A. Rubio y Lluch, *Documents per l'Historia de la Cultura Catalana Migeval* (Barcelona, 1908), I, 159.
[66] *Jaufré*, ed., H. Breuer (Göttingen, 1925), v. 58 ff.

mance of the young hero who came to seek adventure at Arthur's court was portrayed on the palace walls at Saragossa.

Whether King Pedro himself or one of his predecessors was responsible for the paintings at Saragossa, we do not know, but we do know that he was an amateur of Arthurian romance. In Professor Entwistle's pages we read[67] that a copy of the *Lancelot* was completed for him in 1339, and another in 1346, both made by chaplains; that he bought a *Meliadus* in 1339, wrote a letter concerning a *Queste del Saint Graal* in 1342 on behalf of the princesses Blanca and Maria, and had copies of the *Tabula Rotunda* made in 1349 and 1356.

But the letters of principal interest to us are those in which Pedro IV requires Pedro Palau to return to him the book of *Lancalot en Catala*, which the duke primogenitus had been reading. They are dated respectively 17th February and 16th March 1362, and the prince was then eleven years of age. . . . We are strangely drawn to a king wise enough to know that *Lancelot du Lac* is incomparably the best book for boys, who considered archbishops the fit porters of such a treasure, and whose librarians had the good taste to retain it for a whole month after his peremptory demand.

It is an odd coincidence that in the very year 1356, when the king had a second copy of the *Tabula Rotunda* made, his queen, Leonor, bought for the Infantas at Montpellier and Avignon, besides certain tapestries illustrating the stories of Virgil, Charlemagne, and the Castle of Love, an arras, 36 palms in height, costing 32 florins, 9 grossi, "on which was depicted the story of the knights of the Round Table."[68] In 1368 Pedro himself bought in Paris for Donna Leonor a French tapestry, one of those "draps istoriats" for which she seems to have had a special liking, and this one, 4 ells (or about 15 feet) in length, was devoted to the history of Arthur himself.[69]

The taste for Arthurian illustration was by no means confined to northern Aragon; it was known, too, further south. In a record concerning the preparations made for the entry of King Martin into Valencia in 1402 is noted the payment to Bernat Godal for painting fifteen horse trappings with his own gold, silver, and other colors, "to wit, the trapping of Aristotle, and Virgil, and Tristany and Isolda, and Jason and Eropra (Europa?) and Etnas (Æneas?) and Semiramis, and Lancelot and Ginebre (Guinevere), and the Pope, and Saladin"![70] It was a strange company, indeed, in which the immortal lovers of Arthurian romance found themselves.

Crossing the Pyrenees, we find an inventory of King Jean le Bon made in 1353 when Gaucher de Vannes became the royal "argentier" or keeper of the household effects. In the list of silver fountains, appraised by Pierre de Laigny and Pierre Chapelu, changers and burghers of Paris, there is listed one, "a fountain with a vine above the device (*divise*) Tristram and Ysolt."[71]

TAPESTRIES AND ENAMELS OF LOUIS OF ANJOU

In the years 1364 and 1365 the second son of King Jean, Louis, Duke of Anjou, dictated one of the most important of medieval inventories. Louis, in his day, the richest and most powerful noble of France, was born at Vincennes in 1339.[72] At the disaster of Poitiers in 1356 he fought beside his father. In 1359 he was viceregent of his captive father in Anjou and Maine. When as a result of the treaty of Brétigny King Jean returned to France, Louis was obliged to go to London as a hostage, and his father, to sweeten that hard exile, created him Duke of Anjou. Two years later Louis, in violation of his father's pledge, fled back to France, and his father, with a high sense of duty, returned voluntarily to England, and died a prisoner there in 1364. Both his eldest son, who succeeded him as Charles V, and Louis now indulged an expensive taste for great tapestries, glittering jewels, and enameled table service. As rapacious as he was ambitious, Louis was undeterred by the impoverished state of his country. Immediately upon his father's death in 1364 he sent emissaries into his fiefs of Anjou and Touraine, ravaged though they had been by the English, to collect all arrears for thirty years back; the records say that many, not having the means to pay, fled the country, and widows were driven to beg their bread.[73] For twelve years Louis continued these exactions and not until 1376 did he relent. Out of such proceeds he built up his great collections of treasure and art. The very year he began to bleed his subjects of what little substance the English had left, he had drawn up his first inventory. It is well to remember that the treasures of art have often been made only at the cost of blood and tears and ruined lives.

It was this same Louis, we may note, who borrowed from his brother a manuscript of the Apocalypse that it might furnish the basis for the great series of tapestries which to this day is the glory of Angers.[74] In 1380 his royal brother died, and at this

[67] W. Entwistle, *op. cit.*, pp. 89–94.
[68] Rubio y Lluch, *op. cit.*, I, 171.
[69] *Ibid.*, I, 104, n. 1.
[70] A. Bonilla y San Martin, *Tristan de Leonis* (Madrid, 1912), p. xxx.
[71] L. Douet d'Arcq, *Comptes de l'argenterie* (P., 1851), p. 308.

[72] L. E. S. J. Marquis de Laborde, *Notice des émaux du Musée du Louvre* II (P., 1853), vii ff.
[73] *Bibl. de l'École des Chartes*, XXXVI (1875), 300.
[74] L. de Farcy, *Histoire et description des tapisseries de la cathédrale d'Angers* (Angers, 1889).

time Louis had drawn up a second and far more extensive inventory. For a brief time until the coronation of Charles VI, he was regent; but soon afterwards the offer of the the the throne of Naples from Queen Giovanna took him to Italy. There he fought and won his throne but had to melt up most of his vast collection of plate, so recently and carefully catalogued, to do so. He could now call himself King of Naples, Sicily, and Jerusalem, Duke of Apulia, Calabria, Anjou and Touraine, Prince of Capua, and a dozen other titles as well. But the adventure was no happy one and he died of fever near Bari in 1384. To his credit, it should be remembered, at the last he ordered 20,000 francs to be distributed among the poor of Anjou, Touraine and Maine "in return for the burdens and oppressions we have laid upon them."

According to the earlier inventory of 1364–65 he owned the large number of seventy-six tapestries.[75] Among them we find a tapestry of the Nine Worthies;[76] a tapestry of Charlemagne, King Arthur, and Godfrey de Bouillon;[77] a tapestry of Lancelot, "who fights with the knight who said he had been found with the Queen Guemenie (sic)";[78] and a tapestry of Lancelot "how he brings away the Queen Guemenie (sic) to the Castle of the Perilous Garde."[79] These last two hangings were doubtless based on the stirring episode in the *Mort Artu*, when Lancelot rode up to Agravain, who had found the lovers together, and crying, "Coward, traitor!" drove his spear through Agravain's body, and then, when the field was won, brought the Queen on horseback to Joyous Garde, "formerly called the Dolorous Garde."[80]

In this same inventory of 1364–65 there are numerous entries which refer to the legend of Tristram. Among the rich vessels which once adorned the ducal table were: first, a cup, gilded and enameled, on the base of which were Tristram and Ysolt;[81] second, a hanap on the base and cover of which was the history of Tristram and Ysolt;[82] third, a salt-cellar of silver gilt: "The said salere is set upon a foot of which the pillar is of a tree, in which tree is King Mark, and below are Tristram and Ysolt, all carved very beautifully, and before them at the aforesaid foot there is a piece of crystal in the fashion of a

fountain, and within this fountain appears the head of King Mark";[83] fourth, a cup of silver gilt; "Inside the said cup is a blue enamel, in which are Tristram and Ysolt and the head of King Mark in a tree."[84]

This subject of the tryst of the lovers beneath a tree, spied upon by King Mark, is, as we shall see in our study of the Tristram romance, the most familiar, the most stereotyped motif of all in the Arthurian legend. Whether it was the symmetry of the composition or the piquancy of the situation which commended it, the subject caught the imagination of all sorts of craftsmen who repeated it with singular monotony, and used it for singular purposes. In a MS of the *Cy Nous Dit* at Chantilly (No. 1078–79), a book which somewhat vainly sought to moralize popular stories, the well-known scene is reproduced (Fig. 120), and there follows it this interpretation:[85]

Here we are told a Queen and a knight were seated beneath a tree above a fountain to speak of light love; and they turned to speak of good and courtesy because they saw in the fountain the reflection of the King who watched them from the tree above. If we guard ourselves from evil thoughts and evil doing, for the love of our Lord, who sees all our thoughts, we would keep us in His peace, just as the Queen and the knight kept the peace of the King; for there are some who keep better the peace of their temporal lords who see them only outwardly, than they keep the peace of Our Lord, who sees all their thoughts within and without.

The later inventory made by the Duke of Anjou in 1379–80 (when the King, his brother, was dying), shows double the number of vessels enameled with scenes from the same romance, viz., eight.[86] Most of the descriptions give no new details, except for one that adds that Tristram had a falcon on his wrist and Ysolt held a little dog.[87] This object seems to have formed a pair with one which is described as representing the lovers under a tent at a game of chess.[88] A silver gilt flask engraved with "Moorish letters" contained two large round enamels, one depicting a knight and a lady riding, the other "Tristram, who plays the harp before the Queen Ysolt, and behind is King Mark who hurls a lance."[89] This last subject is also found on a silver basin, which showed

---

[75] *Bibl. de l'École des Chartes*, L (1889), 169.

[76] *Ibid.*, 171. A partial list of inventoried tapestries of the Nine Worthies is given in *Rev. archéologique* (1918), pp. 133 f.

[77] *Bibl. de l'École des Chartes*, L, 173.

[78] *Ibid.*, 174.

[79] *Ibid.*, 175.

[80] H. O. Sommer, *Vulgate Version*, VI, 281–283. *Mort le Roi Artu*, ed. Frappier, p. 99. Cf. Malory, *Morte d'Arthur*, Bk. XX, ch. 8. The insignificant fight with Margonde—cf. P. Ackerman, *Tapestry, the Mirror of Civilization* (N. Y., 1933), p. 321,—seems much less likely as a subject than the crucial combat with Agravain.

[81] Laborde, *Notice des émaux*, II, 59, No. 348.

[82] *Ibid.*, 62, No. 370.

[83] *Ibid.*, 52, No. 312.

[84] *Ibid.*, 90, No. 563.

[85] *Mémoires de la Société des Antiquaires du Centre*, II, 18; pl. II. In translating I have omitted a "ne" which makes nonsense of the whole passage. Aroux in *L'hérésie de Dante* (P., 1857), p. 30, finds in the scene "the druidic element reflecting itself powerfully in the doctrine of Love"!—whatever that may mean. On *Ci Nous Dit*, cf. *Histoire litt. de la France*, XXXVI, 237.

[86] H. Moranvillé, *Inventaire de l'orfévrerie et des joyaux de Louis I, Duc d'Anjou* (P., 1906), II, 236, 277, 291 f., 312.

[87] *Ibid.*, III, 493.

[88] *Ibid.*

[89] *Ibid.*, 453.

in enamel "a man and a woman as if in a chamber, and the woman has a little dog in her lap, and the man places his hand on her head, and behind is a man who wears a crown and bears a lance in his hand."[90] These scenes are based on the French *Prose Tristan*, which attributed the death of Tristram to Mark's treacherous blow. (Cf. Fig. 276)

This later inventory also describes a pair of silver vessels of Italian workmanship.[91] One was enameled within "with knights and ladies of old," and recorded their names,—all being associated with the legend of Troy. The mate contained the enameled figures of Charles, Regnaut, Olivier, Geffroit, Orlando, Atsofo (Astolfo?) from the Carolingian cycle, and the following knights of the Round Table: "Galeotho, Febus, Messire Yvain, Galaas, Lancelot, Tristan, Palamedes, Rex Artus, Piercivale, Bordo (Bors)." The strange mingling of French and Italian forms points to a workshop in Northern Italy where the two languages slipped off the tongue with equal readiness. The presence of Febus and Palamedes points to the great prestige of the *Palamedes* in Italy, to which we have so much testimony.

Of this great collection of plate not a single item can be identified in the museums today; and Moranvillé has shown why. Between 1381 and 1384 it all went to the mint to finance the gamble for the Neapolitan throne. Even the crown was broken in pieces and pawned to Louis's creditors, and on his death in far-off Apulia his widow had little left with which to deck her table.[92]

Tapestries of Charles V and His Brothers

Louis's brother, Charles V, had meanwhile been acquiring his own collection of tapestries. In 1368 he bought the "Quest of the Grail" from Huchon Berthélemi,[93] and in the inventory of tapestries at the Louvre made eleven years later when Charles was dying, it is listed with one of "Messire Yvain" and two tapestries of the Nine Worthies.[94]

With the accession in 1379 of the boy, Charles VI, disasters began to multiply for France. In 1391 he complained of having to sell most of his inherited treasures to pay for the wars in Flanders and on the frontiers.[95] Nevertheless, he accumulated a hundred and fifty tapestries, and his wife, Ysabeau of Bavaria, indulged herself likewise. Both seemed to have found romance a haven from reality, for in 1382 the king took out from the library of the Louvre MSS of the *Saint Graal* and *Tristan*, and two years later a *Mort d'Artus*; the queen about 1390 borrowed the *Saint Graal* and a *Bel Escanor*, in 1392 an *Enserrement de Merlin*, and *Torrez, Chevalier au Cercle d'Or*, in 1402 a *Tristan*, in 1404 an *Artus*.[96] Ysabeau's taste found reflection in art, for the keeper of her tapestries acknowledged the receipt in 1398 of a large piece, "Perceval, who conquered the Holy Grail," thirty-four feet wide.[97] It came from Jacques Dourdain, one of the great Parisian weavers of the period, who had been associated with Nicholas Bataille in the famous Apocalypse series now at Angers. Between 1400 and 1410 we hear of the repairing by Jean De Jaudoigne of this same tapestry of the Holy Grail, "where there were several images broken."[98]

Philip the Bold, Duke of Burgundy, brother of Louis of Anjou and Charles V, kept up the family tradition. He seems to have bought two Perceval tapestries. One appears in the inventory made at his death in 1404.[99] and reappears, probably, in the inventory made at Dijon on the accession of Philip the Good, his grandson.[100] In the latter it is called "a tapestry of Orguilleux de la Lande, nommé Parcheval le Galloiz, worked with a little gold [thread]." The title is certainly misleading, for it has been translated, "The Pride of the Land, named Perceval the Gaul."[101] But the hero of Chrétien de Troyes's *Conte del Graal* was not a Gaul but a Welshman, and he is not to be identified with another knight in the same romance called Orgueilleux de la Lande, or the Proud Knight of the Heath.[102] The first adventure of the boy Perceval when he leaves his mother's forest home is to kiss a damsel whom he finds alone in a tent, and to carry off her ring. The suspicions of her lover, the Proud Knight, being aroused, he drives the lady forth shabbily clad until he can meet Perceval and be revenged. When the meeting does take place some time later, Perceval vanquishes the Proud Knight and convinces him of the lady's innocence. That certain scenes from this story of Orgueilleux de la Lande appeared on the tapestry seems clear, but which they were we cannot tell.

The other Perceval tapestry,[103] bought by Philip the Bold in 1390 at Arras of André de Monchi, and measuring almost sixty-four feet in width, he employed as a *douceur* during certain delicate negotiations between England and France.

[90] *Ibid.*, 498.
[91] *Ibid.*, 481 f.
[92] *Ibid.*, I, xii–xvi.
[93] J. Guiffrey, *Hist. générale de la tapisserie* (P., 1878–85), I, 26.
[94] *Ibid.*, 25. J. Labarte, *Inventaire du mobilier de Charles V* (P., 1879), p. 378.
[95] Labarte, *op. cit.*, p. viii.
[96] L. Delisle, *Cabinet des MSS* (P., 1868), I, 49. On Torrez cf. *Hist. litt. de la France*, XXX, 263.

[97] Guiffrey, *op. cit.*, p. 18.
[98] *Ibid.*, p. 22.
[99] A. Pinchart, *Hist. de la tapisserie dans les Flandres* (P., 1878–85), p. 15.
[100] *Ibid.*, p. 24.
[101] W. G. Thomson, *History of Tapestry*, ed. 2 (L., 1930), p. 93.
[102] Christian von Troyes, *Percevalroman*, ed. A. Hilka (Halle, 1932), vv. 635–832, 3691–4085.
[103] Pinchart, *op. cit.*, p. 11.

The Duke of Burgundy, who knew perfectly the dispositions of the English in regard to France and foresaw all the difficulties which would be produced by sour and turbulent spirits, had sent before him in order to sweeten and calm them, certain presents to the lords who had the greatest prestige and authority; to wit, the Dukes of Lancaster, Gloucester, and York.

These presents consisted of three magnificent tapestry hangings, and of these the Perceval went to the Duke of York.

Philip the Bold had also a huge tapestry of King Arthur. This was of such large dimensions that in 1402 he had it divided up by an expert, Colart d'Inchy, living at Hesdin, into four pieces.[104] In the inventory of 1404 it is, however, described as "a tapestry of two pieces of the history of King Arthur."[105]

About 1408 the inventory of Valentine of Orléans records a "tappis à ymages" of the jousts of Lancelot.[106]

TAPESTRIES IN ENGLAND

In England, too, Arthurian tapestries were prized. In addition to the record concerning the three huge tapestries sent across the channel by Duke Philip to the uncles of Richard II, there is a record showing that one of these uncles, Thomas, Duke of Gloucester, before he was smothered to death at the command of his nephew, possessed in 1397 "a piece of cloth of arras, without gold thread, of the battle between Gamlayn and Lancelot."[107] Gamlayn is a name unknown in the roll-call of Arthur's knights.[108] It is almost certainly a misreading of "Gauvain," and the tapestry probably illustrated the last desperate combat which was fought in France between the two former friends and of which the story is told in the *Mort Artu*.[109] The piece may therefore have belonged to the same set as the two *Mort Artu* pieces of Louis of Anjou. Richard II himself at his deposition in 1399 possessed an arras of Perceval,[110] and it may be the same which appears in the inventory of Henry V in 1422 as "another piece of arras which begins the

history of Sir Percyvall: 'Here is the history—' "[111]

It is thus a curious fact that Charles V, Ysabeau of Bavaria, Philip the Bold, Philip the Good, the Duke of York, Richard II, Henry V, all possessed tapestries concerned with Perceval. Though one would have supposed that this hero's fame was on the wane toward the end of the fourteenth and the beginning of the fifteenth countries, the printed editions of Perceval's romance in the sixteenth century show that he still more than held his own.[112] Despite the incompleteness of the records concerning medieval tapestries, it is probably a significant index of the relative popularity that so many survive concerning Perceval tapestries and so few concerning other Arthurian heroes. Of Lancelot there were the tapestries in the possession of Louis of Anjou, Valentine of Orléans, and Thomas of Gloucester; of Arthur himself those in the possession of Leonor of Aragon and Philip the Bold.

The revival of interest in the art and the legends of the Middle Ages which was characteristic of the Romantic and Preraphaelite movements produced, as we should expect, a realization that there had existed a medieval iconography of the Round Table cycle. Scott, in *The Betrothed*, published in 1825, has this passing but natural reference: " 'And be besieged in form,' said the Fleming, 'like the castle of Tintagel in the old hangings, all for the love of fair lady.' " And William Morris in *The Ring Given to Venus* paints a picture on which the imagination lingers:

> a cloister of delight,
> Well wrought of marble green and white,
> Wherein upon a wall of gold
> Of Tristram was the story told,
> Well done by cunning hands that knew
> What form to man and beast was due.

Brief as these two passages are, they prove that Scott and Morris were true heirs of the medieval romancers and poets.

---

[104] *Ibid.*, p. 13.

[105] *Ibid.*, p. 15.

[106] H. Göbel, *Wandteppiche*, Teil I, Bd. I, 63.

[107] *Archaeological Journal*, LIV, 288.

[108] The reference cannot be to *Gamelyn*; see *Middle English Metrical Romances*, ed. W. H. French, C. B. Hale (N. Y., 1930), pp. 209 ff., which has no connection with Lancelot.

[109] H. O. Sommer, *Vulgate Version*, VI, 338–343. *Mort le Roi Artu*, ed. Frappier, 169 ff. Cf. Malory, Bk. XX, ch. 21.

[110] W. G. Thomson, *op. cit.*, p. 85.

[111] Thomson, *Tapestry Weaving in England* (L., 1914), p. 26.

[112] *Perlesvaus*, ed. Nitze, Jenkins, I (Chicago, 1932), p. 12. Christian von Troyes, *Percevalroman*, ed. Hilka, pp. vii, 481 ff. *Perceval le Galloys*, ed. G. Apolinaire (P., 1918).

CHAPTER III

KING ARTHUR

IN THE preceding chapter we have had amazing illustrations of the deceptive power of incomplete evidence. Surviving inventories and historic records give an impression of the countries, the media, and the periods in which illustrations of the Round Table cycle flourished which is utterly different from the impression one derives from the reflection of those illustrations in imaginative literature. When one turns from these two types of evidence, and examines the actual remains of Arthurian illustration, fancying that he now knows what to expect, he will be startled by several novelties—earlier dates, unsuspected phases or branches of the tradition, new media, new territories. Who would have guessed from the preceding chapter that the very earliest surviving illustrations would come from Brittany, Lombardy, and Apulia? that one of them would be in mosaic and would represent the heroic king riding a goat? Pope's warning regarding a little knowledge could hardly be demonstrated more neatly than here. No one of the three sets of facts affords a safe basis for generalization, particularly for negative assertion. Only a combined study of them all would lead to sound conclusions. And even then the argument *ex silentio* might prove fallacious. We cannot say that because we have no trace of Arthurian illustration from Bohemia or Scandinavia or the Latin kingdoms of the East that none such existed.

THE PERROS RELIEF

As one might expect from the history of the Arthurian legend, Brittany has given us what may be—or may not be—the earliest surviving representation of Arthur. There is uncertainty as to both subject and date. Perros, near Lannion, once a quiet fishing village, now a *station balnéaire*, possesses a Romanesque church which is dated vaguely about the year 1100.[1] No one could disprove a date seventy-five years earlier or later. Documents are lacking, and in this out of the way corner there is no sculptural history. On the second pier on the left as one enters the nave from the west is a very crude low relief in red granite. (Fig. 3) At the left is a strange heap, which may connote the coils of a monster. Next is a male figure with exaggerated membrum; the legs are bent back toward the body, and one hand grasps the right ankle. The other hand is grasped by another man, who holds a clearly marked crozier. Between these two lies prostrate what seems to be a third man, equipped, it would seem, with a shield and helmet; according to medieval principles, however, he may be merely a duplicate of the first.

The most plausible conjecture as to the subject is that first put forward by De la Monneraye,[2] to the effect that it is a legend of St. Efflam,[3] to whom the church at Perros is dedicated. The earliest form of the story is a Latin text copied in the seventeenth century from the Legendary of Tréguier, composed about 1400.[4] The passage concerned with Arthur may be summarized as follows:[5]

St. Efflam, an Irish prince, accompanied by devout followers, came ashore in Brittany (near Plestin, southwest of Perros). He observed a dragon entering his cave backwards so that the print of his claws would deceive his pursuers into believing that he was still abroad. Presently Arthur, "fortissimus," who had been long seeking the monster in vain because of this subtle trick, arrived on the scene and was directed by the saint to the lair. With a triple-headed bludgeon and a buckler covered with a lion's pelt, he engaged the dragon in a desperate but indecisive conflict. At evening, exhausted and overcome with thirst, he besought water of the holy man. Efflam prayed, made the sign of the cross, struck a rock, and lo, a spring gushed forth. Arthur drank, fell at the feet of the saint in gratitude, and departed with his blessing. Thereupon Efflam prayed Christ to rid the land of the dragon, and with a roar and a vomit of blood, the creature disappeared over the seas.

Interpreted in the light of this local legend, the lumps on the left may be the dragon; the figure with the crozier, St. Efflam; the prostrate form with helmet and shield and the nude figure whose hand is grasped by the saint may both be taken to represent the exhausted Arthur. The dedication of the church to the saint makes this explanation seem plausible, though it still leaves much to be desired.

The antiquity of the legend itself is not established, but its character does resemble that of certain hagiographic traditions concerning Arthur which certainly date from the twelfth century. These were no doubt the products of monkish scriptoria in Wales and Dumnonia, and they paint no flattering picture of the darling of the laity and the professional storytellers. The *cyfarwyddon* and bards in turn made mock of the shavelings. The old Welsh poem, *The Harryings of Annwn*, which recounts the raid of

---

[1] P. Joanne, *Dictionnaire géographique et administratif* (P., 1899), V, 3483.

[2] *Bulletin archéologique de l'Association Bretonne*, I (1849), livr. 2, 159. H. de la Villemarqué, *Romans de la Table Ronde* (P., 1860), pp. 23, 433. Albert le Grand, *Vies des saints de la Bretagne Armorique*, ed. 5 (Quimper, 1901), p. 590, and B. Jollivet, *Les*

Côtes du Nord (Guingamp, 1859), IV, 88 confuse the interior capital with a sculpture on the south porch.

[3] *Speculum*, VIII (1933), 480.

[4] *Annales de Bretagne*, VII (1891–92), 279.

[5] *Ibid.*, pp. 285–87.

Arthur and his men in the ship Prydwen against the island fortress of the gods, suddenly shifts to an invective against the monks. Some of the lines may be translated, in default of an authoritative rendering, as follows:[6]

> Monks congregate in a choir like dogs. . .
> Monks congregate like wolves. . .
> They know not when midnight and dawn divide,
> Nor what is the course of the wind nor who agitates it,
> In what place it dies away, on what land it roars.

The monks naturally retorted to the raillery of the bards and *cyfarwyddon*, impugned their morals, and depreciated their hero. In the Welsh life of St. Patern,[7] composed probably about 1100, Arthur is called a *tyrannus*, a word which had unpleasant connotations even then. In the contemporary life of St. Cadoc Arthur is represented as seized with a sudden lust and as dissuaded by Cei and Bedwyr from raping a passing damsel. In the life of St. Carantoc[8] we find a story like that of St. Efflam. Carantoc had been given an altar by Christ himself and coming to Severn mouth had set it afloat to see where it might come ashore. Arthur, then reigning over that region, was seeking a huge dragon which was devastating the "field of Carrum." Carantoc met and greeted the king, gave him his benediction, and asked news concerning the floating altar. Arthur cannily demanded as the price of his information that the saint remove the monster. Carantoc knelt in prayer, and behold! the beast came out with a great roar, like a calf to its dam, and bowed its head before him. He threw his stole round its neck and led it away.

Such legends in which the character of Arthur is blackened or his power contrasted unfavorably with that of the saints do not necessarily prove, as M. Faral has maintained,[9] that Arthur had not yet become a celebrated hero. Alexander the Great was idolized by the chivalric world as a pattern of generosity at the same time that he was condemned by the clergy as a supreme example of pride. Theodoric was likewise consigned to hell as an Arian by the clergy, but notwithstanding achieved among the Teutonic laity immortal fame as Theodoric or Dietrich von Bern. It was the popularity of Arthur with a class of entertainers hostile to the monks which led the latter to exalt their saints at the expense of the popular hero. Such must have been the situation out of which the Efflam legend sprang, and such probably is the explanation why Arthur—if it be Arthur

—should appear in this early Breton relief in so inglorious a rôle.

THE MODENA ARCHIVOLT

Let us remind ourselves that in 1114 a Paduan document gives the name Artusius as that of Count Ugo's brother; in 1136 a similar document mentions a Galvanus; in 1125 another Artusius is mentioned among those who transferred the possession of a castle to Modena cathedral; and the names Artusius and Galvanus recur with some variations in spelling throughout the century.[10] These are precisely the Latinized forms employed by Italians in later centuries for Arthur and Gawain.[11] Since the Artusii of the Padua and Modena records appear as grown men in 1114 and 1125, they must have been christened close to the year 1100 or even earlier. Thus we have proof that Italian interest in the *Matière de Bretagne* may be traced back to the eleventh century.

It is not, therefore, so astonishing as it might otherwise seem to discover that iconographic evidence for this interest is found in the Po Valley not long after 1100. The city of Modena boasts a stately cathedral, richly sculptured, which we know from a contemporary document was begun in 1099.[12] Over the north portal known as the Porta della Pescheria there are an architrave and an archivolt, surely of different dates. (Fig. 7) The latter, which is the center of our interest, consists of a semicircular band in somewhat higher relief than that at Perros, and of vastly higher quality. The subject of the sculpture, which is luckily provided with clear-cut names over most of the personages, may be thus described.

In the upper part of the archivolt is a fortress consisting of a central tower, from which a shield is hung, a wall around the tower, a moat outside the wall, defended by a *bretêche*, or wooden tower, on each side. (Fig. 8) Within the wall are a man labeled Mardoc, grasping a joist of the *bretêche* on the right, and a woman labeled Winlogee, both obviously in a state of extreme agitation. From the *bretêche* on the right rides out a knight, Carrado, and against him charge three knights, Galvagin*us* (Fig. 6), Galvariun (Fig. 4), and Che. Before the *bretêche* on the left stands a churl, Burmaltus, brandishing a *baston cornu* in the face of Artus de Bretania, Isdernus (Fig. 5), and a third unnamed knight.

An ordered energy, a driving rhythm dominates these charging knights and their sturdy destriers.

[6] W. F. Skene, *Four Ancient Books of Wales* (Edinb., 1868), I, 266, II, 182. T. Stephens, *Literature of the Kymry* (Llandovery, 1849), p. 194; (L., 1876), p. 186.

[7] E. Faral, *La légende arthurienne, prem. part.*, I, 236, 240.

[8] *Ibid.*, 240 ff.

[9] *Ibid.*, 243 f.

[10] *Romania*, XVII (1888), 161, 355. *Regesta Chartarum Italiae*, XVI (Rome, 1931), p. 295.

[11] G. L. Kittredge, *Study of Gawain and the Green Knight* (Camb., Mass., 1916), p. 96. Cf. Chap. X, n. 34.

[12] A. K. Porter, *Lombard Architecture* (New Haven, L., 1917), III, 10. On architecture of Modena cathedral cf. Frankl in *Jahrbuch f. Kunstwissenschaft*, 1927, p. 39.

Terror is admirably expressed in the huddled figure of Winlogee and in her captor, gripping the joist of the *bretèche*. Though the carving may not be as finely wrought as the famous sculptures on the western façade, there is a striking resemblance between the figure of Burmaltus and that of Cain bringing his sheaf to the altar;[13] there are similarities also in the treatment of hair and the use of the double-ax pattern to depict water. It is therefore possible that the archivolt took shape under the hands of Wiligelmus, the creator of Lombard sculpture; more probably it was the work of an assistant.

When was this work executed? Into all the details of this much controverted question we do not propose to enter. It has been urged that only after the publication of Geoffrey of Monmouth's *History* could the Italians have been interested in the Arthurian legend[14]—an argument refuted by the proper names from Padua and Modena. It has been urged that the cathedral at Modena must postdate the year 1117 because any earlier edifice would have been demolished by a severe earthquake recorded for that year at Milan, Cremona, Parma, Verona, and Venice, though not at Modena[15]—an argument which *a fortiori* demonstrates that, since there was a "scossa fortissima" at Modena itself in 1753,[16] the cathedral and its sculptures belong to the second half of the eighteenth century! It has been urged that the façade sculptures at Modena must postdate 1140 because one of the figures holds the hem of his robe in the same odd fashion as does the statue of a king formerly at S. Denis.[17] By similar reasoning one could prove that the façade sculptures at Modena belong to the twentieth century, for a tablet with two supporters closely resembling the commemorative tablet at Modena adorns the Academy of Medicine Building, New York City, erected in 1925. In both cases it is merely necessary to assume without proof that if marked resemblances occur between Modena workmanship and that found elsewhere, the Modena artist is the debtor. It is obvious that by such arguments one can demonstrate for the Modena sculpture as late a date as one wishes. Perhaps truth may lie in the opposite direction.

The fact is that a good body of evidence, assembled by Porter and others, points in that direction.

1. A contemporary document whose authenticity is unquestioned, supported by the commemorative tablet mentioned above, asserts that the building of the cathedral was commenced in 1099.[18] It states, moreover, that before the year 1106 "effodiuntur marmora insignia, sculpuntur et puliuntur arte mirifica; sublevantur et construuntur magno cum labore et artificum astutia. Crescunt ergo parietes, crescit edifitium."[19] One could hardly wish clearer testimony to the existence at Modena of astonishingly fine sculptures before 1106.

2. A comparison of the armed knights on the Modena archivolt with the picture of Goliath in the Bible of Stephen Harding, dated before 1109,[20] and with the knights of the Spanish Beatus MS of 1109,[21] shows that the shields, the helmets, the hauberks, and the riding equipment of the Modena figures is at least not incompatible with a date in the first decade of the century.[22] The helmet with the profile of an isosceles triangle, worn by Carrado, Galvaginus, and Galvariun, is very rare after that period. Professor Gerould after exhaustive research has been able to discover only three examples, and two of these may possibly belong to the first quarter of the century.[23]

3. Two of the name-forms on the relief are more archaic, closer to the Welsh, than those in Geoffrey of Monmouth's *Historia* of 1136–38, though of course they appear in forms modified by Bretons speaking French. Galvaginus comes closer to its original, the Welsh epithet Gwallt-Avwyn, than do the multifarious forms which the Geoffrey MSS supply: Gualguanus, Galwainus, Gualguainus, Gualwanus, etc.[24] Omitting the Latin termination, we find only on the Lombard relief the three syllables of the Welsh original. Even more convincing is Isdernus, which has preserved the *n* of Welsh Edern, whereas neither in Geoffrey nor in any Continental romance do we find this feature surviving.[25] It is very remarkable indeed if we assume that Geoffrey was responsible for the Continental interest in the Arthurian legend that the Lombard sculptor should have made the necessary research to discover two name-forms that were more primitive and authentic than those which Geoffrey himself used.

These three considerations do not, of course, demonstrate conclusively that the carving was made in the first decade of the century. They merely render it highly probable. The remaining considerations are more cogent.

4. Porter was the first to bring out fully the very important relationship between Modena cathedral and San

[13] *Ibid.*, IV, pl. 144, fig. 2.

[14] *Monuments et mémoires, Fondation Piot*, XXVIII (1926), 72. *Speculum*, X (1935), 376.

[15] *Monuments Piot*, XXVIII, 81.

[16] M. Baratta, *Terremoti d'Italia* (Turin, 1901), p. 241.

[17] *Gazette des beaux arts*, LX (1918), 35.

[18] Bertoni, *Atlante storico-paleografico del duomo di Modena* (Modena, 1909), part 2, tav. 10.

[19] *Ibid.*, 88. Porter, *op. cit.*, III, 13.

[20] *Medieval studies in memory of Gertrude Schoepperle Loomis* (N. Y., 1927), p. 220. C. Oursel, *Miniature du XII siècle à l'abbaye de Citeaux* (Dijon, 1926), pl. V. For date see *ibid.*, 16–23.

[21] Henry Shaw, *Dresses and Decorations of the Middle Ages* (L., 1858), I, pl. 7.

[22] The nasal which Des Noettes cannot find before 1100 is found on the Farfa and Roda Bibles (1000–50 A.D.), is mentioned by Gui d'Amiens who wrote the *De Bello Hastingensi* before 1086, in v. 492: "Per nasum galeae concitus accipiens"; occurs in the *Beatus de S. Sever* (1028–72) and the Bayeux Embroidery (ca. 1070). In the two last is found the curb bit, which Des Noettes cannot find before 1125.

[23] *Speculum*, X (1935), 363–367. *Ibid.*, XIII (1938), 224. A. Gardner, *Medieval Sculpture in France* (L., 1931), fig. 137. M. Longhurst, *English Ivories* (L., 1926), pl. 32. A. Goldschmidt, *Elfenbeinskulpturen*, IV, pl. LXIII, 180 d.

[24] *Pub. Mod. Lang. Assoc.*, XLIII (1928), 388–395.

[25] Geoffrey's form is Hider or Hyder, with or without the Latin termination.

Niccola at Bari, which was begun in 1087 and sufficiently far advanced in 1098 to hold a church council.[26] "The introduction of a wooden roof at Modena, the design of the false triforium gallery, the columns of the intermediate piers—all features hitherto unaccounted for—must be ascribed to the influence of San Niccola." The left supporter of the Bari throne, dated 1098, is easily recognizable as the inspiration of the crouching figure between Cain and Abel on the façade of Modena.[27] The conception of a sculptured archivolt showing mounted knights attacking a central castle from both sides is found at Bari and Modena, and nowhere else in the world. That the Bari relief is earlier is proved by the way in which certain knights carry their lances poised above their shoulders, rather than hugged under the armpit—a valuable point first made by Levé in connection with the Bayeux Embroidery (ca. 1070).[28] The demonstration of this influence exerted by work done at Bari before 1099 on work commenced at Modena in 1099 is, to say the least, a remarkable coincidence.

5. The name Winlogee on the Modena archivolt is clearly derived from the Breton name Winlowen,[29] and points directly to a Breton *conteur* as the source of the tale. It is again a most remarkable coincidence, if nothing more, that the Breton contingent to the First Crusade under their Duke spent four months of the winter of 1096–97 at Bari,[30] the very city in which some of the craftsmen later employed at Modena must have been at this very time. In the train of the Breton nobles we should expect to find one or more of these French-speaking *conteurs* who ere many decades had passed were to infect all Christendom with the Arthurian craze. At about the same time, in the same city, a sculptor must have studied the Porta dei Leoni with its unusual archivolt, for it is that unique arrangement which we find imitated over the Porta della Pescheria within a decade or two. Though it is not impossible that the sculptor may have heard his Arthurian *conte* elsewhere than in Bari, is it likely that he should have been exposed elsewhere to so powerful a histrionic impression as his carving attests and as he would be likely to receive from one of the Duke of Brittany's chosen reciters?

Accordingly we are entitled to use our imaginations on the situation in Bari in the winter months during which the Crusaders waited for fair weather before they risked the perils of the straights of Durazzo. The Duke of Brittany was associated with Robert Curthose, Duke of Normandy, destined to achieve glory at the siege of Antioch. Of Robert, William of Malmesbury records that he "showered infinite wealth into the laps of mimes and worthless fellows"[31]

—a remark, which coupled with the same chronicler's reference to "that Arthur concerning whom the trivial tales of the Bretons rave wildly even today," illustrates the hostility between the secular storytellers and the monks already noted. It is a legitimate conjecture that one of the *mimi* whom the Duke rewarded so lavishly was he whose tale was to be translated into stone not many years later, and we may fancy him standing in the great hall of the Norman Count of Apulia, Roger Bursa, and reciting in French with dramatic gesture and intonation the moving story of "Artus" and his knights.

What was the story? It might seem hazardous to attempt a reconstruction of a narrative antedating by some fifty years the first written Arthurian romance, but if there was a continuous tradition, the task is not impossible. Oddly enough, Foerster, whose authority has tended to minimize the traditional element, himself pointed out certain very striking parallels between the Modena relief and the *Vulgate Lancelot* account of Caradoc of the Dolorous Tower, which is at least a century later.[32] So detailed was the correspondence that M. Mâle accepted Foerster's view completely.[33] But there are discrepancies, and the chief are the absence of Winlogee and Mardoc from the French romance and the substitution of Lancelot for Galvaginus as the hero. It is only when we recognize that the sculpture represents a composite tale centering around the abduction of Arthur's queen, sometimes called Guenloie or Guendoloena, here called Winlogee, that the whole scene and practically every actor in it can be understood, accounted for.[34] We find the explanation of the early twelfth century sculpture not only in the *Vulgate Lancelot*, but also in *Durmart* and other thirteenth-century romances in which Gawain accomplishes the rescue of the abducted queen.[35] In brief, we are dealing with an early but already complicated version of the theme of which Chrétien's *Charrette* is the classic form. By the aid of these literary sources and the indications of the carving itself the story may be retold in brief and tentative outline.

Winlogee, Artus' queen, guarded only by the unarmed knight Isdern, rode out into the forest. A giant knight, Carrado, fully armed, rode down upon them and swung the lady from her saddle to the crupper of his horse. When Isdern interfered, Carrado knocked him from his palfrey,

[26] A. K. Porter, *Romanesque Sculpture of the Pilgrimage Roads* (Boston, 1923), I, 67. *Burlington Mag.*, XLIII (1923), 63. *Art Studies* (1923), I, 12–15.

[27] *Gaz. d. beaux arts*, per. 5, XVIII (1928), 115, 121.

[28] *Bulletin monumental*, LXXVII (1913), 130.

[29] A. de la Borderie, *Hist. de la Bretagne*, II, 280.

[30] C. W. David, *Robert Curthose* (Camb., Mass., 1920), pp. 94, 221.

[31] *Comptes rendus de l'Acad. d. Inscriptions* (1890), p. 208.

[32] *Zeits. f. Romanische Philologie*, XXII (1898), 243.

[33] E. Mâle, *L'art religieux au XII siècle* (P., 1922), p. 269.

[34] *PMLA*, XLV (1930), 418–32. R. S. Loomis, *Celtic Myth*, pp. 7–11, 105, 107.

[35] Gawain's prominence in the rescue, though denied by Miss Hutchings in *Medium Aevum*, I (1932), 204; IV (1935), 61, is assured not only by the sculpture itself and the evidence cited *ibid.*, II, 161, but also by the Guinevere's extraordinary affection for him shown in Wolfram von Eschenbach's *Parzival*, XIII, sec. 645, and Girard d'Amiens's *Escanor*, vv. 7343 f.

carried off the queen to the Dolorous Tower and delivered her over to Mardoc, who loved her. Meanwhile the alarm had been given; Artus, Galvagin, Galvariun, and Che set out on the rescue; Isdern, still suffering from Carrado's blow, managed to pick up shield and spear and joined the troop. They arrived before Carrado's castle and approached it by two opposite wooden *bretêches*. Before one of them Burmalt, a huge churl, brandished his *baston cornu*, and held off Artus, Isdern, and one other knight. Galvagin, however, encountered Carrado at the other *bretêche*. (At this point, there may have stood the tale of Carrado's betrayal and death. A woman named Floree, whom Carrado had likewise seized, placed his sword, with which alone he could be killed, within Galvagin's reach, and with this Galvagin despatched the giant, who deplored the woman's treachery.) Galvagin then proceeded through the castle, saw the shields of vanquished knights adorning the great tower, and discovered Winlogee with Mardoc. Probably the story ended with the sparing of Mardoc's life and the restoration of the queen to her husband.

This, like most versions of the abduction of Arthur's queen including Chrétien's *Charrette*, betrays its debt to Irish saga. Though reconstructed entirely from the indications of the sculpture, the *Vulgate Lancelot*, and *Durmart*, it is manifestly the same story as the famous Irish legend of the abduction of Bláthnat by Cúroi.[36] In both tales a man seizes a woman, strikes down a warrior who interferes, and carries the woman off to his fortress. The humiliated warrior joins with others and attacks the fortress. In the midst of a general struggle, the abducted woman, or another, gives the sword with which alone the abductor could be killed to the leader of the attack, and the abductor dies deploring the perfidy of women. Naturally the woman is restored to her husband. It is interesting to note that whereas in the original Irish version, the humiliated warrior, the leader of the attack, and the husband were identical, in the sculpture the rôles have been distributed among Isdernus, Galvaginus, and Artus—interesting evidence of the complex history of the story's development.

It we accept the date and the interpretation of the sculpture set forth above, there is nothing to surprise the specialist in the history of sculpture or of Arthurian romance; if there is anything to cause astonishment, it is the completeness with which the details dovetail into the other facts and confirm inferences which we should be obliged to make on other

grounds. How fully it harmonizes for instance with Professor Kittredge's statement:[37]

The fact that we can detect so much rationalizing in the French Arthurian material, and that too in very early texts,—in Chrétien, for example,—shows that these texts, even if they do come early in extant French literature, come late in the development of the particular story which each tells. They stand, in a sense, at the end rather than at the beginning of a long course of development. And even the Celtic materials which the French authors followed had already been more or less subjected to the same process before they came into French hands.

The same inference which Kittredge draws from the rationalizing in French romances, we are obliged to make from the extraordinary amount of conflation of variants to be observed in our archivolt.

There is, however, one point which may properly provoke startled inquiry: how did a subject utterly without religious significance find a place in the decoration of the house of God? Bishop Odo's embroidery commissioned for the cathedral of Bayeux[38] is not wholly analogous since the conquest of England was a Crusade sanctioned by the Pope. Likewise the window at Chartres and the mosaic formerly at Brindisi depicting the battle of Roncesvaux[39] are both accounted for by the holy aura which hung around the wars of Charlemagne with the paynim. No such excuse could possibly be invoked to justify the intrusion of the theme of the rescue of Arthur's queen into a sacred edifice.[40] If excuse there was, we do not know and in all probability never will know what it was.

But was an excuse necessary? A study of medieval church decoration reveals a number of instances where scenes and figures wholly unedifying crept within the sacred precincts. St. Bernard about 1125 protested vehemently against certain figures of knights in combat and hunters blowing horns which he had seen carved in monastic cloisters;[41] evidently though Bernard was strict, others were lax in these matters. Pyramus and Thisbe appear on a Romanesque capital of Bâle cathedral.[42] In the Scandinavian North scenes from the Sigurd legend were frequently carved on church doorways,[43] and one door from Iceland portrayed Wolfdietrich freeing a lion from a dragon.[44] From later periods we have many examples: the popularity of Reynard the Fox in church decoration gave scandal to the severer clergy.[45] The

[36] Loomis, *op. cit.*, pp. 12 ff.

[37] Kittredge, *Study of Gawain and Green Knight*, p. 241.

[38] *Art Bulletin*, VI (1923), 5 ff. E. Anquetil, *Antiquité de la tapisserie de Bayeux* (Bayeux, 1912), p. 4. H. Prentout, *Études sur quelques points d'histoire de Normandie* (Caen, 1926), p. 56.

[39] E. Mâle, *op. cit.*, p. 264.

[40] The remarks of Mâle and Olschki on this matter seem rather nebulous. *Ibid.*, p. 268. *Archivum romanicum*, XIX (1935), 159 ff.

[41] Migne, *Pat. Lat.*, CLXXXII, col. 916.

[42] Cahier and Martin, *Nouveaux mélanges d'archéologie, curiosités mystérieuses* (P., 1874), I, 228.

[43] Du Chaillu, *Viking Age* (N. Y., 1889), II, 244, 267.

[44] *Ibid.*, 252. H. Schneider, *Die Gedichte und die Sage von Wolfdietrich*, pp. 230–247. S. Bugge, *Home of the Eddic Poems*, tr. W. H. Schofield, p. 70. Cf. *Aarböger för Nordisk Oldkyndighed* (1882), p. 94. Schück and Warburg, *Illustrerad Svensk Literatur Historia* (1926), I, 432.

[45] *Histoire litt. de la France*, XXXI, 214. *Miracles de la Ste.*

Chertsey and Halesowen tiles paved monastic chapels with scenes from the life of Tristram; and on a capital of one of the churches at Caen Lancelot still crosses the sword-bridge and Gawain lies on the Perilous Bed in full view of the congregation.[46] It would seem that the masons, wood-carvers, and other artisans were not a straight-laced crew, and that sometimes the ecclesiastical authorities were more amused than shocked by what craftsmen provided. Such may well be the explanation for this incongruous element in the adornment of Modena cathedral; and if so, let us be grateful for the laxity which has bequeathed us so animated, so balanced a sculptural pattern and so significant a document in the evolution of Arthurian romance.

THE OTRANTO MOSAIC

Apparently the Arthurian interest in Italy displayed by the names at Padua and Modena and the Modena relief continued to be felt throughout the century. At Otranto, not far from Bari, the nave of the cathedral is covered by a large mosaic of marble and colored stone.[47] It possesses little of the brilliant color and delicate design of contemporary mosaic in Sicily, but is a strange conglomerate of beasts and men, delineated with some animation but little beauty, and though it has escaped the destructive mania of the nineteenth century, has suffered considerably from earthquakes and restorers. Inscriptions tell us that it was precisely in the year 1165 that archbishop Jonathan commissioned the work to be carried out by the priest Pantaleone.[48] Near the sanctuary is a curious group (Fig. 9): a man labeled "Rex Arturus," equipped with crown and sceptre, rides a beast identified clearly (by his horns, short tail, and cloven hoofs) as a goat. In front there leaps up a black panther-like creature. Since the figure of the king has been very crudely restored, we reproduce, in addition to a photograph, a drawing by Millin now in the Cabinet des Estampes, Bibliothèque Nationale. (Fig. 9a)

One thinks at first of Arthur's combat with the giant cat of Lausanne, the Capalus; and this must be an ancient tradition, despite its localization in the Alps, for Graindor de Brie incorporated it in the *Bataille Loquifer* about 1175, and the Welsh original of the Capalus, the Cath Palug, is mentioned in the *Black Book of Carmarthen*, transcribed about the

same time, but containing of course much older material.[49] But the panther may be merely one of the multitude of beasts which sprawl rather carelessly around the mosaic; and it is hard to believe that Arthur would enter a conflict with a monster so formidable armed only with a sceptre and riding on a goat!

Is there any explanation for the goat? Only one, and that purely conjectural, has suggested itself. There is ample testimony that Arthur was supposed to be living on in two supernatural forms,—one as leader of the Wild Hunt,[50] the other as the Maimed King, a sort of year-spirit whose wounds annually reopened. The latter tradition was preserved with peculiar force in Sicily, where it is localized by Gervase of Tilbury.[51] It is therefore possible that other traditions of a supernatural Arthur may have persisted in Apulia. Now the Welsh held one strange conception of a supernatural king which is attested by Walter Map.[52] One of the most ancient of British kings, Herla, it is said, was on a time interviewed by another king who was a pigmy in respect of his low stature, not above that of a monkey. The little creature was mounted on a large goat. The dwarf king resembles the conception of the immortal Arthur in being possessed of infinite riches and dwelling in a mysterious palace entered through a cave. It is possible therefore that Arthur, in assuming the traits of various Otherworld kings, acquired the uncouth mount of the pigmy potentate. It is also easy to see why the grotesque image of Arthur bestriding a goat, the beast associated in the medieval mind, as in Spenser's allegorical pageant, with the sin of lechery,[53] should have been rapidly suppressed, and have left no trace save in the Otranto mosaic. Perhaps a more satisfactory interpretation may be offered, but at least this is a plausible guess.

THE CONSTANCE PAINTING

About the year 1300 an unusual group of secular wall-paintings was executed at Constance in a house behind No. 5 Münsterplatz, sometimes called Der Haus zur Kunkel, that is, "The Distaff House."[54] It is so named because it contains in fair preservation a series of paintings, in square compartments, of women employed in the linen industry. When these were discovered in 1860, they were faced on the oppo-

Vierge, ed. Poquet, p. 509. Cf. *Romania*, XLII, 586 n. 1; *Archiv für das Studium*, LVI (1876), 265; A. Kuhn, *Allgemeine Kunstgeschichte* (1909), III, 1, 204, 207; L. Olschki, *Romanische Literaturen des Mittelalters* (Potsdam, 1928), pp. 140–144.

[46] Cf. infra pp. 44 ff., 71 f.

[47] E. Bertaux, *L'art dans l'Italie méridionale* (Rome, 1904), I, 488–490. *Studi medievali*, II (1906–7), 506.

[48] *Ibid.*, 510.

[49] *Festgabe für G. Gröber* (Halle, 1899), pp. 311 ff.

[50] *Romanic Rev.*, III (1912), 191; XII (1921), 286.

[51] Loomis, *Celtic Myth*, p. 194. L. A. Paton, *Fairy Mythology of Arthurian Romance*, (Boston, 1903), p. 35, n. 1.

[52] W. Map, *De Nugis Curialium*, ed. M. R. James (Oxf., 1914), p. 13. Trans. James (L., 1923), p. 13. Has this association of pigmy and goat been influenced by Pliny? Cf. Trans. Tupper and Ogle, p. 323, note.

[53] Spenser, *Faery Queene*, I, IV, 24. Garnett and Gosse, *English Literature*, I, 171.

[54] *Mitteilungen der antiquarischen Gesellschaft in Zürich*, XV (1866), 227 f.

site wall by another series depicting the male victims of female charms in three rows of four medallions. This second group unfortunately is preserved only in black-and-white copies in the Wessenbergsammlung at Constance. As the surrounding inscriptions show, they were based on a brief poem which condenses into a few lines the famous book of legends and lives of wicked wives with which the fifth husband of the Wife of Bath used to regale her. Ironically enough, this antifeminist poem was written by the Meistersinger Heinrich von Meissen, who won the sobriquet "Frauenlob" because of his habitual praise of ladies.[55]

The poetic procession of male victims is headed inevitably by Adam, but ends curiously with Arthur and Perceval. Frauenlob in Tennysonian fashion places the blame squarely on Guinevere, "who broke the vast design and purpose of the king."

> Artuses scham
> Von wibe kam.[56]

The copy of the Constance painting illustrating this couplet still preserves the word "Arthuses" plainly in the circular inscription which surrounds the medallion. (Fig. 10) The medallion itself depicts the king seated on a throne, his hand raised as if to wipe away a tear, while Guinevere stands in a coquettish pose. The original, in which reds and greens predominated,[57] must have added charm of color to charm of line.

We can say this with greater confidence because there survives an illuminated MS made in Constance certainly by an artist of the same school, in all likelihood by the very painter of the murals.[58] It is the Weingarten MS of Minnesinger lyrics at Stuttgart, from which selected illustrations have been published by Löffler. Even a cursory glance reveals a startling similarity. The rectangular frames, the Lombardic lettering, and the composition of certain figures which we note among the industrious women of the murals correspond especially to the miniatures of Reinmar and Willehalm von Heinzinbruch in the MS.[59] It is hard to believe that it was not the painter of the Arthur medallion who employed the very similar figure as regards crown, mantle, and tippet, seated with outstretched leg on an uncomfortable throne, to represent Bliger von Stainach.[60] With some variations, but with nearly the same posture of arms and

hands, the painter has given us the famous lyrist, Walther von der Vogelweide.[61] It was of course natural that an artist who illuminated a book of lyrics should have chosen a lyric for the basis of his mural decoration, and that his poets should resemble his potentates as Leonardo's Bacchus resembled his St. John.

ARTHUR AMONG THE NINE WORTHIES

About the year 1310, a jongleur, Jacques de Longuyon, composed, at the instance of the Bishop of Liége, the *Vœux du Paon* or "Vows of the Peacock," and inserted therein for the first time a list of the nine famous conquerors of the world and a brief statement of their acts of prowess.[62] With true medieval devotion to schematism these were apportioned among the pagans, the Jews, and the Christians, three to each. It is a motley crew, great military captains and subjugators of large areas of the earth's surface such as Alexander and Charlemagne, together with Joshua and Arthur, whose exploits were of doubtful authenticity and touched but a small corner of the world, libertines like Cæsar together with the noble and self-sacrificing Judas Maccabeus and Godfrey de Bouillon. The schematic list caught on. In 1336 the Nine Worthies appeared in a pageant at Arras, bearing their blazoned shields, and for some three centuries they were familiar in literature, pageantry, and art.[63] Caxton, it will be remembered, in his preface to the *Morte d'Arthur* declares that "it is notoriously known through the universal world that there be nine worthy and the best that ever were."

It might almost be claimed that Jacques de Longuyon did as much for the general reputation of Arthur as did Geoffrey of Monmouth. He devotes to the British hero these lines, inspired ultimately by Geoffrey:[64]

'I know three Christians such that no man alive ever saw one better than they wearing a bright helm. The fame of Arthur, who ruled Britain, witnesses that he slew Ritho (Ruston), a giant, in open field, who was so strong, proud, and orgulous that he made a robe of the beards of kings, which kings were held in obedience to him by force. He desired the beard of Arthur, but in that he failed. Arthur slew also on Mont S. Michel a giant so huge that all the folk of the land marveled thereat. In many other places,

---

[55] *Ibid.*, 229, n. 1.—When he died at Mainz in 1318, the women of that city bore his body from the hospice to the burial place and uttered the greatest lamentations because of the infinite praises which he had heaped on the whole female sex. So great was their gratitude that they poured enough wine into his tomb to flood the church. It would seem that the poem illustrated at Constance was written in a mood of surfeit or disillusionment, for it is not a Dream of Fair and Faithful but of Fatal Women.

[56] Heinrich von Meissen, ed. L. Ettmüller (Quedlinburg: Leipzig, 1843), p. 102.

[57] H. Wienecke, *Konstanzer Malereien des Vierzehnten Jahr-*

hunderts (Halle, 1912), p. 25.

[58] *Ibid.*, p. 22.

[59] K. Löffler, *Die Weingartner Liederhandschrift in Nachbildung* (Stuttgart, 1927), pp. 60, 125.

[60] *Ibid.*, p. 26.

[61] *Ibid.*, p. 139.

[62] J. Barbour, *Buik of Alexander*, ed. R. L. G. Ritchie (Edin., L., 1925), I, xxxv–xli.

[63] The very corrupt text is given *Bull. de la Soc. des Anc. Textes Fr.*, 1883, 47.

[64] Barbour, *Buik of Alexander*, ed. Ritchie, IV, 405.

if the history lie not, this King Arthur vanquished many a haughty prince.'

Arthur and his eight rivals appear frequently in medieval art and with a certain inevitable monotony so that exhaustive enumeration, illustration, and description seem unnecessary.[65]

Perhaps the earliest instance is that in the Hansasaal of the Rathaus at Cologne. (Fig. 11) Though Professor Hamann dates this group of painted stone statues between 1360 and 1370,[66] they must be some forty years older. The costume of Godfrey de Bouillon reproduces closely that of the St. Victor of Xanten, which Hamann himself places in the thirties,[67] and resembles far more closely the tomb effigy of Robert of Artois, who died in 1317, than that of a knight who died in 1335.[68] All the nine statues are obviously of the same date; all have the long surcoat flowing almost to the ankles, and there is no trace of plate armor. Probably they belong to the decade 1320–30.[69] They stand close together on lofty pedestals under Gothic canopies. Blues and reds predominate, the hair and beards are gilded, and canopies of blue with gold stars and of red with gold lilies alternate. Arthur's visage is rather world-weary than handsome, and he raises his hand to doff his helmet with a tired gesture. Hamann concedes the French inspiration of the sculptures.

German examples from the late fourteenth century are those at Schloss Runkelstein, to be described in the next chapter, and the badly damaged frescoes in the castle of the Teutonic Knights at Lochstedt in East Prussia,[70] where possibly the prototype of Chaucer's knight may have seen them "when he hadde the bord bigonne aboven alle nacions in Pruce." The largely restored Schöne Brunnen at Nüremberg (1385–96) is adorned with the Worthies, but Arthur is not included.[71]

French inventories of the second half of the same century mention a hanap and a "thiphenie" enameled with the subject and a tapestry in Louis of Anjou's ill-fated collection;[72] two tapestries belonging to Charles V in 1379;[73] another bought by Philip of

Burgundy in 1388, enriched with gold and silver thread.[74] A similar rich tapestry is listed among the possessions of Jean Duc de Berry in 1416.[75] The Worthies appear as statues on the keep of Maubergeon, Poitiers, done about 1385,[76] and are described as adorning in white stone the great hall at Coucy.[77] But far and away the most imposing of all surviving memorials of the Worthies is the great tapestry of Arthur at the Metropolitan Museum, New York. (Fig. 12)[78] Four others from the same set, though in a mutilated condition are (1938) in the Brummer Gallery of that city. It seems impossible to identify these with any recorded set; they are too late for Charles V; they lack the silver and gold threads of the tapestries of his brothers, Philip and Jean. Surely, however, they emanated from one of the Paris workshops whose output was handled by the dealer Nicholas Bataille, for the figure of Arthur is not unlike the venerable bearded figures seated under a Gothic canopy, which preceded each of the seven great sequences of St. John's vision woven in tapestry for Louis of Anjou and for the most part still preserved at Angers. The Angers series was certainly designed for and largely carried out at the shops of Bataille. The Metropolitan Museum tapestry must have been designed, as the tabard shows, about 1400,[79] perhaps after Bataille's death, but it has suffered from neglect, and the dais and Arthur's feet have been largely restored. The present dimensions are 10 ft. 8½ in. by 8 ft. 8½in.

Arthur himself is easily identified by the three gold crowns repeated on his blue surcoat and pennon. With scowling brow and portentous and predatory nose, "lik a grifphon loketh he aboute." The whole conception is significantly like that of God the Father in majesty painted early in the fifteenth century in the *Missel de l'Église de Paris* and figured in Martin's *Miniature française*, fig. cvi. He is surrounded by obsequious clergy—two archbishops in the upper niches, two bishops in the lower. At the extreme left are two secular lords under somewhat different canopies; they belonged to another figure in the series of

---

[65] *Gazette des beaux arts*, per. 5, XIV (1926), 250. *Annales archéologiques*, XVI, 234. *Zeits. des Harzvereins für Geschichte*, XXII, 359. *Journal of the British Archeological Assoc.*, XX, 315. *Herald and Genealogist*, I, 175.

[66] *Kunstdenkmäler der Rheinprovinz*, ed. P. Clemen, VII, abt. 4, 216–20. Beenken, *Bildhauer des XIV Jahrhunderts* (Leipz., 1927), p. 99. Hamann, *Die Elisabethkirche zu Marburg* (Marburg, 1929), II, 257 f.

[67] *Ibid.*, 168 f.

[68] *Ibid.*, fig. 185, 257.

[69] Cf. *Victoria and Albert Museum List of Rubbings of Brasses* (L., 1915), pl. 2 and 4.

[70] Steinbrecht, *Schloss Lochstedt und seine Malereien* (1910). Clasen, *Die Deutschordensburg Lochstedt* (1927).

[71] *Anzeiger für Kunde der deutschen Vorzeit*, 1854, col. 167; 1866, col. 182.

[72] L. E. S. J. Marquis de Laborde, *Notice des émaux du Musée*

du Louvre, II (P., 1853), 71, 100. *Bibl. de l'École des Chartes*, L (1889), 171.

[73] J. Labarte, *Inventaire du mobilier de Charles V* (P., 1879), p. 378.

[74] Pinchart, *Hist. de la tapisserie dans les Flandres* (P., 1878–85), p. 13. Other tapestries on the subject are listed in this book and in the *Revue archéologique*, ser. 5, VII (1918), 133 ff.

[75] J. Guiffrey, *Inventaires de Jean duc de Berri* (P., 1894–96), II, 209.

[76] A. Michel, *Hist. de l'art*, II, 2, 701.

[77] *Mod. Philology*, XV (1917), 214.

[78] Göbel, *Wandteppiche* (Leipz., 1928), Teil 2, II, fig. 14. G. L. Hunter, *Practical Book of Tapestries* (Phil., L., 1925), pp. 17 ff. Hunter, *Tapestries of C. H. Mackay* (N. Y., 1925), pp. 16 ff. *International Studio*, LXXVI (1922), p. 48.

[79] The tabard cannot be much earlier, and corresponds to that worn by Arthur at La Manta. Fig. 14.

Worthies and have been arbitrarily though skilfully attached to Arthur. On the other hand, some of the small canopied figures of cardinals in the Brummer Gallery must have surmounted originally the Arthur portrait. Harsh though the conception of Arthur is, the tapestry is a fine example of the decorative strength of this great period and of its rich, harmonious coloring.

A series of the Nine Worthies and of the Nine Worthy Women, their bellicose peers, has been excellently preserved at the castle of La Manta in Piedmont.[80] (Fig. 14) They occupy a wall of the great hall, and were done about 1430 for Valerano and Clemensia Provana, whose protraits are introduced as those of Hector and Penthesilea. Tommaso, Duke of Saluzzo, natural father of Valerano, had lived much in France and was thoroughly imbued with its culture. He composed a conventional poem, *Le Chevalier Errant*, in which he described in the palace of Fortuna the seats of the Nine Worthies; those of the Nine whom Fortune had otherthrown had left their seats empty.[81] The MS of the *Chevalier Errant* now at the Bibliothèque Nationale (Fr.12559)[82] or a similar one may have furnished the painter at La Manta with some suggestions. (Fig. 13) In the painting the warriors of life size, fully armed, stand in varying attitudes in a flowery meadow, separated by trees, on which hang their escutcheons. The use of trees as partitions, the outlining of the figures against the sky, the decorative heraldry, suggest a certain relationship to the murals of the Davanzati Palace, Florence, done some thirty years before.[83] Most of the Worthies posture gracefully with sword or sceptre or ax in various costumes and attitudes; but the painter has not been happy in the awkward, limping movement of Arthur, the shortened left arm, and the fixed stare with which the Briton regards either his sword or his shield adorned with three gold crowns. The device is repeated on his blue surcoat. The royal crown rests on a wig-like mop of hair; the face is wrinkled and worried. Arthur is the least successful figure in a stately decorative group. Beneath are the Italo-French lines, which may be translated:[84]

I was king of Britain, Scotland, and England. Five hundred kings I conquered, who held their lands from me. I have slain seven great giants in the midst of their land.

I went to conquer still another on Mont S. Michel. I saw the Holy Grail. Then Modred made war on me, who slew me five hundred years after God came to earth.

To the same half-century belong three windows in the Rathaus at Lüneburg.[85] In the central window the Briton stands belligerently with curved sword in his right hand; his shield is slung about his neck, charged with the three crowns on blue; the visor of his helmet is up; he grasps his curved sword in defiance. The Germanic Museum at Munich contains crude panel paintings of about 1470 from the Alten Hof.[86] Everything has been clumsily daubed over, and Arthur, distinguishable by the three gold crowns on a red field, is labeled "der kunig von Arines." In the castle of Valeria at Sion, Switzerland, there are some badly damaged frescoes of the Worthies from the end of the century.[87] (Fig. 17) The crowned Arthur wears spiked plates on his shoulders and a long mantle reaching the knee. His shield bears gules three crowns or, impaling the Virgin and Child, an attempt to harmonize the conventional charge with the ancient testimony of Geoffrey's that his shield bore the image of the Virgin.[88]

Another Swiss representation of the Worthies is found on a tapestry of about 1475 in the Historical Museum at Bâle.[89] In its incomplete state it measures 5 feet 7 inches in length and 3 feet 8 inches in height, and is made of wool, varied by linen for the whites, by silk for the boar shield, the crowns of David and Charles, and the jewelled collars, and by silver tinsel for David's mantle-clasp. Arthur stands between Judas Maccabeus and Charlemagne—a debonair youth in dull rose, furred kirtle, and light brown sleeves and hose, holding a spear with three white crowns on a pink banner. (Fig. 15) A decorative scroll contains the defective inscription: "Kunig artus min macht und min miltikeit das ich alle lant erstreit." "King Arthur. My power and my generosity [brought it to pass] that I conquered all lands." The Briton is set against a dark green background, and is contrasted deliberately with his fellow worthies. Judas is black-bearded, wears a turban on his head, and holds an oval shield—an outlandish warrior. On the other side of Arthur Charlemagne in his imperial robes is the venerable monarch of the *Chanson de Roland*, "à la barbe fleurie."

---

[80] *L'arte*, VIII (1905), 94, 183. Van Marle, *Italian Schools of Painting*, VII, 190 ff.

[81] E. Gorra, *Studi di critica letteraria* (Bologna, 1892), p. 48.

[82] Fig. *L'arte*, VIII, 192.

[83] *Gazette des beaux arts*, per. 4, VI, 237. *Country Life*, XLV, 11. *Les arts*, Aug. 1911, No. 116.

[84] *Mod. Philology*, XV (1917), 213.

[85] J. L. Fischer, *Handbuch der Glasmalerei* (Leipzig, 1914), pp. 106, fig. 15. *Kunstdenkmäler Hannovers*, IV, 185. *Zeits. des Harzvereins für Geschichte*, XXII (1889), 362, 371.

[86] *Ibid.*, 373.

[87] *Burgwart*, VI (1905), 51–53.

[88] Geoffrey of Monmouth, *Historia*, ed. Griscom (N. Y., 1929), p. 438. Richard Robinson, *Learned and True Assertion of Arthure* (L., 1582), gives on authority of Batman three arms of Arthur; second arms, vert a plain cross argent, in chief the figure of the Virgin Mary with Christ in her arms; third, azure three crowns or. Brit. Mus. MS. Lansdowne 882, f. 29ᵛ gives six arms to Arthur; first, gules Virgin and Child with rays or; fifth, gules three crowns or.

[89] R. F. Burckhardt, *Gewirkte Bildteppiche des XV und XVI Jahrhunderts im Hist. Mus. zu Basel* (Leipzig, 1923), pp. 36 f., col. pl. XIX. H. Göbel, *op. cit.*, pt. 3, I, 46–48.

The little escutcheon at the extreme left gives us a clue to the early history of the tapestry. The boar's head was the device of Mathias Eberler, a wealthy burgher of Bâle, who was born about 1440, died in 1502, and left us several artistic mementos. In 1464 he commissioned an illuminated Bible; a painted chest of his is in the same museum as the tapestry; a beautiful sculptured angel of his period is still at the Engelhof on the Nadelberg. Since he acquired this property in 1477, it is possible that the tapestry was commissioned for his new home. The tapestry belongs to a considerable number of local products which were called "Heidnischwerktücher" because some were influenced by Oriental designs; they were often woven by women.

(Woodcuts on the Nine Worthies theme are briefly treated in Chapter XIII.)

THE COVENTRY WINDOW

Evidence in art of English interest in the Nine Worthies before 1500 seems to be limited to the painting of their coats of arms on the fifteenth-century mortuary chest of Robert Curthose in Gloucester cathedral (where Arthur's device is gules three crowns or)[90] and to the "clothe of ix conquerouris," mentioned in an inventory of the possessions of Sir John Fastolf in 1459.[91] It was not until the sixteenth and seventeenth centuries that the theme became familiar in English pageantry and decoration.[92]

But Arthur was not wholly forgotten in fifteenth-century England. His arms appear on a French tapestry at Winchester College, perhaps commissioned in anticipation of the birth of a new Arthur at Winchester in 1486, the son of Henry Tudor.[93] His figure stands in the north window of the antechapel of All Souls, Oxford. In the nine lights of a window at St. Mary's Hall, Coventry, Arthur appears with Constantine, William the Conqueror, Richard Lion Heart, Edward III, Henry VI, and others as one of the glories of English monarchy.[94] (Fig. 16) The glass has suffered severely and was restored in 1793 and 1893. Though perhaps half of Arthur's light is new, the last restoration has been skillfully and conscientiously done. The old glass survives in a

fragment of the baldachin, the dome of the crown, the face and beard, the middle of the sword, the right forearm, the adjacent ermine robe, part of the triple tiara, part of the lowest decorative crown on the jupon, both legs, and the letters -stor in the inscription. The plate armor, hair, and beard are silvery, and the only colors occur in the yellow crowns, actual and decorative, and the red jupon. Dr. Rackham has dated the window about 1490,[95] but the scalloped coude and the plain knee-cops went out of fashion about 1450 and the exaggerated plate defenses of the Yorkist period came in. Unless there was conscious archaism in the costumes—a very rare phenomenon —the window must have been done before the death of Henry VI in 1461, quite probably immediately before or after the state visit of the king to Coventry in 1451.[96] There is in fact a distinct resemblance to the work which John Prudde, the king's glazier, made in 1447 for St. Mary's, Warwick;[97] a marked resemblance also to the stained glass portrait of Edward IV at Canterbury cathedral, which Mr. Read believes to have been done in Prudde's workshop.[98] Though there is something of the monotony of factory production in the Coventry kings, all being fashioned on the same basic cartoon, they are not without spirit and delicacy.

THE ROUND TABLE, WINCHESTER

To include the Round Table, mounted over the dais in the hall of Winchester castle (Fig. 18), in a book which professes to deal with art may seem profanation. A heavy oaken structure, eighteen feet in diameter, first decorated, it would seem, for Henry VII by some sign-painter, it was repaired in 1517, and repainted at least in 1522 and 1789 and probably oftener by artists of the same order of talent.[99] It can claim no place here as art, but solely as a historic curiosity. It was first mentioned by the chronicler Hardyng about 1450.[100] Caxton in his preface to Malory's *Morte d'Arthur* of 1485 mentions among the proofs of Arthur's existence "at Wynchester the rounde table." Henry VIII, who seems to have tried to impress the emperor Charles V with the memorials of his British predecessor,[101] exhibited it in 1522

[90] *Bristol and Gloucestershire Archaeological Soc.*, XXVIII, 290.

[91] W. G. Thomson, *Tapestry Weaving in England* (L., 1911–12), p. 28.

[92] C. J. Bates, *Border Holds of Northumberland*, I, 301. A. Wood *City of Oxford*, ed. A. Clark, I, 444. Strutt, *Sports and Pastimes*, ed. J. C. Cox, xxxv f., xliii. *Proc. Soc. Antiquaries*, ser. 2, XII (1889), 375 f.

[93] *Burlington Mag.*, VI (1905), 495; pl. IV.

[94] *Annual of Walpole Soc.*, XIX (1931), 103 ff.

[95] *Ibid.*, 110.

[96] *Ibid.*, 108.

[97] *Ibid.* P. Nelson, *Ancient Painted Glass in England* (L., 1913), pp. 41 f.

[98] H. Read, *English Stained Glass* (L., N. Y., 1926), p. 113; pl. 175.

[99] M. Portal, *The Great Hall of Winchester Castle* (Winchester, L., 1899), 87 ff. *Proceedings at Annual Meeting of the Archaeological Institute*, 1846, pp. 61 ff. J. Milner, *History and Survey of Winchester*, ed. 3 (Winchester), II, 204. *Hampshire Field Club, Papers and Proceedings*, 1900, p. 196.

[100] R. H. Fletcher, *Arthurian Materials in the Chronicles* (Boston, 1906), p. 252. As early as 1355 Arthur was reputed to have been crowned at Winchester. *Ibid.*, p. 224.

[101] Besides Portal, *op. cit.*, p. 87, cf. *Letters and Papers, Foreign and Domestic, of the Reign of Henry VIII*, ed. James Gairdner (L., 1880), V, 20.

to his imperial visitor. It was described accurately by a Spaniard who saw it on the occasion of the marriage of Philip and Mary in the city in 1554.[102] But he asserted that one compartment, called the place of Judas or the Siege Perilous, remained always empty; whereas the name of "Gallahalt," Malory's blunder for Galahad, fills the place on Arthur's left hand, which was the Siege Perilous.

The crude figure of Arthur, enthroned, a sword in the right hand, fills the compartment which extends from the Tudor rose at the centre to the circumference. Twenty-four other spokes of alternating white and green—the Tudor colors—radiate outward to a circular band in which the names of twenty-four knights are written in Gothic letters. These now read: galahallt, launcelot deu lake, gauen, percivale, lyonell, trystram de lyens, garethe, bedwere, bloberrys, la cote male-tayle, lucane, plomydes, lamorak, born de ganys, safer, pelleus, kay, Ector de marys, dagonet, degore, brumear, lybyus dysconyus, Alynore, mordrede. Around the Tudor rose there is a circular band with the legend "Thys is the rownde table of Kyng Arthur with xxiiii of hys namyde knyꝫttes." The names of Galahallt and Garethe show that Malory was the source of most of the names, as we should expect. Some are corruptions of well-known forms: lyens for lyones, bloberrys for bleoberys, plomydes for palomydes, born for bors, pelleus for pelleas. Two names are so far distorted that we cannot be sure of their originals: brumear and Alynore. Neither lybyus dysconyus (li biaus desconus) nor degore is mentioned in Malory, and the latter is not known as an Arthurian knight. They were familiar, however, as the heroes of two Middle English romances.

An inspection of the back of the board shows that it originally had legs, and the most plausible account of its origin is that it was constructed for one of those festivities, supposedly held in imitation of the high feasts of King Arthur, and called Round Tables, at which knights distinguished themselves both in the *bohort* and at the board. The earliest mention we possess of such a Round Table refers us to Cyprus in 1223, as we noted in Chapter I,[103] and throughout the rest of the Middle Ages, not only in England but also in France, Spain, and Germany these imitative festivals flourished.[104] Edward III in 1344 created an order which developed into the Order of the Garter but which in the early stages was intended to revive the famous fellowship of Arthur's day and to enroll 300 knights.[105] In all likelihood, then, the Winchester table was made for some more modest occasion, but whether in the thirteenth, fourteenth or early fifteenth centuries it seems impossible to tell, for we have no record of a Round Table tourney at Winchester. By Hardyng's time it was assumed that this was the veritable board of a sixth century king. And possibly it was the presence of the table at Winchester which led Henry VII, with his Welsh ancestry, to ordain that his eldest son should be born there and christened Arthur in the year 1486.[106] Probably at this time the ancient board received the scheme of decoration which we see today. For here are names supplied by Malory's *Morte d'Arthur* of 1485; here in the central rose are reconciled the pretensions of the houses of York and Lancaster; and here in the exaltation of Arthur is suggested the special interest of the house of Tudor in its Welsh descent.

[102] Portal, *op. cit.*, p. 88.
[103] Note 34.
[104] Cf. forthcoming article by R. S. Loomis in *Medieval Studies in Memory of A. Kingsley Porter* (Harvard University Press).
[105] W. H. St. John Hope, *Windsor Castle* (L., 1913), I, 112–128.
[106] C. B. Millican, *Spenser and the Round Table* (Camb., Mass., 1932), 9–18.

CHAPTER IV

TRISTRAM IN THE VERSE ROMANCES

CHAUCER'S friend, the poet John Gower, wrote about 1390:

> In every mannes mouth it is
> How Tristram was of love drunke
> With Bele Isolde, whan they drunke
> The drink which Brangweine hem betok.

The incidents of this love story were not only in every man's mouth; they were, as we saw in Chapter II, the most popular romance subject for enamels, embroideries, and wall-paintings, as described in poet's dream or appraiser's inventory. And the extant remains of medieval art also attest the popularity of the theme. It found as much favor with cloistered nuns bending over their embroidery as with more worldly ivory-carvers turning out mirror-cases and jewel-caskets for wealthy bourgeoise or coquettish countess.

There is no Arthurian romance whose history is clearer.[1] It begins with a king of the Picts, Drust son of Talorc (780–785), whose story furnished the basis for the fight with Morhaut, the wounding, the false claimant, the recognition in the bath. Among the Welsh Drystan mab Tallwch became attached to the Arthurian cycle. The familiar triangle of uncle, uncle's wife, and nephew, and the flight of the lovers to the forest were developed on the model of the Irish romance of Diarmaid and Grainne. As the tradition passed on the lips of the *conteurs* through Cornwall and Brittany, it acquired its permanent center at "high Tintagel fair with famous days," and the localization of the beginning and the end in Brittany. Perhaps in Brittany also the tale of Ysolt of the White Hands was shaped on the model of a celebrated Arabic love-story of Kais and Lobna, and the powerful conclusion was wrought under the influence of classical tales—the death of Paris and Œnone and the return of Theseus. Other motifs, Celtic, Anglo-Norse, Oriental, were likewise absorbed, and it was a highly developed Continental form of the legend which seems to have been told by the professional reciter, Bleheris or Breri by name and a Welshman by birth, to a Count of Poitiers between 1100 and 1137, told in French with such histrionic power that the lovers suddenly became famous and Bleheris' version was recognized as authoritative. The pas-

sionate ancient story fitted exactly the theories of courtly love in southern France in its glorification of love and its rejection of the claims of feudal marriage.

This new cult of love undoubtedly owed much to one of the most famous and influential women of the Middle Ages, Eleanor, Countess of Poitou, Duchess of Aquitaine, who became the wife of Henry of Anjou in 1152 and Queen of England on Henry's accession to the throne in 1154. She may in her youth have heard at her father's court the moving romance even from the lips of Bleheris himself, and without doubt to her own troubadour poet, Bernard de Ventadour, Tristram was a lover *par excellence*.[2] To her as Queen, Wace is said to have dedicated his romanticized Arthurian chronicle with its praise of peace and love and sweet love-service,[3] and Benoît de Ste. Maure his romanticized epic of Troy. And under her influence, it may well have been that about 1185[4] the Anglo-Norman poet Thomas wrote his powerful version of the Tristram legend. Expressly citing Breri (Bleheris) as giving the most authoritative version of the story,[5] he himself, courtly poet that he was, retold the whole legend from its plaintive prelude concerning Tristram's young unhappy parents, through the many adventures of the lovers themselves, up to a superlative tragic climax, with two primary purposes in view,—one the glorification of courtly love, the other the glorification of that Anglo-Norman world in which he envisaged the ancient story as taking place.

Several other versions existed in the second half of the twelfth century. Of those which survive, Marie de France's short lai, *Chievrefoil*, was probably written also at the Anglo-Norman court. Eilhart von Oberg's poem was written in the Rhineland about 1170[6] and doubtless follows an earlier French poem, now lost. Some fragments by the Norman Béroul survive. But a number of versions circulated orally by the *conteurs* or committed to writing have disappeared. We have two witnesses to a poem by one Le Chévre;[7] Chrétien de Troyes says he wrote a poem, now lost, concerning King Mark and Ysolt the Fair-Haired; Eilhart, Thomas of Britain, and Marie de France assert their knowledge of various versions of the story;[8] and we have seen in Chapter II that the author of *L'Escoufle* described scenes from some

---

[1] Thomas of Britain, *Romance of Tristram and Ysolt*, trans. R. S. Loomis (N. Y., 1931), introd. *Neophilologus*, XV, 18, 88, 183. Thomas, *Tristan*, ed. Bédier, II (P., 1905), 105–130. G. Schoepperle, *Tristan and Isolt* (N. Y., Frankfort, 1913). *Beiblatt zur Anglia*, XV, 16.

[2] *Mod. Phil.*, XIX (1922), 287. On Eleanor's influence cf. Amy Kelly, *Speculum*, XII (1937), 3.

[3] Layamon, *Brut*, ed. F. Madden, vv. 42 f.

[4] *Romania*, LIII (1927), 100. *Ibid.*, LV (1929), 1.

[5] Ed. Bédier, v. 2119. *Romania*, LIII, 82 ff.

[6] *Neophilologus*, XV, 193. Cf., however, W. Stammler, *Verfasserlexikon des deutschen Mittelalters* (Leipz., 1932), I, col. 522 f.

[7] Kelemina, *Geschichte der Tristansage* (Vienna, 1923), p. 29.

[8] Schoepperle, *op. cit.*, I, 115 f. Marie de France, *Lais*, ed. Warnke (Halle, 1925), p. 181. Cf. Robert Mannyng, *Chronicle* (finished 1338), ed. Furnivall, vv. 93 ff.

perished Tristram romance. The earliest illustration of this famous legend, like the earliest Arthurian illustrations, is related to existing versions but does not reproduce faithfully any surviving literary source.

THE FORRER CASKET

This is a casket of ivory or bone in the possession of Dr. Robert Forrer of Strasbourg and is the subject of a monograph by him, which, though marked by several errors, seems sound on the major points.[9] The object, without its modern metal supports, is about 3 inches high, $3\frac{3}{4}$ inches wide, and $5\frac{3}{4}$ inches long. The borders containing rosettes, round arcades, or oblique lines leave no doubt that it came from a school of ivory carvers which produced a large number of religious reliquaries. Professor Goldschmidt has definitely fixed the center of their activity at Cologne;[10] his dating of the school, however, between 1200 and 1250 may well be questioned. Both Koechlin and Dr. Forrer are inclined to place this casket before 1200.[11] M. Hoepffner has argued that the literary source was the famous poem of Thomas and explained the divergences as due merely to the artist's whim;[12] but such an explanation will hardly pass when every divergence can be shown to have some literary support outside of Thomas. It is therefore more likely that the designer followed some unrecorded tale or some MS that has perished. Let us proceed to our identification of the scenes.

BACK. 1. (Fig. 19) We see between two towers and against a background of three trees two knights in combat on foot, one cutting into the top of the other's shield. This scene corresponds not to the version of Thomas, as reconstructed by Bédier, but follows in certain distinctive points Eilhart von Oberg, who says that Tristram undertook to fight Morhaut, the champion of Ireland, unhorsed him, and that in the ensuing fight on foot Morhaut "den schilt vorhau her im genug."[13] Contrast this scene with Chertsey tiles 19 and 20 which were certainly based on Thomas. It is worth noting that not only does Tristram's shield not bear the device of a lion, which Thomas as we shall see, must have attributed to him, but also the device, technically known as a carbuncle, appears on both shields, —an indifference to heraldic distinctions on the part of the carver which would seem more characteristic of the twelfth than of the thirteenth century.

RIGHT SIDE. 2. (Fig. 20) Some time after Tristram's

victory over Morhaut, he made a voyage to Ireland to win the hand of the Princess Ysolt, for his uncle King Mark of Cornwall. The fateful return voyage to Cornwall followed, and the king welcomed his bride. On this side of the casket we see once more two towers occupying the sides; a battlemented wall joins them. Behind this wall King Mark clasps the hand of the Princess with her long tresses. There is no clue to the version followed; in none does the meeting take place in a *verger*, as the tree would seem to indicate.

COVER. 3. (Fig. 21) Under a Romanesque arch, flanked by two towers, we see a bed. Under the coverlet lie a man and a woman, while another woman brings a goblet. No such scene is found in Eilhart, but we have it in Thomas's poem as reconstructed from the Norse saga.[14] After the night of his marriage to Ysolt, King Mark asks for wine, and Bringvain bears in the love-potion which Ysolt's mother has prepared and which has not been entirely consumed on the fateful voyage. The king drinks, but Ysolt secretly pours out her share. It is significant that though Gottfried von Strassburg in his great poem, written about 1210, usually follows Thomas, he expressly rejects this incident,[15] and any possibility that he might have been the inspirer of the casket is therefore excluded.

LEFT SIDE. 4. (Fig. 22) This is almost a duplicate of the right side: flanking towers, wall, man and woman on each side of a tree. The differences are slight except that the man and the woman do not wear crowns and do not join hands. We may safely conclude that they are Tristram and Ysolt, but just which rendezvous is represented we cannot tell. There is no trace of the spying Mark in the foliage nor of the spring below—both familiar in later iconography. One thinks of the parting of the lovers in the garden, movingly told by Thomas, but there is no certainty.

FRONT. 5. (Fig. 23) Here, separated by the lock, are two probably related scenes under two arches. On the right a knight in mail hauberk, a baldric over his shoulder, places his hand on the back of a lady's neck, and addresses her with raised fore-finger. On the left a lady throws an arm about the shoulder of a man playing a harp. Here, oddly enough, we seem to have the episode of the harp and the rote (a guitar-like instrument) as told neither by Thomas nor by Eilhart, but by Gottfried.[16] The knight Gandin, by playing his rote before King Mark, wins from him a promise and thereby claims and carries off the queen. Tristram, returning from the chase, follows Gandin in the guise of a harper, plays to him till he wins his confidence, and then seizes the opportunity to ride away with Ysolt. Now it is in Gottfried alone that Tristram bears the harp, and that Gandin is specifically said to be armed, "under armen."[17] Since Gottfried's poem is

[9] R. Forrer, *Tristan et Yseult sur un coffret inédit du XII siècle*, extract from *Cahiers d'archéologie et d'histoire d'Alsace* (1933), fasc. xxiv, xxv. The connection which Forrer assumes between the inscription and the tile figured on p. 158 I had on p. 68 of my Chertsey tile monograph expressly warned against, and the translation on p. 157 of *Quid baculo* as "Voici le gobelet" is impossible. The embroidery fragment figured on p. 150 is not the Erfurt tablecloth but Wienhausen embroidery I. On p. 177 is the remark: "En France . . . on n'a malheureusement conservé aucun manuscrit illustré de Tristan." This applies only to the verse romances.

[10] A. Goldschmidt, *Elfenbeinskulpturen aus der Romanischen Zeit* (Berlin, 1923), III, 3 f.

[11] Forrer, *op. cit.*, pp. 138, 141.

[12] *Romania*, LIX (1933), 548.

[13] *Quellen u. Forschungen*, XIX (1877), 61 f.

[14] Thomas, *Tristan*, ed. Bédier, I, 157 and n.

[15] Ed. F. Ranke (Berlin, 1930), vv. 12648–56.

[16] *Ibid.*, vv. 13104 ff.

[17] Vv. 13279, 13289.

probably later than the casket, we are obliged to infer some earlier source for these details.

To sum up, the carver of the Forrer casket has followed in the three identifiable scenes versions which correspond to those of Eilhart, Thomas, and Gottfried successively. Probably he worked earlier than the date of Gottfried's poem, possibly earlier than the date of Thomas. Did he follow a version which combined these divergent traditions, more ancient than the surviving texts? Or did he know several versions, and adopt now one, now another, at random? The question will probably he answered only when we learn what song the sirens sang, or what name Achilles assumed when he hid himself among women. As with numerous ivory caskets of the later French school, this was doubtless originally intended as a jewel case for ladies. It may well have been a marriage gift, as Forrer proposes, but his argument that the scenes were chosen that they might suggest only the chaste course of true love ending in faithful matrimony,[18] runs counter to the fact that three of them do not exalt wifely fidelity: Ysolt did not drink the love philtre with her husband; the rendezvous beneath the tree, whatever the precise occasion, was doubtless an illicit assignation; and the episode of the harp and the rote glorified the lover in contrast to the husband.

THE BASLINI CASKET

A bone casket which was included in the Baslini collection in 1886, and whose present whereabouts is unknown, suggests that the Forrer casket was not a unique product of the Cologne school.[19] The top, (Fig. 24) 15¾ inches long, presents, together with six ecclesiastics standing in pairs in compartments, four secular figures which may reasonably be connected with our romance. In one compartment, behind a battlemented wall, stand a harper and a woman so like Tristram and Ysolt on the front of the Forrer casket that we cannot resist an identification, even though the carving is more delicate and the woman holds a round goblet—possibly a reminiscence of the potion. Further confirmation is found in two figures facing each other from opposite ends of the plaque. At the top a knight in hauberk and helmet grasps with his right hand a shield suspended by a guige around his neck, as are the shields of Tristram and Morhaut on the Forrer casket. At the bottom the corresponding figure is a crowned woman, with hands uplifted under her mantle. Since these two figures taken together resemble Gandin and Ysolt on the front of the Forrer casket, it is probable that the carver was again copying a design representing the

harp and the rote episode. But it is quite possible that he was not conscious of the story, since he sets the figures from the romance in such odd juxtaposition to his ecclesiastics. The refinement of the carving offers a hint that the craftsmen of Cologne may have produced illustrations of the great romance more gracious than any now existing.

THE CHERTSEY TILES

If we could see the England of the thirteenth century, we should discover standing on a branch of the clear Thames, about ten miles from the battlemented pile of Windsor Castle, another pile of buildings of white stone, scarcely less imposing,—the rich and venerable Abbey of Chertsey. It had been founded in 666 by the saintly Earconwald before his consecration as Bishop of the East Saxons and had continued through the centuries under Benedictine rule. Six hundred years later it was one of the richest in England, splendid to the eye with stained glass and marble column and magnificent tile pavements. For that very reason, perhaps, at the Dissolution no monastery in England was more effectively "dissolved." In 1752 Dr. Stukeley, the antiquary, recorded:

Of that noble and splendid pile which took up four acres of ground and looked like a town, nothing remains; scarcely a little of the outer walls of the precinctus. . . One may pick up handfuls of bits of bones at once everywhere among the garden stuff. Foundations of the religious buildings have been dug up, carved stones, slender pillars of Sussex marble, monumental stones, effigies, crosses, inscriptions, everywhere.[20]

Yet despite all this lamentable destruction, in 1853 when a retired surgeon, Dr. Manwaring Shurlock, came to live at Chertsey and became interested in the ruins, he was able to make a very considerable collection of the tiles which had once formed part of the pavement of the Abbey. After consultation with Sir Gilbert Scott, Baron de Cosson, and Paulin Paris, he published in 1885 a handsome book about them. In 1922 in a kitchen garden which occupied a part of the Abbey site, new fragments were discovered and also a kiln, probably one of those in which the tiles were baked.[21]

The identification of many of these pictorial tiles was first made by Shurlock.[22] He recognized that many scenes were from the romance of Tristram, together with three from that of Richard Cœur de Lion and some miscellaneous scenes of hunting and combat. In 1870 excavation of the Premonstratensian Abbey of Halesowen near Birmingham, founded in

---

[18] P. 178.
[19] Goldschmidt, *op. cit.*, III, 26.
[20] M. Shurlock, *Tiles from Chertsey Abbey* (L., 1885), p. 6.

[21] The late J. R. Holliday kindly procured copies of these which have been used in Figs. 32, 40, 56.
[22] M. Shurlock, *op. cit.*

1215, revealed fragments of ten tiles evidently made from the same moulds as the Tristram series at Chertsey.[23] Thus it is clear that the thirteenth-century authorities of two religious houses must have approved the execution of a series of tiles from this highly secular romance. Indeed, there is an even earlier record of secular pavements made by a monk from the Cistercian Abbey of Beaubec in Normandy.[24] At a general chapter held in 1210 the Abbot himself was condemned to three days' penance because he had lent a monk of his to persons not belonging to the order for the construction of pavements which "tended to levity and curiosity."

But it may be there was a special reason for the introduction of this subject at Chertsey. Lethaby emphasized the important royal connections of the romance of Tristram, of Chertsey Abbey itself, and the tile designs.[25] The tiles were probably made about 1270, in the last years of Henry III; and it was at the court of his grandfather, Henry II, ninety or a hundred years before, that Thomas and Marie de France composed their poems of Tristram. Among the regalia of his father John was listed in 1207 "ensis Tristrami," of which the present sword Curtana is a modified replica.[26] Prince Edward, the son of King Henry III, took with him to the Holy Land in 1270 a romance which contained many adventures of Tristram.[27] Royal interest in the romance, therefore, is certain. Moreover, Chertsey was not far from Windsor, and in the reign of Edward I there was, as records show, a "King's Chapel" at Chertsey. Lethaby pertinently suggested that this chapel was a royal work of Henry III, and that for it the tiles were made.[28] This hypothesis is reinforced by the similarity of the Chertsey tiles to those which still pave the chapter house of Westminster Abbey and which were surely inspired by Henry III and executed by his craftsmen.

The pictorial tiles were an inch thick and about nine and a half inches in diameter; they were encircled by inscriptions in Lombardic lettering and then set in large foliate patterns.[29] They were of dark red clay, in which the designs had been lightly stamped and the depressions filled with white clay. So hardly have the fragments we possess suffered from fire, falling masonry, and exposure, that it is difficult to imagine the magnificent effect which a

great expanse of this richly decorated tiling would have produced. The authorities agree that there was in all Europe no other pavement in this medium to compare with it.

The Chertsey pavement belongs to the most glorious period of English art, when embroideries known as *opus Anglicanum* were famous throughout Europe, when Westminster Abbey and Salisbury cathedral and the choir of Lincoln were building, when English miniatures rivaled the work of Paris, and the Painted Chamber of Westminster Palace was unsurpassed in Christendom. The tile designs are thoroughly characteristic of the period and of the art of London. Lethaby pointed out how closely the design of tile 1 duplicates the figure of Edward the Confessor receiving the ring from St. Peter on a tile at Westminster chapter house.[30] The costume, the attitude, the treatment of the folds are almost identical. Moreover, the general scheme of decoration had been familiar in England for seventy-five years at least. We find it in another artistic medium on the Warwick ciborium in the South Kensington Museum.[31] Circular medallions enclosed in twining stems and conventional leaves may be seen also, as Miss Saunders notes, on the Manerius Bible from Canterbury and the Huntingfield Psalter. A comparison of the ciborium with Shurlock's plates 36, 39, is enough to demonstrate the affiliation. As for costume, there is the close similarity already noted to the Westminster tile, which Lethaby would date between 1255 and 1265, and to the fine Crusader in MS Royal 2 A XXII of the St. Albans school of almost the same time.[32] The ailette appearing on Morhaut's shoulder in tile 19, however, belongs to a small type depicted several times in the *Psautier de S. Louis*, which may be as late as 1270. We may be fairly safe, then, in setting the tiles within the last decade of Henry III's life (1262–72).

The encircling inscriptions are never attached to the pictorial roundels, so that though they render it certain that the designer followed the Anglo-Norman poem by Thomas, they are almost useless for more specific identifications. Here are some of the more complete:

Ci reprent Tristra(m); en la m(e)r en une; sauvage mer livre; mande le rei; priant kil vienge a; Morehaut; Morgan e se gent; en Engleterre; Sire Ro-; sans governail; en la bataile; Marc.[33]

[23] *Transactions of the Birmingham and Midland Institute* (1871), p. 65.
[24] Martini, *Thesaurus Anecdotorum*, IV, 1308.
[25] *Annual of the Walpole Soc.*, II (1913), 78 f. *Burlington Magazine*, XXX (1917), 133.
[26] *Mod. Lang. Rev.*, XVII (1922), 29. *Burlington Mag.*, XLI, 58 f.
[27] E. Löseth, *Roman en prose de Tristan* (P., 1890), pp. 423 f. E. G. Gardner, *Arthurian Legend in Italian Literature* (L., 1930), pp. 46 f.
[28] *Proceedings of the British Academy*, XIII (1927), 124.

[29] R. L. Hobson, *Catalogue of English Pottery in the British Museum*, pp. 40 ff. L. Haberly, *Mediaeval English Pavingtiles* (Oxf., 1937), pp. 9–15, 26–29, 49.
[30] *Burlington Mag.*, XXX, 133 f.
[31] O. E. Saunders, *History of English Art in the Middle Ages* (Oxf., 1932), p. 95.
[32] *Walpole Soc. Annual*, XIV (1926), pl. XXVII.
[33] Cf. R. S. Loomis, *Illustrations of Medieval Romance on Tiles from Chertsey Abbey* (University of Illinois Studies in Language and Literature, 1916), p. 25.

The cryptic bits of lettering on tiles 11 and 31 will be mentioned below. There are in all thirty-five designs from the Tristram series recoverable in whole or in part. Whether by accident or through deliberate censorship, only three of the surviving scenes depict incidents after the drinking of the potion, and none could be considered offensive to the most extreme modesty.

At present the great bulk of the fragments are in the stores of the British Museum; a few have been pieced together and are on public exhibition there. A few fragments are in the stores of the Victoria and Albert Museum, and others in the Surrey Archaeological Society Museum at Guildford; still others in the chancel of the church at Little Kimble, Bucks. The Duke of Rutland possesses a few at Belvoir Castle, including tiles 7 and 11, but they are inaccessible.

The thirty-five scenes may easily be identified in the translation of Thomas, supplemented from the *Saga*, published by R. S. Loomis in 1931.

1. (Fig. 25) Rivalon, Tristram's father, while on a visit to King Mark's court in Cornwall, receives tidings from a messenger that the Bretons under Duke Morgan are carrying fire and sword into his lands. This is probably the scene depicted on the tile.

2. (Fig. 26) Tristram, the child of Rivalon and King Mark's sister, orphaned soon after his birth, was carefully trained by Roald, his foster father, in all the Seven Arts and in the activities of knighthood. Here we see him, with his foster brothers, a curly headed boy learning to use a bow and arrow.[34]

3. (Fig. 27) Tristram and his foster brothers go aboard a vessel from Norway to buy hawks. Tristram remains to play chess, and the merchants, impressed by his surpassing skill in tongues and crafts, sail away with him. The tile shows us Tristram seated at the chessboard in the bow, a hawk perched on the stern of the boat, and a sailor pushing off.

4. (Fig. 28) Set ashore in Cornwall, Tristram meets first two pilgrims from St. Michael's Mount, and then a hunting party, who ride by blowing their horns. The fragment showing a man with puckered brow, the mouthpiece of a horn at his lips, probably belongs here.

5. (Fig. 29) Just as the huntsmen are about to cut up the stag, Tristram, who in later centuries was famous as a master of the art of venerye, shows them the latest French fashion and dresses a stake with certain parts of the beast including the head. Thus accompanied by the pilgrims and the huntsmen, the youth goes to the castle of Tintagel, comes before King Mark, and presents him with the stake. In the tile the two pilgrims are easily recognizable by the slavin, scrip, and bourdon. Tristram stands in the center, glove in hand, while a huntsman, kneeling, points back at him, and presents the stake gift. The stag's head, however, does not appear.

6. (Fig. 30) The same evening in the castle hall Tristram asks leave to play the harp and so pleases the king

that he declares, "Thou shalt be in my chamber by night and solace me by thy skill and harping while I lie waking."

7. (Fig. 31) Roald, after long wandering in search of his foster son, makes his way to Tintagel, gives the porter a gift, and is admitted to the hall. The figure on the tile standing in the doorway, key in hand, is certainly a porter, and this would seem to be the occasion depicted, though there survives no corresponding figure of Roald.

8. (Fig. 32) Roald reveals to King Mark that Tristram is the son of Rivalon and the King's sister, and Mark, at the request of the youth, equips him with arms and gives him the accolade. The fragment representing a king embracing an armed knight may well apply here.

9. (Fig. 33) Mark sends his nephew to Brittany to reclaim his paternal lands from Duke Morgan. On Tristram's landing he receives homage from his father's vassals. The design shows a vassal kneeling, and swearing an oath of allegiance, while he places his hands between those of Tristram.

10, 11. (Figs. 34, 35) Tristram rides with twenty knights to Duke Morgan's court and in full audience claims his heritage of the usurper. The two beautiful figures on the tiles probably represent this scene. A fragment of tile 11 in the possession of the Duke of Rutland contains lettering between Morgan's right forearm and the edge: above NOS; below EUIS. The meaning is as mysterious as is the inscription on tile 31. (Fig. 55a)

12. (Fig. 36) Duke Morgan defies Tristram, calls him a whoreson, and strikes him with his fist in the teeth. Whereupon Tristram draws his sword.

13. (Fig. 37) Tristram cleaves the Duke's head down to the eyes before all the court, and makes his escape. Though Tristram seems to have changed suddenly to a coat of mail since we last saw him in tiles 10 and 12, there is little doubt that this tile continues the dramatic episode at Duke Morgan's court.

14. (Fig. 38) After recovering his patrimony in Brittany Tristram goes to Tintagel, only to find the nobles of the land assembled lamenting over their sons, of whom sixty were to be selected by lot to be sent as truage to the King of Ireland. This lugubrious scene is represented on the tile by the two boys squatting on the floor and the five mourning men.

15. (Fig. 39) When Tristram enters the hall he sees the barons kneeling before those who are to draw lots, beseeching God to have pity on them.

16. (Fig. 40) Tristram, having learned that the truage is being enforced by Morhaut, brother-in-law of the Irish king, a redoubtable knight whom no man dares oppose in single combat, offers himself as champion of the rights of Cornwall. Here we are obliged to guess, for the tile shows simply two men in traveling costume, gesticulating with some violence, and behind them a third man holding a mace. The first two may be Tristram and one of his knights, just returned from Brittany, and the man with the mace may be Morhaut, the ambassador, since a mace was a recognized symbol of the ambassadorial office as early as the *Chanson de Roland* (c. 1080)[35] and as late as the Sicilian coverlet (c. 1395) which we shall study on p. 64.

[34] Gottfried von Strassburg, ed. Ranke (1930), v. 2115.

[35] Vv. 247, 268, 281.

17. (Fig. 41) As soon as Tristram has undertaken the combat, his uncle calls him, kisses and embraces him,—a scene easily recognizable on the tiles.

18. (Fig. 42) The king's example is followed by the Cornish barons; in fact, in the Saga we read that Tristram kissed all the vassals and knights that were there. The occasion depicted on the tile is determined by the two curly-headed boys, sons of the barons, on the left.

19. (Fig. 43) Tristram and Morhaut arm, mount, encounter, break their spears, and Morhaut deals Tristram a wound in the left side with his poisoned sword. The design representing this incident is noteworthy, because it shows a lion rampant on Tristram's shield; the Middle English *Sir Tristrem* also mentions the "lyoun" on the hero's shield; and the Norse Saga in describing the knighting of Tristram says that his horse's housing was red embroidered with golden lions. The logical inference from all this is that Thomas, from whose version the tiles, *Sir Tristrem*, and the Saga are all derived, attributed to his hero, as his armorial charge, gules a lion rampant or. The significance of this becomes patent when we note that the daughter of Henry II and Eleanor wore a gown of red silk embroidered with a golden lion, and that before 1163 Henry's brother William bore a rampant lion on shield and housings.[36] Though we have no other record, this must have been the royal device of the first Angevin king. In the reign of his son, Richard Cœur de Lion, the device was used of two golden lions rampant, each facing the other.

20. (Fig. 44) In spite of his wound, Tristram deals Morhaut a stroke on the helm that pierces his skull to the brain, and in withdrawing the sword leaves a splinter wedged in the skull.

21. (Fig. 45) When Morhaut falls from his horse dead, Tristram bids the ambassadors of Ireland carry his body back as the only tribute the Cornish will yield them. And the ambassadors bear his body away with great sorrow.

22. (Fig. 46) When the ambassadors arrive in Dublin and carry Morhaut's body to the castle, the barons run to meet them and the King of Ireland is overcome with sorrow. The design, representing a king in great agitation, apparently running, fits this scene.

23. (Fig. 47) Tristram's poisoned wound does not yield to the efforts of the leeches; he lies in great agony and the stench from his body drives his friends away. Mark, however, visits his sick-bed and Tristram beseeches that he be allowed to depart "wheresoever God will suffer him to go."

24. (Fig. 48) At King Mark's command, Tristram is set alone in a boat, with only his harp for solace and drifts across the sea. It is probably to this scene that the inscription "sans governail," "without a rudder," belongs.

25. (Fig. 49) Carried by chance to Dublin, Tristram gives his name as Tantris, and attracts attention by his mastery of arts. The Queen of Ireland, who alone has the skill to heal the wound dealt by Morhaut, works the cure of the accomplished stranger. Tristram, once healed, teaches her daughter, Ysolt, to play the harp, to write letters, and to excel in other arts. This situation has inspired the loveliest of all the designs.

36 *Mod. Lang. Rev.*, XVII, 24 ff. *Romania*, LIII, 100. *Apollo*, XXV (1937), 240.

26. (Fig. 50) Without ever revealing his identity or destination, Tristram gains leave of the Queen to set sail, and presently lands in the haven under King Mark's castle, in that little cove at Tintagel which we can still see under the headland with its broken battlements. That the fragmentary design showing a youth wading ashore from a boat represents this scene, is pure conjecture.

27. (Fig. 51) The people of Tintagel recognize Tristram's boat, hasten down to greet him, bring him a great horse, and he rides up to the castle. Again, the identification of this group of riders is only a guess.

28, 29. (Figs. 52, 53) King Mark is persuaded by his barons to wed and to send Tristram to Dublin to fetch the daughter of his mortal foe as a bride. The hero arrives in Ireland incognito, and as luck would have it learns that the King has promised his daughter to whoever would kill a devastating dragon. Tristram boldly undertakes the adventure, and drives his spear down the throat of the dragon with fatal effect.

30, 31. (Figs. 54, 55) Tristram, being overpowered by poison from the dragon's tongue, is once more healed by the Queen. And when a cowardly seneschal pretends that he has killed the dragon and claims the Princess, Tristram arises in court to deny his story and to challenge him to single combat. Tristram gives the King his glove as pledge of his good faith. The two tiles may possibly illustrate an earlier scene when Tristram gives Mark his glove as a pledge that he will undertake the battle with Morhaut. But the expression on the King's countenance seems that of anxiety and surprise rather than of joy, and seems to suit the King of Ireland better than King Mark. On one fragment of tile 31 appears the cryptic lettering shown in the illustration: in the first line G:, in the second ANNO, in the third OR(?)IE.

32. (Fig. 56) As is well known, Tristram finally wins the Princess Ysolt as a bride for Mark, and on the voyage to Cornwall, when the heat is great, he asks for drink. By the mistake of a page, the drink which Tristram takes first and then gives to Ysolt, is the love-potion intended for her and Mark. The tile shows us Tristram kneeling and presenting the hanap to the Princess Ysolt.

33. (Fig. 57) Now we have a long gap in the narrative. Ysolt, suspected of infidelity to King Mark, is adjudged to endure the ordeal of redhot iron. In order that she may swear to the truth, though without revealing her guilt, she arranges that Tristram, disguised as a pilgrim, shall meet her boat at the crossing of a river, carry her ashore, and fall with her as if by accident. This stratagem is carried out; she makes a sign to her lover from the boat, and he comes up and takes her in his arms. We need have little doubt that this is the scene depicted on the tile, even though the man ascending the ladder wears nothing distinctive of a pilgrim.

34. (Fig. 58) Another long gap in the series brings us close to the final tragedy. Tristram lies fatally wounded in his Breton castle and sends his brother-in-law, Kaherdin, to London to implore Queen Ysolt, renowned for her healing arts, to bring aid. Ysolt returns with Kaherdin, but when their ship is in sight of the Breton coast, they are becalmed. Ysolt is tortured at the delay,—the delay which keeps her from her lover's side till after his death. Several features of the design identify this scene,—the

drooping sail, the sailor in the bow, pulling at the oar, the agitated gestures of the two figures beside the mast, Ysolt in her broad hat and traveling robe and Kaherdin in his coif.

35. (Fig. 59) The last of the roundels apparently depicts the funeral rites over Tristram's bier. Four candles stand beside him and two priests chant the dirge.

THE RUNKELSTEIN MURALS

In a sunbathed valley of the southern Tyrol lies the town of Bozen (now Bolzano). To the northeast the great Brenner pass ascends over the Alps into Germany; to the south it follows the Adige down to Verona; to the east rise mountain masses and the flushed summits of the Rosengarten. Leading into this enchanted valley from the north is the dark gorge of the Talfer, and guarding the entrance of the gorge, stands on a crag of porphyry Schloss Runkelstein, or, as it is called by the Italians, Castello Roncolo. The dark-red tiles cap a dark-red block of buildings; and a low tower juts upward: here and there battlements crop out. A path leads steeply up to the castle across a bridge over a dry moat and into a cobbled courtyard surrounded by ivied walls. Here one can mount into a little embrasure in the wall and while sipping a glass of the long famous wine of Bozen,[37] look down at the Talfer, brawling among its boulders beneath, on its way to mingle with the Adige and the Po, or look across the courtyard to the open gallery, with its painted figures of the Nine Worthies and the triads of knights, giants, and giantesses. It is these and its cycles of other four-teenth century paintings that have made the place famous.[38]

Though the castle was founded in 1237, its history, as it concerns us, begins with its purchase in 1385 by the Tyrolese bankers, Niklas and Franz Vintler. An inscription, now vanished, went on to record:[39]

Ego Nicolaus Vintler hoc castrum Runkelstain nun-cupatum legaliter comparavi. Tandem anno 1388 mense Augusti posessionem eiusdem castri corporaliter subinivi. Quod quidem castrum . . . edificiis, fossato, antimuralibus, canipis, cisternis, salis, stubis, et pluribus commodis augendo, a novo edidi et reformavi.

Niklas was the Rothschild of his day. A count of Wolkenstein once remarked that "where no money is there no Vintler may be found." Farmer general of taxes, holder of many mortgages on castles and lands, holder of the purse strings of the spendthrift

Duke Friedrich "of the Empty Pocket," he was the financial power of the Tyrol. As patron of the arts, he assembled at Runkelstein a large library; and it was here that his chaplain, Heinz Sentlinger, com-posed his chronicle in rime, and his cousin, Hans Vintler, translated from Italian the *Pluemen der Tugent*.[40] It was probably within five years of his occupation of Runkelstein that Niklas had executed the series of paintings which glow on the walls of the older buildings.[41] At the same time he built the charming Summer House, with its open loggia and gallery, and about the end of the century he adorned it with murals.

When Niklas died in 1413, the castle passed first to his brother Franz and then to various owners till it came about 1500 into the possession of the Emperor Maximilian. Between 1503 and 1511 he employed three court painters, Jörg Kölderer, Friedrich Leben-bacher, and Max Reichlich, to restore the old work. "Das Sloss Runckelstain mit dem gemel lassen zu vernewen von wegen der guten alten Istory und dieselben Istory in schrift zuwegen bringen." The castle in the middle of the nineteenth century was in a somewhat dilapidated condition, but was bought and presented to the Emperor Franz Josef, restored by him at great cost, and given in 1893 to the town of Bozen.

If we ascend the stairs to the gallery of the Summer House overlooking the courtyard, we may look more closely at the somewhat weatherbeaten but still richly glowing figures painted on the walls. First come the Nine Worthies.[42] The three pagans and the three Jews are shown standing, in knightly armor. The three Christians, however, (Fig. 60) are seated on a paneled stall, and Arthur and Charlemagne wear robes of state over their arms. Here Arthur appears as a once august figure,—now badly blurred,— bearded and crowned, a sceptre in his left hand. Beyond the Worthies are three knights of the Round Table (Fig. 61) seated on the same paneled stall, wearing ample surcoats over their armor, each with a spear in his right hand and an armorial shield over his left side. First, Perceval (or Parzival) is distin-guished by the heraldic device of an anchor argent on a field of gules, which is ascribed to his father by Wolfram von Eschenbach.[43] He wears a red surcoat with dagged sleeves, and a helmet with beaklike visor—characteristics of the late fourteenth or early fifteenth century.[44] Next is "Her Gavein" in a *chapel de fer* and a green surcoat; a white hart upon his

[37] A. Schultz, *Höfisches Leben* (Leipz., 1879), I, 297 n. 3; *Deutsches Leben im XIV u. XV Jh.* (Vienna, 1892), II, 507.

[38] For earlier bibliography of Runkelstein cf. P. Clemen, *Tyroler Burgen* (1894), pp. 74–76. For recent bibliography cf. A. Morassi, *Storia della pittura nella Venezia Tridentina* (Rome, 1934), 347. For architecture and history cf. J. Weingartner, *Bozner Burgen* (Innsbrück, 1922), pp. 149 ff.

[39] *Archiv f. Geschichte u. Alterthumskunde Tirols*, I(1864), 296 n.

[40] *Ibid.*, 297.

[41] *Atti del Reale Istituto Veneto*, LXXII, pt. 2, 511–518. Cf. costume with that figured in 1387 MS of *Wilhelm von Oranse*, A. Schultz, *Deutsches Leben im XIV u. XV Jh.* (1892), pl. 12, 14, 15.

[42] Cf. *supra* pp. 37 ff.

[43] *Parzival*, 99, 13–16.

[44] Hefner-Alteneck, *Trachten des Christlichen Mittelalters*, II, pl. 35, 57, 92.

shield. Toward him leans Ivain as if to ask news of Chateau Merveil. His surcoat is white, his cognizance a spread eagle. Then follows a group of three pairs of lovers—Wilhelm von Oesterreich and Aglei, Wilhelm von Orleans and Amaley, and in the midst, Tristram and Ysolt. (Fig. 62) Above Tristram's head is a shield (partly visible in the reproduction) blazoned with a boar, the cognizance which Gottfried von Strassburg assigns him.[45] He wears a light-red, loose tunic with wide sleeves; a wallet hangs from a girdle about his hips. He holds out his hand to Ysolt, a full-bosomed lady in a blue gown, a crown encircling her head. Germanic romance now has its turn with the three heroes (Dietrich von Bern, Siegfried, and Dietleib von Steier), the three strongest giants, and the three wildest giantesses. Above these last (Fig. 63) runs the inscription: "Under allen ungeheurn under allen mag man sy fir di ungeheirigsten schreiben."[46] The first of these formidable hags has some claim to be an Arthurian personage, for above her Zingerle read the words, "Fraw riel nagelringen," and pointed out that there was a giantess Ruel in Wirnt von Gravenberg's poem *Wigalois*, which (as we shall see in Chapter VII) is illustrated at length in other paintings at Runkelstein. According to this romance a monstrous unarmed female attacks the hero, snatches his sword from his side, binds him and is about to behead him, when his horse whinnies opportunely and the monster flees thinking a dragon is approaching.[47] Wirnt described the giantess at length. She was black in color and shaggy as a bear; her hair and eyebrows were long; her head was large, nose flat, teeth big, mouth wide; her ears and breasts pendulous, her back bent, her legs strong, feet crooked, and she had claws like a gryphon's. Manifestly the painter has not followed this description and particularly in equipping the woman with a sword, Nagelringen, which is that of the giantess Hilde in *Thidrekssaga*.[48]

Between the triad of lovers and Dietrich a doorway leads from the gallery. Over the round arch are the Vintler arms, two white bear-paws and three black bear-paws quarterly—arms based upon a legend to the effect that a Vintler had once fought with a monstrous white bear in a public theater and had lopped off the two forepaws. Through the doorway is the passage to the Ladies' Chamber of the Summer House. The walls were originally covered completely with scenes from the romance of Tristram but half of them were smeared over with theatrical decorations in the 1850's and two scenes and part of a third were destroyed when a section of the north wall collapsed in 1868. Luckily the latter had already

been published as somewhat crude drawings by Seelos in 1857.[49] The surviving frescoes follow closely the great poem composed by Gottfried von Strassburg about 1210, and were done by a different artist from the painter of the gallery. The coloring is a uniform greenish grisaille, the high lights being indicated by white, and a few blood spots picked out in red. Certain features, particularly the beaked visor of "Marolt" in Scene 1, indicate that the original painting was done before 1413. On the other hand, drastic repainting has been carried out, probably in the sixteenth century: beards of a cut that was not seen in the fourteenth century adorn the chins of Mark and Tristram; plumes wave from nearly every helmet; and the architecture in scene 8 is certainly not Gothic, whatever else it may be. Maximilian's painters must have done a thorough job. It is curiously uneven in quality, however. The head of Ysolt in the upper part of Scene 8 and in the lower part of Scene 9 actually is alluring; there is vigor in Tristram's stroke in Scene 1, but there is little charm or strength or even plain competence in Scene 13. In the lower part of Scene 8 re-painting has given us two bearded crowned figures in the doorway, and were it not for the inscriptions, it would be hard to tell which was Mark. The reproductions tell more of the treatment than any verbal description, and the scenes are easily identifiable in Jessie L. Weston's fine translation of Gottfried:

1. (Fig. 64) The end of the judicial combat between Tristram and "Marolt," whose names appear. Against a rocky background Tristram stands with feet apart, both hands gripping his sword and swinging it far back to deal a final stroke at "Marolt," who has fallen groveling to the stony ground.

2. (Figs. 64-65) This probably represents Tristram's first voyage to Ireland since Gottfried, unlike Thomas, says that the hero was accompanied by eight men, and since he seems to be leaning against the mast for support. Yet it does seem strange that he should not have been relieved of his armor. The beaker which is apparently offered to him is also hard to explain. Above, perched perilously on a cliff, are the houses of Dublin.

3. (Fig. 65) The second voyage to Ireland. Tristram stands armed by the mast, surrounded by his people, while a boy in the bow points to the castle of Wexford.

4. (Fig. 66) Tristram, afoot, cuts the tongue from the dragon's mouth with a knife, while the seneschal of Ireland and two other knights gallop from the scene; Gottfried mentions the hero's meeting four knights before he encounters the dragon.

5. (Fig. 67, 70) The Princess "Isalde," two maids and a squire revive Tristram, as he lies with his sword and gauntlet beside him, overpowered by the poison of the

[45] Ed. Ranke, v. 4942. Cf. *Mod. Lang. Rev.*, XVII (1922), 24 f.
[46] *Germania* (Vienna), 1878, p. 28.
[47] Wirnt v. Gravenberc, ed. J. M. N. Kapteyn (Bonn, 1926), vv. 6285-433. H. Schneider, *Germanische Heldensage* (Berlin,

1928), I, 265.
[48] *Thidrekssaga*, ed. Bertelsen, I, 11 ff.
[49] I. V. Zingerle, I. Seelos, *Freskenzyklus des Schlosses Runkelstein* (Innsbrück, 1857).

dragon's tongue. Here the painter has deviated from the text in omitting the Queen, Ysolt's mother.

From this point on the paintings are badly damaged. So much is indistinguishable in the photographs that for scenes 5, 6, 7, and 9 it has seemed desirable to reproduce also Seelos' plates. (Figs. 70, 72a)

6. (Fig. 68, 70) The Princess "Isalde" in the background draws Tristram's sword from its sheath. She appears again threatening him with the same sword as he sits in the bath while "Bragene" grips her hand. The scene by no means corresponds to Gottfried, who tells us that Ysolt after her discovery approached Tristram, sword in hand, her mother entered and intervened to save him, and not till later did "Bragene" enter and advise his safe-keeping. The painter could not have had Gottfried's text very precisely in mind. In the tower above is a head blowing a horn, and two heads, one that of a king, looking out over a wall. These represent doubtless the King and Queen of Ireland gazing out at the departing vessel of their daughter which we find in the next scene.

7. (Fig. 69, 70) In the stern of a vessel, Tristram holds out his hand, and Ysolt takes from it the fatal goblet. The waist of the boat is full of figures, among whom can be distinguished two trumpeters, and "Bragene" identified by her name.

8. (Fig. 71) This has been drastically repainted. The architecture, the costumes, the beards are obviously not of the fourteenth or even the late fifteenth century. In the doorway stands a mysterious crowned figure with a sword. At his left "Marck" extends both hands to "Isalde," who is attended by her ladies and a bearded Tristram. To the right of the doorway are courtiers and a figure who seems to be blowing both a serpentine and a straight trumpet. Above in an arched window appear the heads and shoulders of three persons—on the left a venerable bearded face, which is identified by an inscription below as Mark's; on the right, a crowned head of a man, who is likewise identified as Tristram, and between them a full face of Ysolt, perhaps the loveliest bit of painting in the whole castle.

9. (Fig. 72, 72a) Here are three successive scenes in the repulsive episode of "Isalde's" attempt to procure the murder of her faithful "Bragene." In the upper background "Isalde" gives her instructions to the two henchmen. On the right above, "Bragene" sits alone in the forest, while the two men return with the false report of her murder. In the fore-ground below, "Bragene" is brought back by one of the men, and "Isalde" takes her into her arms. Once more the artist has not belied the Queen's reputation for beauty.

The next two scenes are those destroyed by the collapse of the north wall.

10. (Fig. 73) Tristram and "Isalde" lie in bed together under a canopy-like building. A chessboard shades the candle light from the lovers, and Bragene watches beside it. Tristram's friend, Mariodoc, has followed Tristram's track through the snow and spies upon him.

11. (Fig. 73) This represents the famous tryst beneath the tree as described by Gottfried. By "Bragene's" advice, Tristram has informed "Isalde" that he is waiting for her by casting into a little brook, which flows past her bower, a chip of wood carved with the letters I and T. King Mark and his dwarf Melot have learned the stratagem, and have mounted into an olive tree above the brook where Tristram is waiting. Tristram observes the shadow of the two men in the tree, and so, presently, does "Isalde" when she arrives, accompanied by "Bragene." Both the lovers then assume so distant and reproachful a demeanor toward each other that Mark is absolutely deceived.

12. (Figs. 73, 74) The dwarf, nevertheless, determines to track and trap the lovers. One night Mark, "Isalde," Tristram, "Bragene," and the dwarf, are all, by the surgeon's orders, occupying one chamber. The King arises to go to matins, and Melot accompanies him, as we see on the right, first sprinkling the space about the royal bed with flour. "Bragene," however, notices the flour and warns Tristram, but he will not be dissuaded and springs from his bed to "Isalde's," as he is represented in the fresco.

13. (Fig. 75) Here we have the scene, already depicted on the Chertsey tiles. Tristram, disguised as a pilgrim, walks up the gang plank to carry "Isalde" ashore. Behind her is "Bragene" and a shipful of courtiers.

14. (Fig. 75) "Isalde" in her shift stands before a bishop and making oath that she has never lain with any man except the pilgrim who has just fallen with her, she is able to take into her bare hands, without injury, the redhot iron.

Still further interest in the Tristram legend on the part of the Vintler family may be indicated by the fact that in the Schrofenstein, Bozen, where perhaps Niklas Vintler died, there were paintings, and the word *Tristan* was legible.[50]

German poetry inspired, besides the paintings at Runkelstein, six fourteenth-century embroideries of Tristram: three at Wienhausen, one at Erfurt, one at South Kensington, and fragments at Lüneburg. These embroideries are based apparently on a lost source, which follows the version of Eilhart von Oberg more often than Gottfried's version, and sometimes introduces features unknown to either Gottfried or Eilhart.

At Wienhausen in Hanover rise the dark-red brick walls and high-peaked roof of a former Cistercian nunnery of the thirteenth century. Within, the place shows how completely the early severity of ornament and the old strictness of Cistercian discipline yielded to the prevailing medieval love of beauty and romance. The founders of Citeaux had proscribed in their constitution stained glass, wall paintings (save those of Christ himself), sculptured ornament, and jeweled chalices. But Wienhausen was and is still famous for the rich painting of its Chapel and its extraordinary collection of embroideries, including subjects religious and secular, both kinds worked

---

[50] C. Höffinger, *Burg Runkelstein bei Bozen* (Munich, n. d.), p. 5.

probably by the nuns themselves. If what Winter says in his *Cistercienser des Nordöstlichen Deutschlands* be true, that games and dances in lay costumes were popular at many festivities within the cloisters, and that nuns even gave birth to children, then it would seem as if the barriers between religious and lay were nearly all down, and there need be no astonishment over the probability that the three Wienhausen Tristram embroideries as well as others on secular subjects were the handiwork of nuns. In the fourteenth and fifteenth centuries, five abbesses of Wienhausen were daughters or granddaughters of the Dukes of Brunswick.[51]

The Wienhausen embroideries have often been mentioned and studied in German publications,[52] but far and away the most scholarly and sumptuous work is Fräulein Marie Schuette's *Gestickte Bildteppiche und Decken des Mittelalters*, to which the present account is much indebted. All the embroideries were doubtless designed and drawn in black on a linen base, and the spaces stitched in wools dyed with mineral oxides in vivid and appropriate colors.

WIENHAUSEN EMBROIDERY I

The first of the three hangings dates from the first quarter of the fourteenth century and is well preserved. (Figs. 76, 77) Its dimensions are 13 feet 3 inches by 7 feet 8 inches. On the left there is a border of roses and rose leaves intertwined; on the right, one of oak leaves and acorns. Running horizontally between these occur in alternation four rows of heraldic shields under an arcading and three rows of scenes from the romance. The colors are dark turquoise, rose, pea-green, straw, light blue, and white. The background of nearly all the scenes is dark blue. The armorial shields in the first row are those of the Empire, Brunswick, France, Bohemia, Greece, Castile or Portugal, Hungary, and others; in the second row we recognize the three gold leopards of England; in the third row are the shields of Thuringia, Saxony, Bavaria, the Palatinate, Lüneburg, Austria, Silesia, Pomerania; and in the fourth those of minor German houses.

The complete inscription, written in the local dialect, runs:

Tristram de bat den koning dat he mote striden vveder Morolde. De koning sprac, ec vvile de levere gheven min koningrike half. Tristram de kerde sec umme unde sette uppe dat pert unde stridde an des koniges danc. Do quam he vor den koning unde claghede dat he vervundet vvare. Do quam vrue Brangiele unde vru Isalde, legheden ene in en scip unde vorden ene to der stad, dar me ene salven scolde. Do steg he uteme scepe. Do stunt he unde

vedelede. Do quam vru Braniele unde toch ene up de norch (*leg.* borch). Do stot vru Braniele unde hel ene. Vru Isalde salvete ene. Do badde se ene. Vru Isalde helt dat svert. Braniele dvoch ene.

Tristram asked the king that he might fight against Morold. The king said, 'I will rather give thee half my kingdom.' Tristram turned about and mounted his horse and fought without the King's thanks. There he came before the King and lamented that he was wounded. There came Lady Brangiele and Lady Isalde, and laid him in a ship, and brought him to the city, where he would be salved. There he stepped out of the ship. There he stood and played the viol. There came Lady Braniele and brought him to the castle. There stood Lady Braniele and held him. Lady Isalde salved him; there she bathed him. Lady Isalde held that sword. Braniele washed him.

This inscription cannot be the work of the designer, since it does not follow the scenes precisely, and in three scenes the persons have been wrongly identified. In Scene 9 we have surely Mark standing grief-stricken on the shore, while a man pushes off the boat in which Tristram lies; but the inscription identifies the two standing figures as "Brangiele" and Ysolt. In Scene 12 Ysolt, crowned, holds Tristram's wrist, while "Braniele," crownless, holds up a box of salve. The inscription reverses the roles. In Scene 20 it is only the uncrowned "Braniele" who bathes Tristram; the inscription mentions both Ysolt and "Braniele."

The designer himself followed a version differing from any surviving. The form of the name Tristram and Mark's reference to half his kingdom are not found in either Eilhart or Gottfried; Tristram's viol and his healing by Bringvain and Ysolt are features standing in flat contradiction to both poets, who provide him with a harp and attribute his healing either to a messenger or to Ysolt's mother.

Most of the other distinctive details parallel Eilhart's account, of which Miss Schoepperle gives a convenient summary at the beginning of her *Tristan and Isolt*. In Scene 9 Tristram lies alone in his boat; whereas Gottfried, as we saw at Runkelstein, supplies a crew for the first voyage to Ireland. In Scene 14 we see two birds between Tristram and the throned Mark—a clear indication that the designer followed, though not precisely, Eilhart's story that while Mark was seeking to evade the barons' demand that he should take a wife, he saw two swallows quarreling, and a golden hair falling from their beaks. When the barons and Tristram entered, he declared he would marry only the woman to whom the hair belonged, and Tristram undertook to find her. As in Eilhart, moreover, the Queen of Ireland, Ysolt's mother, does not appear. Only one feature, the exhi-

[51] M. Schuette, *Gestickte Bildteppiche des Mittelalters*, I (Leipzig, 1927), i, xvi.

[52] H. W. H. Mithoff, *Archiv für Niedersachsens Kunstgeschichte*

(Hanover, 1849), II, 9. J. Lessing, *Wandteppiche u. Decken des Mittelalters*, Pl. 11–13. *Pantheon*, I (1928), 89. *Burlington Mag.*, LII (1928), 27.

bition in Scene 22 of the tongueless dragon's head as evidence that the false seneschal had not slain the monster, parallels Gottfried.

Below is a brief identification of the scenes: (Figs. 76, 77)

FIRST ROW. 1. Tristram with hands crossed stands before Mark's throne and undertakes the combat with Morhaut.

2. He rides out armed from the castle.

3. He paddles a boat, containing his horse, to the isle of combat.

4. He fights with Morhaut, whose shield is adorned with a Saracen's head.

5. Tristram kills Morhaut.

6. He paddles back from the island.

7. He rides out of the gateway,—a scene probably intended to represent his return to Tintagel Castle.

SECOND ROW. 8. He appears before Mark to lament his wound.

9. Mark weeps, and a courtier consigns Tristram's boat to the waves.

10. Ysolt and Bringvain listen from a tower to Tristram playing the viol.

11. Bringvain leans out of a tower and draws Tristram in, while Ysolt looks on.

12. Tristram, his head tonsured, squats on the ground, while Ysolt holds his wrist and Bringvain holds a box of salve.

13. A ship under sail carries Tristram back to Cornwall.

14. Tristram addresses Mark while two swallows flutter overhead.

THIRD ROW. 15. Tristram returns to Ireland to seek the hand of the Princess Ysolt for his uncle.

16. He encounters the dragon.

17. He cuts out its tongue.

18. Poisoned by the venom, he lies in a swoon among the reeds, and is discovered by Ysolt and Bringvain.

19. He rides up to the palace, supported by Ysolt.

20. Bringvain bathes Tristram.

21. She restrains Ysolt, who brandishes a sword.

22. Ysolt and Tristram (?) at the left. The false seneschal, who has found the dead monster and claims to be the slayer, holds up the dragon's head before the King and Queen of Ireland.

23. A crowded vessel. In the bow Tristram and Ysolt lie embracing, while an attendant holds up the fatal goblet.

WIENHAUSEN EMBROIDERY II

The second embroidery at Wienhausen, judging by the costumes, was probably made a few years later than the first, perhaps about 1325. (Fig. 78) It has suffered much worse usage, for it once covered the altar steps. It now measures 4 feet 5 inches by 5 feet 5 inches, but it consists of two clumsily joined fragments of a much larger hanging. All the faces and shoes, as well as other details, have been crudely restored. The colors are dark and light blue, pea-green, red, ochre, black, and white. Three odd fea-

tures, Ysolt's hat with peacock feathers, the half-mullet decoration on Tristram's helm, and the trefoil design on Mark's bed quilt, appear also on the contemporary Gawain embroidery at Brunswick, but the treatment of the scenes, except one, is so close to that on Wienhausen I that detailed identification is unnecessary. The inscription consists mainly of the names of the characters underneath:

Rex Marchis Tristra-	Marrolf Tristra-
Markis Rex Tristram	istram Sarpant Ma-
Tristram Isalde Bra-	-am du heft ghe sclaen

The word *Sarpant* refers, of course, to the dragon. The last words apparently represent the exclamation of Ysolt on discovering Tristram's identity by the tell-tale breach: "Tristram, thou has slain [mine uncle!]"[53] In the first scene the kneeling Morhaut holds a scroll with the words "Tint mime heren," which mean "Tribute for my lord."

The name-forms with the exception of "Isalde" are strange. Tristram, as has already been pointed out, occurs in neither Eilhart nor Gottfried. The names Marchis and Marrolf seem influenced by the analogy of the French title *marquis* and the literary name Marcolf. Every scene here represented is common to both Eilhart and Gottfried except one. The first scene in the second row depicts King Mark lying in bed; a garment is draped over the canopy; a single bird with a clover leaf in its beak flies above him. The leaf must be a blundering substitution, made perhaps by the embroidress, for the golden hair; but Mark's lying in bed suggests that the original design followed some other version than Eilhart's, for he does not place the scene in the royal bedchamber.

WIENHAUSEN EMBROIDERY III

The third embroidery may be assigned on the basis of costume to about 1340, the long surcoats in Scenes 5 and 6 dating it certainly before 1350. (Fig. 79) It has been cut up, has lost all its left border and part of the right and until 1924 parts of it were attached to a hanging containing scenes from the life of St. Elizabeth. Its dimensions are about 8 feet 5 inches by 13 feet 2 inches, but it was, of course, somewhat longer before the left border was cut away. Apart from this dismemberment the piece has suffered little; the general color effect is lighter and gayer than that of the others,—indigo, pale blue, deep red, straw, rust, pea-green, and white. While this embroidery bears almost no resemblance in design to Wienhausen I, it displays marked analogies to Wienhausen II; for example, the inscriptions, the little trees and narrow towers which form partitions between the scenes,

[53] Or perhaps the "serpent." Cf. Eilhart, ed. F. Lichtenstein (Strasbourg, 1877), v. 1894.

the costumes of the ladies; and certain scenes also correspond strikingly, such as Mark seeing the swallow with the golden hair, Tristram cutting out the dragon's tongue, Tristram in the bath. Also striking is the similarity of Wienhausen III to the Gawain embroidery at Brunswick (Figs. 143, 144) in costume both male and female, in the partitions of towers and trees, in the variegated boats, and in the banquet scenes. Ysolt riding side-saddle in the lowest row (Scene 21) is almost identical with the riding figure of Orgeluse at Brunswick. (Fig. 143) The dyes, however, are different, and so is the treatment of waves.

Both inscription and illustrative design show a marked variance from any surviving source. The former may be translated:

Konich Markes sande ut zinen om na der iunen vrowen de hede alzo dan har alz . . . hede vorde in dat palas. He vor over de ze. Do sloch he dot Morholte, Isalde broer. Do sloch he den worm un sche vom en de tucnen ut. De rode ridder—

King Markes sent forth his nephew for the young damsel who had the hair such as . . . had brought into the palace. He went over sea. There he slew the Morholt, Isalde's brother. There he slew the dragon and cut out his tongue. The Red Knight—

The scenes run as follows:

FIRST ROW. 1. Mark in bed sees the two swallows.
2. Mark, throned, converses with Tristram.
3. Tristram, unarmed, rides out with an attendant.
4. Tristram and two men in a sailing vessel.
5. Tristram fights Morhaut while their horses fight beside them. No literary version mentions the horse combat, or places the fight with Morhaut at this point. Tristram wears the strange crest of a Saracen's head on his helmet.
6. Tristram cuts out the tongue of the dragon.
7. He lies in a swoon, his horse and shield beside him, his sword hanging from a tree.
SECOND ROW. 8. The seneschal cuts off the dragon's head.
9. He presents the dragon's head before Bringvain, the Princess, the King and Queen, while Tristram holds up the tongue. This scene illustrates Gottfried, but it should follow the scene of recognition.
10. Tristram in his bath-tub is recognized by Ysolt, who holds his sword and the telltale fragment.
11. A ship contains a helmsman and Bringvain, while under an awning Tristram hands the goblet to Ysolt.
12. Mark and Ysolt sit at the wedding banquet, the ring hovering in the air between them.
13. Bringvain and Mark lie in bed together, while Ysolt stands on the further side.
THIRD ROW. 14. Bringvain and the two murderers are in the forest. One of them holds a hound, which is

killed in her stead; the other holds a mysterious shirt, which finds no mention in any text.
15. Tristram and Ysolt, lying together in a love grotto, are discovered by Mark. The sword does not separate the lovers, but lies by Ysolt's side on the coverlet, where also Mark has placed his glove. This scene is closer to Eilhart than to Gottfried.
16. The tryst beneath the tree. Mark sits among the branches accompanied by a dwarf. Since there is no spring at the base of the tree, the design is closer to Gottfried's version, where the spies are revealed by shadows but not by their reflection in water.
17. Tristram, banished from Cornwall by the King, sails to Brittany.
18. A priest, in the center, joins Tristram in matrimony with Ysolt of Brittany. Apparently Ysolt's mother gives the bride away, and her brother Kehenis, is, in modern parlance, "best man."
19. The wedding banquet. Tristram toasts the bride. At the right two minstrels blow their trumpets.
FOURTH ROW. 20. The bridal night, when Tristram, torn between desire and his love for Ysolt of Ireland, leaves his bride a virgin.
21. Tristram boasts that his love Ysolt treats his dog with greater honor than his wife Ysolt treats him. And in this scene we see Tristram's hound Hodain carried on a horse litter and displaying an hauteur worthy of a Castilian noble. In front ride Bringvain and Ysolt. Eilhart says that Tristram and Kehenis watch this procession from behind a bush, but here we have a man and two women behind the mound-like obstruction. Was there then a version, followed by the designer, which represented Tristram as making his boast not to Kehenis but to his wife, and revealing to her how precious his very hound is to her rival? Something like this seems probable and certainly makes for a more dramatic effect.
22. Tristram, accompanied apparently by his wife and an attendant, returns to Brittany.

THE LÜNEBURG EMBROIDERY

In 1895 there were discovered in the village church of Emern and later deposited in the Lüneburg Museum the tattered and faded fragments of an embroidery.[54] Three scenes under trefoil arches are all that can be connected with our romance. (Figs. 80–82) The piece is not embroidered solidly like the Wienhausen hangings, but like the Erfurt tablecover shows the white linen ground; against this the designs are worked in white linen, and the outlines in faded silks of yellow and green. The date, according to Fraülein Schuette, is early fourteenth century and the provenance lower Saxony.[55]

1. (Fig. 80) Here is the familiar detection of Tristram in his bath. Ysolt holds the sword, and points to the telltale notch, while Bringvain lifts her hands in astonishment.

[54] *Karl Koetschau von seinen Freunden u. Verehrern zum 60 Geburtstag* (Düsseldorf, 1928), p. 35.
[55] Another fragment was associated by Fraülein Schuette with the Tristram scenes (*ibid.*, Pl. 2, p. 38), but the cinquefoil arch

seems to connect it rather with the embroidery of the Virgin, found at the same time and place and employing the same arch. Cf. W. Reinecke, *Wegweiser durch die Sammlungen des Museumvereins für das Fürstentum Lüneburg*, ed. 3 (1927), p. 17.

2. (Fig. 81) Ysolt, crowned, and Tristram stand on either side of a tree. Behind her a dog rises on its hind legs. This scene surely represents a tryst, but as with the similar scene on the Forrer casket, it seems impossible to specify the occasion.

3. (Figs. 81–82) The mast and sail of a ship appear. On one side a man, on the other a woman raise their hands as if conversing. Below there is a very decorative pattern of waves and dolphins. Again the particular occasion is impossible to determine.

The Erfurt Tablecloth

In the cathedral museum of Erfurt there is a linen tablecloth from a Benedictine nunnery at Würzburg, gaily embroidered in blues and reds.[56] Figs. 83–85) It is 14 feet and 1 inch long, and 3 feet wide. Two rows of thirteen scenes run the length of the piece, each row set to face those who sat before it. A border, surrounding these scenes and the inscriptions, consists of a foliate design and grotesque figures of men and women, whose legs are replaced by the bodies, wings, and feet of birds. Each scene is placed under an arch, and the spandrels are occupied alternately by courtly ladies sprouting wings and by gentlemen equally angelic. The costumes place the date about 1370. The inscription, in Gothic, not Roman letters, runs:

Hie hebit sich dye materie von Tristram unde von der schon Ysalden. Hy ersleit he den worm. Hie brengit der rote ritter daz hobt vor den kong. Hi vint Yzalde Tristam in dem rore. Hi wist Tristar*m* die sunge*n* dem konge. Hi vurt Tr*i*stram die schon Ysalden mitem heym zcu lande. Hi rit Tristram von houe. Hi kumt Yzalde zu Tristra*m* in den garte*n*.

Here is the matter of Tristram and the Fair Ysalde. Here he slays the dragon. Here the Red Knight brings the head before the King. Here Yzalde finds Tristam in the rushes. Here Tristarm shows the tongue to the King. Here Tristram brings the fair Ysalde home with him to land. Here Tristram rides from court. Here Yzalde comes to Tristram in the garden.

Once more Eilhart seems the main source, but the punishments of the Red Knight and of the dwarf are found in no extant version, and, as we have seen, the exhibition of the dragon's head is peculiar to Gottfried. The mention of the Red Knight here and in Wienhausen III makes it certain that there once existed a romance in which the false seneschal bore that name. He is here represented with red hair and beard. A list of the scenes follows:

LOWER ROW. 1. (Fig. 83) King Mark and Tristram seated. A swallow with a hair in its mouth flutters above them.

2. King Mark, standing in a gateway, takes the hand of Tristram riding away.

3. Tristram encounters the fire-breathing dragon.

4. He slays the dragon with his sword.

5. (Fig. 84) He cuts out the dragon's tongue.

6. The Red Knight rides out with a companion.

7. He swears three knights to secrecy on his sword.

8. He cuts off the dragon's head.

9. He shows it to the King of Ireland.

10. (Fig. 85) Ysolt and Bringvain leave the castle on foot.

11. They find Tristram lying among the rushes, the tongue in his hand.

12. They bring him to the castle.

13. Ysolt threatens Tristram in the bath, while Bringvain restrains her.

UPPER ROW. 14. Ysolt and Bringvain reveal their discovery to the King of Ireland.

15. Tristram, kneeling, shows the tongue to the King.

16. The Red Knight is brought by two men before the King.

17. The Red Knight's head is struck off in the presence of the King and of another knight.

18. (Fig. 84) The Queen of Ireland standing in a gateway hands the potion to Bringvain, who stands in the ship with Tristram and Ysolt.

19. Tristram and Bringvain stand in the ship, while King Mark in a gateway assists Ysolt to disembark.

20. Tristram brings Bringvain in Ysolt's stead to King Mark's bed.

21. Mark, Ysolt, Bringvain, and Tristram, at a feast.

22. Ysolt clasps Tristram's hand as he rides away into banishment.

23. (Fig. 83) Tristram carves chips into the stream.

24. The dwarf reveals the assignation to Mark.

25. Tristram and Ysolt meet beneath the tree. The heads of Mark and the dwarf appear among the leaves and are reflected in the fountain below.

26. After the lovers' departure, Mark, convinced of their innocence, seizes the dwarf by the legs, as if to plunge him into the stream.

The South Kensington Embroidery

This richly colored hanging adorns the walls of the Victoria and Albert Museum, South Kensington.[57] (Fig. 86) It is closely related to the Erfurt tablecover; the design, the costume, the close resemblance in several scenes—all point to the same date and probably to the same designer for both. Though it still measures 8 feet by 3 feet 6 inches, it has been barbarously mutilated and is in fact a composite of at least three fragmentary embroideries stitched together. The colors range from pea-green to indigo and from a rich pink to plum. The figures are outlined by parchment strips, once gilt, now black; and the belts of the knights and the gowns of the ladies

---

[56] *Anzeiger für Kunde der Deutschen Vorzeit*, 1866, col. 14. A. Overmann, *Aeltere Kunstdenkmäler . . . der Stadt Erfurt* (Erfurt, 1911), p. 344.

[57] D. Rock, *South Kensington Museum, Textile Fabrics, Catalogue of the Collection* (1870), p. 77.

are studded with the same material. Ysolt's hair is naturalistically represented by undulating threads, but all the faces are oval blanks—not a mouth, nose, or eye being indicated.

In the top row are alternating figures of ladies and gentlemen, all engaged in flirtatious converse, but all, alas, decapitated by some vandal's scissors. Below are two rows of five scenes each, under triple trefoil arches with alternating backgrounds of blue and red, the spandrels occupied by birds. The scenes require no elucidation since they correspond so obviously to those on the Erfurt tablecover, except for Scene 4, which apparently depicts Tristram's squire asking the whereabouts of the dragon from the fleeing seneschal. In the lower right hand corner a scene from a second embroidery has been added, depicting two lovers under a double cusped arch. Above this running vertically is a scene from a third hanging, similar in decorative scheme to the large embroidery, but on a smaller scale. It must represent King Mark and an attendant riding out from a castle, and Tristram and Ysolt in the grotto, lying beside each other on a white bed. Only the lovers' heads appear because of mutilation.

Another fragment of this third embroidery is attached in the upper right corner, and a comparison with the Erfurt cover, Scene 25 (Fig. 83, upper row), leaves no doubt that this is the Tryst beneath the Tree, though Mark's head is not discernible either in the tree or the spring below.

THE HERMITAGE CASKET I

We have now studied the reflections in art of the poems of Thomas and Gottfried and of the lost romance, akin to Eilhart's, which seems to have inspired the German embroideries. Béroul's version, composed about 1190, was, if not the source, at least the nearest relative to the source of the designs on an ivory casket now in the Hermitage Museum, Leningrad. Béroul's poem is a fragment, so that for only two of the eight scenes shown on the casket can we make a direct and assured comparison. The vigorous and spirited poem has inspired a graceful and spirited work of art.

The casket belongs to a large group of secular ivory carvings produced at Paris in the first forty years of the fourteenth century, of which we shall note many other examples ere we are done. The Parisian connoisseur, Raymond Koechlin, ever to be remembered with grateful veneration by those who knew him, has appropriately given us a corpus and a history of these "articles de Paris."[58] The elephant tusks from the west coast of Africa, the Sahara, or Nubia were imported into France and were worked over by the

members of the carving guilds—*imagiers* (figure sculptors), *pigniers* (comb-makers), *tabletiers* (writing-tablet carvers)—who lived in or near the Rue de la Tableterie near the Porte S. Denis. Hither the great lords and ladies sent their *valets de chambre*, ladies in waiting, or barbers, or came in person to select a set of toilet articles neatly packed in a case of *cuir bouilli*, or a casket handsomely lined with velvet to accommodate their jewels. The records of these purchases possess something of the melancholy charm of Villon's famous refrain.

To Jehan Girost, *pignier*, dwelling at Paris, for moneys paid to him, which were due him, for a little mirror of ivory with the case hanging from a silken lace, bought by him April 16, 1387 for the said Madame the Queen [Ysabeau of Bavaria].

To Jehan Cyme of Paris for a fair mirror of ivory, fitted with two combs of wood; for a case of cuir bouilli to hold the said mirror and combs; for six *palettes* of ivory and wood to hold candles for reading romances, which my lord [Jean Duc de Berry] himself took and bought at Paris, February 4, 1378.

The costumes on nearly all the extant secular ivories from Paris point to the period between 1300 and 1340 as the period of production; it is incredible that objects destined for people of fashion in their most fashionable moods should have continued to reproduce the modes of a past generation. What, then, has happened to the ivories carved at Paris in the second half of the century, of which comparatively few remain? That is an unsolved riddle.

The Hermitage casket has been known and described since 1837,[59] but not until 1878 is it mentioned as equipped with a lid. Since Von Falke has proved that this part is a forgery,[60] it is here omitted from consideration. The scenes on the four sides are enclosed in quatrefoil frames.

FRONT. 1. (Fig. 87) In the left quatrefoil is a boat on the water; the Princess Ysolt fondles a lapdog on the gunwhale; a youth, perhaps Tristram, offers a goblet; another youth urges her acceptance; Bringvain appears with her small cask, and a helmsman with two steering oars. The drinking of the potion, here illustrated, is referred to but not related in the Béroul fragment. Vv. 2206–09.

2. Beneath the lock of the casket is depicted the effect of the potion, the first delirious embrace of the lovers.

3. In the right quatrefoil King Mark welcomes Ysolt to Cornwall, while Tristram and Bringvain and three courtiers look on.

RIGHT SIDE. 4. (Fig. 88) The plot of the marriage night is shown. Bringvain, persuaded to substitute herself for her mistress in the dark, appears in the bed with Mark, while the Queen steals away with her lover.

[58] Cf. especially Koechlin, *Ivoires gothiques* (P., 1924), I, 7–33, 360–367.

[59] *Ibid.*, I, 517; II, 465. *Romanic Review*, VIII (1917), 196.
[60] *Pantheon*, I (1928), 75–80.

BACK. 5. (Fig. 89) In the left quatrefoil the lovers are shown in bed together. It may be the very same night represented in 4; but as Professor Ranke has plausibly argued,[61] it may be supposed to represent the occasion when the lovers were discovered together, an occasion which led to Ysolt's purgation through the ambiguous oath. Such a discovery in *flagrante delicto* is not found in Béroul before the purgation, but Professor Ranke has offered reason to believe that it may have stood in that position in some lost version akin to Béroul's. We can only conjecture.

6. In the first half of the next quatrefoil Ysolt is shown carried on the back of Tristram, disguised as a leper, a *botele* hanging from his waist, a cape over his shoulders, just as he is described by Béroul. Ysolt seems to be slipping from her lover's back into the arms of a knight who approaches to receive her. Vv. 3304–08, 3572–76, 3939–42, 3953–57.

7. In the right half Ysolt is kneeling, her hand on a book or reliquary held by a bishop, while Mark stands beside her. She is swearing the ambiguous oath.

LEFT SIDE. 8. (Fig. 90) The scene does not correspond precisely to anything in the extant versions, but very probably was included in the lost part of Béroul. It comes closest to one narrated in the Norse *Tristramssaga*,[62] and evidently represents Tristram and Kaherdin, his brother-in-law, who have come from Brittany, as pilgrims with scrip and bourdon, meeting Ysolt as she rides with her attendant. She recognizes Tristram and drops her ring into his begging bowl as a sign of recognition.

Hermitage Casket II

From the same Parisian workshops that produced the casket just described came another one, likewise now possessed by the Hermitage Museum.[63] The sides and the cover show a number of conventional love scenes. The front, however, is devoted to the romance of Tristram.

1. (Fig. 91) The first panel obviously depicts the Tryst beneath the Tree, the Queen on one side with a lapdog on her arm, her lover on the other with a falcon on his gloved fist. The three following scenes are based on one or other of the two episodic poems called the *Folie Tristan*,[64] which relate how Tristram in the guise of a court fool came to Mark's court, imposed on the royal dupe with his jests, and found access to Ysolt. But she, unable to recognize him in his disguise, was only convinced when he related many incidents in the history of their love which only Tristram could know.

2. The second panel is strongly reminiscent of the scene in the illuminated psalters, where the words, *Dixit insipiens in corde suo*, are usually illustrated by a court jester standing before King David. The figure of Tristram with his club in hand and the attitude of the king on his throne were probably inspired by some such miniature in a Psalter. The peculiar fool's tonsure is well described in the fourteenth century poem *King Robert of Sicily*:[65]

He heet a barbur him bifore
That as a fool he schulde be schore,
Al around lich a frere,
An hondebrede bove either ere,
And on his croune make a crois.

3. The third panel probably represents the Queen, in the presence of her ladies, incredulously mocking the unknown fool.

4. The fourth represents her yielding to her lover's embrace; a damsel holds a goblet and a cruse at the side.

[61] *Medieval Studies in Memory of Gertrude Schoepperle Loomis* (N. Y., 1927), p. 87.

[62] *Tristramssaga*, ed. E. Kölbing, chap. 87. Cf. *Romanic Rev.*, VIII, 203 f.

[63] A. Darcel, *Collection Basilewsky* (1874), *Texte*, p. 196. *Pantheon*, I, 77, 80.

[64] *Folie Tristan*, ed. Bédier (P., 1907). *Folie Tristan de Berne*, ed. Hoepffner (P., 1934).

[65] W. H. French, C. B. Hale, *Middle English Metrical Romances* (N. Y., 1930), p. 938, vv. 169–173. Cf. *Oxford Folie*, vv. 209 ff.

CHAPTER V

TRISTRAM IN THE PROSE ROMANCES

WE have already made the acquaintance of the *Prose Tristan* and the *Tavola Ritonda* in Chapter II, and have also had a taste of their quality and have not found it high. About the year 1230 a curious fate overtook the legend of Tristram in the Latin countries; for some unaccountable reason, the glorious poems of the twelfth century ceased to enchant, ceased to be copied, so that Thomas and Béroul survive only in fragments, and Chrétien's poem has vanished. Their place was taken by an inferior brood of prose romances, beginning with the *Prose Tristan* and the *Palamedes*. Italy, Spain, and Portugal followed suit with equally prolix and tasteless fictions. Despite their banality their reflections in the decorative arts are perhaps as interesting as the reflections of the poems.

THE S. FLORET MURALS

The gorge of the Talfer, above which rises Runkelstein, has its rival in the valley of the Couze in Auvergne, where stands the bronze-dark tower of S. Floret. From Issoire leads a straight road flanked by acacias and bordered by wide fields, where (in season) the poppy and the cornflower mingle with the yellow wheat. The road swings on under the hill of Perrier, with its overhanging rock-pinnacles and grottoes, into a valley of apple orchards and vineyards, and presently nears, on the left, the olive-gray waters of the Couze, flowing between the poplars. A church spire pricks the skyline ahead, and soon appears the village of S. Floret with its red-tiled roofs and the remains of a castle,—a round turret, haunted now by pigeons, and a square tower containing what was once the great hall. Within the hall there are, high up on the walls, near the vaulted ceiling, the faded but still charming remains of fresco painting.

The castle was probably built late in the thirteenth century, and early in the fourteenth it was the property of Athon de S. Floret.[1] In 1364 he made his will bequeathing all he possessed at S. Floret and Rambeau to his daughter, Alienor, and directing that he be buried in the cemetery or church of S. Floret du Chateau, where across the valley, probably, his bones still lie. Since the paintings date from the middle of the century, the armor in them being clearly of that date,

it was doubtless this same Athon de S. Floret who commissioned them.

With the passing of the centuries the great tower of S. Floret was subdued to humble uses.[2] Before the French Revolution it served as a barn and a threshing floor. About 1860 it was sold, except for the wine cellars, for 350 francs to a laborer. A year or two later an Italian workman, employed in decorating the church at Issoire under Viollet-le-Duc, happened to stray as far as S. Floret, entered the old castle, and noticed the dusty, cobwebbed paintings, scratched by the tines of hayforks. He announced his discovery to Anatole Dauvergne, non-resident member of the Comité des Travaux Historiques. In 1862 Dauvergne with the aid of Italian workmen removed the dust and cobwebs, soaked the painted surfaces in a preparation of wax and linseed oil to bring out the colors, and made full-size tracings. These seem to have been sent to the Ministère de l'Instruction Publique, and destroyed in the fire in the Tuileries, 1870.[3] Luckily Dauvergne's report to the Sorbonne had already been published,[4] and some crude lithographs of a few scenes had been reproduced in Racinet's *Costume historique*.[5] In 1902 and 1909 M. Yperman made a nearly complete series of very accurate watercolor copies from the frescoes, which are now preserved in the Library of the Musée des Monuments Français, Paris. In 1930 the castle was bought by the State, the hay and farm implements were removed, and it is to be hoped that this rare vestige of feudal art may suffer no longer from gross neglect.

The surviving paintings are all found on the north and south walls, except for a single detail from the east wall.[6] There are such marked resemblances in costume and drawing between these paintings and the miniatures of a codex done for Louis of Taranto between 1352 and 1362 by Neapolitan artists under strong French influence, that there can be no doubt of their contemporaneity. The drawing of the horses, especially in Figs. 100, 105, with their round bellies, short legs, and small heads, is strongly reminiscent of those in the MS. The attitude and costume of Tristram in Fig. 101 resemble closely those of the courtier with folded arms in Fig. 309. Tristram's tippet in Fig. 96 is of the same style as those in Fig. 308. The gorget and hair of Ysolt in Fig. 98 resemble, though

---

[1] The following facts are found in *Moyen âge*, XXXIII (1922), 174 f.

[2] The following facts are found in *Mémoires lus à la Sorbonne, archéologie*, 1863, p. 67.

[3] Such was the substance of a reply from the Ministry to my inquiry.

[4] Cf. Note 2.

[5] A. Racinet, *Costume historique*, IV, pl. 4, 5.

[6] These paintings have received comparatively little attention.

They are mentioned in *Moyen âge*, XXXIII, 153 f., in *Les arts*, No. 169, p. 16, in Enlart, *Manuel d'archéologie, architecture civile* (P., 1904), II, 165. They have been inaccurately reproduced by Racinet, by Gélis-Didot and Laffillée (*Peinture décorative en France du XI au XVI siècle*), who copy Racinet, except for the color, which is fanciful; and by Michel (*Hist. de l'art*, II, 1, p. 405) who reproduces Gélis-Didot. The remarks of M. Mâle in Michel's *Histoire* and of M. Lemoisne (*Gothic Painting in France*, [Florence, N. Y.], p. 11) are unreliable.

not exactly, those of a lady in Fig. 306. Many of the backgrounds show conventional plant patterns in black on brown. The legs of the knights and their mounts are unnaturally short, and the horses are barrel-bellied. Nevertheless, despite these blemishes and the scratched and broken plaster, the general impression is delightful. The battle scenes with their swords and spears against the sky have the decorative effect of a Paolo Uccello. The colors are harmonious. The tryst beneath the tree (Figs. 96, 97, 98) is certainly one of the most charming of all the illustrations of Arthurian romance.

The reproductions in this book are from Yperman's very faithful watercolor copies, supplemented in some cases by the corresponding pictures from Racinet, or from Gélis-Didot, which are based on Racinet. For Racinet and Gélis-Didot, though much less faithful, nevertheless preserve features obliterated in Yperman's day. The head of King Mark alone has been photographed directly from the original.

The fragmentary inscriptions in Gothic lettering under the paintings were printed by Dauvergne with many inaccuracies.[7] The readings given below and in footnote 22 have been carefully corrected by a study of the original, though much has disappeared in the interval, and by consultation of the romance text. When Dauvergne's reading makes no sense and cannot be emended, it is given in brackets with a question mark. When it can be safely emended on the basis of the sense or the MS text, the emendation is merely placed between brackets. When it is emended on the basis of the original inscription, the correct reading is substituted.

These inscriptions make it certain that the paintings illustrate the curious compilation from the *Prose Tristan* and the *Palamedes* made in French by Rusticiano da Pisa shortly after 1270 and called by him the *Meliadus*.[8] According to the prolog, it was "translated from the book of Sir Edward, King of England, at the time that he passed beyond the sea in the service of our Lord God, to conquer the Holy Sepulchre"; namely, in 1270–71, when as Prince he spent the winter in Sicily on his way to the Holy Land. The first four scenes of Rusticiano's romance illustrated at S. Floret may also be identified near the beginning of *Guiron le Courtois*, of which in the sixteenth century printed editions appeared both in French and Italian. Since the text is difficult of access, except for Löseth's very brief synopsis, the narrative is here given in some detail. The first three large paintings spread across the north wall. They set forth the deeds of Branor le Brun, a huge but aged knight who appeared incognito

at Arthur's court on a day of Pentecost, overthrew the chief knights of the Table Round, undertook the cause of a besieged countess, and issued forth from her castle to chastise her enemies.[9]

1. (Figs. 92, 92a) On the left side of the north wall we see the resulting mêlée against a background of conventional flowers and a single tree. On the left Branor, bearing a shield party argent and sable, rides with upraised sword-arm against the foe, "like a wolf among sheep." The same device is repeated on his housings; the fanlike crests on his horse's head and his own helmet are half black, half white. The shields of the knights he encounters are adorned with a flaming sun on a green field and an escutcheon on a sable field. Two knights of his own party show a star and crescent on a green field, and a field party white and red, cross-hatched with green. On the earth lies a knight with a shield gules a bend engrailed argent.

2. (Figs. 93, 93a) To the right of 1, in the middle of the wall, Branor is seen against a red background and green trees, rescuing a damsel and slaying her abductor, the gigantic Caracados.[10] On the left the damsel in white sits on her palfrey and holds the rein of Branor's destrier, while on the right stands Caracados' destrier. In the middle the two knights are engaged on foot. Caracados is covered with wounds and his sword, shield, and helm have fallen to the ground; and Branor, seizing him by the camail, drives a sword into his arm. "These two knights," says the romancer, "were without fail the greatest and the most puissant that could be found in all the world. . . . The ancient knight (Branor) said within his heart, 'Verily this is one of the good knights of the world and it is no marvel, for I see that he possesses a body like that of a giant. But come what may, I will fight to the end, for I have promised the lady to bring back her daughter.' . . . They shattered the shields and broke the mail of their hauberks. The place where they fought was covered with pieces of shield and mail."

3. (Figs. 94, 94a) North wall, to right of 2. Branor has met four armed knights leading an unarmed knight with his arms tied and his feet bound under the belly of his horse.[11] The wife of the captive calls on Branor: "O generous knight, for God's sake succor this knight who is my baron, whom the evil and disloyal men lead to his death." Branor promptly challenges the four, takes his shield and spear from his squire, and encounters one of the knights, breaks his spear, and hurls him to the earth. The other three then agree to attack in a body, and Branor rides against them with lowered spear and breaks all their spears in the shock. In the painting we see the prisoner and his wife at the left; Branor in the center, with leveled lance, bearing back a knight with shield argent a pale sable. The helms and the broken lances of two other knights appear. On the ground is another broken spear and the body of a knight, and his horse, its head averted, closes the picture on the right.

4. (Fig. 95) East wall, above lower north window. A

[7] *Mémoires lus à la Sorbonne, arch.*, 1863, pp. 77 ff. For other inscriptions cf. note 22.

[8] E. G. Gardner, *Arthurian Romance in Italian Literature*, p. 47. E. Löseth, *Roman de Tristan*, pp. 423 f.

[9] Löseth, p. 428. The details of the narrative have been taken

from Bib. Nat., fr. 1463, f. 9 v. They may also be found near the beginning of printed editions of *Guiron le Courtois* and in *Girone il Cortese*, ed. F. Tassi (Florence, 1855).

[10] Löseth, p. 428. Fr. 1463, f. 13 r, v.

[11] Löseth, p. 428. Fr. 1463, f. 14 v.

scroll below the painting is apparently intended to represent the speech of some person whose figure has vanished. It reads: "sire roi, le ch*eualie*r qui abati ta*nt* de votres le iour de la pantecoste . . ." Translation: "'Sir King, the knight who overthrew so many of your [knights] the day of Pentecost . . .'"

Dauvergne describes this scroll as attached to a scene in which three ladies and an old man appear. The old man has vanished, but the figures of a queen and two damsels, with the peaks of two tents, are plainly visible. The scroll, of course, refers to Branor, who had overthrown many knights, fourteen kings, and Arthur himself at the feast of Pentecost. The speaker is probably a messenger whom Branor sent, after the adventures already depicted, to announce Branor's name at Arthur's court and to reveal his motive for jousting with his knights.[12] The old man who formerly appeared in this painting was perhaps Arthur, and the queen is probably Guinevere with her maidens.

(This is the last of the scenes connected with Branor, and we now enter the romantic story of Tristram.)

5, 6, 7. (Figs. 96, 97, 98) South wall, middle embrasure. Inscription under painting, left jamb: "uesi pourcoy m*on*seignor *tristan* de lionois se*n* pa*r*ti du reaume de cornoalha e sen uint au reaume de logres pourseq*ue* li roys mar . . . [es poi*n*t lieu(?)]." Translation: "This is why Sir Tristan de Lionois departed from the realm of Cornwall and came to the realm of Logres, because King Mark . . . (??)." Inscription under painting, right jamb: " . . . [reina; lors] dit ela: *tristan*, que poysun uoy ie? ie ne ui tel molt lonc tans a. dama, ie le bie*n* coneu quar ie lay autrefois ueu." Translation: " . . . [queen; then] said she: 'Tristan, what fish do I see? I have not seen such for a very long time.' 'Lady, I recognized it well, for I have seen it before.'"

The painting covering the two jambs and the arch of the embrasure make up one scene, the tryst beneath the tree, and it is executed with far greater delicacy than the others. The proportions of the figures are not distorted, with the exception of Ysolt's elongated fingers. Beneath both seated figures we see the buttressed garden wall. On the left jamb, Tristram sits in white cotehardie and red tippet, "his lokkes crulle as they were laid in presse." He points upward, as does the queen on the opposite jamb. She wears a blue-green gown with dull violet sleeves; a gorget covers her neck and chin; a crown rests on her brown hair. Below the window a fountain was once painted, showing the reflection of Mark's head, but rains entering freely have long since washed it away. Above the lovers, in the arch appears the mournful head of King Mark against the rounded foliage of a pine tree. These three figures constitute the chef-d'œuvre of the painter of S. Floret.

The famous scene of the tryst is not found in Rusticiano at all, and we cannot identify the painter's source. He has clearly depicted the cones of a pine, and, as we see from the right inscription, he must have depicted a fountain; this combination occurs only in Béroul and the Italian *novellino*.[13] But neither text, so far as we know, contains any such dialog as that recorded in the right inscription. Ap-

parently it is only here and on the Bamberg comb[14] that we find a trace of an ingenious version in which Ysolt calls the attention of her lover to the reflection in the fountain by pretending to descry a remarkable fish.

The left inscription indicates that its composer had some notion of making the outcome of the tryst the cause of Tristram's wandering in the realm of Logres in Scene 8, but neither Rusticiano nor any other surviving source makes such a connection. The explanation, however, may be this: whoever chose and arranged the murals was determined to insert the tryst somewhere; Rusticiano, when he turns abruptly from Branor to Tristram, describes the latter as newly come to the realm of Logres,[15] and in the *Prose Tristan* during the interview beneath the tree Tristram expresses his intention of departing to the realm of Logres.[16] Of course, he is lying and only too gladly remains in Cornwall to be near the Queen, but in this false declaration the author of the S. Floret inscriptions may have found his excuse for linking the rendezvous at the fountain to Tristram's adventure in Logres. This, however, is simply a guess.

8. (Fig. 99) South wall, west embrasure, left jamb. Inscription: "uesi come m*onseignor* *tristan* chiuachoyt pour le reaume de logres quetant aua*n*ture, e uint [uers la nuit] . . ." Translation: "This is how Sir Tristan rode through the realm of Logres seeking adventure, and came [toward nightfall] . . ."

Returning to Rusticiano's romance,[17] we read that in the year in which Tristram wedded Ysolt à Blanche Main he rode through the largest and most adventurous forest of Logres, but met no one. When night came on and he could no longer see the road, he dismounted among some fair trees. He relieved his horse of saddle and bridle, and let it pasture; then doffed his helm and sword, lay down upon his shield, and went to sleep. The painting shows on the left the fore part of a horse; the diagonal line across the picture is the hero's spear; Tristram himself is shown reclining in his surcoat, argent a bend gules, his hand on his breast, his knees crossed. His sword and shield are behind him. His head with its wavy hair, closed eyes, full lips, is delicately, if somewhat effeminately painted. Indeed the artist throughout seems to conceive of Tristram, the oft wounded hero of a hundred desperate encounters, as a youth of unblemished beauty.

9. (Fig. 100) South wall, west embrasure, right jamb. Inscription: "uesi se cocha en la forest entre [beaus] a[rbres e dor]mi sur sun ecut, e aui*n*t a*n*si com aua*n*ture . . . enemi mortel se cocha e se co[m]ple[int] . . . e pourquoy se cocha si . . . si fort q*an*t . . ." Translation: "Here he lay down in the forest between fair trees and slept on his shield and it happened by chance . . . mortal enemy lay down and lamented . . . why he lay down so . . . so mighty when . . ."

The story relates[18] that by chance Palamedes, the jealous rival of Tristram for the love of Ysolt of Ireland, came to the same spot and, unaware of the nearness of his mortal enemy, dismounted and lay down on his shield. Unable to

---

[12] Löseth, p. 428. Fr. 1463, f. 16.

[13] Gabrici, Levi, *Lo Steri di Palermo* (Milan), 98. Béroul, ed. Muret (P., 1915), vv. 351, 404.

[14] Cf. *infra* pp. 68 f.

[15] Löseth, p. 429. Fr. 1463, f. 16 v.

[16] Löseth, p. 202. Bib. Nat., fr. 757, f. 39.

[17] Löseth, p. 429. Fr. 1463, f. 16 v.

[18] *Ibid.*

sleep, he stood up and began to lament his unhappy fate: "Ah, Palamedes, now art thou the most unhappy knight on earth, for thou lovest the flower and rose of the world!" The painting shows Palamedes recumbent in surcoat of argent, a chief gules, his eyes open, and his head resting on his left hand. His spear lies beside him, his sword and shield behind him, and his saddle in front. The background is of trees and grasses.

10. (Figs. 101, 101a) North wall, under vaulting, above 2. Inscription: "uesi come m*onseignor* pal*amedes* deliura m*onseignor* t*ristan* de lionoys que un uauasor tenoyt pris et li uoloyt fere coper la teta pourse q*ue* il li tua su*n* fis an la perilhue forest q*ui* estoyt un de xxvi ch*eualie*rs a la fey morgain; e por se fit pes m*onseignor* t*ristan* a m*onseignor* pal*amedes*; si estoyt il le gregnor enemis mortel du munde." Translation: "See how Sir Palamedes delivered Sir Tristan of Lionoys, whom a vavasour held as prisoner and wished to have his head cut off, because he had slain his son in the Perilous Forest, who was one of twenty-six knights of Morgain la Fey; and because of this Sir Tristan made peace with Sir Palamedes; yet he was his greatest mortal enemy in the world."

Except for the inscription, most of the adventures which once occupied the space around the west embrasure have now vanished. But in the scene above the inscription just given we see Tristram, captured by a vavasour, led out by a troop of fifty knights to be beheaded.[19] He goes afoot, his hands tied behind his back. He is mourned by the people. Palamedes, helm on head, accompanies the cavalcade, and Tristram, recognizing something familiar in his carriage, beseeches him to carry his last salutation to Arthur's court and to cause his shield to be hung in the great hall as a memorial. Palamedes weeping says to himself, "Ah, Palamedes, evil knight, how dost thou suffer that before thee the best knight of the world should suffer death. So help me God, though he be my mortal enemy, I shall not reck, come what may, for I shall put me in adventure for his deliverance." When the vavasour gives the command for Tristram's beheading, Palamedes forbids it and laying spear in rest, runs him through the body and striking blows to right and left, does deeds of arms beyond the prowess of man. The painting shows Tristram on the left with hands bound; and Palamedes, with surcoat and shield argent a chief gules, riding with brandished sword against a troop of knights, while shattered lances and dismembered bodies strew the earth.

11, 12. (Figs. 102, 103) North wall, east embrasure, left and right jambs. Left inscription: "apres la deliura*n*se de m*onseignor* t*ristan* chiuauchoye*n*t m*onseignor* pal*amedes* e m*onseignor* t*ristan* ensenble e enco*n*trerent m*onseignor* galaaz e le fire*n*t ioster ansi come [paur (?)]." Translation: "After the deliverance of Sir Tristan Sir Palamedes and Sir Tristan rode together and met Sir Galaad and made him joust as if [fear (?)] . . . " Right inscription: " . . . les abatit il tous deus; tant mis m*onseignor* t*ristan* a [trousa si (?)] e li autre dit sun non; apres quil ot dit . . [s]e conoy-tre*n*t e se alere*n*t [au mostier] e les troua m*onseignor* banis e lor dit les noueles que uos aues . . . " Translation: " . . . he smote them both down; then Sir Tristan (. . ??) and the other told his name; after he had told . . . knew each other

and departed [to the monastery], and Sir Banis found them and told them the news that you have . . . "

After Palamedes had rescued Tristram from death,[20] the two knights rode together in friendly wise till they met Galaad alone. The romance says that his shield was covered with a vermeil case, but the painting shows it uncovered, argent a cross gules, and a surcoat of the same device. There is the customary challenge, and Galahad easily hurls Palamedes to earth and proceeds on his way. Tristram, astonished, demands combat, and Galahad consenting, the two knights rode against each other "as if the lightning were chasing them." Galahad unhorses Tristram. After a long combat on foot and many wounds, they reveal their names, and all three embrace and repair to a monastery near by. There their wounds are washed and bound up, and there Banin finds them at supper and tells them evil news.

The left jamb painting depicts Galahad riding to the encounter and the right jamb shows Tristram riding against him, and Palamedes following him on foot. Tristram's surcoat shows gules a bend argent, and Palamedes' shield and surcoat argent a chief gules.

13, 14. (Figs. 104, 104a, 105) South wall, east embrasure, left and right jambs. Left inscription: "uesi come m*onseignor* t*ristan* saco*m*pagna au ch*evalie*r a lescu uermeil e est u[enu] e*n* pais que estoyt garde de plus de c*ent* ch*eualie*rs; m*onseignor* t*ristan* leu[r] pria qui il le lesasent esprouer a seta aua*n*ture." Translation: "See how Sir Tristan accompanied the knight of the red shield and has come into a land which was guarded by more than a hundred knights; Sir Tristan asked them that they would let him essay this adventure." Right inscription: "[le] ch*eualie*r a lescu uermeil li otrea, e il li desconfis a layde de ses conpagnons." Translation: "The knight of the red shield granted it to him, and he discomfited them with the aid of his companions."

According to the story,[21] Tristram, Ivain, Gaheris, and Brunor le Noir, under the alias of the *Chevalier à l'escu vermeil au lyon d'argent rampant*, come to a bridge over a deep river. Two knights are on guard. Tristram demands the adventure and hurls both knights into the river. The *Chevalier à l'escu vermeil* marvels at the deeds of the "Knight of the black shield, for Tristram then wore black armor." After crossing the bridge, the companions are menaced by seventy other knights. Tristram again spurs against them alone. After he has battered them sufficiently, the *Chevalier à l'escu vermeil* calls on Ivain and Gaheris to join in the mêlée, with the result that the four put the whole band of seventy to flight.

The painting on the left jamb shows the *Chevalier à l'escu vermeil*, with shield and surcoat gules a lion rampant or, charging the foe with brandished sword. He is supported by two companions, one of whom, by a curious violation of perspective, though his horse is on the further side of the Chevalier, reaches his sword around the nearer side and deals a blow on the helmet of an adversary, forcing him to stoop and butt helm-foremost into the Chevalier's shield. The right jamb shows Tristram, with shield and surcoat argent a bend gules, accompanied by three knights (at least, three horses are visible!) riding with

[19] Löseth, p. 430. Fr. 1463, f. 24 v, 35 r, v.

[20] Löseth, p. 430. Fr. 1463, f. 27 r, v.
[21] Löseth, p. 326. Fr. 1463, f. 46 v, 47 r, v.

uplifted sword against the enemy. These two paintings must be taken together to represent the last joint charge of the four companions, but there seem to be at least seven knights on the one side. And Tristram described at this point as wearing black arms, actually wears the white arms with a bend "de bellie," which are ascribed to him earlier in the romance.[22]

THE PALERMO CEILING

Palermo possesses besides its Capella Palatina and its many churches another architectural treasure, less overwhelming and far less famous, but as interesting from the point of view of secular as the others from that of religious art. The great hall of the old Palazzo Chiaramonte is covered with a painted wooden ceiling which is a veritable florilegium of medieval secular iconography. Here, together with a few scenes from the Old Testament, the Apocalypse, a figure of St. George, and the heads of the prophets, are painted Aristotle and Phyllis, the Fountain of Youth, Jason, the Argo, the Golden Fleece, the Judgment of Paris, the Rape of Helen, the Sacrifice of Iphigenia, the Death of Dido, a Carolingian *cantare* on the Cymbeline theme, and a few inevitable scenes from the romance of Tristram. Unfortunately the ceiling is over 26 feet from the floor, and many of the painted panels are set in a vertical, not a horizontal, plane, so that even with opera glasses and a gutta percha neck, it is difficult to study the scenes. The recent publication of all the details, accompanied by an illuminating commentary by Professors Gabrici and Levi,[23] makes it possible to scrutinize the ceiling much better in one's own library than at Palermo.

The Chiaramonti, whose palace boasts this painted ceiling, claimed descent from Charlemagne and seem as a matter of fact to have been a branch of the Clermont family of Dauphiné, which established itself in Sicily under the Norman régime of the twelfth century. Manfredi I, head of the house, was instrumental in bringing to the throne of Sicily Federigo of Aragon, who on his coronation in 1296 displayed his gratitude by creating Manfredi Count of Modica and Seneschal of the Realm. In 1307 Manfredi began the building of

his great stone palace, and had probably brought it near completion before his death in 1321. The vast possessions of the family were gradually concentrated under Manfredi III, who enjoyed the favor of King Federigo III, with the title of Grand Admiral. In 1374 and 1377 he inherited large lands; in 1378, a year after the king's death, he became the most powerful of the four Vicars of Sicily and the unquestioned ruler of Palermo. It was precisely in these years of supreme affluence and power that Manfredi had his three painters at work on the ceiling of his great hall. But his successor offered resistance to King Martin I, was executed in the piazza before his own palace in 1396, and the new king promptly took possession of the palace. In Chapter II we have seen this same King Martin entering Valencia in 1402, his horse-trappings painted with figures of Lancelot and Guinevere, Tristram and Ysolt. At Palermo, doubtless, he dined in state under the ceiling which still contains scenes from the romance of Tristram. After his death his widow was pursued by the ambitious and amorous old Count of Modica; in 1410 she was nearly seized by his troops in the Chiaramonte palace. But she and her damsels escaped in the middle of the night, fled down to the harbor, and found refuge in a friendly galley. For a while the palace was the residence of the Spanish viceroys; in 1535 the Emperor Charles V held a parliament there. In 1601 the painted ceiling looked down on the grim tribunal of the Inquisition, and today it looks down on the sessions of the Court of Appeals. Such in brief is the history of the Chiaramonte palace, or, as it is popularly called, the Steri.

The ceiling of the great hall on the second floor (the first above the ground floor) was painted by three artists between 1377 and 1380. Their names are recorded on the ceiling itself: "Mastru Chicu pinturi di Naru, Mastru Simuni pinturi di Curiglu[ni], Mastru . . . Darenu pigituri di Palermo."[24] All three were Sicilians, from Naro, Corleone, and Palermo respectively. Though Gabrici is inclined to attribute the paintings up to beam 11 to Chicu di Naru, including the Tristram group,[25] yet two hands can clearly be differentiated within that group and it seems impossible to determine which of the three names should be

---

[22] Dauvergne published, though quite inaccurately, certain inscriptions which have outlived the paintings they described. These I have revised as far as possible on the basis of direct examination and of the MS text. 1. North wall, west window, left jamb. Cf. Löseth, p. 429. This adventure occurs between scenes 9 and 10. Inscription: "[tristan de liono]is deliura dina[dan] . . . [e]stoyent a la fey . . . i auantura que. . . ." Translation: "Tristan de Lionois delivered Dinadan . . . belonged to the Fay . . . an adventure which. . . ." 2. North wall, west window, right jamb. Cf. Löseth, p. 429. Inscription: " . . . [con]pagnon de la tabala . . . [ica eleh(?)] . . . [nin(?)] an la perilluse [for]est uii iors apres quil fu pa(r)tis de camelot." Translation: " . . . companion of the table . . . (?) . . . in the Perilous Forest seven days after he had departed from Camelot." 3. East wall, north side, right of window. Cf. Löseth, p. 430. This adventure follows Scene 12.

Inscription: "uesi come *m*onseignor banis emmena *m*onseignor galaas . . . [lors (?)] que helis li roy tenoy en sa prison [pal (?)] . . . de la tabla round. a seli point fu desconfis elis . . . estoy m . . . " Translation: "See how Sir Banin led away Sir Galaas . . . [when (?)] Helis the King held in his prison [Palamedes (?)] . . . of the Table Round. At this time Elis was discomfited . . . was . . . " 4. East wall, south corner near Scene 13. Cf. Löseth, p. 325. Inscription: "[arri(?)]ue deuant la tor . . . iostasent au che*v*alier de . . . acheua seta auanture et li o[trea (?)]" Translation: "[arrives (?)] before the tower . . . should joust with the knight of . . . achieved this adventure and [granted (?)] him."

[23] Gabrici, Levi, *op. cit.*

[24] *Ibid.*, p. 65.

[25] *Ibid.*, p. 66.

attached to them. This work on the great wooden ceiling bears great resemblance in construction and in the purely decorative patterns to contemporary work in Spain, where Moorish artists carried to a high point of skill and elaboration the decoration of wooden ceilings.[26] It was natural that Sicily, which had been for a hundred years a jewel in the crown of Aragon, and the Chiaramonti, who were among the most loyal upholders of the Aragonese dynasty, should have submitted in a measure to the influence of Spanish art. It was not a felicitous idea, as Levi has observed,[27] to combine the decorative scheme of Spanish ceilings with the illustrative materials of French mural painting. Scenes from romance which were easily decipherable and most delectable on walls two or three yards away and only a few feet above the level of one's eye became undecipherable when reduced in scale, elevated to a height of 26 feet and set at strange angles to the line of vision. The coloring of red, ochre, various shades of brown, and occasionally pale blue and pink, against black backgrounds, is, though intense and striking, hardly to be called beautiful.[28]

The first group of scenes which Levi hesitatingly connected with Tristram (Trave III, 167 a–d)[29] seems very questionable, and therefore is not here reproduced. The knight fighting a dragon protects his left arm with a cloth—a curious feature not found in any account of Tristram's combat; and there is nothing of the dragon's tongue or of the false seneschal—features which are essential to that account. In the love scenes which follow, the damsel does not wear the crown which usually identifies the Princess Ysolt. The final scene, where a youth, a crowned damsel, and an old man and woman hold hands, while two youths sound trumpets, seems to fit no situation in the romance.

The rest of Levi's identifications we may safely accept. The source is the *Tristano Riccardiano*, a free redaction of the French prose romance written about 1275.[30] When Tristram brought Ysolt to Tintagel after the fateful voyage, he sent a letter to his uncle announcing the arrival of the bride; but Mark, in a gloomy mood, refused to welcome her, and sent barons down to the port to meet her in his stead. But when he saw her beauty, he embraced his nephew, and with great pomp and joy brought him and Ysolt to his castle. These events seem to be clearly depicted in two scenes.

1. (Fig. 106) On the left there is the galley from Ireland, the rowers at their oars. A white banner, with two blue crescents and diagonal and horizontal blue stripes, floats above them. The blazoning apparently bears some relation to the indications of the *Tavola Ritonda*,[31] which states that the arms of Tristram were "a field azure with a bend argent, with a border of gold on each side of the bend," and of the German embroidery at South Kensington, which shows the hero bearing a shield with blue and white bars. Governal stands in the galley, while Ysolt, crowned, her arms resting on her lover's shoulder, walks with Bringvain down the gang-plank. Tristram, stepping ashore, is warmly grasped by the hand by one of the barons.

2. (Fig. 107) Here we see a group on horseback. Tristram, lifting his visor, and the mounted courtiers look on, while the bearded king throws his arms about his bride.

On another beam we have four exquisite scenes from the life of the lovers in the Forest of Morrois.

3. (Fig. 108) On the left against a rocky landscape we see the queen placing a wreath on the head of her kneeling lover. On the right is a mounted squire, Perinis, holding a hunting javelin. Two antlered stags and a thickly leaved tree suggest a forest.

4. (Fig. 109) Perinis with his hunting javelin follows on foot; his master rides beside his lady, his arm clasping her neck.

5. The lovers are picnicking on a rocky knoll, while the faithful squire holds two palfreys. Ysolt is not eating, but stretches out her hand in a gesture of sympathy to him for whose sake she had left the luxurious life of Tintagel.

6. (Fig. 110) According to the *Tristano Riccardiano* (p. 173), the idyl ended, the lovers left the forest, rode to the house of a Cornish knight, were gladly welcomed and served to their heart's desire. This seems to be the occasion represented by the lovers riding, followed by Perinis, and met by two horsemen issuing from a castle.

Three scenes cannot be identified with any particular incidents in the texts, yet love-scenes involving a youth and a crowned lady are in all likelihood intended to illustrate this romance.

7. (Fig. 111) A palfrey stands observantly in its stable. Tristram presents the queen with a bouquet.

8. (Fig. 112) Tristram, mounted on his palfrey, is just departing or arriving, and leans forward to grasp Ysolt's hand.

9. (Fig. 113) The palfrey stands tethered to a tree; the lovers are wrapped in close embrace. From the accompanying decorative portion of the ceiling one may gather an impression of its character.

On another beam there is a group of three scenes done by a much cruder artist. His representation of Tristram's feet is not flattering, and Ysolt, as he represents her, would send no one into ecstasies. The *Tristano Riccardiano* (ch. 75) relates that King Mark ordered five pavilions to be pitched by the seashore, at Tintagel, and the lovers began to play a game of chess at the foot of one of them.

10. (Figs. 114, 115) Against the background of a pavilion, Tristram is welcomed to a game of chess, by the queen. His squire holds the horse from which presumably Tristram has just dismounted, and Bringvain stands behind her mistress.

11. (Fig. 115) Like the preceding, except that Tristram is seated and makes a move on the board, and his squire stands with arms crossed over his chest.

[26] *Ibid.*, p. 54, 144.
[27] *Ibid.*, p. 142.
[28] Pl. II, III.

[29] Pl. LV–LVIII.
[30] Ed. E. G. Parodi (Bologna, 1896).
[31] Ed. F. L. Polidori (Bologna, 1864), p. 513.

12. (Fig. 116) The familiar tryst beneath the tree. Here the tree is a laurel, as in the French *Prose Tristan*, and from it the crownless head of Mark looks sternly at Tristram. The fountain consists of a square marble laver. On the left Tristram advances with hawk on wrist; on the right the queen gazes at the troubled reflection in the water, while Bringvain points a warning finger at the head above.

This juxtaposition of the tryst and the chess-game recalls the pair of basins in the inventory of Louis of Anjou, mentioned in Chapter II. In the first, "Tristram has a falcon on his fist, and Ysolt holds a little dog, and on a tree is King Mark, whose head appears in a fountain"; in the mate "are Tristram and Ysolt beneath a pavilion, and they play at chess."

Besides these scenes remaining *in situ* there are, according to Levi, a few others which were removed at the time of the first restoration and are now preserved, though in a bad state, at the Sovrintendenza dei Monumenti of Sicily.[32] Among them can be recognized the regal figure of Ysolt, in the embraces of a man clad partly as a knight, partly as a minstrel, with many colored festoons hanging from his tight robe. This must be the occasion when Tristram obtained access to his lady in the disguise of a minstrel.[33]

The South Kensington and Bargello Quilts

The *Tristano Riccardiano* seems to be one of the chief sources of the *Tavola Ritonda*, a composite romance written fifty or more years later. Akin to these is the Spanish *Cuento de Tristan de Leonis*. But none of these could have been used by the designer of a pair of Sicilian bed-quilts now in the Victoria and Albert Museum, South Kensington, and the Bargello, Florence, respectively. (Figs. 117, 118) He must have used a manuscript which approximates now one, now another, of the Italian texts; now finds its closest analogue in the Spanish *Cuento* or Malory's *Morte d'Arthur*, and now furnishes scenes or details found in no other version. The quilts have been the subject of a thorough study in *Romania* by Pio Rajna, of revered memory,[34] and though in a few details the present account ventures to dissent from his, it is none the less deeply indebted to him.

Sicily in the fourteenth century seems to have made a business of exporting pictured coverlets, for the Florentine inventory of Bartolomeo Boscoli in 1386 mentions "a Sicilian coverlet of cloth with arms and paintings in several colors."[35] No others, apparently, are extant except those mentioned and one in private possession still to be described, but the dialect of the inscriptions determines their Sicilian origin. The quilt at South Kensington measures 10 feet 6 inches by 9 feet; the one at the Bargello meas-

ures 8 by 7 feet. The former, still complete, consists of an oblong space filled by six nearly square compartments, separated from each other by a strip of florets; and this oblong space in turn is bordered on three sides by scenes separated from each other by graceful patterns of oak leaf and grape. The Bargello quilt has lost altogether the right border, the upper two scenes of the central space, and the upper part of the left border. The fabric of both quilts is linen; the background is covered with fine needle-work; the figures, the foliage patterns, and the architectural details are padded out with cotton. Though the drawing is not remarkable for grace, the labor involved must have been considerable, and except for the mutilation of the Bargello quilt, both quilts are in a good state of preservation. Their size and the arrangement of the scenes are adapted to the function of a quilt covering a bed eight feet long, such as one mentioned in the year 1342. The three horns which recur on the shield and jupon of Tristram were the arms of the very Guicciardini family of Florence, in whose possession the Bargello quilt was found. The three lilies, which similarly form the cognizance of the Irish champion and adorn the pennant floating from the Irish ships in Scenes 4, 10, 11, and the shields of the knights in Scene 9, may perhaps be related to the three lilies on a banner which appeared between the paws of a lion in the arms of the Acciaiuoli family. It may be coincidence that in 1395 Piero di Luigi Guicciardini married a Laodamia Acciaiuoli—a marriage which terminated unhappily with the lady's death two years later.[36] At any rate, the costume depicted on the quilts seems to harmonize with the date, and we have already seen an instance of heraldic flattery of a literary patron in Thomas's assignment of the royal arms to Tristram. The Neapolitan MS, British Museum Add. 12228, assigns the royal arms of Naples to the hero Meliadus, and an embroidery at Freiburg combines the names of Johannes Malterer and his wife Anna.[37] It is therefore a plausible hypothesis that the two coverlets were ordered for the wedding of 1395.

The scenes represented do not begin with one quilt and then pass to the other, but are so intertwined that it seems best in identifying them to pass back and forth as the story leads. We shall designate the South Kensington and Bargello quilts by S.K. and B. (Figs. 117, 118)

1. B. Left border, middle. Inscription: "Comu Tristainu *et* Guvirnal si parteru dalu rre Feramonti." "How Tristainu and Guvirnal departed from King Feramonti." According to the *Tavola Ritonda*, Tristram and his master Governal went to Paris after the death of his father, and

---

[32] Gabrici, Levi, *op. cit.*, p. 103.

[33] *Romania*, XXXV, 497.

[34] *Ibid.*, XLII (1913), 517. Cf. also *Dedalo*, II (1922), 770; *Journal of Royal Institution of Cornwall*, XVII, 142; *Monats-*

heftef. Kunstwissenschaft, XII (1919), 166.

[35] *Romania*, XLII, 579.

[36] *Ibid.*, 560.

[37] Cf. *infra* pp. 78 f.

there dwelt at the court of King Pharamond till he was fifteen years of age. The Princess Bellices pressed her love upon the fair youth so ardently that Governal deemed it prudent to leave.[38] The quilt shows Governal and his charge riding.

2. B. Left border, top. Inscription: "Comu lu misageri e vinutu a Trist[a]inu." "How the messenger has come to Tristainu." The *Tristano Riccardiano* and the Spanish *Cuento* relate that the Princess Bellices slew herself after writing a letter to Tristram, and sending him a messenger, with a sword, a brachet, and a horse.[39] A squire took the letter, sword and brachet, mounted and set forth after Tristram. We see him in the embroidery riding, the sword held forth in his left hand, a tiny hound in his right.

3. B. Left border, bottom. Inscription: "Comu T*ristainu et* Guvirnal so vinuti allu rre Marcu." "How Tristainu and Guvirnal have come to King Marcu." The *Tavola Ritonda* tells us that the pair rode through Cornwall till they came to Tintagel, and the hero offered Mark his service.[40]

4. S.K. Right border, bottom. Inscription: "Comu lu rre Langui*s* manda p*er* lu trabutu *in* Cornualia." "How King Languis sends for the tribute to Cornwall." The King of Ireland bears this name only in the Italian texts; the French prose has Hanguin, Anguyn, Angyn. It is very curious that neither the Italian nor the French texts mention the King of Ireland at this point as sending a vain expedition to demand tribute, but Malory, Book VIII, ch. 4, says: "Then it befell that King Anguish of Ireland sent unto King Mark of Cornwall for his truage, that Cornwall had paid many winters." On the quilt we see a ship filled with rowing knights; two messengers stand on the poop.

5. B. Lower border. Inscription: "Comu lu rre Marcu fechi cavalieri Tristainu." "How King Marcu made Tristainu a knight." According to the *Tavola Ritonda*, Tristram, after learning of the demand for tribute, besought King Mark to knight him, and after keeping vigil in the church, he went to the piazza, was duly given the accolade and girded with a sword by the King.[41] The towers filled with ladies and trumpeters, the piazza filled with courtiers, Tristram kneeling, arms crossed on his breast, Governal holding his shoulder, the King about to raise him from the ground—all are visible in the embroidery.

6. S.K. Lower border. Inscription: "Comu [li m]issagieri so vinuti a[llu] rre Marcu p[er] lu tributu di secti anni." "How the messengers have come to King Marcu for the tribute of seven years." Once more it is noteworthy that the inscription departs from the Italian and French texts as to the number of years, but agrees with the Spanish *Cuento*[42] and Malory, who writes: "And all that time King Mark was behind of the truage seven years."[43] But the scene corresponds closely to one in the *Tavola Ritonda*,[44] in which two ambassadors from Morhaut, returning to King Mark for an answer to the demand for tribute, were unexpectedly answered by the youthful Tristram, who rose, challenged the right of Ireland, and undertook to defend the right of Cornwall by single combat. On the quilt the King, the ambassadors, and Tristram, with the three horns on his jupon, are easily recognizable.

7. S.K. Right border, middle. Inscription: "Comu lu rre Languis cumanda chi vaia lo osti [in] Cornuaglia." "How King Languis commands that the host go into Cornwall." Here again Malory offers the closest parallel:[45] "With this answer the messengers departed into Ireland. And when King Anguish understood the answer of the messengers, he was wonderly wroth. And then he called unto him Sir Marhaus ... Then the King said: 'Fair brother, Sir Marhaus, I pray you go into Cornwall for my sake, and do battle for our truage.'" The two messengers are represented kneeling before King Languis, holding out to him the message from Mark refusing the tribute. The King points to Morhaut, who holds in his hand the glove and mace, symbols of ambassadorial office since the time of the *Chanson de Roland* (c. 1080), in which Charlemagne appoints Ganelon ambassador to Marsile with the words, "Si recevez le baston e le guant."

8. S.K. Right border, top. Inscription: "Comu lu Amoroldu fa bandiri lu osti *in* Cornuvalgia." "How Amoroldu has proclaimed the expedition into Cornwall." This scene corresponds fairly well to an earlier scene in the *Tavola Ritonda*,[46] where Morhaut assembles a great multitude of knights and footsoldiers and announces his purpose to besiege Tintagel.

9. S.K. Left border, lower middle. Inscription: "Comu lu Amoroldu fa suldari la genti." "How Amoroldu has the men hired." There is nothing of this in any version. A man in courtly robes is depicted tossing, as it were, coins into the hands of soldiers. The end of the trumpet in 8 appears on the left and shows that the two scenes originally formed a solid strip with 4, 7, and 8, and are now wrongly placed after 11 and 12.

10. S.K. Left border, bottom. Inscription: "Comu lu Amoroldu vai *in* Cornuvalgia." "How Amoroldu goes into Cornwall." There is a passage corresponding in the *Tavola Ritonda*,[47] where we read of the embarkation of Morhaut's troops and a fair passage to Cornwall. The text, however, speaks of setting sail, whereas the quilt shows only the soldiers pulling at their oars. Their strokes seem to be timed by a rowing master with a whistle in his mouth. Morhaut stands in the poop.

11. S.K. Left border, top. Inscription: "Comu lu Amoroldu e vinutu in Cornuvalgia cu*n* xxxx galei." "How Amoroldu has come into Cornwall with forty galleys." The rowing master seems to have supplanted Amoroldu in the poop.

12. S.K. Left border, upper middle. Inscription: "Comu T*ristainu* dai lu gua*n*tu allu Amoroldu de la bactaglia." "How Tristainu gives the glove of battle to Amoroldu." There is no scene of this kind in the Italian, English or French prose texts.

13. B. Middle, lower left. Inscription: "Comu lu Amoroldu vai alla isolecta." "How Amoroldu goes to the islet." The quilt does not correspond exactly to the *Tavola*

---

[38] *Tavola ritonda*, ed. Polidori, p. 61.
[39] *Cuento de Tristan*, ed. G. T. Northup (Chicago, 1928), p. 83.
[40] *Tav. rit.*, p. 63.
[41] *Ibid.*, p. 66.
[42] *Cuento*, p. 85.

[43] Book VIII, ch. 4.
[44] *Tav. rit.*, p. 67.
[45] Bk. VIII, ch. 4.
[46] *Tav. rit.*, p. 64.
[47] *Ibid.*

Ritonda, since that does not mention the horse in the boat and expressly says that Morhaut went alone, whereas the quilt shows a squire plying the oars.[48]

14. B. Middle, lower right. Inscription: "Comu Tri*stainu* vai nella isola *per cum*bactiri locu." "How Tristainu goes to the island to fight there." The quilt here reflects most closely the *Tristano Riccardiano*,[49] which mentions the hero's entering a boat with his destrier.

15. S.K. Middle, bottom left. Inscription: "Comu Tristainu aspecta lu Amoroldu alla isola dilu maru Sanca Vintura." "How Tristainu waits for Amoroldu in the island of the sea, Sanca Vintura (Without Adventure)." The name of the island is thus given by the Italian texts, but the *Tavola* says that Morhaut arrived first.

16. S.K. Middle, bottom right. Inscription: "Comu Tristainu bucta la varca arretu intu allu maru." "How Tristainu thrust the boat back into the sea." The Spanish, which alone says that the hero used his foot to thrust his boat into the sea: "dio un golpe del pie a la varca e botola an la mar," comes closest to the scene depicted on the quilt.[50]

17. B. Middle, upper right. Inscription: "Comu lu Amoroldu combactiu cu*n* Tristainu a c[a]vallu." "How Amoroldu fought with Tristainu on horseback." The *Tavola* is followed in this and the next two scenes.[51]

18. B. Middle, upper left. Inscription: "Comu Tristainu combactiu cullu Amoroldo *et* speciaru li la*n*ci." "How Tristainu fought with Amoroldo and they splintered the lances."

19. S.K. Middle, left center. Inscription: "Comu Tristainu feriu lu Amorolldo *in* testa." "How Tristainu smote Amorolldo in the head."

20. S.K. Middle, right center. Inscription: "Comu lu i*n*fa delu Amoroldu aspecttava lu patrunu." "How the servant of Amoroldu waited for his master." Though, as we have seen, this squire appears already in Scene 13, there is no mention of him in the Italian texts.

21. S.K. Middle, upper left. Inscription: "Comu lu Amoro[l]du feriu Tristainu a tr[a]dimentu." "How Amoroldu smote Tristainu by treachery." The quilt shows the Irish champion in his boat shooting a poisoned arrow at his victorious enemy, and except for the squire, it reproduces the account in the *Tavola*.[52]

22. S.K. Middle, upper right. Inscription: "Sitati de Irlandia." "Cities of Ireland." This characteristic piece of Italian Gothic architecture, from which appear the heads of a king, a queen, and three other persons, is obviously an anticipation of the return of Morhaut fatally wounded to his home.[53]

THE PIANETTI QUILT

Rajna described minutely a quilt, then in the possession of the Marchese di Azzolino, in 1935 in that of the Marchesi Pianetti, Florence, which must have been made in the same Sicilian workshop and at about the same time as those just treated.[54] (Fig. 119) The upper half and both side borders are lost, and the dimensions are at present about 8 feet 2 inches square. It is easy to recognize the same technique of needlework and padding as in the other Sicilian coverlets, the same Lombardic lettering, the same foliage patterns twining between the human figures. The main field, however, is filled with *fleurs de lis* and suggests a patron of the house of Anjou. The lower border contains three allegorical crowned figures of *Curtisia*, *Gula* and *Astinencia*, with their appropriate animals—the eagle, the fox, and the camel. The large central field is sown with heraldic *fleurs de lis* and suggests that the work was done for some member of the French dynasty of Naples, perhaps for that Louis I of Anjou, who gambled his life and fortune away in the venture for the Neapolitan throne between 1381 and 1384, or more probably for Louis II, who occupied Naples between 1390 and 1399.

The centre of the coverlet in its original state was filled by a circular frame containing two figures and their names. In the half which is left we see a woman's skirt and feet, a man's legs and girdled waist, and a tasseled cord like that which hangs from the back of Amoroldu in the right border of the South Kensington coverlet. Rajna read the lettering, "-vallia" to the left of the man, "-unda" to the right of the woman, and proposed that the complete inscriptions were, "Tristainu di Cornuvallia" and "Isotta la Biunda." He was surely right. These mutilated figures must be all that is left of the famous lovers.

THE TRYST BENEATH THE TREE

Religious iconography of the Middle Ages contained many motifs which were repeated endlessly apart from their narrative context and were easily recognized and interpreted by layman and cleric. The Harrowing of Hell, St. Martin dividing his cloak, the Resurrection, St. Lawrence with his griddle, were familiar all over Christendom as separate motifs.

[48] *Ibid.*, p. 69.
[49] *Tristano riccardiano*, ed. Parodi, p. 37.
[50] *Cuento*, p. 87.
[51] *Tav. rit.*, pp. 69–71.
[52] *Ibid.*, p. 71.
[53] *Ibid.*, p. 72.—It may be noted that this sequence differs from that proposed by Rajna in regard to the positions of Scenes 13 and 20, which are kept in their original relation on the coverlet to 14 and 19 respectively. The order here assigned to 13 and 14 is further supported by the *Tavola*, which mentions Morhaut's embarkation before Tristram's. Some of the inscriptions differ from Rajna's readings and may be easily verified from the reproductions. It seems probable too that Rajna overestimated the designer's inventive tendency. So many instances in which the quilts differ from the *Tavola* agree with a variant literary source that it seems probable that the remaining variations and additions such as the presence of Morhaut's squire at the island combat and Morhaut's proclaiming the expedition and hiring the soldiers were suggested by a lost text.
[54] *Romania*, XLII, 562 ff. *Monatshefte für Kunstwissenschaft*, XII, 169.

They occur isolated on pilgrim's medal, on tympanum sculpture, in the niche of burgher's house, in the illumination of a manuscript. Comparatively few single scenes from secular literature enjoyed any such wide dispersion, any such constant repetition. To be sure, Alexander's celestial flight was carved from Greece to Gloucestershire, but it seems to have owed its remarkable diffusion to religious interpretation as an analogue to the fall of Lucifer and thus belongs to sacred rather than to profane art.[55] Scenes from the beast epic, however, such as Reynard preaching to a congregation of geese, though often found in churches, can hardly be called religious either in origin or in intent. The motifs of Aristotle bestridden by Phyllis and of Virgil dangling in a basket were perhaps used as exempla to point a moral and do occur rarely in ecclesiastical surroundings, but were in the main popularized by secular art. So too in the fourteenth and fifteenth centuries was the Fountain of Youth.

Arthurian romance provided only one such scene, occurring apart from any illustrations of the narrative context and recurring far and wide throughout Christendom; namely, the meeting of Tristram and Ysolt beneath a tree, in which lurks the royal spy, King Mark. Though the theme occurs in its context, as we have seen, on some German embroideries, on two Parisian ivory caskets, on the Palermo ceiling, and among the frescoes at S. Floret and Runkelstein, it enjoyed a remarkable independent popularity. We have noticed it already as one of the stereotyped motifs on the enameled vessels listed in the inventories of Louis of Anjou. Why it should have caught the fancy of craftsmen so that they reproduced it independently at Paris, Chester, Bourges, and Ratisbon, is hard to say. Was it the piquancy of the situation, or was it the opportunity for symmetrical treatment? At any rate, it is probably due to the predilection of the artists that we find the theme of the tryst beneath the tree treated separately in literature—in the Italian *novellino* and in the moralized exegesis of the *Cy Nous Dit*.[56] A miniature from Chantilly MS. 1078–9 illustrates the latter. (Fig. 120)

The Parisian Ivories

The earliest instances in art of the tryst apart from other illustrations of the same romance are found on Parisian ivories of the first quarter of the fourteenth century. It appears on seven caskets together with the Hunting of the Unicorn and other romantic sub-jects; on two mirror-backs and one handle of a *gravoir* or hair-parter it appears alone. The caskets on which it occurs on the same panel with the unicorn theme are at the Metropolitan Museum, New York, the British and Victoria and Albert Museums, London, the Bargello, Florence, the cathedral treasury, Cracow, the Walters Gallery, Baltimore, and in the possession of Mrs. St. John Mildmay (1862).[57] The iconography of these caskets is now completely elucidated: the lid is usually filled by the Siege of the Castle of Love, the front by the Humiliation of Aristotle and the Fountain of Youth, the back by Lancelot on the Sword-Bridge and Gawain in the Chateau Merveil, one side by Enyas and the Wodehouse, and Galahad receiving the keys to the Castle of Maidens, the other side by the Tryst and the Unicorn.[58] As Antoniewicz noted,[59] a scheme of contrasts is to be detected here. The senile infatuation of Aristotle for Phyllis is set off against the fresh ardors produced by the Fountain of Youth, the carnal passion of Tristram and Ysolt against the unicorn, symbol of virginity. Probably Galahad, the virgin knight, stands in contrast to the wodehouse, the medieval caveman; and possibly Lancelot's perilous quest of Guinevere is intended as a foil to Gawain's adventure in quest of the Bleeding Lance of the Grail Castle. In the last instance, however, the Lancelot and Gawain scenes are so badly muddled and the connection of Gawain's adventure with the holy quest is so remote that it is doubtful whether one out of a hundred who saw the four scenes ever caught the contrast in the motives of the two knights—even if it was ever intended.

The representations of the tryst on the caskets differ little from one another except in the quality of workmanship. The Metropolitan example is perhaps the finest. (Fig. 122) King Mark's countenance is that of a mature and troubled man, watching intently his suspected wife, not the bland youth of the British Museum example. The gestures of the lovers are natural; the drapery falls in appropriate curves; even Tristram's falcon and Ysolt's pet dog are alive. The reflection of Mark's head in the fountain hardly lends itself to realistic handling in low relief, but otherwise there is little to cavil at, much to praise in the grace and sincerity of the craftsmanship. The British Museum casket 368 (Fig. 121) depicts the rendezvous more crudely, but with little difference except that the position of the lovers is reversed and the sculptured spout of the fountain is omitted.

The mirror-back in the Vatican Library (Fig. 123)

[55] *Burlington Mag.*, XXXII (1918), 136, 177.
[56] Cf. *supra* p. 28.
[57] Koechlin, *Ivoires gothiques* (P., 1924), II, 449–455. The Mildmay casket is Koechlin's No. 1287. Cf. *Catalogue of the Special Exhibition of Works of Art on Loan at South Kensington Museum*, 1862, ed. J. C. Robinson (1863), p. 19. The Walters

casket is Koechlin's No. 1281. Cf. also M. H. Longhurst, *Cat. of Carvings in Ivory* (L., 1929), II, 53.
[58] *Art in America*, V (1917), 19. *Romanische Forschungen*, V (1890), 248.
[59] *Ibid.*, 255.

is the work of a tyro.[60] The foliage, Ysolt's dog, the carved animal head from which the water gushes in the form of seven straight scratches, Mark's head in odd juxtaposition to his knee and foot, are clumsy in the extreme. On the other hand, a mirror-back at the Musée de Cluny (Fig. 124), made if one may judge by Tristram's costume about 1340, is delicate in detail and charming in the ensemble.[61] A curious attempt to fit the scene to the handle of a hair-parter is to be found at the Museo Civico, Turin. (Fig. 125) The tree and the King have been eliminated; Ysolt with her dog and Tristram with his falcon stand close together above a laver, decorated with grotesque spouts, in which is mirrored the face of Mark.[62]

The Milan Hanap

There is in the Poldi Pezzoli Museum, Milan, a cup of crystal, mounted on an exquisitely shaped stem and base of silver gilt, equipped with a covercle,[63] altogether almost ten inches high. (Fig. 126) Both base and covercle are inlaid with translucent enamels, in a charming symphony of green, orange, lilac, yellow, and gray, against a background of blue. For purposes of reproduction the crystal cup itself has been removed so that the pattern of the base can be clearly discerned. The background is diapered and, in five of the eight compartments, sprinkled with rosettes. Six of the compartments are filled with such romantic scenes as appear on the secular ivories and in Queen Mary's Psalter: a youth is presented by his lady with a wreath; two knights, one followed by a squire, canter from two sides toward a maiden and take the spears which she holds out to them. In the remaining two compartments we have the familiar tryst. The date must be about 1335, but the provenance is somewhat puzzling.

The authorities who have pronounced on the matter seem to agree that it issued from the workshop of Ugolino, the famous goldsmith of Siena, who created the Bolsena reliquary at Orvieto in 1338 and the reliquary of St. Juvenal. Certainly there are marked resemblances.[64] On the other hand, the figure drawing seems more French than Italian; the subjects are typical of the Parisian school of ivory-carvers; and the sprinkling of rosettes in the background appears on the translucent enamels at the base of the statue of the Virgin presented by Jeanne d'Evreux to S. Denis in 1339.[65] Now this work supposedly emanated from Paris, and Dr. Marvin Ross gives his expert opinion in favor of North French origin for the cup also.

The Namur Tablet-Case

A unique cuir-bouilli case for writing tablets has been preserved at the Museum of Namur.[66] (Fig. 127) It is probably of French workmanship and may be dated about 1340. At the top are a crowned lion and a grotesque monster, quite unconcerned with the scene below. The foliage pattern, the lozenge background, the rendering of the fountain, Ysolt pointing to the reflection are reminiscent of the Milan hanap. The King's forearms and buttoned sleeves are new features. On the other side of the case two gentlemen and ladies converse, and below them a monk gives absolution to a kneeling nun.

The South Kensington Wooden Casket

A wooden casket of the middle of the fourteenth century at the Victoria and Albert Museum furnishes another illustration.[67] (Fig. 129) The lid is reinforced by decorative iron bands, dividing it into four panels. At the two sides stand the two lovers, very slender, Ysolt pointing at the pool at the bottom of the two middle panels. Two lion-headed bosses, to which the handle is attached, were suggested perhaps by the lion-headed spouts which adorn the fountain in some of the ivories. Mark's head is not mirrored in the pool, but in the tree above it he appears in half length, brandishing a sword in his right hand and with his left seizing a barely discernible dwarf, who raises his hand in supplication. The casket was probably carved in England, but, strange to say, no English or French version mentions the dwarf in the tree.

The Ratisbon Embroidery

About 1370 there was prepared, very probably at Ratisbon, a richly colored embroidery, called the "Teppich der Medaillons," which still hangs in the Gothic townhall of that city.[68] (Detail, Fig. 128) Like other German work of the same kind, it is stitched in colored wools, covering the linen base; its dimensions are about 9 by 11 feet. Against a deep rose-red background are set medallions with alternating backgrounds of pea-green and indigo. The other colors are lilac, light blue, and ochre. The niches of the border and the medallions contain fifty pairs of lovers, among them a lady leading a wodehouse by a chain, Aristotle ridden by Phyllis, and the familiar tryst. The medallions are $18\frac{1}{2}$ inches in diameter and include each an encircling inscription in the Bavarian dialect. That around the tryst scene runs: "ich sieh

[60] Koechlin, II, 385.

[61] *Ibid.*

[62] *Ibid.*, p. 408.

[63] *Zts. f. Christliche Kunst*, XIV (1901), col. 65.

[64] Molinier, *Orfévrerie religieuse et civile* (P.), p. 251. Michel, *Hist. de l'art*, II, 2, p. 980. R. Jean, *Arts de la terre*, (P., 1911), p. 331.

[65] Molinier, *op. cit.*, p. 213. Jean, *op. cit.*, p. 333.

[66] Viollet-le-Duc, *Dictionnaire raisonné du mobilier français* (P., 1871), II, 156 f.

[67] R. Kohlhausen, *Minnekästchen im Mittelalter* (Berlin, 1928), pp. 35, 88 f., pl. 33.

[68] F. von der Leyen, A. Spamer, *Die altdeutschen Wandteppiche im Regensburger Rathause* (Regensburg, 1910), pp. 2–8.

in des prune sche*in* auf d*em* paum de herre*n* mein."
"I see in the shine of the spring my lord in the tree."
Mark's head looks out from a corolla of linden leaves
and is repeated against a pale blue, pear-shaped pattern, which one must interpret as a spring. Apart
from the charm of the rich indigo, ochre, and green,
the design is a preposterous parody.

The Bruges Corbel

Between January 14, 1376, and May, 1387, the
façade of the town hall of Bruges was erected. On the
earlier date Louis de Maele, the fickle and cruel
Count of Flanders, laid the cornerstone; on the latter
Gilles de Man was busy gilding the statues and
niches, and at the beginning of the next century no
less a man than Jan van Eyck was engaged in the
same task.[69] Much of the sculpture was executed by
Jean de Valenciennes, and it is quite possible that it
was he who carved the corbel which supported a
statue of a Count of Flanders on the façade and
which represents the tryst. (Fig. 130) For some 525
years it looked down on the little Place du Bourg.
When it was set in place, Bruges was at the apex of
its prosperity. Merchants from every country in
Europe bought and sold in her markets, and her
population is said to have numbered a quarter of a
million.

The sculpture of the tryst was removed during the
restoration of the town hall about 1854 to the Gruthuyse Museum.[70] King Mark's head is surrounded by
a sort of Christmas wreath. On the left is the queen,
pointing with her finger to the pool. A bearded Tristram in buttoned *cote-hardie,* a garland on his head,
sits on the other side. A falcon, which once perched
on his left fist, has been broken off, leaving only its
talons and tail. Though the sculptor has handled
hair, drapery, and foliage clumsily, the faces of the
lovers possess a certain placid comeliness.

The Chester Misericord

Of the same approximate date (c. 1380) is a misericord at Chester cathedral.[71] (Fig. 131) As every amateur of ecclesiastical antiquities knows, the seats of
choir-stalls could be tilted up, and a bracket, carved
on the under side, could be used by the clergy as a
prop to support them as they stood during the long
hours of the service,[72]—one of the many devices by
which medieval ingenuity evaded the austerities imposed by religious ritual and discipline. The craftsman at Chester displayed skill in undercutting the

foliage and branches, but his work is otherwise undistinguished, and he surely did not understand his
subject. Tristram stands somewhat awkwardly avert-
ing his face from some annoying oak-leaves, and presents to the queen a ring just under the angry eyes
and curling beard of the jealous king. There is no
trace of the fountain, though Ysolt's dog seems
poised as if to lap up water. On the left is a squire,
equipped with sword, buckler, and dagger; on the
right an attendant bears the queen's cloak and a
second dog. The costume is interesting: the buttoned
cote-hardie with accentuated waist and the girdle
round the hips worn by Tristram; Ysolt's kirtle
buttoned half way down the front and up to the
throat; the ample liripipes of the squire and damsel,
and the latter's rectangular head-dress.

The Lincoln Misericord

Lincoln cathedral possesses what is perhaps a copy
of the Chester misericord. (Fig. 132)[73] Unfortunately
the tree has been broken away, the faces of Mark and
Tristram damaged, and the squire decapitated.
Though most of the characteristic features of the
Chester carving—the two attendants, the little dog
at the base of the tree, the meeting of the lovers'
hands beneath Mark's head—are present, yet the
Lincoln craftsman introduces changes in the costume
of Ysolt, her attendant, and the squire, and by
omitting the crowns of the King and Queen shows
that he has no notion of the story.

The Bamberg Comb

A remarkable version of the same scene is carved
on a boxwood comb in the possession of the His-
torische Verein at Bamberg. (Fig. 133) The long,
elaborately dagged sleeves and the sweeping trains
of the *houppelandes* set the date early in the fifteenth
century. The comb has been mistakenly described as
an ivory and said to be of French or Catalan provenance; but Koechlin, whose judgment in such matters is hardly to be questioned, called it German
work, and a glance at the two wooden caskets of the
same period figured by Kohlhausen[74] suggests an
origin in Westphalia or the Middle Rhine. It contains decorative scrolls, on which are incised the
speeches of three persons, couched in a barbaric
French. Ysolt, the crowned lady at the left, says in
a whisper of warning: "Tristram, gardes de dire
vilane por la pisson de la fonteine." "Tristram, guard
against speaking shame because of the fish of the

[69] E. Gilliat-Smith, *Story of Bruges* (L., 1909), pp. 206 f.
[70] Information kindly supplied by M. Albert Viscomte de
Bocarmé.
[71] *Journal of Architectural, Archaeological, and Historical Society for the County and City of Chester and North Wales,* N.S.,

V (1895), 52. The reference to a similar misericord at Bristol is
probably a mistake for Lincoln.
[72] Francis Bond, *Woodcarvings in English Churches, Misericords* (Oxford, 1910).
[73] M. D. Anderson, *Medieval Carver* (Cambridge, 1935), p. 105.
[74] Kohlhausen, *op. cit.,* pl. 56, 57.

fountain." Tristram, having noticed the "fish," says aloud to deceive the King: "Dame, ie voroi per ma foi qu'i fu ave nos monsingor le roi." "Lady, I should wish by my faith that my lord the King were with us." Mark, reassured by this speech, in a stage whisper curses the dwarf who has informed on the lovers: "De deu sot il condana qui dementi la dame loial." "May he be damned of God who slandered the loyal lady." It is plain that we have here once more the version of the assignation unrecorded in literature but preserved at S. Floret, where one lover warns the other of the King's presence by calling attention to a supposititious fish in the fountain.

The Bourges Corbel

The latest and one of the most interesting of the illustrations of the tryst is that in the Chambre du Trésor of Jacques Cœur's palace at Bourges. (Fig. 134)[75] The undercutting of the trees suggests comparison with the Chester misericord; the scroll which waves on each side of Mark's head and which doubtless once bore an inscription reminds one of the Bamberg comb; the use of a corbel recalls the Bruges sculpture. The date is determined by the fact that the palace was begun in 1443 and completed in 1450.

Bazin, Bishop of Lisieux, thus writes of the days of Charles VII:[76]

The King's household was at this period administered by a man of the utmost industry and genius, Jacques Cœur of Bourges, of a plebeian family, but endowed with great mental ability, unflagging perseverance, and rare prudence. Lord Steward of the household of the King, in addition to the tasks of this office he continued to devote himself as before to vast commercial operations, which brought him great riches and with them high place and renown. The first in his day, he caused to be constructed and equipped ships which transported to Africa, throughout the Levant, and even to Alexandria in Egypt cloths, woolens, and other articles fabricated within the realm. On the return voyage these ships brought back different varieties of silks and all sorts of spices and perfumes, which were marketed in the provinces reached by the waters of the Rhone or in Catalonia and other neighboring lands, a practice which was then entirely new in France, for theretofore this commerce had long been carried on through the medium of other nations, notably the Venetians, the Genoese, and the Barcelonians. Such was the source of the immense riches amassed by Jacques Cœur. Among other ways he gave proof of his opulence in causing to be erected with such unusual despatch at Bourges, his native city,

that house so richly ornamented, so spacious, and yet withal so magnificent that neither princes of the blood nor the King himself had any residence comparable to it.

This merchant prince seems to have been a man of great wealth who owed his fortune not to deceit or oppression but to enterprise and honesty. His patriotic loans to the penniless Charles VII were as essential to the recovery of France as the inspired valor of Jeanne d'Arc. Yet such was the gratitude of his royal master, such the instability of fortune, that in the year after the completion of his palace, Cœur was charged with all manner of crimes—from poisoning the King's mistress, Agnes Sorel, to supplying the Turks with arms. In 1453, on the very day of the fall of Constantinople, he was deprived of all his offices, heavily mulcted, and imprisoned. He escaped, and three years later in the island of Chios sacrificed his life in the struggle with the triumphant Ottomans. His motto, often repeated in the decoration of his palace, "A vaillants cœurs rien impossible," inspires mixed emotions of admiration and irony, for it became true in a sense which he little anticipated.

The building rises from the old Roman walls of Bourges, and in the third story of the largest tower is the so-called Chambre du Trésor, protected by an iron door and a complicated lock. In this tower room, patently intended for the preservation of valuables, we find the corbel which interests us. For long this sculpture was explained by an ingenious *concierge* as a surreptitious visit of Jacques Cœur himself to Agnes Sorel, of which Charles VII was an unobserved observer. There can be no doubt of the true subject. To the left, the dwarf in the guise of a court jester, bauble in hand, a bell attached to his long sleeve, lurks behind a tree. Tristram advances across a flowery lawn, his right hand resting on an elaborate collar; his left, which probably pointed to the spring, is broken off. In the spring, the reflection of the King's head is handled more realistically than in any previous sculpture, being almost flat and upside down. To the right and left of Mark's head waves a scroll. The queen reclines at the right, her right arm curiously raised to her crown, her head finely rendered. The total effect is one of realism triumphing over design; and even the realism, when one contrasts the size of the tree in which Mark is hiding with the size of the flower beneath it, does not extend to a sense of proportion. Thus ends the series of representations of the Tryst beneath the Tree.

[75] Viollet-le-Duc, *Dictionnaire de l'architecture franç.* (P., 1856) IV, 503, 505.

[76] A. B. Kerr, *Jacques Cœur* (N. Y., L., 1927), pp. 83 f.

CHAPTER VI

LANCELOT, GAWAIN, PERCEVAL, AND GALAHAD

LANCELOT DU LAC is a hero whose prominence in the Arthurian cycle seems to date from his assumption of the rôle of Guinevere's lover in Chrétien de Troyes's *Chevalier de la Charrette* about 1170, and whose reputation was finally made by the author of the *Vulgate Lancelot* some fifty years later. But appearances in this case may be deceptive. Evidence too complex to set forth here suggests his connection with Geoffrey of Monmouth's Lucius Hiberus, with a Llwch Lleminawc of the old Welsh *Harryings of Annwn*, with the Irish god Lugh Loinnbheimionach.[1] Strange to relate, Lancelot, the immortal lover, the central figure of the *Vulgate Lancelot* and next in prominence to the central figures in the *Queste del Saint Graal* and the *Mort Artu*, scarcely makes his appearance, outside books, in extant medieval art. Only in a group of ivory caskets from Paris already mentioned, in a single sculpture at Caen, and among other famous lovers on an Italian *plateau d'accouchement* does Tristram's great rival appear. This despite the fact that manuscripts filled with miniatures of his exploits and his amours must have stood in every courtly library and must have been easily accessible to practitioners of the decorative arts.

TRISTRAM AND LANCELOT ON THE LOUVRE TRAY

There arose late in the fourteenth century and extended into the fifteenth a curious custom of providing for women of Tuscany and Northern Italy while they were in childbed special painted trays on which their meals were served. Baldinucci in the seventeenth century describes them as about a fathom in diameter and adorned with religious subjects,[2] but neither the dimensions nor the subject matter seems to fit many extant examples. Often the Triumphs of Petrarch and other subjects familiar to the cassone painters appear on the *plateaux d'accouchement*, as they are sometimes called. One tray of this type originating in the late fourteenth century passed from the Arconati-Visconti Collection to the Louvre; and is frankly sensual. (Fig. 135) A nude, winged Venus hovers above in a mandorla, attended by two cupids with clawed feet. Golden rays stream from her body toward a group of knights kneeling in adoration in a flowery mead. These devotees of Venus (and of Mars as well, for all were famed in battle) are identified by the inscriptions on their very contemporary costumes as, from left to right, Achilles,

"Tristan, Lancelot, Sanson," Paris, Troilus. It is odd that the French forms of the names should have been employed in so many cases in preference to the Italian.

Whereas Achilles and Samson are bearded and perhaps middle-aged, Tristram and Lancelot possess in this painting that immortal youth which clings to them in the romances: Tristram has long locks of hair, and Lancelot has an almost feminine softness. Both stretch out hands of supplication toward the goddess. Parodies on sacred things and a bold adoration of Venus were far from unknown to the Goliards and other wayward spirits of the twelfth and thirteenth centuries. But here we have in art a clear prognostic of the paganism of the Renaissance, the idolization of the flesh set up in opposition to the idealization of the spirit.

LANCELOT ON THE IVORIES

On the group of early fourteenth-century ivory caskets from Paris described in the previous chapter there recurs a little scene from the famous poem of Chrétien de Troyes, *Le Chevalier de la Charrette*. Lancelot in his endeavor to deliver the Queen from the hands of an abductor, Meleagant, has reached the banks of a torrent which alone separates him from the castle of her captor. The black, raging stream is spanned only by a bright sword as long as two lances, each end fixed in a tree-trunk. Beyond the stream Lancelot descries two lions chained but ready to devour him. Nevertheless, Love inspires him to remove the mail from his hands and feet and creep across the scythelike blade. Bleeding he arrives on the other side, to discover that the lions were an illusion.[3]

No miniature illustrating the scene in the *Charrette* has survived, but certain miniatures of the same adventure in the *Vulgate Lancelot* have simplified the subject so that we have merely wavy lines at the bottom to indicate the stream, a large but not particularly long sword, Lancelot in surcoat and chain armor crossing it on his hands and knees. It was in some such simplified miniature that the design for the ivory carvings must have had its source.

The caskets on which the crossing of the sword bridge is carved are in the British Museum (Fig. 136), the South Kensington Museum, the Metropolitan Museum, New York (Fig. 137), the Bargello, Florence, Cracow cathedral, and the Walters Art

---

[1] R. S. Loomis, *Celtic Myth and Arthurian Romance* (N. Y., 1927), pp. 91–93.

[2] *Monuments Piot*, I (1894), 218.

[3] *Karrenritter u. Wilhelmsleben*, ed. W. Foerster (Halle, 1899), vv. 3021 ff.

Gallery, Baltimore;[4] sides of a casket containing the scene are in the British Museum and in the collection of Robert von Hirsch, Bâle.[5] In all except the last, Lancelot on the sword bridge has curiously taken his place with three other panels on the same side,—panels which are devoted to Gawain's adventures in the Chateau Merveil. And this juxtaposition is responsible for the intrusion of alien elements, for in every instance the shower of spears and swords descending from the conventionalized cloud above has been mistakenly carried over from the scene on the right, where, as we shall see, it properly belongs. The South Kensington example goes even further in appropriating for Lancelot the shield with the infixed lion's claw, which likewise belongs to Gawain in the scene on the left.

It becomes clear from this confusion that the atelier of the ivory carvers could boast little first-hand acquaintance with the Arthurian story. Someone who did possess that knowledge must have selected two of the most famous marvels of the legend for illustration—Lancelot on the Sword Bridge and Gawain on the Perilous Bed. And one may commend his excellent instinct for the exotic and strange. But somehow in the shop the designs were mixed: the Sword Bridge was allotted only one panel, whereas Gawain's exploits were allotted three; the order of the scenes was jumbled; and, as we have seen, features from the Gawain adventure transferred to Lancelot. Of all these products of the Parisian workshops, the Walters casket depicts Lancelot with the greatest delicacy; the British Museum plaque with the greatest crudity.

LANCELOT ON THE CAEN CAPITAL

Fifty or more years after the production of the ivory workers' model of the romance caskets, a sculptor at S. Pierre, Caen, adopted four of the same subjects for a capital of the nave: Lancelot on the Sword Bridge, Gawain on the Perilous Bed, the Virgin and the Unicorn, and Aristotle ridden by Phyllis.[6] To these he added Virgil's assignation, Samson and the Lion, and the Pelican in her Piety. His treatment of the Sword Bridge (Fig. 138) is striking; the intrusive missiles are not there; the lions of the romance are recalled by the figure of a single lion sitting on its hauches; and above a tower appears the head of a woman, doubtless Guinevere herself. The hero is clad in armor of the second half of the century. Certainly this relief is not based directly on the

ivories, though together with the other three subjects it may have been suggested by a casket. In that case, the sculptor has deliberately reconciled his design with the *Vulgate Lancelot* and suppressed the errors of the ivory carvers. Otherwise, he must have had access to a series of designs of the Sword Bridge, the Perilous Bed, the Unicorn, and the Humiliation of Aristotle anterior to and free from the corruptions of the ivory carvers.

At any rate, it is odd to find a group of four subjects familiar to the ladies of the fourteenth century as motifs adorning jewel cases, mirror-backs, and other ministrants to their vanity, appearing thus conspicuously in the nave of a church. Doubtless a pious moral was easily extracted from the tales of Aristotle, Virgil, Samson, the unicorn, and the pelican, but it is a little difficult to see what Lancelot and Gawain were doing *dans cette galère*. The medieval exegetist, of course, was equal to anything; if he could interpret Europa and the Bull as Christ, the sacrificial ox, bearing the sins of the world, he doubtless found symbolism in the parlous adventures of Arthur's knights. Such speculations are vain; we may have to do merely with the fancy of an irresponsible artist.

GAWAIN ON THE IVORIES

The adventures of Gawain in the Chateau Merveil, we have just noted, occur both on certain ivory caskets and also at Caen in conjunction with carvings of the Sword Bridge. Gawain himself we have encountered as an old Arthurian hero on the Modena archivolt.[7] He seems to have inherited some of the adventures of the Ulster hero Cúchulainn, and even as late as 1485, when Malory's *Morte d'Arthur* was published, he retains the solar character of increasing in strength till noon and of waning in strength thereafter. One of the adventures which he inherited from Cúchulainn was that of Chateau Merveil, which occurs in Arthurian romance in many forms.[8] As told of Cúchulainn in *Bricriu's Feast* (c. 750)[9] the story runs that he came to the perilous revolving fortress of Cúroi in Cúroi's absence, was hospitably entertained by the lady Bláthnat, took the seat of watch one night, heard a great noise, slew a monster which attacked him, vanquished a giant hurling branches, and was greeted as victor by Bláthnat and by Cúroi, his returned host. As told by Chrétien de Troyes in the *Conte del Graal* (c. 1175),[10] Gawain entered the hall of a magic castle, sat upon a perilous

[4] Koechlin, *Ivoires gothiques français*, II, 451–454. The Walters casket is No. 1281.

[5] Formerly in the Trivulzio collection, Milan. *Ibid.*, 455. O. M. Dalton, *Catalogue of Ivory Carvings* (L., 1909), p. 127, No. 370, pl. LXXXVII.

[6] E. de Robillard de Beaurepaire, *Caen illustré* (1896), pp. 177 ff.

[7] Cf. *supra* pp. 32–34.

[8] R. S. Loomis, *op. cit.*, 159–176. *PMLA*, XLVIII (1933), 1011–18.

[9] *Bricriu's Feast*, ed. G. Henderson (L., 1899), pp. 101–113.

[10] Ed. A. Hilka (Halle, 1932), vv. 7676 ff.

bed, equipped with wheels and bells; at once there was a great noise, arrows and bolts rained down upon his shield; when this attack ceased, a churl loosed a lion upon Gawain, and the knight succeeded in cutting off the claws which the beast had fixed in his shield, and the head also. He was then congratulated by his host of the night before and by the lady of the castle through her damsels. The derivation of this adventure from that of Cúchulainn may not be immediately patent, but it is confirmed by remarkable correspondences between the Irish saga and other romance versions of the Perilous Bed motif.

It was probably Chrétien's version which was the basis of the ivory carver's designs, but as with the Sword Bridge, so here there are signs of confusion. On all the caskets, enumerated above in connection with Lancelot except the Von Hirsch plaque we find to the right of the Sword Bridge motif, in the third panel, Gawain lying on the bed, partly protected by his shield, his head propped on his hand. Beneath the bed the wheels and bells are faithfully portrayed, and above are quarrels and swords descending from a cloud. Most of these panels represent the claws of the lion fixed in the hero's shield, and three at least show the muzzle of the lion appearing at the left—both features anticipating the combat with the lion which followed the adventure of the bed.

On all the ivories including the Von Hirsch plaque, the panel to the left of the Sword Bridge contains the lion combat itself, in which the severing of the lion's paw and head is quite clearly marked, except in the Metropolitan Museum example. The third Gawain scene is found in the fourth panel, to the right of the bed adventure. Three swaying damsels in flowing robes advance with their congratulations toward the hero. In the South Kensington and Metropolitan Museum caskets once more the carver's literary ignorance is revealed, for he introduces foliage into this interior scene.

We know of two instances in which the Perilous Bed motif, instead of fitting in with other scenes to form the long side of a casket, filled one of the narrower sides. One included in the Manzi sale in 1919 was of the normal type;[11] but the De Boze casket, described and figured in 1753 but long since lost except for one side, furnishes an amazing example of artistic libertinism. Into one panel (Fig. 142) the carver crowded the bed scene, with Gawain recumbent under the flight of swords and bolts, the lion with a missing paw, another lion, a horse protruding its head from a gateway, a queen and two damsels above the gateway, three more damsels above a battlemented wall, a tree and two falling birds. For the horse, the birds, and the placing of the scene outdoors, the artisan could have had no literary authority; he was merely indulging his fancy.

The Museo Civico, Bologna, possesses a mirror-back illustrating the Perilous Bed adventure (Fig. 140), and the Musée Archéologique, Niort, contains a writing tablet. (Fig. 141) Both ivories introduce the lion and the damsels into the scene, somewhat prematurely. On the Bologna ivory five damsels, one with a poodle, two with wreaths, stand in a gallery looking down upon Gawain's heroism.

Of all these illustrations of the exploits of Gawain on the ivories, the Metropolitan Museum casket is the most natural and the most graceful.

GAWAIN ON THE CAEN CAPITAL

As has already been mentioned, the capital at S. Pierre, Caen, from the second half of the fourteenth century contains four scenes often found together on ivory caskets destined for a lady's boudoir, and one of them is that of the Perilous Bed. This particular scene has suffered from some domestic Hun, but the head of Gawain, the darts, two wheels and two bells are still clearly to be seen. (Fig. 139)

GAWAIN ON THE BRUNSWICK EMBROIDERY

In the Landesmuseum at Brunswick there are two large pieces and one small fragment of an embroidery representing the adventures of Gawain (Figs. 143, 144) as narrated by the Bavarian knight, Wolfram von Eschenbach, in his *Parzifal* (c. 1205).[12] They were discovered in 1877 in the Kreuzkloster, which had been a Benedictine nunnery between 1230 and 1398. They have been badly cut up and partly restored; when the rectangle of which they form parts was complete, it measured about 5 feet 1 inch by 14 feet 4 inches. There was doubtless a border of at least 3 inches additional at the bottom, and probably another row of scenes, an inscription, and a border at the top. The style and costume are very close to those of a Solomon embroidery from the same Kreuzkloster and also to Wienhausen Tristram III. The long surcoat of the knights, as on the Tristram hanging, indicates a date not later than 1340 for the design. The feminine costume is distinguished by remarkable crested hats and very long liripipes. Since the dyes employed on these three embroideries are quite different, it may be surmised that though the cartoons of all came from the same hand, the dyeing and needlework were done separately. The Gawain hanging uses a blue with a turquoise tint for a background, and against this sets patterns of strawberry red, pink, ochre, pea-green, rust, white, lilac, and robin's egg blue.

---

[11] *Collection Manzi, sculptures, tableaux, tapisseries* (P.,1919), p. 16, fig. 48.
[12] *Romanische Forschungen*, V (1890), 274. M. Schuette, *Gestickte Bildteppiche des Mittelalters*, II (Leipzig, 1930), pp. 8–10, pl. 3, colored pl. 4.

The inscriptions run thus:

... vrowen up dat pert. de v[er] wundede ritter spr[anc]
... dat scep. Gawan mit Lisoys streit un crec h[e s]in
pert weder. de scepman wolde den tolen han. Gaw[an]
... dar n[a] quam he up Castel Marveile dar e[m] vel ...

... woman on the horse. The wounded knight sprang ...
the boat. Gawan fought with Lisoys, and he won his horse
back. The boatman wished to have the toll. Gawan ...
Thereafter he came to the Castle Marveile, there to him
many ...

As we shall presently see, the inscriptions do not fit
the scenes under which they are placed but lag considerably behind, so that the first fragment of the inscription refers to events antecedent to those depicted in the first row, and the scenes in the lowest
row are not covered by the inscription beneath. A
similar maladjustment may be observed on Tristram
embroidery I at Wienhausen. Since the story of Gawain's affair with Orgeluse here begins *in medias
res*, it is probable that there was at least one additional row at the top containing the opening scenes,
and that the length of the accompanying inscriptions
was so badly calculated that the words describing the
original first row occupied two lines instead of one,
and thus it must have been something of a puzzle for
medieval beholders, as for us, to relate the words to
the pictures. In its original state the embroidery
must have contained one or more rows representing
how Gawain rode forth in quest of the Grail, came
upon a wounded knight, Urian, fetched him a healing
herb, and applied it to his wound. He then swung
Urian's lady upon her palfrey (*Parz.* 522), whereupon
Urian sprang on Gawain's destrier and rode away,
mocking. The first inscription, of course, refers to this
last incident. The scenes may be conveniently followed in Miss J. L. Weston's translation, II, 16–75,
but the references below are to sections in the German
text.

FIRST ROW. 1. (Fig. 143) Gawain, who has met and
become enamoured of the scornful beauty, Orgeluse of
Logrois, rides after her on a feeble mare since his own
mount has been stolen. The squire Malcreature, who in the
poem has departed, is shown on the embroidery riding after
them. (*Parz.* 535)

2. Orgeluse is ferried over a river, while Gawain stands
disconsolate on the shore. (*Parz.* 535, 536)

3. Gawain on his feeble steed encounters the redoubtable Lischoys Gwelljus, who has in the meantime won
Gawain's horse from the wily Urian. (*Parz.* 537)

4. The fight continues on foot: Gawain is victor and
thus reconquers his steed. (*Parz.* 537)

5. A badly damaged figure of Gawain.

Separate scene, end of FIRST ROW. 6. (Fig. 144) Gawain, having given the vanquished Lischoys to the ferryman in payment of toll, and having been ferried over and

sumptuously entertained over night by the ferryman, is
seen riding away the next morning from his host and
daughter to essay the adventure of Chateau Merveil.
(*Parz.* 562)

SECOND ROW. 7. (Fig. 143) Outside the gate of the
castle he meets the mysterious merchant with his rich
wares, and leaves his destrier in his keeping. (*Parz.* 563)

8. Gawain approaches the Perilous Bed as it rolls about
the hall on wheels. (*Parz.* 566)

9. As he lies on the bed, Gawain is the target for stone
missiles and of crossbow bolts, which according to the
poem were shot by unseen hands, but in the embroidery
are discharged by three men. (*Parz.* 568)

10. A peasant with a club, standing in a doorway, looses
a lion, the last of the terrors of Chateau Merveil, at the
hero. The lion fixes his claws in Gawain's shield; Gawain
cuts off the two forepaws, which in succeeding scenes
remain as his cognizance. (*Parz.* 571)

11. In this much damaged scene two damsels are visible,
sent by Queen Arnive to see how the hero has fared. The
head over the arch is perhaps that of the queen. (*Parz.*
574–575)

THIRD ROW. 12. Gawain, the next morning, having
descried the lovely Orgeluse riding in a meadow beyond
the river with a knight, is ferried over, encounters his rival,
strikes off his helm and lays him low. (*Parz.* 597–598)

13. Gawain then rides with the still scornful Orgeluse
to further adventure. (*Parz.* 601)

14. Leaving Orgeluse, he rides to the perilous tree.
(*Parz.* 602)

15. He plucks a bough. (*Parz.* 603)

16. King Gramoflanz, guardian of the tree, rides up unarmed to meet Gawain. The king's figure is badly damaged. (*Parz.* 604)

17. (Fig. 144) After coming to a friendly arrangement
with Gramoflanz to meet in combat later, Gawain rides
back with the bough to Orgeluse, who at last begs forgive-
ness on her knees for her cruelty. (*Parz.* 611)

18. The ferryman rows them both over the river. (*Parz.*
621–622)

19. Riding together up to Chateau Merveil, they are
met by an escort of knights and trumpeters, while on the
right Queen Arnive and her ladies look out from a tower.
(*Parz.* 624)

20. At the banquet which followed Gawain's return to
Chateau Merveil, he placed his sister Itonje by his side;
it is they probably whom the artist has placed together in
the middle, toasting each other, while on the left are Queen
Arnive and Orgeluse. At the right is a seated gentleman
and a servitor entering through a door. (*Parz.* 636)

THE PERCEVAL CASKET

Perceval is associated in the minds of most lovers
of music and literature with the legend of the Grail,
and rightly so. There is no legend of which the Celtic
provenance can be more fully demonstrated, though
the case is complicated.[13] The youth of Perceval bears

[13] *Speculum*, VIII (1933), 415. *Romanische Forschungen* XLV
(1931), 66.

a marked affinity to that of the Irish hero Finn.[14] This Celtic tradition, introduced by the Bretons to the French, provoked endless curiosity and demanded a solution even more urgently than the passage of the bleeding spear and the grail through the hall of the Fisher King's castle required a question of Perceval. What did it all mean? Much misguided ingenuity, true religious fervor, and a high literary genius eventually supplied answers, confused and conflicting though the answers were.[15] The spear was the lance of Longinus,[16] and the grail or platter was the dish of the Last Supper and the vessel in which Joseph of Arimathea caught the blood which flowed from the side of the Savior.

Three versions of the legend are important for iconographical study: the *Conte del Graal*, begun by Chrétien de Troyes about 1175 and completed by a series of continuators in the next fifty years or so; the *Parzival* of Wolfram von Eschenbach, which is apparently based in part on Chrétien and in part on a lost poem by Kyot; the *Estoire* and the *Queste del Saint Graal*, written between 1210 and 1223, and forming parts of the great Vulgate cycle in prose.

An ivory casket of the early fourteenth century illustrates several scenes of Perceval's youth, together with figures of St. Christopher, St. Martin, St. George, and St. Eustace on the lid.[17] (Figs. 145–148) It came probably from a Paris workshop and is now in the Louvre. It has naturally been taken for granted that the scenes from Perceval's boyhood were inspired by Chrétien's poem, but Professor A. C. L. Brown first raised the interesting issue whether there had not been at least some other influence.[18] It is a pretty question. On four points the carving diverges from Chrétien; on two of these it corresponds to other versions of the same story; on one it corresponds to a cognate Arthurian tale of boyhood as well as to Irish and Welsh practice; on the remaining point it is at least not inconsistent with another version of Perceval's youth. In Scene 1 he carries a bow as in Wolfram, and meets three knights as in Wolfram, *Peredur*, and *Sir Percyvelle*. In Scene 4 he carries two javelins according to ancient Celtic custom, which seems to be preserved in *Carduino*,[19] an Italian poem which tells of an Arthurian hero's youth, much like that of Perceval. In Scene 6 Guinevere is sitting at the table when the uncouth lad rides in, and there is nothing to the contrary in *Peredur*. It would seem plausible, then, to attribute three of these divergences from Chrétien to other traditions. But the strange thing is that two of these divergences from Chrétien's text occur in

miniatures of the *Conte del Graal* itself, the two javelins in the Mons MS, the bow in Bib. Nat. fr. 12577.[20] In the latter MS, moreover, we find a queen seated at table beside the Grail King when, of course, there should be none. Are we to argue that these divergences also are not fortuitous but due to the influence of other traditions known to the illustrator? The presence of the queens at the high table is doubtless due to mere force of habit; the royal couple could not be rent asunder. Perhaps the bow is equally inevitable. As for the other variations upon Chrétien, no confident decision seems possible. It is hard to believe that the illustrator of a MS abandoned the text before him for some hypothetical version which he had heard or read; on the other hand, the coincidences in regard to the two javelins and the three knights are abnormal. At any rate, it will do no harm to identify the scenes on the Perceval casket by means of the *Conte del Graal*, according to Hilka's edition.[21] An English translation is that of W. W. Newell in his *King Arthur and the Table Round*, II, pp. 3–23.

LEFT SIDE. (Fig. 145) 1. The youth in his rude "Welsh" garb, a bow on his shoulder, kneels before three knights of Arthur's. Vv. 100 ff.

BACK. (Fig. 146) 2. Perceval receives his mother's advice before his departure. Vv. 496 ff. 3. His mother swoons over the parapet of the drawbridge. Vv. 620–625. 4. The youth rides through the forest. Vv. 626–632. 5. He kisses the damsel of the tent. Vv. 670 ff.

RIGHT SIDE. (Fig. 147) 6. He rides into Arthur's hall and asks to be knighted. A damsel prophesies that he will be the best knight in the world, and Kay strikes her in the face with the palm of his hand. Vv. 903 ff.

FRONT. (Fig. 148) 7. The Red Knight scornfully strikes Perceval with the butt of his spear, and the youth, enraged, drives his javelin through the knight's eye. Vv. 1076 ff. 8. Perceval clumsily endeavors to remove the dead knight's helm. Vv. 1120 ff. 9. The squire Yonet laces the knight's mail hose on Perceval. Vv. 1176 ff.

THE PERCEVAL FRESCO AT CONSTANCE

The paintings which once adorned the house "Zur Kunkel" at Constance have already been introduced to the reader in Chapter III. Their date is about 1300, their subject the downfall of men because of women, and the particular source a lyric by the Meistersinger "Frauenlob." A pair of embracing lovers in the third row have been identified for no reason at all as Tristram and Ysolt or Paris and Helen. (Fig. 149) The words *sorge nam* were legible in the encircling inscription, and undoubtedly they are derived from

[14] *Folklore Record*, IV, 7–21. *Mod. Philology*, XVIII (1920), 211–218.
[15] A. Pauphilet, *Etudes sur la Queste del S. Graal* (P., 1921).
[16] R. J. Peebles, *Legend of Longinus* (Baltimore, 1911).
[17] Koechlin, *op. cit.*, I, 513; II, 463.

[18] *Mod. Lang. Notes*, XL (1925), 70.
[19] *Ibid.*, 68 f. *White Book Mabinogion*, ed. J. G. Evans (Pwllheli), col. 455, "deu par . . . yny law."
[20] Cf. Figs. 263, 264.
[21] Christian v. Troyes, *Percevalroman* (Halle, 1932).

Frauenlob's line: "Parcival groze sorge nam," "Parcival took great sorrow," presumably because of his lady.[22] But Frauenlob has, consciously or unconsciously, perpetrated an anticlimax in thus concluding his list of men brought low by women with Wolfram von Eschenbach's Parzival, for if there is one hero above another in medieval history or fable whose love for his lady elevates and protects, it is this very hero. Nor is there any spiritual kinship between his wife Kondwiramur and Delilah, Guinevere, Phyllis, or even Judith and Bathsheba, conspicuous in Frauenlob's list.

The painting, which survives only in an outline copy, has little to distinguish it.

THE PERCEVAL MURALS AT LÜBECK

In 1929, during the demolition of a house at Lübeck, mural paintings of the Perceval story were discovered under layers of later decoration.[23] They were already in deplorable condition, and since funds were not available, they could not be removed and preserved. Water-color copies by Wilhelm Boht are now in the St. Annen Museum, and are here reproduced. The color was, to judge by the copies, drab brown, dull green, blue-gray, with a little salmon pink, and terra cotta. Between 1323 and 1339 the house belonged to Johannes Saffran, and it is probably to this period that we must assign the paintings on the basis of style and costume. They were found in the original dining hall on the ground floor, on the east and north walls, at a height of about 3 yards 10 inches above the floor. They consisted of two rows, the lower of small scenes under a series of round arches; the upper of medallions about 30 inches in diameter, the interspaces being filled with grotesques and animals. The scenes in the lower row, hitherto unidentified, are surely a sort of chronicle of the life of Man from the baptismal font and the cradle, through the games of boyhood, to the old man toasting his feet before a fire and to the final death-bed. Corroboration may be found in a group of medallions in the contemporary English psalter of Robert de Lisle, where we follow the life of Man from his mother's arms to his tomb.[24] The upper row of medallions at Lübeck was promptly identified as scenes from the adventures of Perceval. Unhappily, a floor had been carried right through the the middle of them, so that many details are lost and the effect is spoiled.

Burmeister's dating, about 1350, must be mistaken, especially if, as he thinks, the work was done by a Frenchman. There is nothing to indicate that these paintings were contemporary with the S. Floret paintings or with the Garderobe paintings at Avignon of about 1340. The peaked cap worn by the knight in 3 is precisely the same as that found in the slayer of the unicorn on early fourteenth-century ivories; the hat of state in 7 reminds one of the Munich *Tristan* MS;[25] and the long surcoats in 9 did not long outlast the year 1325. A probable date would therefore be the second or third decade of the fourteenth century. Burmeister was probably right in emphasizing English influence, for though there is no marked resemblance to the Chertsey tiles, the general treatment of the medallions is similar. French influence seems less obvious, apart from the *fleur de lis* on the north wall between 8 and 9.[26] Whereas the hats of state in 7 and the way in which the foreleg of the horses is regularly raised remind one of the Munich *Tristan* MS, (Figs. 359, 361) and the very flat bowl of the Grail harks back to the form depicted in the Munich *Parzival* MS. (Fig. 358) That the painter was a German, influenced by contemporary English art, as were most of his confreres of the Hanseatic towns, is a legitimate conclusion. His source may have been Wolfram,[27] yet there are marked discrepancies. A convenient translation is that of Miss Margaret Richey, *The Story of Parzival and the Graal*, pp. 32 ff., but the following references are to sections of the German poem.

1. (Fig. 150) Perceval's mother, seated, talks with the lad, who is distinguished by bare feet and a curious horn on his hood. (*Parz.* 119)

2. Perceval runs barefoot after a stag or other cloven-hoofed beast. (*Parz.* 120)

3. (Fig. 151) At the left the lower part of the youth's kneeling figure is visible; at the right an unarmed knight and, apparently, a lady riding the same white horse appear. This may represent some confusion between Perceval's kneeling before the four knights as in Wolfram, and the two knights who abducted a lady concerning whom the four knights inquired of the innocent youth. (*Parz.* 122)

4. (Fig. 152) Perceval's mother stands with lowered head, while her son rides away on a white horse, bearing a bow. (*Parz.* 128)

5. At the top is a tent striped red and white; below we see the forelegs of a white horse and Perceval advancing toward the seated lady of the tent. (*Parz.* 131)

6. (Fig. 153) At the left the youth rides his horse; at the right we see lumpy waves and the side of a boat. This probably illustrated *Parz.* 142, where we read that the youth lodges in a fisherman's hut, though no river or boat is mentioned.

7. Perceval rides into Arthur's hall, where the King and another person in hats of state sit at table. (*Parz.* 147–148)

[22] Heinrich v. Meissen, ed. Ettmüller (Quedlinburg, Leipzig, 1843), p. 102.

[23] *Zts. des Vereins f. Lübeckische Geschichte u. Altertumskunde*, XXVI (1930), 113.

[24] *British Museum, Reproductions from Illuminated MSS*, Ser. 3, pl. XXIV. Cf. *Hymns to the Virgin and Christ*, ed. Furnivall (E.E.T.S., 1867), p. xvii.

[25] Cf. Fig. 364.

[26] *Niedersachsen*, XXXVII (1932), 112, 235.

[27] Wolfram v. Eschenbach, *Parzival u. Titurel*, ed. E. Martin (Halle, 1903), I, 42 ff.

(The following scenes from the end of the story were on the north wall.)

8. (Fig. 154) In the upper left, a crested helm, the torso and shield of a charging knight; at right a horse's tail. This probably represented Perceval's encounter with his half-brother Feirefis. (*Parz.* 737)

9. The legs of two knightly figures in long surcoats reaching to the ankle are all that we have left of what was probably the scene of mutual recognition by the two brothers. (*Parz.* 748)

10. The meagre remains show a seated figure holding a chalice. In all probability this is Perceval become King of the Grail, though there is nothing in Book XVI to correspond to the picture and it is well known that Wolfram did not conceive the Grail as a chalice.

GALAHAD ON THE IVORIES

The composite romance caskets emanating from Paris in the early fourteenth century displayed an acquaintance not only with outstanding figures like Tristram, Gawain, and Lancelot, but also with Galahad,—the hero of the *Queste del Saint Graal* and, as we have seen in earlier chapters, an incongruous intruder in the later elaborations of the *Prose Tristan*. His history is simple. His name is the form of Gilead furnished by the Vulgate Bible—Galaad.[28] It forms part of a most ingenious attempt to spiritualize the character of the hero of the Grail quest and adapt it to the monastic ideal of Christianity.

The scene chosen from the *Queste* for the ivory carvings seems odd, pointless; it is in no sense an obvious choice as are the scenes from the stories of

Tristram, Lancelot, and Gawain. Galahad, setting forth on the quest of the Grail, came, after some adventures, to the Chateau des Pucelles, fought with the seven brethren who maintained there an evil custom, and put them to flight at the hour of noon.[29] At the bridge which led to the castle Galahad met a white-haired man in religious garb, who brought him the keys of the castle, saying: "Sir take these keys; now you may do what you will with this castle and those who are therein, for you have so wrought that the castle is yours."

This scene occupies alone the side panel of caskets at the South Kensington Museum (Fig. 155), the British Museum (No. 368. Fig. 156), and the Walters Gallery.[30] In these three Galahad is depicted as just dismounted from his destrier, clasping the hand of a bearded man in religious garb with a large key, and striding toward the gate of a castle. The same scene without the horse is carved in combination with Enyas's rescue of the damsel from the wodehouse, or wild man, on a plaque at the British Museum (No. 369. Fig. 158), on caskets in the Metropolitan Museum, New York, the Bargello, Florence (Fig. 157), and Cracow cathedral.[31] This juxtaposition of Galahad and the wodehouse is probably a part of the symbolic scheme of these caskets.[32] Here the wodehouse is the incarnation of brutal lust; Galahad the type of chastity. On a plaque now in the collection of Robert von Hirsch, Bâle, Galahad's coming to the Chateau des Pucelles is attached to the Lancelot and Gawain scenes.[33]

---

[28] Heinzel, *Über die altfranzösischen Gralromane* (Vienna, 1892), pp. 134 f.
[29] *Queste del S. Graal*, ed. Pauphilet (P., 1923), pp. 47 f. Cf. Malory, *Morte d'Arthur*, Bk. XIII, ch. 15.

[30] Koechlin, *op. cit.*, II, 450, 452.
[31] *Ibid.*, 453 f., 459.
[32] Cf. *supra* p. 66.
[33] Koechlin, *op. cit.*, II, 455, No. 1288.

CHAPTER VII

IVAIN, WIGALOIS, AND GAREL

IN THE inventory of Charles V made in 1379 we have noted a tapestry of "Messire Yvain," one of the chief secondary personages of Arthurian romance. His name, like Arthur and Tristram, is that of a historic figure, Owain son of Urien, a Briton of Cumbria or Strathclyde, who fought the Angles in the second half of the sixth century.[1] His fame survived among the Welsh as one of the heroes of the *Gododin*. But he was caught up in the current of Arthurian myth and folklore; when he appears in French romance, he is no longer a foe of the Anglo-Saxons, but the inheritor of marvelous tales told long before of Cúchulainn in Ireland. His most famous adventure, originating perhaps in the encounter of Cúchulainn with the storm-demon Cúroi beside a loch,[2] was localized by the Bretons at a famous storm-making spring in the Forest of Broceliande.[3] His adventures with the grateful lion, on the other hand, which gave him his title of the Knight of the Lion, represent a tradition brought back by some Crusader or minstrel from the Orient.[4] One version of the composite French tale made its way back to Wales and was there written down and preserved as *The Lady of the Fountain*;[5] another slightly variant version furnished the plot of Chrétien de Troyes's *Ivain* or *Le Chevalier au Lion*, composed about 1173, one of the most successful efforts to combine the Celtic tales of strange customs and enchantments with French chivalric and amatory psychology. This in turn was rendered closely into German by Hartmann von Aue in 1203 as *Iwein*.

THE IVAIN MURALS AT SCHMALKALDEN

In the little Thuringian hill-town of Schmalkalden there stands an old house which for centuries served as the residence of the Landgrave's steward; since the town from the fourteenth century belonged to the Landgrave of Hesse, the house was and is still called the Hessenhof. In the cellar, once the ground-floor, is a room, measuring about 11 by 14 feet, which has passed through successive vicissitudes as a "Trinkstube" and as a coal-cellar. It was the latter humiliating function which saved it from redecoration so that its vaulted ceiling and upper walls retain in fair preservation paintings from the thirteenth century. They were first mentioned in 1862; in the nineties they were twice published, and in 1901 most fully by Paul Weber,[6] whose illustrations are here reproduced as well as two photographs from the original paintings. (Figs. 159–166) Seven bands of painting cover the uneven surface of the plaster, each over 31 inches wide and about 14 feet long. One of these bands is nearly obliterated. The main outlines were done with a brush in brown, and then the finer lines of face, hands, and garments were rendered in black. The intervening spaces were then filled with the same brown or a rich yellow, or were left white, and the whole surface was covered with a wax solution. The name IWAN is discernible between the rows over scenes 17 and 20, and leaves no doubt that the subject is derived from some MS of Hartmann's romance.[7] The slight differences between the painting and the poem do not force us to presuppose any other source. The story may be easily followed in the Everyman translation of Chrétien's romances.

As we enter the room from the hall, we are greeted on the right by the painted figure of a man, lifting a cup and doubtless pledging our healths,—a broad hint as to the original uses of the room. If we follow the painting along this side past a door, we come to the opening scene.

FIRST ROW. Upper west wall. (Fig. 161) 1. After a great feast at Whitsuntide, Arthur and his queen retire to their chamber to sleep, while outside four knights listen to the story of Calogrenant's eerie adventures at the storm-making spring. Of all this, little is discernible save a bed, a crown upon it, and the partition between the bedchamber and the adjoining room. Vv. 77–98.

2. Determined to outshine Calogrenant, Ivain sets out from the court. One can see only his helmet, the outline of his shoulders and shield, and the head and neck of his horse. Behind him is a tower and before him a tree. Vv. 963–973.

3. Here Ivain stretches out his arm to greet the Giant Herdsman, seated on a mound, a club in his left hand. Behind the giant stand three of the wild animals which constitute his herd. Vv. 980–988.

SECOND ROW. Above Row 1 on vault. (Fig. 162) 4. Directed by the Herdsman, Ivain comes to the storm-making spring in the forest of Broceliande. His dark brown steed, dappled with red and white, is tethered to a tree. He takes the golden bowl chained to another tree and is about to pour water from the spring upon a slab supported by columns. Two birds fly about in alarm. Vv. 989–998.

---

[1] J. Loth, *Mabinogion* (P., 1913), II, 1 n. C. Oman, *England before the Norman Conquest*, ed. 7 (L.), p. 243.

[2] *Fled Bricrend*, ed. G. Henderson (L., 1899), pp. 97–101. Cf. R. S. Loomis, *Celtic Myth*, pp. 68–71.

[3] *Beihefte zur Zeits. f. Romanische Phil.*, LXX, 131 ff.

[4] *PMLA*, XXXIX (1924), 485.

[5] J. G. Evans, *White Book Mabinogion* (Pwllheli, 1907), p. 112.

[6] *Zeits. f. Bildende Kunst*, N. F., XII (1901), 73. Cf. also O. Gerland, *Die Spätromanischen Wandmalereien im Hessenhof zu Schmalkalden* (Leipzig, 1896); *Bau- und Kunstdenkmäler im Regierungsbezirk Cassel*, V (Marburg, 1913), Textband, pp. 206–215; Tafelband, pl. 119–122.

[7] Hartmann v. Aue, *Iwein*, ed. E. Henrici (Halle, 1891). Certain MSS give the form Iwan or Ywan; cf. *ibid.*, pp. 522 f.

5. Ivain encounters on horseback the lord of the spring, whom Hartmann calls Ascalon, Chrétien Esclados, and who bears the charge of an eagle on his shield. Vv. 999–1028.

6. Ivain gallops after the fatally wounded Ascalon, who turns in his saddle to ward off a blow. Vv. 1051–61.

7. Ivain, passing under the gate-tower of Ascalon's castle, is trapped by the fall of a portcullis, and his steed is cut in two. The halves of the animal are barely traceable on the two sides of the tower. The lovely maiden Lunete is shown reaching out from the window of a second tower and giving the hero a ring, which renders him invisible. Vv. 1111–1210.

THIRD ROW. Above Row 2 on vault. (Fig. 163) 8. Ascalon lies dead in his armor on a bed. Beside him stand three courtiers and his wife Laudine, wringing her hands. Vv. 1305–16.

9. Between two towers Ivain stands, rendered invisible by the ring, while several knights search the space with their swords in vain. Vv. 1370–80.

10. Ivain's friend, Lunete, kneels before her mistress, Laudine, and urges her to take Ivain for her husband. Vv. 1788–862.

11. Ivain stands meekly with hands crossed, before Laudine, while Lunete, holding his sword (?), pleads his cause. Vv. 2248–81.

FOURTH ROW. Middle of vault. (Fig. 164) 12. With Lunete standing at her right, Ivain at her left, Laudine, seated in state, proclaims to her vassals her choice of a husband. Vv. 2385–415. This scene is reproduced from the original wall painting in Fig. 159.

13. Ivain clasps Laudine in his arms, while three courtiers and a priest witness their raptures. Vv. 2418–20.

14. Ivain and Laudine lie in bed together. Vv. 2422–23.

NORTH WALL, LUNETTE. (Fig. 160) 15. Under a conventional foliate border we see the wedding banquet, painted at the moment when Laudine proposes a toast to her husband. She raises her cup, as do other courtiers, both seated and standing. At the right a minstrel in yellow and white robe of a zigzag pattern beats a drum and plays a flute. Weber was able to discern in front of the table, below the figure of Ivain and at the left, the almost obliterated figures of a fiddler and a flute-player.

FIFTH ROW. Below Row 4 on vault. (Fig. 165) This row reverses the usual order and runs from right to left. 16. Arthur, who has come with his knights to try the adventure of the spring, pours water on the slab. The ensuing tempest is indicated by hail-stones before his face. Vv. 2529–39.

17. Ivain, who is now the defender of the spring, hurls Kay from his saddle. Storm clouds hang above their heads. Vv. 2551–86.

18. Ivain, bearing the eagle shield of Ascalon, rides toward Arthur, leading Kay's captured horse. Vv. 2601–02.

19. All that we can reconstruct of this scene is a knight with a sword on the right, and two ladies on the left. Probably this depicts the return of Ivain to his castle. Vv. 2653–82.

SIXTH ROW. Below Row 5 on vault. (Fig. 166) 20. Probably we have here the departure of Ivain from his bride. The figures on the left are perhaps Lunete, Laudine, and Arthur. Vv. 2956–68.

21. After a long gap in the story, Ivain rides forth into the forest after taking leave of the Lady of Noroison. Vv. 3819–27.

22. Intervening in a fight between a lion and a dragon, he strikes with his sword at the dragon's head. He thus wins the gratitude and loyal service of the lion. Vv. 3834–64.

Weber noted a marked resemblance between these paintings and the illustrations of the Munich *Tristan* MS. (Figs. 359–366) In both, the rows are divided by plain narrow borders, in which the names of the characters are written over their heads; trees are similar and show the same heart-shaped leaves; crowns are rendered by simple circlets, sometimes broadening to a blunt apex in front; Laudine always, Ysolt often, wears a band reaching from her crown under her chin; dappled horses are common, and those painted in scenes 4 and 16 at Schmalkalden display the same bulging chests as does Kaherdin's horse figured by Weber in Abb. 10. There are differences, however, which point to a later date for the MS: men's robes are shorter; horses frequently wear housings; helms show a simple convex outline in front; and the fashion of emphasizing the waist has come in.

It seems that the paintings date about 1250. The most archaic feature is the helm, with its flat, projecting top, which is found on German seals used in the second decade of the century.[8] How much longer it remained fashionable is uncertain. Knee-cops, on the other hand, seem not to have come in till after 1250, and chin-bands as a part of a lady's coiffure are found in the lovely *Poire* MS. (Figs. 202, 203) The latter may be dated about 1260,[9] and a slightly earlier date seems appropriate for the Schmalkalden frescoes.

IVAIN ON THE FREIBURG EMBROIDERY

Two scenes from the romance of Ivain occur on an embroidery in the Augustinermuseum at Freiburg in Breisgau.[10] It came from Kloster Adelhausen, but was originally made, as the armorial shields and the names Anna and Iohannes at the two ends indicate, for Johannes Malterer and his wife, of Freiburg. He was, like Niklas Vintler of Schloss Runkelstein, a banker and made a fortune by loans to spendthrift nobles. Though in a document of 1323 he is styled "der mezzier" (butcher), it is probable that this means simply that he was overseer or owner of a

---

[8] G. A. Seyler, *Geschichte der Siegel* (Leipzig, 1894), fig. 132, 211.

[9] Cf. *infra* p. 89.

[10] H. Schweitzer, "*Bilderteppiche und Stickereien in der städtischen Altertümersammlung zu Freiburg*," Sonderabdruck, *Schauinsland*, XXXI (1904).

slaughter-house; at any rate, his trade connections did not prevent his marrying his daughters to a "Markgraf" and a "Ritter." Two years before his death in 1360 the name of his wife is recorded as Gisela, and he is supposed to have wedded her about 1335. By inference, the name Anna, which appears on the embroidery, is that of an earlier wife, and these facts fit in with the style of the embroidery to place it about 1325. The embroidery is 16 feet long by 26 inches wide, and is in excellent condition. As usual, the design is worked on linen with a woolen flat stitch. The whole is surrounded with a border of light brown with a wild-rose pattern running through it.[11] Within this border is a series of eleven yellow decorative frames reminiscent of stained-glass design. The spaces between them are red, filled with a white and green flower pattern. In the frames, against a blue background, are the two armorial shields mentioned above, and nine scenes representing: Samson and the lion, Delilah cutting Samson's locks, Aristotle in his study tempted by Phyllis, Aristotle ridden by Phyllis, Virgil arranging an assignation with his mistress, Virgil hanging in a basket from a tower, the two scenes from Ivain, and the virgin and the unicorn. As Schweitzer remarked, there is in all this a clear-cut moral for womankind, to be compared with that in the Constance murals and the Parisian romance caskets.[12] Samson, Aristotle, and Virgil were the stock examples of men brought to shame by female wiles. Laudine, we have observed, married all too hastily her husband's slayer, whereas the unicorn could only be attracted and conquered by a chaste woman.

The first illustration of the Ivain romance (Fig. 167) depicts a light blue spring, a brown block of stone, and a cup standing on it. A gray cloud hangs above, from which red rays of lightning and huge balls of hail descend. Ivain, a brown lion's head decorating his helm, crumples Ascalon with a blow on his crowned helm. The designer in an effort to adjust the figures to his space has represented both combatants on foot, not mounted, as in the literary versions or the Schmalkalden paintings.

In the next frame we see Lunete in a white robe holding up the magic ring and presenting to her mistress Ivain, who wears a red surcoat and carries a white shield with a brown rampant lion. Laudine sits on a throne, clasping her hands in the stress of conflicting emotions.

IVAIN ON ENGLISH MISERICORDS

Ivain is the only romance of Chrétien's of which an English redaction has survived, *Ywain and Gawain*, one of the best English Arthurian poems, composed in the North in the first half of the fourteenth cen-

tury.[13] One scene (vv. 673–683) seems to have struck the fancy of some English carver in wood, just as it later appealed to the inventor of Baron Munchausen; namely, the portcullis slicing the hero's horse in two. The carver had several imitators, for there are five misericords on which Bond identified the scene:[14] at Chester Cathedral, at Lincoln Cathedral, at Boston church, in the chapel at New College, Oxford, and (formerly) at St. Peter per Mountergate church, Norwich. The similarity of treatment renders unnecessary the reproduction of more than three examples. Unlike the Parisian miniaturist (Fig. 261) and the Schmalkalden painter (Fig. 162), the original carver visualized the incident from the rear, so that we see the front of the towered gateway, the descending portcullis, and the rump of the unfortunate steed.

The Lincoln misericord (Fig. 168) is not only an excellent bit of carving but also deserves from one author of this book grateful notice as the seed from which the work has grown. Mr. S. Smith, of Lincoln, generously lent to an unknown American student in 1911 Bond's book on misericords, which first suggested a comprehensive study of the iconography of Arthurian romance. The Boston misericord (Fig. 169), made in the same county, is perhaps a copy, though very crude, of the Lincoln example. Both probably date from the last quarter of the fourteenth century. The carving from New College, Oxford, (Fig. 170) dates from about 1480.

THE WIGALOIS MURALS AT RUNKELSTEIN

Gawain's son Guiglain or Guinglain appears fleetingly in some confused and obviously traditional episodes of the *Conte del Graal*. He is also the hero of the early French romance, *Le Bel Inconnu*, by Renaut de Beaujeu, and of its English cognate, *Libeaus Desconus*. His name recalls that of the famous Ulster hero Cúchulainn, though there is little close parallelism between their stories.[15] The name Guiglain was influenced probably by the name of the Breton saint Guingalois (the French form of Winwaloe), passed on to Germany, and was given the form Wigalois by the Austrian poet Wirnt von Gravenberg, when he adapted a long French version of the hero's adventures, now lost.[16] A zealous admirer of Hartmann von Aue and Wolfram von Eschenbach, Wirnt finished about 1210 a poem concerning Wigalois' birth in the faery world and the many perils through which he passed to find his father and to win fame and a bride. To his French source Wirnt doubtless added some features, such as

---

[11] Cf. colored pl. in Schweitzer's article.
[12] Cf. *supra* pp. 37, 66.
[13] Ed. G. Schleich (Oppeln, Leipzig, 1887).
[14] Francis Bond, *Woodcarvings in English Churches, Miseri-*

cords (Oxford, 1910), pp. 76 f. Dates pp. 226 f.
[15] *PMLA*, XLIII (1928), 394 f.
[16] Wirnt v. Gravenberc, *Wigalois*, ed. J. M. Kapteyn (Bonn, 1926).

the giantess Ruel, for such ferocious females are absent from the matter of Britain. The *Wigalois* achieved great popularity, as is shown by the thirty-five medieval MSS extant in whole or in part, by the *Volksbuch* of 1472, and by the inspiration it afforded the miniaturist of the Leyden MS[17] and one of the painters at Runkelstein.

This Tyrolese castle has already been described in connection with the paintings of Gottfried's *Tristan* and the triads which adorn the second storey of the Summer House. Beneath this storey is a *loggia*, cut off from the courtyard by arches but open to the air. It was doubtless cooler on summer evenings than the rooms overhead, and furnished the Vintlers and their ladies a pleasant retreat for sweetmeats and drink and chat while the sunlight faded slowly from the mountain-tops. The upper surfaces of the walls were once covered with murals in black and white on a pale green ground, and the subjects were the Liberal Arts and the adventures of Wigalois.

Exposure to the weather, the signatures of countless fools, the collapse of a part of the north wall, which also carried away scenes from the Tristram and Garel series above, have left these paintings in a bad state. Rather than attempt photographs of the poor remains, it has seemed better to reproduce the copies which Graf Waldstein published in 1892.[18] He identified the subjects through the occurrence of the name "Vigelas" in several scenes, and pointed out the mention of a "Vigelas sal" in an inventory of 1493. This series has suffered less apparently from the restorer than the paintings above, for he confined himself to inserting red splotches to represent blood and flames. The original painter was perhaps the same as that of the Tristram series, also done in grisaille, but the latter have been so drastically restored that accurate conclusions are difficult. Waldstein believed that only half of the original number of Wigalois subjects were left; these run in two rows around the south and west walls.

UPPER ROW, beginning at left end of west wall.
1. (Fig. 171) On the left, Guinevere from the battlements of Karidol returns the magic girdle to King Joram, which he, a stranger knight, had given her. At the right the knights of the Round Table sally forth from the gates to accept Joram's challenge to fight for the girdle. Vv. 407–450.

2. (Fig. 172) Joram overthrows all his antagonists. When Gawain appears on the scene, the stranger dons his magic girdle and by its virtue wins first with spear and then with sword until the usually invincible Gawain is forced to yield. Then they ride off together through a rocky wood, and Joram bestows the girdle on Gawain. The painter shows the ground strewn with knights and horses, "Gavein" raising his right hand in surrender, and again riding away with the victor. Vv. 559–627.

3. (Fig. 173) As the two knights approach King Joram's castle, they are welcomed by knights and squires. The painting here seems to abandon the standard MS version and to follow that which is represented by the *Volksbuch* of 1472, which mentions the fair Florie, Joram's niece, as the first to meet her uncle and his guest. Vv. 680–84.

A gap occurs at this point, for a part of 4 and the whole of 5, 6, and 7 were removed during the restoration under the Emperor Franz Joseph. According to Waldstein, 4 depicted Gawain feasting beside his host; 5 and 6 could not be identified, and 7 showed Gawain riding away from Lady Florie, to whom, as his wife, he had given the magic girdle. Beyond this point the collapse of the north wall carried away still other scenes, of which we have no record whatsoever. When the paintings recommence over one of the arches of the south wall, they concern the adventures of Gawain's son, Wigalois, "der Ritter mit dem Rade," immediately after his defeat of Hojir, the Red Knight. The wheel which decks his helm may have a remote connection with one or another of Cúchulainn's adventures with a wheel, and possibly originated in a solar symbol.

8. (Fig. 174) With the maiden messenger Nereja, the hero comes one evening upon a rich pavilion, with fifty spears set up around it. King Schaffilun entertains them that night, but requires the satisfaction of a combat the next morning, giving Wigalois a fresh horse, twenty-five spears, and six squires. The outcome is fatal for the king. The painter has shown Nereja and the squires in the background, the slain knight and his horse beside the pavilion with its spears, and Wigalois in an attitude of triumph. The curved extensions of the saddle-bow which protect the hero's legs are noticeable in this and the following scenes. Vv. 3297–564.

9. (Fig. 175) Wigalois and Nereja approach the city of Roimunt. The steward rides out to meet them, and, after some militant preliminaries, respectfully invites them in. He does not bear as his crest the prosaic dish which the poet ascribes to him as the badge of his office. Vv. 3885–966.

10. (Fig. 176) Wigalois follows the crowned beast, the dead King of Korntin. Though Wirnt described it as having a leopard's head (vv. 3877–8) the painter has given it a human face, perhaps to suggest the human nature of the transformed king, "Jorel." Vv. 4504–09.

11. (Fig. 177) Within the precincts of the night-burning castle to which the hero has been led, Wigalois encounters a great number of knights in black armor, the souls of those who have been slain with their king and had to endure with him a purgatorial penance. As they encounter Wigalois, their spear-heads and shafts burst into flame and force him to withdraw. Vv. 4555–83.

12. (Fig. 178) The King of Korntin, transformed back into human shape, holds in his hands the spear which alone could avail in Wigalois' coming combat with the dragon Pfetan. According to the poet, the king shone like the sun and merely pointed to the spear stuck in the wall of his castle,—two features which the artist has disregarded. Vv. 4626–761.

---

[17] Cf. *infra* pp. 134 f.

[18] *Mittheilungen der K. K. Centralcommision*, N. F., XVIII (1892), 34, 83, 129.

13. (Fig. 179) After telling Wigalois that he is Gawain's son and encouraging him to win the Princess Larie, the spectral king returns to the form of a beast and enters his castle followed by the black knights. Above their heads the painter has written the words "die brinnenselen," (the burning souls), and below the beast is the name "Jorel," which Wirnt did use twice, though elsewhere he gave the king the name "Lar." Vv. 4836–58.

The LOWER ROW of paintings on the west wall begins under the scene numbered 1.

14. (Fig. 180) "Vigelas," riding with the magic spear in hand, meets the disconsolate lady "Belekar." She is mourning for her husband "Moral," who lies clutched in the coils of the dragon "Pfetan." Vv. 4866–960.

15. (Fig. 181) Wigalois rides against the rampant dragon, whose tail is still coiled about "Graf Moral." Vv. 5012–99.

16. (Fig. 182) On the ceiling of the embrasure, on the right, is represented the dead dragon, his tail coiled around Wigalois' horse. On the left is the unconscious hero being stripped of his armor by a fisherman and his wife. Vv. 5288–360.

17. (Fig. 183) On the right wall of the embrasure is shown "Belekar" coming with her maidens to the hero's aid. According to the poem, he came to life as he lay on the seashore, and recovered his memory by virtue of some magic bread and a blossom which he carried in his pouch. He then, on the approach of the ladies, retired to a cave. The painter has synchronized these two incidents. A little further on, Wigalois is depicted on foot entering the castle of Belekar, and finally at the extreme right, riding forth from the castle to punish the enchanter Roaz. Vv. 5917–6253.

Many and terrible were the adventures which Wirnt related of this journey, but of the paintings which reproduced them nothing is left. Before the last "restoration," which destroyed them entirely, Waldstein identified the following scenes but left no record of the details. 18. Wigalois is carried away into a cave by the gigantic wild woman Ruel, who is probably the "Riel" painted on the balcony above among the three giantesses, as described on p. 49. The painting showed a rocky cave and Ruel herself. 19. The hero fights with the dwarf knight Karrioz, who guards the road to Glois. Vv. 6601 ff. 20. He finds in the gateway at the end of a bridge a turning water-wheel, from which swords and clubs project. Vv. 6775 ff. 21. He pursues the monster, half man, half beast, whose name "Maryen" was recorded in the picture. Vv. 6932 ff.

A comparison of these paintings with the miniatures of the Leyden MS of *Wigalois* (Figs. 367–373), some of which are described in Chapter XII, demonstrates the far superior imaginative power of the monk of Amelungsborn, Jan von Brunswik. This miniaturist was a romantic soul, who retained the uncanny details of his original with obvious delight. Flaming knights, enchanted beasts, a combat by candlelight—all are done not only with rich color and dramatic force, but also with a sense of glamor. The Tyrolese painter was a dull soul. The flaming knights in scenes 11 and 13 are reduced to commonplace types; the spectral king, Jorel, in scenes 10 and 13 owes his eerie smile not to the painter's original fancy but to the picture of an Apocalyptic beast in a French MS now in Dresden.[19] As an imaginative conception, he cannot approach the sinister black panther, mounting the amazing battlements of the purgatorial castle as depicted by Jan von Brunswik. (Fig. 370)

THE GAREL MURALS AT RUNKELSTEIN

Niklas Vintler, or whoever chose the subjects to be painted in his Summer House at Runkelstein, selected besides Gottfried's *Tristan* and Wirnt von Gravenberg's *Wigalois* the long romance of *Garel von dem Blühenden Tal*, composed between 1260 and 1280 by Der Pleier, a prolific author of the Salzburg district.[20] The hero owes his name probably to the Welsh Gware of the Golden Hair, who became in French Gaeres or Gaheret and in Malory Gareth, who, be it remembered, was still to be singled out in the *mêlée* by his yellow hair,—perhaps a survival of earlier tradition, since in the twelfth century and later the hair of the knight in combat was hidden under his helm.[21] But the Austrian poet knew no French romance of his hero; he simply took the name in the form Garel from one of the German poems with which he was familiar, borrowed the designation, *von dem Blühenden Tal*, and concocted a new story which had nothing to do with the Gaheret or Gareth of traditional romance. To be sure, Garel is still a nephew of Arthur's, like his prototype, but he is not even a brother of Gawain's, and his home is not Lothian or Orkney, but the Austrian province of Styria, which in 1240 saw that historic Don Quixote, Ulrich von Lichtenstein, riding at adventure in the guise of King Arthur and breaking spears with knights whom he addressed as Kalocriant, Lanzilet, and Ywan. In fact, *Garel* like the author's other romances, is devoid of all Celtic glamour, and except for a few giants and dwarfs is an idealized picture of thirteenth-century war and chivalry. The Round Table feast owes nothing to the baffling traditions of the Bretons,[22] but seems to reflect the contemporary festivals, called Round Tables, of which we hear in the chronicles of Cyprus, England, Germany, and France.[23] Der Pleier has used Arthurian names and a few of the most banal situations from Hartmann, Wolfram, and Wirnt, has fitted them together into a

[19] R. Bruck, *Malereien in den Handschriften des Königreichs Sachsen* (1906), p. 151.
[20] Ed. M. Walz (Freiburg, 1892). Paintings identified, p. 329.
[21] R. S. Loomis, *Celtic Myth*, pp. 84, 86 f.

[22] *Mod. Lang. Notes*, XLIV (1929), 511.
[23] R. S. Loomis, article in *Medieval Studies in Memory of A. Kingsley Porter* (Harvard University Press).

coherent plot, and concluded most edifyingly with the chivalrous treatment of enemies, the marriage of all the gallant princes to the unattached ladies, and the founding of a monastery on the site of the great battle. But his work is a document in the *Kulturgeschichte* of High Germany rather than a great poem.

The illustrations at Runkelstein adorn the walls of what has been called the library, in the northwest corner of the Summer House over the Wigalois *Saal*, but if the room served any such purpose, there are no signs of it. (Fig. 184) It boasts a stone chimney-piece, carved with heraldic escutcheons, as if it had been a gathering place in winter, as was the Wigalois *Saal* in summer. The history of the frescoes is much like that of the Tristram and Wigalois series; they were made probably about 1400, were repainted in the sixteenth century, and suffered much from neglect and damage in the nineteenth. They have fared better than the Wigalois paintings, but not so well as the Tristram group. Of the original twenty-two, only ten are preserved; of the rest which have perished, seven are known through the crude outlines published by Seelos. Probably the original painter was the same who did the triads in the gallery outside; he uses similar color. Since he depicts the same wide-sleeved surcoats and beak-like helms as are found in the Tristram and Wigalois series, his date cannot be far distant. It may be noted that his method of painting plant-forms over some of his foregrounds is reminiscent of the garderobe frescoes at Avignon (c. 1340) and the S. Floret paintings already described (c. 1350).[24] Apparently he worked not directly from the poem but from instructions which were very explicit on certain matters, such as heraldry, but vague on what may seem more important matters, such as the shape of the monster Vulgan. This supposition would also explain why in Scene 12 we find such an extraordinary blunder as the name "Amurat" inscribed over Garel himself. The romance frescoes begin at the right of the fireplace and run around the room. Below them is a series of half-figures of Old Testament men and women, now badly damaged.

Der Pleier opens his romance by telling us that Arthur was holding his Whitsun feast at Dinazarun before the forest of Priziljan,—the first place being Dinas Bran in North Wales,[25] and the second Broceliande in Brittany. Of course, geography in Arthurian romance is seldom consistent, but obviously we are here far from any authentic Celtic tradition. With this situation the paintings begin.

1. (Fig. 185) Before Arthur and his courtiers the notorious Meleagant (Meljacanz) rides up and demands

the queen. Arthur, having pledged his word, is obliged to yield, and the stranger rides away with her. We see Arthur enthroned on the left, pointing with outstretched arm to the abductor and his queen, mounted on the same horse, riding across the meadow. Vv. 45–60.

2. (Fig. 186) Consequent on this calamity, there arrives a young giant, "Karabin," in full armor, equipped with round shield, sword, helm, and a long pole, and delivers the defiance of King Ekunaver of Kanadic and the threat of invasion a year later. The painting represents "Artus," his courtiers, and a tower, much as in the previous scene. The giant kneels before the king, his hands crossed according to the best German etiquette. The painter has departed from the text in allowing Karabin to retain his arms instead of casting them aside. Vv. 220–280.

3. (Fig. 187) Meanwhile Garel, Prince of Styria, has returned to Arthur's court, and he now undertakes to follow the giant and spy out the land of Kanadic. He approaches the castle of Merkanie on a high hill, and sees before it sitting under a linden, an aged lord, a sparrowhawk on his fist, attended by his two sons. Above the hero is written "Her Garel," above the castle, "Merkanie," and above the lord of the castle appear "-sabin" and "-fabier," evidently the names of his daughter Sabie and of the commander of his knights Tjofabier, neither of whom is visible. Nor has the painter depicted the linden or the sons of the lord. The extreme clumsiness with which some restorer has done the arms and legs of Karabin contrasts strangely with the unusual realism of his face and that of the lord of Merkanie. Vv. 743–805.

4. (Fig. 188) Having learned that the next day Graf Gerhart will assault the castle, demanding the lovely Sabie as his bride, Garel sallies forth, hurls Rialt, a kinsman of Gerhart's, out of his saddle, sends him a prisoner back to Sabie, and then overthrows "Gerhart" himself. In typical medieval fashion the artist has represented both contests at once, and has shown Rialt as fallen under his destrier instead of lying a spear-length behind. Nor is there a trace of the onlookers. Vv. 1351–481.

Scenes 5 to 9 are known only from descriptions. 5. Garel is shown once more following the giant Karabin. Vv. 2134–47. 6. Garel and a newly acquired liegeman ride to the adventurous garden of Belamunt, where its guardian, a squire, stretches out his hand to them in courteous welcome. Vv. 3205–439. 7. Garel vanquishes Eskilabon, whose crest is an eagle, and claims his allegiance. Vv. 3490–626. 8. Nothing was visible except a richly caparisoned horse. 9. Garel overcomes a giant, Purdan, who blocks the road to Kanadic. Little was visible in the painting except Purdan's severed head, his armed trunk, and his steel pole. Vv. 5683–805.

10. (Fig. 189) Garel finds in Purdan's palace the Prince Claris in chains, releases him, blows a horn, and then hides with Claris. When three dwarfs enter bringing food and drink for the giant, Garel steps forth and with sword swung high bars the door. The dwarf king, Albewin, then offers his fealty. Later he gives Garel a magic ring and sword, of which the latter only is to be seen in the painting. Once more we have a synchronizing of two separate incidents.

[24] Cf. *supra* pp. 57 ff.

[25] *Miscellany of Studies in Honour of L. E. Kastner* (Camb., 1932), p. 342.

It is possible that the structure at the windows of which two persons appear is intended to depict the prison of Duzabel and her eleven maidens, whom Garel delivered on the same occasion. Vv. 6235–302, 6519–76.

Scenes 11 to 16 and scene 19 are known only from Seelos' published copies.

11. (Fig. 190) Duzabel and her maidens thank Garel for their deliverance. Garel is accompanied by Claris, and both are already armed and mounted,—features which do not accord with the text. In the background a solitary knight rides away, whose mysterious identity is hardly solved by the word "Ritter" over his head. Vv. 6728–61.

12. (Fig. 191) Duzabel and her maidens are welcomed back to the city of Turtus by her father Amurat and her kinsfolk. Her mother, whose name, Klarine, was once visible on the gate-tower, looks down with other ladies. Above to the left, Garel and Claris are riding on their way to the latter's home. The painter has departed from the text since he has shown the dwarf king accompanying Duzabel instead of Garel, and has inscribed the name "Amurat" over the hero. Vv. 6937–7018.

13. (Fig. 192) Implored by Laudamie, lady of the land of Anferre, Garel issues from her castle to do battle with the monster Vulgan, and strikes it with his spear. Here it would seem that the artist had only the vaguest directions to go by, for his monster is unrecognizable as the centaur, equipped with a club and magic shield, described by Der Pleier. Vv. 8141–55. Garel, forced to fight on foot, strikes off Vulgan's hand, the club falls, and the monster is promptly decapitated. As in previous pictures, the artist has treated the subject with complete independence and introduced an unmentioned victim, prostrate under Vulgan's attack. Vv. 8277–85.

14. (Fig. 193) Laudamie and her maidens welcome Garel back from his desperate conflict. The painting again differs from its source, since the poem expressly describes Garel as returning without shield and as meeting the ladies in the castle courtyard. Vv. 8529–51.

15. (Fig. 194) Laudamie in gratitude gives herself and her land to her deliverer and summons her vassals to swear allegiance to the new King of Anferre. The poem seems to place the recognition of Garel's sovranty as taking place in the palace, but the painter has shown the royal pair sitting on a platform under a pavilion. Above are the shields of Styria and Anferre. Vv. 9107–114.

16. (Fig. 195) On the left we see the huge army which Garel has assembled under his banner, marching against King Ekunaver. In the front rank we can distinguish Eskilabon with his eagle crest, Garel with his panther shield, and probably Tjofabier with his white and blue shield. The text, however, places Garel and his division in the rear. On the right, Garel accepts the outstretched hand of the giant Malseron, whom he has defeated in single combat. Vv. 10797–977, 11514–692.

17. (Fig. 196) Malseron with his three giant companions goes to the camp of Ekunaver, asks to be relieved of his oath of service, now transferred to Garel, and departs. Ekunaver summons his allied kings to council in a tent and receives Tjofrit, Garel's messenger, and hears his challenge. Once more the painter has combined two scenes in one. Malseron, with his pole, still stands with hand outstretched in entreaty before the king, but the rest of the details illustrate the later scene: Ekunaver with his five royal allies seated under a tent; their heraldic shields above them, the devices of which must have been carefully gleaned from a later passage (Vv. 14031–183); the armed retinue of Tjofrit under Garel's banner in the background; Tjofrit himself, dismounted from his horse and humbly approaching the tent with hands crossed. Vv. 12330–549.

18. (Fig. 197) The painting brings into one single mêlée the chief incidents of Garel's battle with Ekunaver. Near the centre the young hero with crowned helm is apparently thrusting a dagger into Ekunaver's arm. Above the combatants, the banner of Garel floats triumphant, while on the earth below lies the gryphon banner of his enemy. Above to the left, Gerhart holds down and with uplifted sword threatens King Helpherich, identified by the dragon on his jupon. Below, a knight in beaked helmet. who should be Eskilabon, is giving the *coup de grace* to Salatrias, recognizable by the winged Jupiter on the back of his white surcoat. Nevertheless, Eskilabon, with his eagle crest, appears to the right of the great banner, holding down and threatening with his sword some other royal foe. Further to the right, Gilan, with a rampant lion on his surcoat and a lion's head as his crest, attacks from behind King Angenis with a dragon shield. On the ground, crushed under his horse, lies Rubert von Gandin, identified by the stag banner beside him. Under the hind hoofs of Garel's horse is the wolf banner of Ardan. In view of the painter's carelessness in other matters, it is curious that he has scrupulously preserved every heraldic device of the potentates of heathenesse, except the rose of Amillot. Despite the confusion, this is the most effective of the murals in vigor of action, richness of color, the massing of blue helmets, and the patterning of swords and spears against the sky. Vv. 15421–978.

19. (Fig. 198) On the anniversary of the delivery of Ekunaver's challenge by Karabin, Arthur holds court again at Dinazarun. Guinevere has already been brought back by Lancelot. Garel is leading his victorious host to Dinazarun, including the four giants and the captive kings. Alone he encounters Kay, defeats him easily, and as he lies stunned, takes away his helm and sword, and sends him back horseless and weaponless to Arthur. Garel then sends Malseron as an emissary to Arthur with the spoils of Kay. Finding a horse much too small for him, the giant turns it over to a squire and stalks away as fast as the mounted squire can follow. At the left of the painting we see Garel's army; in the foreground the horses of Garel and Kay cropping the grass, and Garel taking the helm and sword of Kay, whose shattered spear and shield lie beside him. In the upper right corner are the badly damaged figures of Malseron and the squire. Vv. 17864–8381.

20. (Fig. 199) Accompanied by his princely companions and the four giants, Garel is welcomed by Arthur. The painter on his own initiative introduces among Garel's lords two captive kings, whereas according to the romance Ekunaver, Ardan, and Helpherich have already been received by Arthur. He also introduces Guinevere, mounted on a palfrey, at Arthur's left, and displays against the sky not only Garel's panther banner, but also Arthur's banner with the traditional device of three gold crowns. Vv. 19260–79.

21. (Fig. 200) Arthur, having been reconciled to Ekunaver and the other captive kings, accepts them and
Garel's princely allies into the order of the Table Round,
and the whole company and their wives take their places
at the famous table set out in a meadow. The poet's conception of the table is strange, for he speaks of it as having
four ends and capable of accommodating hundreds of
lords and ladies. The painter has naturally simplified this
in accordance with more traditional ideas: the table is
round, there are no ladies, and but eleven seated lords.
Arthur himself sits directly in front of the tree-trunk, Garel
on his right, and two captive kings on his left. The remaining seven cannot be identified. The standing seneschal on
the right has lifted his hand; a trumpeter and a flutist
sound a joyous note, and one hungry companion of the
order already reaches out to help himself from the large
central platter. The pennant attached to the trumpet
bears the device of three crowns. Vv. 20012–93.

22. (Fig. 201) The last painting of the series is the
hardest to connect with any particular situation. Obviously we have the return of Garel and his army under
the panther banner, his helm perched on his right shoulder
and his shield hung on his left arm, just as we see Wigalois
in scenes 12 and 13 of his series. But which of various
castles Garel is approaching, what old gentleman is politely
raising his cap, and what crowned lady observes the arrival from a balcony, seems impossible to tell. Of course,
the natural supposition is that Garel is returning to his
queen, Laudamie of Anferre, but if so, the painter has
been remarkably successful in rendering her insignificant,
if not invisible. Vv. 21010–34(?)

Thus ends this series of mural paintings at Runkelstein, and with it our consideration of the illustrations of the *Matière de Bretagne* in the decorative
arts, outside the MSS and printed books. It is an
ironic circumstance that the art of mural painting,
which reached such heights of splendor in the religious art of the Middle Ages,—and which to judge
from the literary descriptions quoted in Chapter II,
should have furnished plentiful and lavish illustration of the legends of Arthur—is represented in extant remains only by the frescoes of S. Floret and
Runkelstein, two small and inconsiderable provincial
castles, and by the decorations of two obscure houses
at Schmalkalden and Lübeck. Of the great royal and
princely castles, of the tremendous fortresses of the
knightly orders in Prussia and the Holy Land, of the
larger town-houses and palaces, not one has preserved
on its walls a trace of Arthurian story. Partly the
result of pure accident, this state of things is also the
result of the fact that the great buildings were more
likely to be renovated than the obscure towers and
holds in the mountains. We are more fortunate in
our MSS, for there are still preserved not a few richly
illustrated books which were destined for royal and
princely patrons. We know that it was a common
practice to use illuminated MSS as sources for wall
designs, and if we may be permitted to use our imaginations upon these surviving miniatures, and en-
large them to the proper scale, we may form some
conception of what we have lost in the great murals
that have perished.

PART II

BOOK ILLUSTRATION

ABBREVIATIONS AND BRIEF REFERENCES
FOR MANUSCRIPTS*

Additional	MS Additional, British Museum, London
Ars.	MS in Bibliothèque de l'Arsenal, Paris
Berlin	MS in Preussische Staatsbibliothek, Berlin
B. N.	MS in Bibliothèque Nationale, Paris
Berne	MS in Stadtbibliothek, Berne
Brussels	MS in Bibliothèque Royale, Brussels
Chantilly	MS in Musée Condé, Chantilly
Cotton	MS in Cotton Collection, British Museum
Douce	MS in Douce Collection, Bodleian Library, Oxford
Dresden	MS in Sächsische Landesbibliothek, Dresden
Egerton	MS in Egerton Collection, British Museum
Florence	MS in Biblioteca Nazionale, Florence
Fr.	MS in Cabinet des MSS, Fonds français, Bibliothèque Nationale, Paris
Harl.	MS in Harleian Collection, British Museum
Lambeth	MS in Lambeth Palace Library, London
Leyden	MS in Bibl. Ryks-Universitet, Leyden
Munich	MS in Bayerische Staatsbibliothek, Munich
Nouv. acq.	MSS nouvelles acquisitions, Bibliothèque Nationale, Paris
Pal. germ.	MS in Collection Palatina germ., Universitäts-Bibliothek, Heidelberg
Phillipps	MS in Phillipps Collection, Thirlestane House, Cheltenham, England
Royal	MS in Royal Collection, British Museum
Rylands	MS in John Rylands Library, Manchester, England
SFRMP	Bulletin de la Société Française de Reproductions de Miniatures à Peinture
Vienna	MS in Stadtsbibliothek, Vienna

* On the selection and arrangement of MS material in Part II see *supra*, pp. 7–8.

1274   Paris B. N. Fr. 342, f. 234 v. Vulgate Cycle. Dated by scribe. (Cf. Frappier, *Mort Artu*, p. xvi). *Infra*, p. 93, Figs. 213–216 (N. French).

1278   Paris B. N. Fr. 750, f. 316. Prose *Tristan*. Dated and signed by scribe, Petrus de Tiergevilla. (Cf. Vinaver, *Tristan, Études*, p. 42). *Infra*, p. 92, Figs. 210–212 (Spanish).

1286   Bonn Univ. Bibl. 526, f. 489 v. Vulgate Cycle. Dated and signed by scribe, Arnulfus de Kayo qui est Ambianis. (Cf. Frappier, *Mort Artu*, p. xxv). *Infra*, p. 94, Figs. 217–223 (N. French).

1303   Rennes Bibl. Munic. 593, f. 170 v, 284, 299 v. *Prophecies de Merlin*. Dated and signed three times by scribe, Robin de Boutemont. (Cf. Paton, *Prophecies*, p. 4). *Infra*, p. 91 n. 15.

1316   London Br. Mus. Add. 10292, f. 55 v. Vulgate Cycle. Miniature bears date on tomb. (Sommer, *Estoire*, I, xxvi). *Infra*, p. 97, Fig. 248 (N. French).

1323   Cologne Hist. Archiv 88, f. 263. *Tristan*. Dated by scribe. (Cf. Gottfried von Strassburg, *Tristan*, ed. K. Marold, Leipzig, 1912, p. xli). *Infra*, p. 134 n. 15 (German).

1344   Paris B. N. Fr. 122, f. 322. Vulgate Cycle. Dated by scribe. (Cf. Frappier, *op. cit.*, p. xiv.) *Infra*, p. 103, Figs. 267–268 (French).

1350   Leyden Rijks-Univ. 195, f. 182. *Walewein*. Dated by scribe. (Byvanck, *MSS . . . des Pays-Bas*, p. 93). *Infra*, p. 124 (Dutch).

1351   Paris Ars. 5218, f. 91 v. *Queste*. Dated, signed, and illuminated by scribe, Pierart dou Tielt. (Cf. Martin, *Gaz. des Beaux-Arts*, CIII, 90). *Infra*, p. 123, Fig. 341 (Flemish).

1357   Cheltenham, Phillipps 1045, f. 631. *Estoire, Merlin*. Dated by scribe Jehan de Loles, niés de Hainaut. *Infra*, p. 91 n. 16 (N. French).

1372   Leyden Rijks-Univ. 537, f. 118. *Wigalois*. Dated, signed, and illuminated by scribe, Jan von Brunswik. (Cf. Byvanck, *MSS . . . des Pays-Bas*, p. 96). *Infra*, p. 134, Figs. 367–374 (German).

1399   Paris B. N. 335–336. Prose *Tristan*. Dated by scribe. (Cf. Vinaver, *Tristan, Études*, p. 41). *Infra*, p. 105, Figs. 277–278 (French).

1420   Heidelberg Univ. Bibl. Palzgerm. 371, f. 177. *Lanzelot*. Dated by scribe. (Cf. Wegener, *HSS. Heidelberger Bibl.*, p. 18). *Infra*, p. 136, Fig. 375–376 (German).

1463   Paris B. N. Fr. 99, f. 775. Prose *Tristan*. Dated and signed by scribe, Micheau Gonnot de la Brouce, prestre, demourant a Crousant. (Cf. Vinaver, *Tristan, Études*, p. 38). *Infra*, p. 109, Figs. 292–295 (French).

1466   Vienna 2539–2540. Prose *Tristan*. Dated by scribe. (Cf. Vinaver, *Tristan, Études*, p. 57).

1467   Berne Stadtbibl. AA 91, *Parzival*. Dated and signed by scribe, Joh. Stemhein de Constanica. (Cf. Benziger, *Parzival*, p. 7). *Infra*, p. 137, Figs. 380–383 (German).

1468   Brussels Bibl. Roy. 9243, f. 295 v. *Chroniques de Hainaut*. Signed and dated by scribe, Jacotin de Bos on Dec. 8, 1449. Illuminated in 1468 by Guillaume Vrelant and payments recorded. (Cf. Leroquais, *Brév. de Phillippe le Bon*, p. 150). *Infra*, p. 126, Figs. 343–348 (Flemish).

1470   Paris B. N. Fr. 112, f. 233. Prose *Lancelot*. Dated and signed by scribe, Micheau Gantelet, prestre, demeurant an la ville de Tournay. (Frappier, p. xiii). *Infra*, p. 110, Figs. 297–298 (French).

1479–80   Chantilly Condé 315–317. Prose *Tristan*. Signed by scribe, Gilles Gassien natif de la ville de Poictiers. (Vinaver, *Tristan*, *Études*, p. 50.) Illuminated by Evrard d'Espingues and payments recorded. (Cf. Guibert, *Ext. Mem. Soc. Nat. et Arch. de la Creuse*, 1895, p. 8.) *Infra*, p. 110, Fig. 296 (French).

1480   Brussels Bibl. Roy. 9246, f. *Estoire*. Dated and signed by scribe, Guillaume de la Pierre. *Infra*, p. 111, Figs. 299–302 (French).

CHAPTER VIII

FRENCH MANUSCRIPTS, 1250-1340

LITERARY romance, as we have already seen, flowered suddenly and richly in France in the second half of the twelfth century. Chrétien de Troyes in his *Ivain* gives a pleasant picture of a lord in his garden, lying on a silken rug, enjoying a maiden's reading of some romance. To provide such a gracious diversion, both in France and in the French-speaking court of Anglo-Norman England, French Arthurian poems were composed in abundance: short lais, like the *Lai du Cor* (c. 1150) by Robert Biket, or the *Lanval* and *Chievrefoil* of that witty lady who called herself Marie de France; long verse translations by the Norman poet Wace and others of Geoffrey of Monmouth's renowned *Historia*, and still longer courtly romances in verse by Chrétien, by the Anglo-Norman Thomas, by poets such as Béroul, Robert de Boron, Renaut de Beaujeu, Raoul de Houdenc, Paien de Maisiéres, and others whose names have been lost in the vast anonymity of the Middle Ages.[1]

Despite this prolific production of French Arthurian poets, despite the amazing diffusion of Arthurian stories, it is probable that before 1200 there were comparatively few copies of the romances. No twelfth-century MS of any Arthurian poem is known. Like practically all the contemporary texts of Geoffrey of Monmouth's *Historia*,[2] which (being generally regarded as true) was often copied in monastic scriptoria, the poems too must have been copied in small, plain, unadorned MSS. Monks alone in that century were the masters of beautiful bookmaking, and they were not to be tempted from their slowly learned and deeply conventionalized craft by the new and unholy glorifications of mundane love and adventure. The Arthurian romances of the day were meant to be read aloud by clerks of princely households or by maidens who did not count; the manuscripts were not intended for the aesthetic delight of lordly owners, many of whom were not, even in the late twelfth century, any too literate themselves. Even the remarkably cultured Baldwin, Count of Guines (1165-1205), who had a large private library of his own, a rare thing at the time, nevertheless seems to have preferred to hear, rather than to read, tales of Tristram and Ysolt, of Arthur and Merlin, of Roland and Charlemagne, and of Crusaders in Jerusalem and Antioch.[3]

In the thirteenth century the spread of courtly culture created a demand which lay scribes found it more and more profitable to satisfy, and MSS of chronicles, romances, fabliaux, songs, and treatises of a moral and didactic sort, rapidly multiplied. In the last quarter of this century lay illuminators began seriously to concern themselves with these secular MSS. By 1292 there were in Paris, according to the Tax Book[4] of that year, at least seventeen lay illuminators who lived in the city, mainly in the neighborhood of the University, some in the street now known as Rue de la Boutebrie. Among the native French scribes and illuminators were also a few foreigners, Jehan l'Englois and Guillaume l'Écossais, who shared in this, the beginning of true trade competition in the making of books.

Although lay illuminators are thus first heard of in Paris, where a notable school of French illumination, under the encouragement of Saint Louis and his royal mother, Blanche of Castile, was brilliantly developed before 1270, it was not in courtly Paris that the larger number of extant thirteenth-century illustrated copies of Arthurian romances were produced. The majority of these were written by Picard scribes and decorated by North French and early Franco-Flemish artists. In wealthy Picardy and the Pas de Calais, in Artois, in Hainaut, in Flanders, the nobility seem to have had a special enthusiasm for Arthurian legend,[5] and the artists of these regions became the first regular illuminators of Arthurian texts. They lacked the extreme refinement and sophistication of the best Parisian artists, but they shared in the freer artistic impulses that came from across the Channel.

THE *ROMAN LE LA POIRE*

To this North French, Franco-Flemish region has been ascribed a MS containing two of the earliest and most charming illustrations of Arthurian poetry, though the text itself is not of the romances. This beautiful little volume contains the *Roman de la Poire* (Fr. 2186), a poem composed, copied, and decorated about 1260. Though the poet praises Paris as the place "ou Amors fu nez et noris" (v. 1332), the rimes show traces of Picard influence, and the broad round handwriting with its flat-headed *t*'s is of a type unlike Parisian script.[6] The aristocratic poet tells of his love for a high-born lady who had

---

[1] Cf. U. T. Holmes, *History of Old French Literature* (Chapel Hill, 1937), pp. 157-184, 278-299, for convenient bibliographical treatment of Arthurian literature.

[2] See *infra*, p. 122.

[3] Lambert of Ardres, *Mon. Germ. Hist. Scriptorum* (Hanover, 1879), XXIV, 607; A. Luchaire, *Social France* (N. Y., 1929), pp. 372, 379.

[4] Henry Martin, *La miniature française du XIII au XV siècle* (P., 1923), pp. 13 ff.

[5] R. S. Loomis, "Chivalric and Dramatic Imitations of Arthurian Romance," in *Medieval Studies in Memory of A. Kingsley Porter* (Harvard University Press).

[6] Ed. by F. Stehlich, *Li Romanz de la Poire* (Halle, 1881), pp. 13, 30. See also G. Graf von Vitzthum von Eckstaedt, *Die*

once given him a miraculous pear, and the artist has several times represented the lover and his lady.[7] Always they wear royal blue crossed with gold and starred with the golden lilies of France, a costume suggestive of royal connections. The lover-poet has much to say of Fortune, the goddess who, with her wheel, is represented on f. 2 v, and also of the great lovers of story who have suffered Fortune's weal and woe. The illustrations depicting these legendary lovers show Pyramus and Thisbe (f. 7 v), whispering through little tubes into the unfeeling wall, Paris and Helen (f. 9 v), and most notably, two pairs of Arthurian lovers, Cliges and his Fenice (Fig. 202), and Tristram and Ysolt[8] (Fig. 203).

On each of the two leaves devoted to the Arthurian lovers two scenes are set forth in golden quatrefoils, one below the other, against a chequered background, and the whole is set within a patterned frame. On a small scale the decorative plan is the same, in regard to the smaller inset quatrefoils decorated with white flourishes, as that used in the great volumes of the *Bible Moralisée*, of which the illustrations were begun in Paris about 1260.[9] In the two upper Arthurian miniatures of the *Poire*, the lovers, clad in deep blues and reds, sit on a bench, and the man's outstretched arm touches the lady's shoulder. The bench, the placing of the two figures, the gesture, show that the lay artist has simply secularized some design of the Coronation of the Virgin, such as that found, also in medallion form, in the Psalter of Blanche of Castile (Ars. 1186).[10] In the lower *Cliges* miniature, Fenice lies in a death-like swoon, which two bearded doctors test by dropping hot lead into her outflung, helpless hand. She rests on a jade green couch, and a small orange pillow is beneath her fair head. In Chrétien's *Cliges* (v. 5989) she thus sought, by seeming death, to escape from her husband. This is the one medieval illustration of this poem that has been preserved. Below the seated lovers, Tristram and Ysolt, is the scene already mentioned in Chapter IV, in which Mark finds them asleep in a forest lodge and, touched by the Sword of Chastity between them, puts his glove over a gap in the foliage to keep the sun from Ysolt's cheek. Elsewhere the only illustrations for this episode occur in German sources, in the Munich *Tristan* MS (cf. p. 133, Fig. 365) and the German embroideries (cf. pp. 53, 55, Figs. 79, 86) preserved at Wienhausen and in the South Kensing-

ton Museum. But here in the *Poire* MS a French artist has more graciously created the tender scene.[11] The sunbeam is represented by a bar of gold running from the bright orb of the sun, half emerging from a cloud. Symbolism has here perfectly achieved its purpose, and thirteenth-century indifference to realism is as delightfully illustrated by Mark's blue horse as by the little red cave patterned with three dots and by the two symmetrically tufted trees. The orange-colored dress of Ysolt, the pale green of the trees, blend with the deep blue, the rose reds, darkening to mulberry or fading to ash rose, colors which give a special harmony to the miniatures as a whole.

These two Arthurian pages, like others in the nine full-page miniatures of the *Poire*, with their historiated quatrefoils and medallions, their clear black outlines, their restrained use of drapery, are strongly suggestive of Gothic stained glass. But the *Poire*, by the manner of its representations of Love's saints, is most of all like one of those beautiful Psalters into which went so much of the best thirteenth-century illumination of France. It might indeed be called a Psalter of Love. In costume and figure style, the lovers of the *Poire*, finely aristocratic as to feature, slender and supple of body, and clad in open mantle and bliaut, the ladies with pretty rolled or netted chignons and soft narrow chin bands, the young men with curled bangs, are all akin to the delicate yet vital creatures in King Louis's matchless Psalter (Bib. Nat. Lat. 10525).[12] But the *Poire* has nothing of the radiant color, the architectural finesse, the exquisite sophistication of the Paris Psalter. The *Poire* miniatures charm by their grave simplicity and softness of style and color.

THE VERSE AND PROSE ROMANCES

Despite the early vogue of French Arthurian poetry, comparatively few books containing the poems were illustrated, and only those produced late in the thirteenth century or in the early years of the fourteenth were of any artistic note. The earliest surviving illustrated MS of Chrétien's poems seems to be the Picard text in three columns, Fr. 12576, of the first half of the thirteenth century.[13] The MS contains the *Conte del Graal*, including Gerbert's continuation; the last of its miniatures shows grotesquely ugly angels taking the Grail back to Heaven. (Fig.

Pariser Miniaturmalerei (Leipzig, 1907), pp. 88, 97, and Taf. xxi; Fred. Lyna, *De Vlaamsche Miniatuur, 1200–1530* (Brussels, 1933), p. 21.

[7] Reproduced (inaccurately) by C. V. Langlois, *La vie en France au Moyen Age* (P., 1926), I, 96; cf. also pp. 40, 108, 112. Langlois, p. 359, thought this MS the masterpiece "of English illuminators living in Paris," c. 1285.

[8] The two Arthurian miniatures were reproduced in color by Suchier, Birch-Hirschfeld, *Geschichte d. franz. Lit.* (Leipzig, 1913), I, 115.

[9] Cf. A. de Laborde, *La Bible Moralisée* (P., 1911–27), Pl. 278; Martin, *op. cit.*, fig. 12.

[10] Cf. A. Michel, *Histoire de l'art* (P., 1906), II, 333, fig. 252.

[11] On this episode see Thomas, *Tristan*, ed. Bédier (P., 1902), I, 241.

[12] Cf. reproduction "reduite" by Henri Omont, *Psautier de S. Louis* (Paris, n.d.), Pl. XIX, LV.

[13] The MS is described by A. Hilka, *Der Percevalroman* (Halle, 1932), p. vi.

204) The poverty of illustration here and elsewhere in the poetic MSS is to be accounted for by the fact that before secular illustration was really well under way, the Arthurian poems in France were outmoded by new prose redactions. How completely this change took place is indicated by the fact that no single text survives which contains the whole (or even the major portion) of Thomas' memorable poem of *Tristan*, but of the *Prose Tristan* there are forty-seven MSS, of which twelve date from the thirteenth century.[14] The prose texts only were in demand; with these and the special problems they created, the new lay ateliers had to deal.

Aside from the *Meliadus* of Rusticiano da Pisa, in addition to certain prose redactions concerned with Perceval, Tristan and the French *Prophécies de Merlin*,[15] the great corpus known as the Vulgate Cycle of Arthurian romance was made up before the middle of the century, of five huge prose romances. These were: the *Estoire del Saint Graal*, which began with the Crucifixion and told the early history of the Grail; the *Merlin*, the *Lancelot* (the last in two or three parts of great length), the *Queste del Saint Graal*, or the Galahad story, and the *Mort Artu*.[16] Each of these "branches" was a vast romance in itself, deliberately spun out for the pleasure of long continued reading. Each branch might be copied as a complete text in itself or in combination with other branches, but not infrequently all of them were copied together. The resultant folio, written in three or two columns of text, contained between five and seven hundred leaves.

The task of writing and decorating these bulky volumes could not have been undertaken by any except fairly experienced and substantial ateliers. How rapidly these must have developed, particularly in the last three decades of the thirteenth and the first years of the fourteenth centuries, is indicated, even apart from all other evidence, by the large number of extant Arthurian MSS. The craftsmen employed on their decoration were laymen, some of very mediocre ability, but they were familiar with the conventions of contemporary illustration established in both secular and religious books. Whether for the great illustrated Bibles of the time or for the romances, the illuminators, untroubled as always in the Middle Ages by any concern for historic verisimilitude, used equally a host of generalized subjects: knights fighting, hunting, feasting; knights in converse with each other or with one or more ladies; lords or ladies in bed; a scribe reading or writing or receiving dictation; a person at prayer; a priest at the altar; a bishop in the act of blessing; a king enthroned receiving or sending away a messenger, giving commands, taking council with his court. These subjects were of a sort that could be and were endlessly reproduced in all sorts of texts. King David in Gothic Bibles and Psalters is not to be differentiated from King Arthur in the romances. Alike they sit, crowned and sceptered, with legs royally crossed, the higher the better. The attitude was itself symbolic of active power.[17] The Arthurian illustrators, moreover, could and often did borrow familiar themes of religious art. In the *Estoire* which told of the time of Christ, or in the *Queste* with its mystical visions and ritualistic episodes, the miniaturists set forth pictures of Adam and Eve beneath the tree, or of their being driven from Paradise, of Cain murdering Abel, of the Annunciation, the Nativity, the Crucifixion, the Deposition and Entombment, Saint Veronica with her handkerchief, the Harrowing of Hell, and the Trinity enthroned. Sometimes by a slight transformation of the original religious scene, like that of the Coronation of the Virgin in the *Poire*, they made it serve the new purpose of romance. The Nativity was the usual model for birth scenes and influenced many representations of a person in bed; it accounts for the attitude of the

[14] E. Vinaver, *Études sur le 'Tristan' en prose* (Paris, 1925), pp. 37–58, describes 47 MSS. Twenty-nine have miniatures.

[15] For the *Meliadus* see Löseth, *Le roman en prose de Tristan* (Paris, 1890), pp. 433 ff. Two of these MSS from the thirteenth century are finely illuminated. See Fr. 350 (Vitzthum, *op. cit.*, p. 140); and Ars. 3325. For *Perlesvaus* see *infra*, p. 106, Fig. 280. For the *Prophécies de Merlin* see the edition by Miss Lucy Paton (N. Y., 1926), who describes 13 French MSS, four of which have miniatures. The one at Rennes, 593, dated 1303 by the scribe Robin de Boutemont, has 83 miniatures.

[16] Cf. H. O. Sommer, *Vulgate Version of the Arthurian Romances*, 7 vols. (Washington, 1909–16); Bruce, *Evolution of Arthurian Romance* (Baltimore, 1923), I, 368 ff. For convenient but incomplete lists of the MSS, see Sommer, I, xxx. His index of names to vols. I–VII (1916), and his marginal notes to the text provide the means of identifying the episodes alluded to in this book. A. Pauphilet, *Études sur la Queste del Saint Graal* (P., 1921), pp. v–x, describes 38 MSS (13–15 century) and specifies those which have the best miniatures. Miss Marjorie Fox, *La Mort le Roi Artus, Étude sur les MSS, les sources et la composition* (P., 1933), pp. 3–23, describes 43 MSS of the *Mort Artu*

and notes 36 that have miniatures; Jean Frappier, *La Mort Artu* (Paris, 1936), pp. ix–xxx, describes 45 MSS. Mead, *Merlin*, Early English Text Society, X (1899), cxxxvi–clxxxi, enumerates 29 MSS of the prose *Merlin*, and notes some miniatures. The MSS of the *Estoire* have not been specifically described. For illustrated late 13th century MSS of the *Estoire* see Fr. 95; Fr. 110; Fr. 344; Fr. 748; Fr. 749; Fr. 770; Fr. 1047; Fr. 19162; Fr. 24394; Cheltenham, Phillipps 1046 (many traditional religious scenes); for 14th century MSS, *ibid.*, 1045; Fr. 105; Fr. 9123; cf. Vitzthum, p. 176; London, Br. Mus. Add. 10292; Add. 38117 (Huth); Roy. 14 E III; Oxford, Douce 178; for 15th century MSS Fr. 96, Fr. 113, Fr. 117; Brussels, Bibl. Roy. 9246. F. Lot, *Étude sur le Lancelot en prose* (P., 1918), 1 n., notes 28 MSS of the *Lancelot* alone, 13 of them from the 13th century. Cf. Sommer, I, xxxi ff. Miss Paton, *Lancelot of the Lake* (N. Y., 1929) gives many illustrations from *Lancelot* MSS of the 13th century through the 15th: Fr. 113, 114, 115, 116, 118, 119, 120, 122, 342, 344, Ars. 3479–80, 3482, Br. Mus. Add. 10293–94. See her list of illustrations, p. xvii ff. The dating needs revision.

[17] Martin, "Les enseignements des miniatures: attitude royale," *Gaz. des beaux arts*, Ser. IV, vol. IX (1913), 173 ff. (Illus.)

dreaming lover in bed in MSS of the *Roman de la Rose*,[18] the allegory which vied with the romances in popularity and as a subject for illustration. In the early Arthurian miniatures the birth of Merlin and the birth of Arthur are reminiscent of the Nativity. Feast scenes, though supposed to take place at Arthur's Round Table, were always in the thirteenth century represented as taking place at a long straight table, as in a royal hall of the day or in contemporary representations of the Last Supper. The tendency to transfer the familiar patterns of religious to secular illustration was inevitable, and only in the more costly manuscripts, under the guidance of rubrics calling for scenes more precisely related to the text, or of lightly drawn but sometimes masterful sketches, whether in the space left for the miniature or at the side or the bottom of the page, by the Master of the atelier,[19] did the illustrators depict, with more originality and increasing attention to detail, the specific scenes of the story. But how casually the traditional religious scenes or the most solemn religious episodes of the stories themselves could be treated by the ordinary workmen of the average atelier is indicated in the cyclic MS Fr. 110.[20] (Fig. 205) In one of its most impressive scenes, the *Queste* tells of the coming of the mystic hero Galahad to take his place at the Round Table. The illustrator, altogether neglecting to represent the hero's coming on foot and clad in Pentecostal red, as the story demanded, shows him instead in blue, riding his horse up to the table, where (most inappropriately) a vivacious young Arthur appears to be chucking a youth under the chin! The companion miniature shows Galahad in light mauve tunic, a red ailette on his shoulder, drawing the sword from the stone.

Apart from the large frontispieces, commonly divided into four or more compartments and surrounded by a more or less elaborate architectural framework—frontispieces now for the most part blurred and ruined—the late thirteenth-century Arthurian illustrators, like others working on secular MSS, confined their efforts chiefly to historiated letters and to small framed rectangles, about two inches wide, or to the width of the column of text into which they were fitted. The historiated letter, as an illustrative device, was destined to give way to the rectangular miniature, but many of the books of the period contain only these historiated letters. Small clear little scenes, framed and historiated, appear in the Brussels *Queste* and *Mort Artu* (Bibl. Roy. 9627–28, Figs. 206–207),[21] where Modred's war on London and Guinevere's reception by the nuns are portrayed. The historiated letter was sometimes much larger. A *Guiron* (Ars. 3325) has twenty-one of these large letters with the figures generally represented against those golden backgrounds which were used so constantly in the thirteenth century as to justify the name, the "goldfoil" style. Sometimes the letter, escaping its frame, became an elaborate decorative device combined with bar and stem prolongations with strong cusped edges and enclosed leaf patterns of a type particularly favored in North-French and Flemish illumination. A *Prose Tristan* (Fr. 776, Fig. 208), of about 1280, not only aptly illustrates these features but also, with its occasional birds, dogs, rabbits, and a grotesque or two, heralds the drolleries which in England and these Franco-Flemish regions were alike becoming so popular. Of special interest in this manuscript are the folios with musical notations; one decorated leaf (Fig. 209) combines the music with a picture of Mark listening to the lay of Dinadan's harper. The musical notation and the decorative devices on this folio and others are close to those in the *Chansonnier d'Arras* (Arras, no. 139). Another part of MS 139 bears an inscription to the effect that it was written in 1278 by "Jehans damiens li petis" (f. 212 v).[22] The vividly decorative details of Fr. 776 surpass in interest the illustrations, which, like most of those in contemporary *Tristans*, show little feeling for the story.

Another French *Prose Tristan* (Fr. 750, Figs. 210–212), itself dated and signed by the scribe, Pierre de Tiergeville (Petrus de Tiergevilla) in 1278, is of special interest because, though the scribe was from a little town in Normandy, near Yvetot, the illuminator was unquestionably Spanish and the manuscript preserves our only known Spanish instance of Arthurian illumination in the thirteenth century. Many of the miniatures seem to have been washed out, but the three here reproduced show clearly the arms of Castile, gules a castle with three towers or, introduced on f. 287 v. The black color, the textile suggestions, the bold decorative devices are all in Spanish style.[23] The historiated letters are commonly divided into three compartments with gold back-

---

[18] Kuhn, "Die Illustration des Rosenromans," *Jahrbuch der Kunsthist. Sammlungen*, XXXI (1912), 20.

[19] Martin, "Les esquisses des miniatures," *Rev. archéol.*, IV (1904), 22 ff.

[20] Fr. 110 is described by Miss Fox, *op. cit.*, p. 3; by Frappier, *op. cit.*, p. x.

[21] The MS is described by C. Gaspar, F. Lyna, *Les princ. MSS à peintures de la Bibl. Roy. de Belgique* (P., 1937), SFRMP, I, 163. They call it Flemish.

[22] Arras, no. 139, is reproduced by A. Jeanroy, *Le chansonnier d'Arras* (P., 1925). Cf. also the figure style and decorative details of the *Tristan* with those in the large Flemish Antiphoner of Beaupré near Grammont, formerly in the Yates Thompson coll.; cf. *Illustrations from the 100 Best MSS*, VI (L., 1916), Pl. XII–XXIII; E. Millar, *Descriptive Cat. of MSS of A. C. Beatty* (Oxford, 1930) II, 83 ff. The *Tristan*, Fr. 776, is described by Vinaver, *Études sur le Tristan en prose* (P., 1925), p. 44.

[23] On its characteristics see J. Dominguez Bordona, *Spanish Illumination* (N. Y., Pantheon Ser., n.d.); cf. Pl. 82, 92, especially for ornament. The only other example of Spanish

grounds. The subjects of the miniatures are as follows:

(Fig. 210) 1. The Chevalier à la Cote Mal Taillée and his squires find a damsel weeping over the body of Lyas.

2. The body of Lyas is given Christian burial.

3. The Chevalier and his squires meet a damsel fleeing from a knight. He bears a shield argent a bend gules.

(Fig. 211) 1. "Yselt" weeps over the news of her lover. Mark rides away on a pretended hunt.

2. "Yselt" harps in the garden while Mark watches from a window. She attempts to slay herself but Mark seizes the sword.

(Fig. 212) 1. King "March" and Andred arm themselves at "Tyntayol."

2. Black shields on their arms, they go forth and find two squires with two horses covered with black *couvertures*.

3. At the Lac Aventurous they encounter Kay, who bears the arms of Castile on his shield.

Two Dated Cyclic Manuscripts
1. Fr. 342, Dated 1274

The progress in illustration as an art in itself can best be followed in the framed rectangular miniatures which came, more and more, to be the typical form in the numerous cyclic MSS produced in the North-French ateliers in the late thirteenth century. One of these is the earliest dated Arthurian MS now known. The scribe's colophon in Fr. 342, f. 234 v., dates his work as written in 1274 "le samedi apries les octaues de la Trinite." This book, which contains the third part of the *Lancelot*, the *Queste*, and the *Mort Artu*, is illustrated with 95 miniatures running (usually) panelwise across two columns of text. This design, with identical framework patterns, appears in one of the earliest known MSS of the famous romance, the *Chevalier au Cygne* (Ars. 3139),[24] which was possibly decorated in the same workshop, but by a better artist. Crude as it is, the Arthurian manuscript, Fr. 342, is historically interesting as the beginning, according to Vitzthum,[25] of the typical "Romanen-illustrationen," which were soon to have such enormous vogue.

The miniaturist was here guided in part by red rubrics written above the panel space, and by direc-

tions, some of which still remain in the lower margin, as on f. 9, where the meeting of Bors with a religious is thus indicated: "Si com boort encontre . . . home de religion qui portoit corpus domini." Just as in Fr. 110, the illustrator here did not fulfill the requirements of the rubricator, for in the vision of the sleeping Lancelot (Fig. 213), the chapel, the candles, the Cross, the sick, praying knight of the story appear, but the healing Grail itself is omitted though the rubric begins "Si com Lan(celot) uit le sant graal"; likewise, in representing Lancelot's rescue of Guinevere from the fire (Fig. 215), though the artist has roughly suggested the flames at the right of his picture, he has omitted the lady. Against flat gold backgrounds are placed ball-headed trees, and squat puppet-like figures with ugly, snub-nosed heads. The physical type is well represented in the miniature representing the mass heard in a hermitage by the maimed king and Perceval (Fig. 214), or in that which begins the *Mort Artu* section. (Fig. 216) In the lower part King Henry, clad in blue and mulberry robes, an orange-colored crown on his head, dictates to his scribe, who works at his MS with knife and quill in hand. In the upper part Bors, eagle argent showing on his orange-colored ailette, returns from Jerusalem, and is received with joy by his comrades. The artist was most at home in scenes of combat, where he constantly repeated his favorite device of representing the rear half of the horses' caparison with a forward right angle, and a single pointed flap at the horse's tail. Black outlines are heavily drawn; there is little or no shading. The draftsman frequently simplifies the scene. Thus, when the lady falls from the tower in the temptation of Bors, but one of her twelve companions is represented, and when Modred begins the Siege of the Tower of London, he is alone, with only a catapult for company. Of the three Arthurian branches in the book, the *Queste* is the most fully illustrated, but the *Mort Artu* section of this textually important MS, which was used by Bruce as the basis of his edition (Halle, 1910), contains 33 miniatures, a fact worth noting because in the later cyclic MSS, probably on account of their ever increasing bulk and cost, fewer and fewer illustrations are found for this, the last, but from the literary point of view, the most dramatic and powerful section of the whole prose cycle.

Arthurian illumination known to us is that dating from the second half of the 14th century in a Castilian *Tristan* (better called *Guiron*) noted by A. Bonilla y San Martin, *Anales de la literatura espanola* (Madrid, 1904), p. 26. Here the miniature shows a mounted troop, the old knight Branor le Brun (already encountered in the S. Floret paintings), a lady and her daughter, who had brought the old knight from Arthur's court. (Cf. Löseth, *Tristan en prose*, p. 427.) Bordona, p. 45, speaks of the scarcity of illuminated books in Castile in the second half of the 14th century. But there was no scarcity of Arthurian MSS and tapes-

tries in Spain at large. Cf. Entwistle, *Arthurian Legend in the Literatures of the Spanish Peninsula* (L., 1925). He refers (p. 109) to the Branor illustration. The *Tristan* MS, Fr. 750, is described by Vinaver, *op. cit.*, p. 41.

[24] Cf. H. Martin, P. Lauer, *Les principaux MSS à peintures de l'Arsenal*, SFRMP (P., 1929), Pl. X.

[25] Vitzthum, *op. cit.*, pp. 122–123, groups with this MS the cyclic MS, Fr. 344; The *Estoire-Merlin*, Fr. 770; the *Prophécies de Merlin*, Harl. 1629 (two poor miniatures). MS. 342 is described by Miss Fox, *Mort Artus*, p. 8; by Frappier, *Mort Artu*, p. xvi.

11. Bonn 526, Dated 1286

A second dated MS of greater artistic interest is the complete cycle now in the University Library of Bonn (MS. 82, cat. no. 526).[26] It is not only dated but signed:

Explicit. Arnulfus de Kayo scripsit istum librum, qui est ambianis. En lan del incarnation M.CCIIII^{xx}VI el mois daoust le jour le s. iehan decolase. Ici fenist la mort dou roy Artu et des autres . . . Et tout le romans de Lancelot.

Nothing else is known of this excellent scribe of Amiens, whose sigh of satisfaction seems almost as palpable as it was on August 27, 1286, when he ended his long task. Patiently he wrote the whole volume with his own hand, just as one unknown illustrator seems to have been responsible for the miniatures that adorn almost every one of the 489 leaves of the volume. Like the scribe, he was probably a Picard.

A distinctive trait in this and other MSS of what might be termed the Amiens school, is the use of illuminated initial letters, usually O(r) or E(t), of a distinctive simple type. The plain rounded letter itself is flat gold against a background of blue or red decorated with a few curving lines in white, which occasionally form a small center flower pattern. The letter is inset in a small unframed rectangular space, which is sometimes prolonged into a border ornament. With a few exceptions, like that on the more elaborate first page, this simple design is regularly used and can be recognized in other products of the same school, especially in those most notable Arthurian MSS, Fr. 95 at Paris, and Phillipps 130 at Cheltenham.

The bold simplicity of these initials is characteristic of all the decorative features of the Bonn volume. The first page (Fig. 217) has a more elaborate aspect, to be sure, for each of the three columns is topped by two miniatures, and each miniature has its own architectural setting with towers or floriated finials extending beyond the framework of the picture. These pictures, like most of those beginning the *Estoire*, have a strong reminiscence of religious iconography, especially in the representation of the figure of Christ, whether on the Cross, or being entombed by Joseph. In the first scene Christ appears

to a sleeping hermit; in the second Christ gives the hermit the *Estoire;* in the third the hermit is led by a strange beast to a house of religion; in the fourth he copies from Christ's book the early history of the Grail. The gold backgrounds on this first page are worn away so that the figures do not now appear with the sharp distinctness to be noted elsewhere. In contrast with the sobriety of the six miniatures at the top of the page are the winged harpy figure, armed with sword and shield, that mounts the border ornament at the left, the stag, with horns meeting in a point, in full career at the bottom of the page, and a graceful minstrel with his psaltery at the right. These are again early intimations of the grotesques which almost at once abound in other books of this region.

The Bonn miniatures are usually framed rectangles introduced at will into the text itself. Occasionally a small part of the picture, human feet or a horse's tail, overlaps the frame. The colors are clear and bright, with a predominant use of blue, coral red, light green, mauve, dark grey. All the interest is concentrated in the figures, almost no accessories being used, the wooden font in which the leprous king "de la terre forainne" (Fig. 218) received baptism and healing, or the high trestle-like chair in which Guinevere witnesses Lancelot's fight in tourney (Fig. 219), being of the simplest sort. Architectural details such as the tower defended by the copper men whom Lancelot overcomes (Fig. 220), or the "palais auenturous," orange colored, with touches of brown and mauve, in which Bors endured the perils of falling arrows (Fig. 221), are rare. The story is told almost entirely by means of figures, robust rather than graceful. The inexpressive faces show little dissimilarity of type; only in the representation of Lancelot as a madman (Fig. 222) is there some attempt to give an emotional quality. The figures gesture with broad upraised hands, as when Guinevere lifts hers in prayer to the nuns. (Fig. 223) The lack of modeling in the white hands, feet and faces, is peculiarly evident. All the emphasis in these miniatures is on bold and simple contours, on broad surfaces. Clumsy though much of the drawing is, the pictures as a whole make a vivid impression. They are concrete illustrations of the story, sufficiently varied, sufficiently original, to set a model far superior to that in Fr. 342 for pictorial Arthurian sequences.

[26] The MS is described by L. Olschki, *MSS français à peintures des bibliothèques d'Allemagne* (Geneva, 1932), and many miniatures are reproduced, Pl. LXXIII–LXXIV. In *Die romanischen Lit. des Mittelalters* (Potsdam, 1928) Olschki reproduced, Abb. 61–66, Lancelot's vision of the Grail; Merlin, book in hand, taking leave of Cæsar; Gawain and a maiden; Lancelot in the cart; Lancelot crowned by a lady; Galehaut's death, his soul coming from his mouth. In Taf. IV Olschki reproduced in color two miniatures, one of the Pentecost feast, when the maiden arrives

to ask for Lancelot, and one of two knights confronting two white nuns. A colored reproduction of six miniatures in Suchier und Birch-Hirschfeld, *Gesch. d. frz. Lit.* (Leipzig, 1913), opposite p. 165, shows Merlin in the form of a stag before Cæsar, f. 125; Galahad, Perceval, Bors, at table in Pelles' Castle, f. 451 v; Lancelot in the cart, f. 296; Lancelot, mad, rushing from the castle where he has been faithless to Guinevere; Gawain on the perilous bed, f. 339 v: Ivain freeing Sagremor and his love from the tree to which they are bound, f. 282 v.

A Masterpiece of Thirteenth Century Illustration
Fr. 95 and Phillipps 130

Incomparably more brilliant and beautiful, but likewise written by Picard scribes and not improbably decorated in the same region, are those magnificent volumes, Fr. 95 at Paris (B. N.) and its long severed and unrecognized companion volume, MS 130 in the Phillipps collection at Cheltenham, of which it is, unfortunately, impossible to obtain photographs. The two volumes are of the same size, written with two columns of text, and illuminated on the same plan. Both volumes, by some happy chance, have been marvelously well preserved. On the great vellum pages the finely written text is as clear, the colors of the miniatures with gold backgrounds and radiant hues, almost as undimmed, as unmarred, as when they first issued from the atelier. No expense, no effort, was spared for these volumes, and the technical facility of the artists was matched only by their amazing inventiveness, by the easy grace and undying charm with which they translated into vivid pictorial form the cycle of stories. Without the exquisite delicacy of the Parisian artists who fashioned the *Psautier de S. Louis*, there is in these Arthurian manuscripts a verve and animation, an enchanting humor and sheer gusto, that captivate the imagination. Partly, of course, the effect is due to the wildly delicious grotesqueries which scamper over almost every page. Here in gay profusion are all sorts of strange hybrids, a birdman with a bagpipe, and lively medieval centaurs, armed with sword and shield, charging at each other across towers and finials above a stately court scene. Here in Fr. 95 we observe monkeys in every guise, one carrying a whole basketload of little monkeys on his back, while another, a monkey cripple, plays a bagpipe (f. 64 v), or another teaches a monkey school (f. 299) or birches bad monkey students (f. 394); yet another monkey sticks out his tongue at a peering archer whose great arrow has already impaled a bird. (Fig. 224) Here as elsewhere the bold border ornaments swirl unexpectedly into bright wings and finely drawn human heads. Little men are busy with little deeds, shooting stags (f. 39), fighting each other with sword and buckler (f. 42), playing ball (f. 61 v), juggling with swords (f. 237, 318); the tumbling girl tumbles while the bagpiper plays (f. 262), and two men, mounted on the backs of others, claw each other as best they can (f. 327). From the middle of a tall upright gray body surmounted by a stag's head, a small human face looks out (f. 201), as some mummer must have done whom the artist thus remembered so realistically. In the Phillipps MS 130, where the grotesques have the same air of inimitable life and foolery, a man is represented sitting delicately on

eggs and holding one aloft; another man balances a sword on his nose.

Fr. 95, though not wholly Arthurian in its present content, is illustrated throughout by the same artists. It contains altogether 394 large folios, and in the Arthurian section, ff. 1–355, a total of 249 miniatures, many of them in pairs, one above the other, and all, except for 24 small ones, the width of one of the two wide columns of text on each page. The Phillipps volume—still alas! with no pagination—has 363 folios with 82 large and 80 small miniatures, placed in the same way. Fr. 95 begins with *Estoire*, ff. 1–113 v, followed by the *Merlin*, ff. 114–355; then the non-Arthurian pieces.[27] Phillipps MS 130 begins with the so-called *Agravain* or the third part of the *Lancelot* and continues through the *Queste* and the *Mort Artu*. In all probability there was once another great volume containing the intervening section, for we can hardly imagine that it was not intended that the cycle should be complete in this princely form.

In both MSS, in addition to the enlivening profusion of grotesques, there is in the miniatures themselves an air of fresh and lively originality. Rarely did the lay mind of lay artists in the thirteenth century reveal itself more clearly than here. Even where the traditional patterns are to some extent followed, as in the Descent from the Cross and the Entombment (Fig. 225), with what a difference after all are they presented! The ancient Jews all wear Jews' hats, their long curling locks and beards are in the "tormented" style; their faces with peaked, worried brows, have an air of anxiety or animated grief. So, too, has St. John, holding his hand to his mouth. Merlin's face (Fig. 226), thin and venerable, is always impressive; the head of the man possessed by a devil shows the wild elf locks rising as if in horror from his head. (Fig. 227) The faces, almost uncolored, but often dotted with pink in a fashion common among North French artists, faces executed with delicate pen work, are at times emotionally expressive, but in general they have, as in the picture of Celidoine (Fig. 228), an incredible youthfulness, a bland sweetness, a slightly astonished expression. Fitly enough, the artists have represented the Arthurian world filled with timelessly young and beautiful people, whose svelte bodies, from the tops of their fair heads to the tips of their long, slender feet, are the embodiment of courtly grace. It is a very young Josephe, son of Joseph of Arimathea, who in the *Estoire* officiates at the first Mass (Fig. 229), and a very boyish Chanaan who slays his twelve sleeping brothers (Fig. 230); in the *Merlin* a young lad, Arthur, drawing the sword from the anvil, is surrounded by a charming, youthful clergy. (Fig. 235) No single scene, perhaps, more completely suggests all these

[27] The non-Arthurian pieces that follow are the *Sept Sages*, ff. 115–379; *La pénitence Adam*, ff. 380–398.

qualities and grace and courtliness and youth than the brilliant one (Fig. 239) representing Arthur and Ban in converse about tourneys, with Guinevere caressing her little dog, and other members of the court, listening pleasantly. The noble lords wear or hold their white gloves, a constantly recurring detail, and one young man at the left feeds the falcon perched on his wrist. The figures stand against a bright gold background, their under-robes are sometimes of gold, with surcoats and mantles of blue or mauve or pink lilac, with touches of orange color. Guinevere, with loose white veil falling beneath her crown, holds her rich mantle caught up beneath her arm in the most fashionable manner. The drapery is treated more dexterously than in the Bonn MS, with more shading and more numerous but still simple and heavy folds. The well-modeled figures are outlined in black with frequently an inset line of white. The men's surcoats reach well below the knees. Armor is of the same type as that in the Bonn MS but is done here a little differently, the chain mail being represented by long, up and down, instead of horizontal lines, with dots between.

Notably in Fr. 95 and the Phillipps MS. 130 are illustrated a certain real power in composition, a perception of balance, an instinct for dramatic focus, that are of high artistic quality. In the scene of Arthur's combat with the ten rebel kings (Fr. 95, Fig. 236), the impact of the opposing armies is admirably conveyed. The lines of the lifted spears make effective diagonals; the central standard with the great red Pendragon head seeming to scream defiance gives a touch of startling color. A mounted knight falls limply from his saddle; another with powerful, uplifted arm swings on high his deadly sword. The artist enjoyed the representation of the famous standard and repeated it in Fr. 95 on ff. 162 v, 190, 191 v, 230 v, 327 v, etc. Arthur's combat is repeated identically in the Phillipps MS, with the exception that banners are represented on the spears and not the dragon standard. There the composition represents Arthur's combat with Modred and the knight with upraised sword is threatening Arthur himself. The figure and the gesture are of common occurrence, especially in Fr. 95. In both books scenes are rarely presented which do not include a number of figures and these are arranged in effectively balanced groups with an interesting trick of massing heads of figures one behind the other. Naïve as is the artist's representation in Fr. 95 of the burial alive of Chanaan (Fig. 232) or of the fulfillment of Merlin's prophecy of the Triple Death (Fig. 234), still there is amazing ingenuity in both miniatures. In the first the central figure of Chanaan is matched in the miniature im-

mediately above it by the figure of Symeu carried away by fiery, flying men, and there is a deliberate parallelism of line between the Bishop's staff in the top miniature and the spade of the digger below. In the picture of the Triple Death, by falling, by hanging, by drowning, the central figure of the unfortunate who, as prophesied by Merlin, experienced all three deaths, is made dramatically effective by outflung hands and tossing feet, and the amazement of the mounted beholders is even reflected in the eyes of the horses. However odd the cleated bridge, the composition of the picture, for the story it had to tell, could hardly be improved upon. With skill and economy the essential symbolism of act and emotion is achieved.

The decorative devices of these books are simple but effective. Long red and blue "filets-bordures"[28] or thread-like flourishes stretching from the top to the bottom of the page separate the two columns of text. At the left is often a long bar prolongation ending in two or three projections, curved at the ends and set off with sharply cusped edges. (Figs. 224, 239) The bars and arms are lightly patterned with small designs in white. The miniatures themselves are usually placed within narrow gold, or red and blue bands, but occasionally the frame itself is decorated with simple designs, or, strikingly, as in the picture of Nascien being carried away in a cloud (Fig. 231), in patterned gold. The neck-entwined serpents with human heads and vivid wings, which top this miniature, again illustrate the exuberance with which grotesques crowd the pages of Fr. 95, and there can be no doubt that in this manuscript the designer of the grotesques was the same artist who executed the miniatures. One has but to look at the Council of Demons (Fig. 233), at the monkey-like heads, the fantastic bodies, with little heads grinning from knee and thigh, to recognize the kinship with the marginal figures.

In the miniatures of these books there is, in comparison with those of the Bonn MS, a more skillful use of detail, though of essentially the same kind. Trees are altogether stylized, but with some variations of leaf patterns. Scrolls are frequently used, flying from the hands or lips of the speakers. Accessories, such as weapons, standards, ceremonial crosses, altar-vessels, and altars with fringed altar cloths, are done with care. Particularly did the artist delight in the faithful representation of Romanesque beds, for in this detail he seems to have followed an older tradition. Certainly the bed in which Merlin's mother sleeps (Fig. 233) suggests that in which the Virgin lies on the west front of Chartres, and it is repeated in Fr. 95 (ff. 12 v, 52, 82 v, 113 v, 261 v)

---

[28] Martin, *Miniature franç.* (1923), p. 21, speaks of "filets-bordures" as characteristic of the school of the Ile de France, but they were widely used. Vitzthum, *op. cit.*, p. 143 compared

Fr. 95 in style with the *Liber Floridus* (Paris, B. N. Lat. 8865) and stressed the transition from pure French to Franco-Belgian style.

with the same care for the round-ringed posts, the center opening, the ornamentation of the sides with either a spindle pattern or a quatrefoil inset in a round disc; in the Phillipps MS it is notably represented in the beautifully executed scene of Mordrain's death in the *Queste*, about three-fourths of the way through the manuscript. The dead king lies in bed; from his mouth his soul departs, to be received by angels; Galahad supports the figure of Mordrain. In the *Mort Artu* section the same elaborate bed appears in the scene representing Lancelot sick and being visited by the Maid of Astolat and his brother knights.

In these MSS, Fr. 95 and Phillipps 130, the apex of North-French Arthurian illumination in the thirteenth century was reached. Within the limits of an unrealistic art, unconscious as yet of space and perspective, and with no suggestion of nature other than that afforded by a stylized tree or two, the MSS show a vitality and originality, a technical and decorative skill that makes them preeminent. For the study of secular art in general they offer superb illustrations of the Picard school, which may well have been centered at Amiens.

RELATED CYCLIC MANUSCRIPTS

Not much later than these two MSS and related to them is a resplendent group made up of the following MSS: two volumes of the *Vulgate Lancelot*, the *Queste* and the *Mort Artu*, in the John Rylands Library, Manchester (French, 1, 2); the sumptuous British Museum MS, Royal 14 E III,[29] containing the *Estoire*, the *Queste*, the *Mort Artu*, a royal volume indeed; and finally the three large volumes, also in the British Museum, Add. 10292–94, a complete cyclic MS which Sommer has made the basis of his edition of the Vulgate Version of Arthurian romance. All these books may be dated approximately by a miniature which occurs in Add. 10292. (Fig. 248) The artist has represented masons chiseling on the flat surface of two tomb-slabs inscriptions, which read:

(1) "en cheste tombe gist ch*evalie*rs crueus si morut le dousime iour de feueir." "In this tomb lies a cruel knight; he died the twelfth day of February."

(2) "karabel et nabor ki mo—par dev*er*s len—en lan de grace m.ccc & xvi." "Karabel and Nabor who (died?)—near the (entry?)—in the year of grace 1316."

Sommer's transcript of the inscriptions is inaccurate,

but his suggestion[30] that February 12, 1316, was the very date on which the miniature was made is most probable. Certainly the artist could never have supposed that it applied to the deaths of Karabel and Nabor, who were suddenly slain by the intervention of God, and whose tombs were set up by the command of Flegetine, wife of Nascien, "par deuers l'entree de babylone," "near the entry of Cairo," some time in the first century. The date 1316 may also be regarded, because of the close family resemblance among the MSS, as approximately that of the whole group.

Though the work of production must have taken a considerable space of time, for all these MSS are profusely illustrated, the Additional MSS alone containing a total of 748 miniatures,[31] the group was probably complete by 1320. A glance shows they all came from the same atelier, which must, indeed, have been one of outstanding importance, to produce volumes of such cost and elaboration. Vitzthum[32] conjectured that this atelier was in the ancient Belgian city of Maastricht, and thought Royal 14 E III the finest product of that workshop. This seems a doubtful provenance. With Bonn 526 established as a Picard MS, its similarities with these later MSS cannot be ignored. Its architectural details, the very matter Vitzthum stressed as a supposed Maastricht peculiarity, its similar drolleries, its use of the bold simple type of initial letter, already described, and its method of framing the illustrations in white-patterned blue and red bands with little squares in each corner,—in short, its decorative plan and details relate it to the later MSS and them to it. Fr. 95, also written by a Picard scribe, though outside the group, has many resemblances to it, especially in figure style. The Rylands MS is closest to Fr. 95; the miniature showing Arthur listening to the knights tell of their Grail quests (Fig. 237) might have been made by the artist of Fr. 95 himself. The exceptionally well-preserved frontispiece (Fig. 240) of the Rylands MS has, however, signs in the decorative elements, in the more leaf-like sprays in which the sharp cusps end, in the combination of plain gold with a chequered background, of a later date than Fr. 95. Moreover, many of the Rylands miniatures, like that showing Lancelot carrying his grandfather's head from the boiling fountain (Fig. 238), might have been done by the fourteenth century workers on the Royal or Additional MS. Trees, horses, figures, are identical.

Several artists of varying degrees of ability worked on this group of MSS. Royal 14 E III is the best,

---

[29] For description of Royal 14 E III see *The Brit. Mus. Catalogue of Royal MSS* (L., 1921), II, 140, which speaks doubtfully of the illuminations as "perhaps of English rather than French origin."

[30] *L'Estoire*, ed. H. O. Sommer, I, xxvi. His frontispiece is an enlarged reproduction of this miniature.

[31] *Ibid.*, p. xxvi f. Throughout his whole edition of these MSS Sommer indicates the occurrence of the miniatures and quotes their rubrics. These rubrics serve as a fair index to the usual miniatures in a complete cyclic MS.

[32] Vitzthum, *Die Pariser Miniaturmalerei*, pp. 133 ff. He does not speak of the Rylands MS.

especially in the three frontispieces to the various branches of the cycle. The blurred but once beautiful first page, the feast scene at the beginning of the *Queste* (Fig. 242), and the miniature at the beginning of the *Mort Artu* (Fig. 241), showing King Henry dictating to Walter Map "les auentures del saint Graal," display the exuberance in drolleries and architectural details, the delightful fresh color and softness of touch so characteristic of the MS as a whole; it shows also in the large miniatures the concern, already affecting the best miniaturists of the day, with space considerations; with the attempt to represent a standing plane, instead of the mere base line which had sufficed before. In the feast scene the tiled floor, the red-robed servitor who kneels before the white table, the figures behind the table, suggest that second stage in Gothic illumination when figures were beginning to be represented with some sense of space about them.[33] Royal 14 E III exhibits, as do all these MSS, with an artless naïveté of treatment, a new joy in primitive landscape motifs, in grassy fields, trees, rocks even of the most lump-like variety as in the *Queste* miniature (Fig. 243), representing Perceval's sister and the three knights coming on the ship of the strange spindles. Water and fishes are constantly represented; the odd fishes may, indeed, constitute a kind of signature of one of the illustrators.

The Royal MS has 105 miniatures. How closely they sometimes correspond with those in Add. 10292–94 may be seen by comparing the two miniatures showing the Maid of Astolat coming in her barge to Camelot. (Figs. 246–247) A great number of the miniatures are as nearly identical as are these two, though those in the Additional MSS are somewhat poorer in execution. If not copied from Royal 14 E III, the Add. MSS must have been copied from the same model. With almost machine-like facility the illustrators carried out the directions of the red rubrics which in these books refer to the subject of the picture, not to the content of the chapter. Tirelessly they represented the same figures, in the small miniatures always too short and with over-large heads, always with the same wide-opened eyes, the thick, curled short hair. Tirelessly they set forth columns, buttresses, arches cusped and crocketted, windows with stone tracery, gables, towers, finials, slates on roofs. With naïve instinct for a certain sort of realism they pictured not only masons at work on stone tombs and carpenters building boats, but the building of an abbey, the siege of a castle, a

novice getting her hair shorn by an abbess, a lady looking into her hand mirror, a minstrel sitting on a banquet table, his dog at his feet, and many another scene of contemporary interest. They were particularly unsuccessful, as illustrators, in the supernatural or tragic scenes. Unable to cope with such a vision as that in the *Estoire* when Christ appears as the Divine Stag accompanied by four lions, the miniature (Fig. 244) attempting to represent it becomes innocently absurd; as also do the miniatures representing Arthur on the Wheel of Fortune (Fig. 245) or the woeful Arthur when Excalibur was given back to the waters from which it came. (Fig. 249) Yet for all the faults of the smaller miniatures in this group of MSS, they do present a wonderfully vivid pictorial sequence of the whole cycle. Their variety, their literalness, are noteworthy. They turn Arthurian romance into the bright colors of chivalric fairy tale.

AN EARLY FOURTEENTH CENTURY MASTERPIECE

Among all the North-French Arthurian MSS produced between 1274–1330—it was the period of their greatest production—the one which perhaps comes nearest to reproducing by its own beauty and dignity something of the high romantic quality of Arthurian story at its best is the *Lancelot* once owned by Henry Yates Thompson and included by him among his *One Hundred Best Manuscripts*.[34] It contains one hundred and thirty-six historiated letters and thirty-nine large miniatures. These wide framed panels run horizontally across the three columns of text; each panel is carefully divided in its background, one half being gold, one half of a chequered color, often pale rose or blue. Generally this division emphasizes the difference between separate episodes; but at times the whole panel is devoted to one scene, which thus gains an impressive scope rare in miniature painting. There is nothing here of that belittling in scale or that lack of discrimination which lessens the artistic and illustrative value of Royal 14 E III and other cyclic MSS. More thought was given to the selection of subjects for this *Lancelot*; greater skill was employed in its execution.

One of the famous episodes of the *Vulgate Lancelot*, an episode made yet more famous by Dante's reference to it in the *Inferno*,[35] was the first kiss of Lancelot and Guinevere. In this MS it receives its most perfect medieval illustration (Frontispiece, Fig. 1),[36]

---

[33] Erwin Panofsky, *Lectures on Gothic and Late Medieval Illuminated Manuscripts*, New York University (N. Y., 1935, mimeographed), pp. 27–28.

[34] See *Illustrations from 100 MSS in the Library of Henry Yates Thompson* (L., 1916), VI, 10–20; Pl. XXXI–XLV reproduce all the larger miniatures and six historiated letters. Cf. Seymour de Ricci, *Les MSS de la Collection H. Y. Thompson*, Bull. SFRMP,

1926. From 1921–1936 the MS was owned by the late Cortlandt F. Bishop. It was sold (April, 1938) to the Morgan Library, New York City.

[35] *Inferno*, V, 133 ff., trans. J. B. Fletcher (N. Y., 1931).

[36] For contrast see the same episode in a good later miniature (Fr. 118, f. 219 v, reproduced by Lot, *Étude sur le Lancelot*, p. 310). See *infra*, p. 105.

one not unworthy to have been seen by Dante's Paolo and Francesca the day they read of this very scene:

> When we read there how the longed-for smile
> Was kissed by such a lover, this one then,
> Who parts not from me this eternal while,
> Kissed me upon the mouth all tremblingly.

Rarely does a medieval miniature convey, as this one does, the sense of a poignant moment; it is enhanced rather than lessened by the insouciance of the companion scene at the right, a lively outdoor conversation between Galehaut's seneschal and the Lady of Malohaut and Laura of Carduel. In the scene of the kiss before the seated, protecting figure of Galehaut the High Prince, the lovers bend with eager outreaching arms to each other. They are stately creatures, the three thus brought together in a design deliberately contrived to suggest, by fluid lines and graceful symmetry, the harmonious sense of union. The tall figure of Guinevere, elongated almost in the English style, with her delicate face and long wimpled throat, is remarkably akin to the representation of Jeanne, Countess of Eu and Guines, kneeling before the Virgin[37] in the *Somme du Roi* (Ars. 6329, f. 1), a manuscript written in 1311. Both faces have the same aspects, with the same shaped line for brow and nose, the eyes sharply indicated, the same tiny mouth. But the *Lancelot* seems nearer in its more restrained treatment of drapery to Fr. 95 than to the *Somme du Roi*, and the best figures have that finer modeling which developed in Paris at the end of the thirteenth and the beginning of the fourteenth century. Something of the rounded, monumental style which distinguishes the figures of David and Goliath,[38] in the splendid Breviary of 1296 (Lat. 1023, f. 7 v) of Philippe le Bel and usually attributed to the celebrated Parisian "enlumineur" Honoré, is to be felt in the beautifully colored miniature (Frontispiece, Fig. 2) representing Lancelot's arrival at a church wherein, grief-stricken, he finds Galehaut's tomb guarded by five knights; it is to be felt still more strongly in the miniature that shows him opening the tomb of his ancestor, the son of Joseph of Arimathea. (Fig. 250) A certain reaction against this finely plastic style took place about 1317, to judge from the Bible written by the Parisian clerk, Jean Papelu,[39] in that year, but the *Lancelot* as a whole escapes that retrogressive tendency. Since it suggests, however, some of the new attempts at space representation, and has palpable kinship with Royal 14 E III it may tentatively be assigned to a

period about 1316, though possibly earlier, and to illuminators who, especially in their decorative devices, seem of North-French origin.

As illustration this manuscript is peculiarly effective. It avoids that multiplicity of combats which was as great a fault in most illustrations, as it was in the original romances; it emphasizes in a way suggestive of medieval pageantry the more picturesque incidents. Thus, in representing the episode first celebrated by Chrétien de Troyes in his *Chevalier de la Charrette*, and preserved in the prose versions, alike telling how Lancelot, for Love's sake, rode in the ignominious cart of the dwarf who alone could take him to rescue Queen Guinevere, and of how Gawain also rode on the same quest, the miniature (Fig. 251) has a processional dignity that escapes the absurdity so commonly found in representations of this scene.[40] So, too, does that famous scene (Fig. 252) in which Lancelot crawls across the sword bridge while puppy-like lions look on. The human figures, Guinevere and King Baudemagus in the centre tower, or at the right the King and his courtiers receiving Lancelot, have dramatic animation; their upraised hands indicate their surprise at Lancelot's feat. The composition, graceful, well-balanced, is far from being the mere costume piece it became in a later MS such as Fr. 122. (Fig. 267) In the earlier, finer *Lancelot* it should be noted, moreover, that the illustrators succeeded more nearly than anywhere else, in picturing the strange perils, the monsters and marvels, of Arthurian romance without merely rendering them grotesque. Here (f. 139) Lancelot in the Valley of False Lovers, strangles with his mailed hands a fearsome dragon; here he walks on a dangerous plank across a river; or in the Perilous Cemetery Gawain and Hector behold the ever-flaming tombs with pointed swords erect on them of Chanaan's twelve brothers. (Fig. 253) When these illustrators treat more familiar things they do so in a way more realistic than any we have yet encountered. The architecture is less elaborated than in Royal 14 E III, but many other things are more veraciously rendered. There are rich pavilions of striped silks, Arthur's dog-headed throne, horse-litters and carts, long tongs and the bellows for the fire to burn the false Guinevere (f. 119 v), Gawain's *flabellum*, or light extinguisher (f. 99), a picnic party feasting on the grass (f. 213); even, in one miniature, the architectural detail, rare in northern painting, of a coffered ceiling (f. 135). For the first time in the MSS so far noted heraldry assumes an important place. The heroes are rather carefully distinguished by their

---

[37] Cf. Martin, *Miniature franç.*, fig. XXVIII.

[38] On Honoré see Martin, *op. cit.*, p. 12, fig. XXII; *Les joyaux de l'enluminure*, p. 35, 102, fig. XLI. Leroquais, *Bréviaires manuscrits*, II, 474, disputes the attribution to Honoré.

[39] Panofsky, *Lectures on Gothic MSS*, pp. 43–45; Bella Martens,

Meister Francke (Hamburg, 1929), p. 85. For miniatures from the Papelu Bible see Martin, *Miniature franç.*, figs. XXXII ff.

[40] For one of the better representations of the cart episode see Fr. 119, f. 312, reprod. by Miss Paton, *Lancelot*, p. 266.

arms, and their shields become an important part of the decorative design. The tall knights in chain mail and conical helms are impressive figures, full of knightly grace, and far from the awkward puppets of the *Lancelot* of 1274 (Fr. 342). Knights dominate the scenes; the women's figures are less distinctive, less frequent. It is a book for a noble lord and nobly wrought. Beyond compare, it is the finest *Lancelot*.

AVERAGE ILLUSTRATED MANUSCRIPTS

Because of their superior number and quality attention has so far been given chiefly to the cyclic collections of Arthurian romance and to certain luxury books, like the *Lancelot* just described and the earlier Fr. 95 and Phillipps 130, which were masterpieces of illumination. But many single texts of far less cost were, of course, produced between 1274 and 1330, the period when the demand for Arthurian MSS seems to have been at its height. Two good *Lancelots* now at Oxford (Ashmole 828 and Rawlinson Q. b. 6)[41] both dating about 1320–30, continue the North-French and specifically Amiens characteristics. Many MSS are, from the artistic point of view, negligible, but a few, of some merit in themselves and of particular interest to Arthurian readers as illustrations of notable texts, may now be considered.

A comparatively modest manuscript of 226 leaves contains the unique text of the prose romance formerly known as the *Huth Merlin*[42] but now as Add. 38117 in the British Museum. It has 71 large miniatures, usually in the form of framed historiated letters with leaves branching from the corners; it has foliated bars for ornament, gay drolleries, and a pleasant charm of soft color. Its North-French illustrators were of average skill; one of them showed marked enjoyment of trees and birds, which he represented exactly as did the illustrator of a late thirteenth-century copy of Marie de France's *Fables* (Ars. 3142, f. 266 v).[43] Our reproductions from the *Merlin* show Balin meeting his damsel in the wood (Fig. 254); Arthur's massacre of the children, here represented by a remarkable bowlful of babies putting out to sea (Fig. 255); Merlin and his false love Nimue being entertained by musicians who play on bright red harps that match the bright arches overhead (Fig. 256); and finally Arthur hunting (Fig. 257), a typical French scene of the chase. The same type of composition is found in a manuscript of 1250, the *Vie et Histoire de S. Denis* (Nouv. Acq. 1099, f. 51 v); it persists in a fifteenth-century copy

of Gaston Phebus' *Livre de la Chasse* (Fr. 619). In Arthurian illustration it is also found in the historiated letter of a *Tristan* (Fr. 772, f. 3 v),[44] which represents King Mark hunting, or in that one illustration of Chrétien's *Erec* in a Picard MS (Fr. 24403, Fig. 258) which shows the hero blowing his horn and chasing a leaping stag.

Of special interest likewise, from the fame of the texts and the rarity of their illustration, are two manuscripts of Chrétien de Troyes's two poems, the *Conte del Graal* (Fr. 12577) and the *Ivain* (Fr. 1433). This last manuscript begins with the late thirteenth-century Gawain-poem, *L'Atre Périlleux* (Perilous Churchyard), and concludes this romance with an admirable miniature representing the marriage scene (Fig. 259) of three maidens and their loves. The style of this miniature and others corresponds too closely to that in the later Paris MS, the *Vie de Saint Louis* (Fr. 5716) by Guillaume de Saint Pathus,[45] not to make us suspect that the Arthurian illustrator had already experienced Parisian influence and that the MS, though attributed textually to the thirteenth century, cannot have been illuminated at so early a date.

Chrétien's Ivain, Fr. 1433

This Picard copy contains the only known French miniatures illustrating Chrétien's famous poem.[46] Two full-page miniatures begin the series, the first made up of five, the second of seven scenes. The later miniatures, being less crowded, are more effective. Among them we may note the following:

Fig. 260. Ivain, prematurely distinguished by a yellow lion adorning his blue horse-trappings and surcoat, dismounts before a gaily colored castle, and is welcomed by the hospitable host and his daughter. Vv. 777–786.
Fig. 261. Three compartments. 1. The next day, Ivain in desperate combat cleaves the shield of Esclados. As he pursues him into his castle, the portcullis drops, slices Ivain's horse in two and clips the spurs from his heels. Vv. 824–952. 2. Trapped between two gateways, Ivain is visited by Lunete. Vv. 970–992. 3. The body of Esclados in its winding sheet lies in a stone coffin, surrounded by mourning courtiers and ladies. Vv. 1178–79. Compare the similar scenes in the mural paintings at Schmalkalden (Fig. 162), and misericords of the dropping portcullis. (Figs. 168–170)
Fig. 262. Three compartments. 1. Lunete, imprisoned in a chapel on the accusation of a false seneschal, overhears Ivain's lament for his faithlessness to Laudine. He hears of her plight, undertakes to defend her the next day, and

---

[41] For these MSS see G. Hutchings, *Medium Aevum*, III (1934), 189–194; Frappier, *Mort Artu*, p. xxix, for the Rawl. Q. b. 6.
[42] The MS is described in the *Catalogue of the 50 MSS and Printed Books Bequeathed to the British Museum by Alfred Huth* (L., 1912), pp. 4 f.; *Cat. Brit. Mus. Add. MSS, 1911–15*, p. 16.
[43] Cf. Martin, *Miniature franç.*, fig. XVIII.

[44] Hunting scenes: *Vie de S. Denis*, Martin, *Joyaux de l'enluminure*, fig. XXXV; *Livre de la chasse*, Martin, *Miniature franç.*, fig. CVIII. For conflicting dates on the *Tristan*, Fr. 772, see Vinaver, *Études sur le Tristan*, p. 44.
[45] Martin, *Miniature franç.*, fig. XXXIX.
[46] The MS is described by Wendelin Foerster, *Löwenritter* (Halle, 1887), p. vii.

rides away. Vv. 3563–770. 2. The giant Harpin comes before a castle to slay four young knights. They are clothed only in their shirts, are mounted on feeble nags, and are continually lashed by a dwarf. Ivain rides out and attacks Harpin. Vv. 4088–212. 3. At the right, Lunete, with hands bound, awaits the fire, while Laudine and her courtiers look on from the gateway of a tower. Ivain has already unhorsed the false seneschal, and the faithful lion is tearing his body. Ivain is still in fight with his brothers. At the left, the victorious hero leads Lunete away to safety. Vv. 4385–567.

The *Ivain* has miniatures on fourteen leaves; many of them are now much rubbed but still show the blue tones of which this illustrator was so fond. The hero himself is nearly always distinguished by the device of a buff lion; the heraldic beast is more satisfactory than the puppy-like lion which companions Ivain in some of the miniatures. Art had not yet achieved realism in depicting wild beasts. In general the illustrator was faithful to his text, but it will be observed in Fig. 262 that the giant Harpin does not wear the bearskin nor wield the stake of which the poem told.

Chrétien's Conte del Graal, Fr. 12577

Likewise dating from the first quarter of the fourteenth century is this copy of Chrétien's Grail romance,[47] fols. 1–53, with a continuation to f. 272. Altogether, the one large and fifty-one smaller miniatures make this the best of the illustrated MSS of the poem. It is obvious, however, that the illustrator had no familiarity with the story but merely filled in, according to such indications as the rubrics afforded, the blank spaces left for him. Translated, the rubric for the famous visit to the Grail Castle reads:

Here is described how Perceval came to the abode of the Fisher King, and there came a varlet to the door, who brought a sword, and the King handed it to Perceval. And afterwards is described how they sat at table before a fair fire, and the varlet came who bore the Bleeding Lance and the damsels the Holy Grail.

Guided by these meagre sentences, the artist has depicted, first, a king issuing from a door and handing a sword to a mounted knight; and second, a damsel with a chalice and a "varlet" with a lance approaching a table, at which are seated a king and a queen, and beyond which is a fire under a chimney-hood. (Fig. 264) Evidently he has failed to realize that both scenes should be interiors, that Perceval should be on foot rather than on horseback, that the Fisher King should be reclining on a couch, and that queen there should be none. Besides, like most of his *confrères* in the craft, he thought that *graal* meant

"chalice." The consequences of illustration according to summary are here glaringly exemplified. Elsewhere the miniaturist's erratic fancy led him to supply the boy hero with a bow, as in the lower part of f. 1, or to reclothe him in the Welsh garb of his boyhood long after he had discarded it, as in the first compartment on f. 169.

We recognize several scenes already made familiar to us by the ivories of Perceval and Gawain and the Lübeck murals. Cf. pp. 71–75, Figs. 140–152.

Fig. 263. Above: Perceval rides out from his mother's home in his red 'Welsh' garment. He meets five knights of the Round Table and taking them for angels, kneels before them. Below: He announces to his mother that he will go to Arthur's court in spite of her command, and she swoons as he rides away. He strikes the Red Knight through the body with his javelin, and holds up the stolen cup.

Fig. 264. Left: The Fisher King gives Perceval the sword. Right: The Grail and the Bleeding Spear are borne through the hall.

Fig. 265. Left: Gawain on the Perilous Bed. Right: Gawain encounters the lion in the Chateau Merveil.

Fig. 266. Left: Perceval's sister points out to him the bier of his mother, surrounded by candles. Right: Perceval confesses his sins to his uncle the hermit.

Of all these miniatures the most interesting for comparative purposes is that of Gawain on the Perilous Bed. In mauve tunic he lies on the red-covered bed with its golden bells beneath; from the blue cloud hurtle down arrows and even a sturdy arbalest. The design is sufficiently close to that on the ivory caskets discussed in Chapter VI to make it probable that the ivory carvers worked from some miniatures such as this. It is far, indeed, from the attempted realism of the fifteenth-century German *Parzival* (Berne, AA. 91) discussed in Chapter XII, Fig. 382, in which the same adventure is set forth.

The Gawain miniature is the only one in the *Graal* MS to have a gold background; all the rest have the colored diapered backgrounds made up of squares and lozenges picked out in white with a net design, or with crosses, crosslets, *fleurs-de-lys*, and other flower patterns. This type of background had been used in Parisian miniatures to suggest interiors even in the thirteenth century, and had been inspired in all probability, as Kuhn[48] suggests, by patterned textiles; the vogue for it is shown by Fr. 12577 to be completely established. So likewise does the far more important dated Bible of Robert Billyng (Bib. Nat. Lat. 11935), illuminated and signed by the famous Parisian, Jean Pucelle, and other members of his atelier in 1327.[49] The *Graal*, like most Paris books of

---

[47] The MS is described by A. Hilka, *Der Percevalroman, Li Contes del Graal* (Halle, 1932), p. vi. On p. xliii, Hilka enumerates the miniatures in all the illustrated *Conte del Graal* MSS.

[48] Kuhn, "*Die Illustration des Rosenromans,*" *Jahrb. der Kunsthist. Sammlungen,* XXXI (1912), 10–12.

[49] Cf. Martin, *Miniature franç.,* figs. XLIII–XLV.

the period, has ivy tendrils at the corners of the miniatures; on the first page a flowing circular pattern of ivy vine encloses on the right and lower sides six medallions inset with heads of knights and their shields. The new vogue of the elaborate decorative ivy border has begun. In this *Graal*, none too distinguished from an artistic point of view, we have a fair instance of an Arthurian MS produced in one of the humbler ateliers of the great city that was, during a good part of the fourteenth century, the most famous center for the production in France of illuminated books.

CHAPTER IX

FRENCH MANUSCRIPTS, 1340-1500

THE first great battle of the Hundred Years War was fought on the sea in 1340. The date may also serve as the beginning of a period markedly different in external aspect in France from that which preceded it. Concurrently with the horrors of war came an intensification among wealthy aristocrats of the habits and fashions of excessive luxury. The simplicity, uniformity, and relative impersonality in dress of the thirteenth century[1] and the first years of the fourteenth century gave way to elaborations less tasteful than bizarre. The external change leaps to the eye in the *Vulgate Lancelot*, Fr. 122, which is dated 1344 by its colophon.[2] The MS includes the second part of the *Lancelot*, the *Queste*, and the *Mort Artu*.

This volume is decorated with 111 miniatures, four of them of the large type illustrated in Figs. 267–268. Its artistic technique shows no advance, rather a great retrogression from the achievements of Jean Pucelle and his school in the earlier years of the fourteenth century. It shows no modeling of the figures, no spatial sense; nothing of the realistic skill and delightful vivacity which characterized the drolleries of Pucelle's marginal decorations. The *Lancelot* has the leaf tendrils, the diapered backgrounds varying with golden spiral patterns, the small medallioned frames, the stereotyped treatment of Nature and architecture which characterized so many of the Parisian manuscripts of the time. What alone in this *Lancelot* is significant is the precision with which the new fashions of dress are pictured. In the first miniature (Fig. 267) the bearded Lancelot appears crawling over the sword bridge, then encountering the phantom lions, then meeting the charge of Meleagant, who rides forth from his castle, while his father and the abducted Queen Guinevere look down. Lancelot wears partly chain, partly plate mail; a short jupon with decorated edge, a longer hauberk of chain mail, a girdle clasped about his hips, a pointed basinet on his head. His knees and elbows are protected by special plates, his legs by greaves. This was the military costume of the time. In the large miniature (Fig. 268), which shows Lancelot releasing certain ensnared lords from a magic carole, the woodland scene of the lady and the stag is separated from the other by a different, diapered background; also by a rainbow colored cloud, supposed to represent the wall of air that encircled the magic garden. The color in this picture is exceptionally harmonious, but the contrast between the unnatural natural objects, especially the strange tree bearing in its top a greenish crown, and the meticulous accuracy of the costumes, gives a sharp sense of incongruity. The men wear carefully scalloped tippets; the ladies have elaborate coiffures with tightly braided side locks of hair; they wear long flowing dresses with marked décolletage. Patterned fabrics, striped and flowered, are indicated.

The first period of the Hundred Years War, the era of terrible French defeats, inevitably halted the production of illuminated books. So far as the Arthurian romances were concerned there was such marked diminution that it may be safely said that after 1344 there was little popular trade production of Arthurian texts. When they began to appear again in the last two decades of the fourteenth century, they were almost exclusively luxury MSS made for a few great patrons. The era of the great libraries had begun.

THE ROYAL LIBRARY

The development of the royal libraries of Charles V (1364–80) and of Charles VI (1380–1422) has been traced by Delisle[3] through the inventories of 1373, 1411, 1413, 1424. The Parisian libraries of the two kings included over 1200 items, in which were some of the most resplendent French MSS. Thirty-eight Arthurian titles[4] are mentioned, some in two or three volumes, and nearly all in prose, though a few in verse, a *Cliges* (No. 1101), a *Meraugis?* (*Merengis*, No. 1141), *L'Atre Périlleux* (No. 1163), and three *Percevals* (Nos. 1151–53), occur. The poems are unadorned. In general the inventories state the nature of the binding, the type of script used, and whether the volume is *très bien escript* or *très mal escript*, the number of columns of text, and the nature of the illuminations, whether *enluminé*, i.e., in the rather careful differentiation of these inventories, "decorated," or whether *historié*, i.e., "illustrated"; also details as to age, size, and value of the volume, whether bound in plain or stamped leather, white, red, or green; and whether clasped with one, two, or even four clasps of latten, brass, or silver.[5] Many interesting details, too, are noted concerning the giving and lending and borrowing of these splendid volumes among members of the royal family,[6] matters which perhaps account for the loss of many books from the royal library. Despite the

---

[1] Enlart, *Manuel d'archéologie française* (P., 1916), III, 70.

[2] The MS is described by M. B. Fox, *La Mort Artus*, p. 7; by J. Frappier, *La Mort Artu* (P., 1936), p. xiv.

[3] Léopold Delisle, *Recherches sur la librairie de Charles V* (Paris, 1907).

[4] *Ibid.*, II, nos. 1081–84, 1101, 1113–1120, 1124, 1131–33, 1139–46, 1151–53, 1163, 1189–90, 1195, 1197–1202.

[5] *Ibid.*, I, pp. 42–48.

[6] *Ibid.*, I, pp. 120 ff., 131 ff.

precise indications of the inventories, however, the listed royal Arthurian MSS cannot be identified to-day, for none of those extant have preserved their original binding; many have lost their title pages, and parts of different MSS have often been bound together. We can only look on certain fine MSS that were produced in the last decades of the fourteenth century and the beginning of the fifteenth, and surmise they may once have belonged to these collections.

There were in the royal library no fewer than six *Tristans*,[7] and three of these great volumes were "enluminé." The two-volume *Tristan* of 814 leaves, now known as Fr. 100–101 (Figs. 269–276), was thought by Paulin Paris to have been written by one of the scribes of Charles V, but its illuminations appear to be closely related to the work of the "Master of 1402."[8] They are original in conception, charming and distinctive in style. They were done in grisaille, a kind of gray or greenish painting which we have already observed in the Runkelstein murals. The backgrounds have a green wash for the earth; a rather deep blue, shading to light, for the sky. The figures are mostly in grisaille, but notes of color are introduced, red in the harness of horses, also in roofs and a rug, yellow and black for a mosaic floor, touches of blue in headdresses, gold for crowns and pendants. The sharply carved rocks, the groups of trees with stippled, pale green tops, the blue water, show a remarkable progress in naturalistic art. Above all the sense of space in these pictures is definitely indicated, for again and again the artist represents, as it were, a little stage, an outward frame, through which we look into actual rooms. He has not complete command of the problems of perspective, but he is well advanced in their mastery. His figures are no longer placed on that foreshortened standing plane which marked the second phase of Gothic illumination, but they belong to the third and last phase, which Professor Panofsky[9] has defined as that in which figures are subordinated to space and the miniatures become pictorial projections of a whole space section. Particularly is this seen in the miniature representing that distinctive episode of the *Prose Tristan*, the murder of Tristram by Mark, who stabs the lover in the back as he sits harping before Ysolt (Fig. 276). The lovers sit on one of those stately medieval beds which served in the day for couch as well. The yellow canopy above the bed is fringed with blue and red, the side curtain is reddish,

the cover lilac; the bed rests on a little platform of its own, and the whole is structurally conceived. Behind Tristram Mark stands on the raised threshold of the door; he comes from one space to another. The figures are proportioned with reference to their surroundings, and are represented throughout in gracious guise. They wear long, gracefully flowing robes with long sleeves; the women's dresses are often high necked and very high waisted. Despite the detail in matters of dress, the elaborate *chaperon* of the men, the heart-shaped or double-pointed headdress of the women, the jeweled belts and necklaces with long pendants, the faces and figures are possessed of romantic charm. The trend toward realism in fashion, already observed in the *Lancelot* of 1344, is here matched also by a realistic presentment of interiors and landscapes with rocks, trees, bridges, and a walled fountain. The realism of detail extends from jeweled drinking horn to great wooden bathtubs bound with hoops. It is significant of the closeness with which contemporary fashions were followed that in Fr. 100 no instance appears of the curious curved leg-protectors which, as we shall see in Fr. 335–336, mounted knights began to use in France about 1400, whereas in Fr. 101, the companion volume to Fr. 100, these leg-protectors do appear. The two volumes were illustrated by the same artists, but in the last a number of miniatures were left incomplete. The frames were drawn but the space left empty.

Despite an excessive number of combat scenes in Fr. 100–101, this *Tristan*, which includes material from the *Queste* is distinguished by the artistic grace and originality of its illustrations. Our reproductions show:

Fr. 100. Fig. 269. The King of Ireland prevents his wife from killing Tristram in his bath when, through his notched sword, she discovers his identity.

Fig. 270. Tristram, hunting in the wood, beholds *la beste glatissante*, the most fantastic of all Arthurian monsters.[10]

Fig. 271. Tristram, having won Ysolt to be the bride of King Mark, embarks with her for Cornwall.

Fig. 272. King Mark receives the magic drinking horn sent to prove Ysolt an unfaithful wife.

Fig. 273. Tristram and Dinadan fight the knights of Morgan le Fay.

Fr. 101. Fig. 274. Perceval comes to Joyous Garde where, above the tomb of Galehaut, the High Prince, he is shown

---

[7] *Ibid.*, II, nos. 1197–1202.

[8] Paulin Paris, *Cat. des MSS français* (P., 1838), I, 134. The MS is described by Vinaver, *Études sur le Tristan*, p. 39. On the work of the "Master of 1402" see Bella Martens, *Meister Francke* (Hamburg, 1929), Index. Cf. Abb. 42–43, 48–50. To this artist has been ascribed the greater part of the illustrations in the Boccaccio (Fr. 12420) of Philip the Bold; the Boccaccio (Fr.

598) of the Duc de Berry to whom also belonged the *Bible Historiale* (Ars. 5057–5058) discussed below. For these and other works of the Master see Martens, p. 241, n. 221.

[9] Panofsky, *Lectures on Gothic and Medieval Illuminated MSS*, p. 28.

[10] On this creature see Bruce, *Evolution of Arth. Romance*, I, 465; Nitze in *Zts. f. rom. Phil.*, LVI (1936), 409 ff.

the painted figures of Lancelot, Tristram, Galahad (cf. p. 20).

Fig. 275. Perceval and the recluse.

Fig. 276. Mark slays Tristram, who was harping before Ysolt.

A second *Tristan* (Fr. 335–336) is dated April 17, 1399, by its colophon. The two volumes, totalling 834 leaves, are far less interesting in their many small, tinted pen drawings than is Fr. 100–101. The draftsman here seemed deliberately to avoid figures difficult to conceive, like the *Beste Glatissante*, or complicated to execute. His pictures are useful chiefly for dating purposes. Through them we may date the curved leg-protector (Fig. 277) and the elaborate headgear for horses, which we find also in the cyclic MS, Ars. 3479–80. (Fig. 284) In the numerous court scenes we observe in Fr. 335–336 the identical fashions in women's dress already noted in Fr. 101. Distinction is given to the volume only by the frontispiece (f. 1, Fig. 278) representing the supposed author of the romance, Luce de Gaut, usually referred to as Luces de Gast,[11] first in the act of compiling his book, another volume on the reading desk beside him, and then, on his knees, in act of presenting his book before various courtiers to the king. This miniature is itself a good Arthurian example of those presentation scenes which were becoming so much the vogue. It is a tinted drawing, a *portrait d'encre*. The faces are mature and individualized; the author represented with his book has the aspect of learning and experience. In this scene too, though the artist has not set himself the space problems found in Fr. 100–101, he has not been unaware of them; he has not created a room with ceiling, receding walls, and floor, but has used the tesselated black and yellow, floor, a chair and throne set at angles to each other, and robust figures beside the throne to suggest a genuine spatial sense. The men in this picture, as sometimes in Fr. 100–101, wear the long cumbersome *houppelande* of the period, but their bodies are felt beneath it.

THE ARTHURIAN MSS OF JEAN DUC DE BERRY

In contrast to his royal brother, Jean, Duc de Berry, did not garner many romances for his library.[12] Religious books, books of history, travel, and didactic import, if they were in sufficiently splendid form, were more pleasing to his eclectic and cosmopolitan taste. On such books, above all on the *Très Riches Heures* (Chantilly, Lat. 1284), painted within 1413–16, he had his own matchless illuminators, the Limbourg brothers—masters of Flemish, French, and Italian styles—spend their efforts and their genius.

But though the Duc de Berry did not, apparently, commission any of his own most distinguished illuminators to work on Arthurian manuscripts, he was not wholly neglectful of the need of such works for the library of a connoisseur. He had a *Lancelot* (No. 270) and a *Guiron* (No. 272). A record tells of his purchase in 1405 of a great one-volume "*Lancelot*," a Vulgate cycle now divided into the MSS known as Fr. 117–120. The record is found in the ducal inventories of 1413 and 1416 and reads:[13]

Un grant livre appelé le Livre de Lancelot du Lac, escript en francois, de lettre de forme, tres bien historié au commencement et en plusiers lieux, lequel Monseigneur acheta, en janvier 1405, de maistre Regnault du Montet, demeurant a Paris, la somme de 300 escus d'or.

The important Parisian bookseller here mentioned was later tried for treason on account of his too frequent visits to England, where he is known, among other things, to have sold a *Tristan*.[14] He may have been the seller, too, in Paris of certain other costly MSS which are connected artistically with Fr. 117–120. One of these was another complete Arthurian cycle, Ars. 3479–80, containing 1300 pages, written in an early fifteenth century hand, and having 125 miniatures; another was the ornate Bible, Ars. 5058. These three huge MSS were all in parts illuminated by the same artists and must have come from the same atelier.

The miniatures in Fr. 117–120 and in Ars. 3479–80 have the same plan and many identical miniatures. Fr. 117, though actually made up only of the *Estoire* and the *Merlin*, contains two miniatures, a large frontispiece, the same in subject as that in Ars. 3479, representing the birth of Lancelot, his life with the Lady of the Lake, a combat of knights, and Lancelot asleep at the wayside cross with two small red-winged angels holding the Grail above. The second miniature in Fr. 117, f. 50, a Harrowing of Hell, is found also in Ars. 3479, p. 109. The *Lancelot* proper begins in Fr. 118, f. 155,[15] and in Ars. 3479, p. 339, with the same miniature showing Ban and Bors as elderly, white-bearded men, and their two fair young queens, all four seated on a throne-like structure, but the Arsenal MS eliminates one of the two small boys. A less successful domestic group appears in the miniature representing Bors beholding the infant Galahad (Ars. 3480, Fig. 279; cf. Fr. 119, f. 466).

---

[11] On this name see Bruce, *Evolution of Arth. Romance*, I, 486 f. For MS 335–336 see Vinaver, *op. cit.*, p. 41.

[12] Delisle, II, 210–297, "*L'inventaire des livres du Duc de Berry*."

[13] Delisle, II, 266 (No. 270).

[14] A. de Champeaux et P. Gaucherey, *Les travaux d'art exécutés pour Jean de France, Duc de Berry* (P., 1894), 126 ff. Guiffrey, *Inventaires de Jean, duc de Berry* (P., 1884), cxliv, notes the frequent occurrence of this bookseller's name in the Duke's accounts. Cf. Nitze, *Mod. Phil.*, XXVIII (1928), p. 365.

[15] Reproduced by L. A. Paton, *Lancelot*, frontispiece.

Of far greater importance, however, than any other correspondence between the two MSS is their identical beginning of the *Queste*. For here, alike, they make a unique, short excerpt from the *Perlesvaus*,[16] that strange romance in which more than anywhere else in Arthurian story "one seems to be passing back and forth between the land of faery and the cloister." Heading this excerpt in each MS is the same Crucifixion (Fr. 120, Fig. 280; Ars. 3480, f. 483), the most beautiful, unquestionably, of the many Crucifixions which appear in MSS of the *Estoire* and the *Queste*. The reason for its distinctive beauty and skill becomes plain when it is compared with the miniature from which it was copied, the Crucifixion in the Brussels *Hours of the Virgin* (Bibl. Roy. 11051, f. 122 v),[17] ascribed to the master[18] of the yet more famous *Hours* (Paris, Mus. Jacquemart-André), made within 1391–1416, for that gallant soldier of France, the Maréchal de Boucicaut. The figures of the Virgin and St. John in the Brussels *Hours* are reproduced in the Arthurian miniatures with almost no change; the touching head of Christ is the same, though the figure hangs straight on the Cross, not with the knees bent as in the Brussels *Hours*. The only significant difference is in the diminutive figure which kneels, in the two Arthurian miniatures, at the foot of the Cross, and holds up the golden chalice of the Grail. Since the twelfth century the chalice had occasionally been represented at the foot of the Cross, and sometimes Mary Magdalene or Adam or an angel had knelt there holding the cup,[19] but here is represented in the kneeling figure either Joseph of Arimathea, whose name occurs in the lines immediately below the miniature, or, if we assume the illustrator read to the bottom of the page, one of those of whom the text says: "they believed fearfully and received the blood." Other miniatures in the *Queste* section of both Fr. 120 and Ars. 3480, likewise have reminiscences of the style of the Boucicaut Master, of the brilliant patterned backgrounds he sometimes used, the limpid clarity of his color, his tender greens and bright vermilion, his stippled trees with yellowish triangular pointed tops, his sharply curving rocks. Particularly reminiscent are the miniatures representing Galahad receiving the key to the Castle of Maidens (Ars. 3480, Fig. 281), or Galahad in combat with the Deadly Sins in the guise of knights on richly caparisoned horses (Fig. 282), or Perceval slaying the dragon (Ars. 3480, Fig. 283). Though this differs in composition, the central figure strongly recalls the St. George of the second Brussels *Hours* (Bibl. Roy. 10767, f. 239),[20] also ascribed to the same Master. None of the *Queste* miniatures attempt the Master's lovely landscapes with their lakes and swans, his outdoor atmospheric effects and subdued interior lighting, his skilled use of perspective. The Arthurian miniatures imitate only the color, the figures, the more easily copied features of the Boucicaut Master.

The connection thus established between the atelier of the Boucicaut Master and these Arthurian MSS is of special interest since the Maréchal de Boucicaut himself was so great a lover and imitator of romance.[21] In 1389 at St. Inglevert near Calais, for a whole month, he undertook jousts with all comers, and with all the apparatus of Arthurian chivalry, shields suspended from trees, a challenging horn, and so forth. In 1399 he is said to have founded the order of *La Dame Blanche à l'Ecu Vert* for the purpose of aiding distressed ladies by force of arms. Such a man would surely have owned his own illuminated Arthurian books, and it may well be that he commissioned the atelier that produced the two Brussels *Hours* to produce for him also one or the other of these sumptuous romance manuscripts.

The rich Bible (Ars. 5058), already noted as being connected with the two Arthurian MSS, Ars. 3479–80 and Fr. 117–20,[22] was, like the latter, once owned by Jean, Duc de Berry, for his signature appears on f. 57 v. The artistic connection is most easily established, perhaps, through the identity in certain miniatures of these MSS of one notable figure. In the Bible the glowing frontispiece sets forth four scenes from the life of Solomon, who is represented as an ancient man with heavy unwieldy body and broad, patriarchal beard. It is this figure, enthroned and receiving the Queen of Sheba, which has also, through the unconscious humor of a busy artist, served for King Arthur. Thus he sits, another Solo-

---

[16] *Perlesvaus*, ed. W. A. Nitze, T. A. Jenkins, I (Chicago, 1932), pp. 10 ff. Of the six known MSS of the *Perlesvaus* the Brussels MS (Bibl. Roy. 11145, f. 1), has one miniature, much effaced, of the angel dictating the work to Josephus (Nitze and Jenkins, p. 4).

[17] Reproduced by J. van den Gheyn, *Deux livres d'heures* (Brussels, 1913), Pl. 42.

[18] For a characterization of the Boucicaut Master see Durrieu, *Revue de l'art chrétien*, LXIII (1913), 301 ff. Van den Gheyn, p. 7, Bella Martens, *Meister Francke*, p. 195, and Durrieu, p. 308, alike ascribe Brussels 11051 to this master.

[19] Cf. Mâle, *Religious Art of the Thirteenth Century* (N. Y., 1913), 223, on the motif of the cup; cf. Lyna, *De Vlaamsche Miniatuur*, Afb. 10, for a 14th century example of the chalice up-

held by Magdalen; Millar, *Eng. Illum. MSS of the XIV and XV Centuries* (P., Brussels, 1928), Pl. XI, for Adam at the foot of the Cross.

[20] Reproduced by Van den Gheyn, *op. cit.*, Pl. 23; also by Bella Martens, *Meister Francke*, Abb. 44: cf. also Abb. 93 (Brussels 10767, f. 222 v) with Fig. 281 here. MS. 10767 is also attributed to the Boucicaut Master by the authorities cited in n. 18.

[21] R. S. Loomis, "Chivalric and Dramatic Imitations of Arthurian Romance," in *Medieval Studies in Memory of A. Kingsley Porter* (Harvard University Press).

[22] Miss Paton, *Lancelot*, reproduces a number of miniatures from this MS. See besides the frontispiece from Fr. 118, pp. 143, 156, 205, 230, 236; from Fr. 119, pp. 266, 292, 300; from Ars. 3480, pp. 328, 330, 343, 346, 384.

mon (Fig. 285),[23] with a courtier behind him when the damsel comes to summon Lancelot for Galahad's knighting. She has but one attendant instead of the Queen's two, but otherwise the composition is the same. In this, as in the Crucifixion from the Brussels *Hours*, the fact of direct copying is certain. The long-bearded, Solomon-like Arthur appears elsewhere in Arsenal 3480, and again very recognizably in Fr. 118, as in the miniature where he receives the messengers of the false Guinevere (f. 264).[24] He serves as a convenient means of tracing the hand of the Bible artist in these romance manuscripts.

The artistic history of Fr. 117–120 was by no means finished when, in all its original freshness, it was sold to the Duc de Berry. Later on it passed into the possession of Jean's grandson, another distinguished bibliophile, Jacques d'Armagnac, Duc de Nemours. To him, accustomed to the realistic art of the mid-fifteenth century, this MS, which must have been first illuminated before 1405, probably seemed old fashioned. Decorative backgrounds had gone as much out of fashion as the style of the clothes represented. So he turned over the volumes to his own illuminator. Long ago Durrieu[25] observed that on numerous pages the paint of these later miniaturists has flaked off, making it possible to see how the new work was superimposed on the old. Many, perhaps most, of the miniatures were subjected to extensive repainting, among them the frontispiece itself. Over the old lozengy backgrounds were painted blue skies and new scenes presented with the new "realism." Though the Crucifixion of Fig. 280, Fr. 120, f. 520, was left untouched, others of that notable group at the beginning of the *Queste* suffered sad changes. In the miniature showing Perceval's fight with the dragon (Fr. 120, f. 537), once no doubt identical with the fine one in Ars. 3480, p. 525, Fig. 283, of which we have spoken in connection with the Brussels *Hours* attributed to the Master of the Boucicaut *Hours*, it is now possible to see beneath the modernizer's duller, darker colors, here a bit of the original bright red of Perceval's jupon beneath the armor painted over it, there a bit of the old background showing through his helmet. Nothing is left of the delicate drawing, the vital freshness of the original. One of these later revisers, whom for convenience we will call reviser B and who may have been that Evrard d'Espingues mentioned below as one of the latest of Arthurian miniaturists, is to be easily distinguished both by his style and his literal

mindedness. In such a scene as that representing Galahad in the Siege Perilous (Fig. 287), Arthur's Round Table is realistically represented with a white table cloth and circular opening in the middle. Over it the Grail hovers supported by two golden angels, and from the Grail, as from a divine presence, radiates effulgence, indicated by finest lines of gold. About the table, sit ten knights—Arthur, with his crown, half turning to Lancelot who sits beside him, Galahad, in white and gold, beneath a rose-colored canopy. The plain but distinctive faces, the arcaded seats, lightly shaded with gold, the tesselated floor, the vista through the open door, here showing Galahad pulling out the stone, are all in the charactistic style of Reviser B. On f. 590 v still another fifteenth century illustrator has revised the fight of Lancelot and Gawain (Fig. 286); he gives us not only his own contemporary costume and heraldry, but also introduces the new landscapes, here a far-off view of the city, with towers and spires, and the wooded banks of a river outside its walls. Arthur is represented, not as a Solomon, but, with realistic appreciation of the probabilities of his appearance, as a man of later middle age, grey-haired, alert and vigorous. He wears his insignia of three crowns; Gawain bears on his shield a double eagle; Lancelot on his shield the three oblique bands, *bandes de bellic*, which regularly distinguish him. The three are clad almost completely in plate mail. The illustrator has emphasized the figures by heavy black outlines drawn on one side and used pen work rather than paint to indicate shadows. It is a different technique as well as a different style from that in the earlier miniatures.

The second Arthurian MS listed among the books acquired by Jean, Duc de Berry, was a *Guiron* in two volumes[26] listed in the inventory of 1416. Though the Duke's *Guiron* has not been identified with any of the fifteen MSS of the *Palamedes*[27] (of which *Guiron* forms the second part) which are now at the Bibliothèque Nationale, it is possible to see in the illustrated *Guiron* (Fr. 356–357) the influence at least of the Duke's illuminators. This *Guiron* is to be dated about 1430 or before, if we may judge from the close resemblances in costume and armor, in its treatment of landscape and marginal decoration, to the probably Parisian Bedford Missal (Brit. Mus. Add. 18850), which was presented in 1430 to Henry VI of England.[28] The *Guiron* was itself later acquired by Jean Louis of Savoy, Bishop of Geneva, who had, as we shall see, a taste for Arthurian romances. His

[23] Reproduced by Martin and Lauer, *Les MSS de l'Arsenal* (P., 1929), Pl. XXXVIII; Martin, *Miniature franç.*, Pl. 75.

[24] Reproduced by L. A. Paton, *Lancelot*, p. 230.

[25] Durrieu, *Les antiquités judaïques* (P., 1908), p.47, for Fr. 118, see f. 204 v, f. 225, f. 252; for Fr. 119, see f. 331 v, 363, 379 v, 391 v, etc.

[26] Delisle, *op. cit.*, II, 286 (No. 270).

[27] Cf. Löseth's enumeration, *Tristan en prose*, 434. The following MSS of the *Guiron-Meliadus* have illustrations: Fr. 338, 350, 356–357, 358–363. Fr. 358 (large miniatures) was made for Louis of Gruthuyse. Cf. Van Praet, *Recherches sur Louis de Bruges* (1831), No. LXIV.

[28] Cf. Blum and Lauer, *Miniature franç., XV–XVI siècles*, Pl. 7. See p. 59 for date of Missal.

arms were added in Fr. 357 on f. 241, the leaf which bears one of the two large miniatures of these volumes. This miniature, which best expresses the trends of interest familiarized by the Duc de Berry's illuminators, represents the scene in which Meliadus and a knight, grieving because his love has been carried off by the King of Scotland, chance to meet the abductor, the lady, and their retinue.[29] (Fig. 288) They ride through a forest of feather-topped trees with well-defined trunks and branches; half-hidden in the trees are animals admirably suggested—a boar, a stag, lightly coursing dogs. A touch of the exotic, the Oriental, is added to this picture of the supposedly Scottish retinue by a camel with red treasure-chests swung from his humps! A wayside cross, a fountain, a monastic church, a windmill on a distant hill, a shaded sky with drifting serpentine clouds, suggest the delight of the Duke's illustrators in both naturalism and the exotic. Here, as with them, is that contrast between the idealized elegance of aristocratic life and a genuine and realistic presentation of humble life. Here the ladies riding in richly patterned dresses recall not too remotely the graceful elegance of the lovely ladies of the Maying party in the *Très Riches Heures*. The contrast between the ladies in the *Guiron* and the booted footman who prods the horses on, or the anxious driver of the packhorse, is marked. Rusticity, the pastoral, the bucolic, is not stressed in the *Guiron* nor is it ever realized with anything of the penetrating realism of the Duke's illuminators; but the feeling for it is present, as in a miniature (Fr. 356 f. 31), where, in a setting of rocks and woods, two knights discourse while a realistic shepherd and his dog watch their sheep. The smaller miniatures of the *Guiron* are not of the delicacy of the large miniature; but here and there, as in the feasting scene with servitors bringing in silver flagons (Fr. 356, f. 83), or in that where the Queen of Scotland and her ladies in a castle by a river (Fr. 356, f. 138) listen to a harpist, there is good measure of aristocratic and artistic charm.

ROMANCE AND REALISM

These two contrasting moods continued to characterize the miniature-painting of the fifteenth century, which had by 1430, in the hands of the greater artists at least, attained the mastery of most technical problems. On the one hand, there was the effort to idealize romantically aristocratic beauty in people and castled landscape; on the other to give a genre-like representation of more varied human types and classes of people; to record more varied emotional experiences; to create atmospheric and seasonal effects; to render buildings, street scenes, shops and houses, as they were actually known to fifteenth century eyes. Italian charm, Flemish realism continued powerfully to affect French illuminators, though the art that was developed, especially by the artists of the Loire valley, of Touraine, Poitou, and Berry, remained more indisputably French than the "international style" developed earlier by the Limbourg brothers and their contemporaries. The supreme artist of the Touraine school was Jean Fouquet (1420–c. 1481), one of the greatest masters of French illumination.[30] He was also the contemporary of and the greatest influence upon one of the latest of our Arthurian illuminators, Jean Colombe. But between Colombe's work in 1480 and the *Guiron* of before 1430, many Arthurian MSS were produced which attest the changing emphasis, by which now realism, now romanticism triumphed in art.

The element of sheer French charm and grace is to be felt chiefly in a delicately executed *Tristan* now at Chantilly (No. 404).[31] It bears the arms of Jean du Mas, Seigneur de l'Isle, that somewhat ruthless collector, but it was undoubtedly not made for him as was the later *Tristan*, illustrated by Evrard d'Espingues, which we shall presently note as also belonging to the Du Mas collection. Into Fr. 404 obtrude no ugly things, no coarse faces: it is graciously refined, altogether courtly. As delightfully as anywhere are to be found here royal hunting parties (f. 21), weddings and funerals, preparations for a feast, with servitors spreading the benches with cloths of various hues (f. 233). There is a consciously rustic scene with a bagpipe-playing shepherd (f. 145); the landscape stretches in fair vistas under blue skies and gold-flecked clouds; the interiors are rich with gold-patterned hangings; the colors have exquisite clarity. But the best miniatures might do for almost any story and there is little of real animation or strength of concept, so far as the story goes, in this *Tristan*.

But the same cannot be said for the MS to which artistically it is closely related, and that is Fr. 96 containing the *Estoire-Merlin-Lancelot* (Figs. 289–291), one of the finest French Arthurian MSS of the fifteenth century. In both alike appear the same chateaux, the same fair distances and skies, the same figures, the same round-cropped heads of youths clad in long hose and short-belted tunics, the same old men. This last MS was taken more seriously by the illustrator, perhaps because of the religious content of the *Estoire*. Certainly it is akin to the notable *Hours* (Chantilly, Lat. 13621), known to have be-

---

[29] For this episode see Löseth, *Tristan en prose*, p. 455, n. 3.
[30] Blum and Lauer, *op. cit.*, ch. IV, "Fouquet"; Pl. 15–20. Cf. Trenchard Cox, *Jehan Foucquet* (L., 1931).

[31] The MS is described by J. Meurgey, *Principaux MSS à Chantilly* (P., 1930), SFRMP, pp. 102–103, Pl. LXVI.

longed much later to Adelaide of Savoy.[32] The *Hours* were made about 1460 in the north, possibly in Paris, but they contain one miniature that might be ascribed to Fouquet himself, and many suggest his influence. The master of the *Hours* was especially interested in genre scenes of everyday life for his illustrations of the labors of the months, but when he or some imitator was at work on the *Estoire* the strangely fantastic yet courtly story allowed no such opportunity. But for the rest there are many resemblances. Both MSS have the same rich brightness and harmony of color, the same interest in depicting landscapes with dim blue distances, cumulus clouds, the rayed, golden glow of late sunset, fresh, verdant slopes, trees with straight clear trunks and round plumy tops. The architecture is so much the same that it seems that the artist must have copied from the same chateau the towers with narrowly peaked slate roofs, the traceried stonework, the topmost grill of iron. In the *Estoire* the artist presents arches and sunny arcades, not without a suggestion of Italy, and many of his scenes are placed beneath an arched or gabled enclosure. The one beside which Christ gives the little red book to the dreaming hermit (Fig. 289) matches the thatched and timbered structure beneath which, in the *Hours*, the Virgin and Joseph worship the Christ-child. The walls open on a vista of far-off hills and buildings. The head of the Christ in the *Estoire* is the head of the Christ of the Last Judgment in the *Hours*, even to the same pointed forelock on the brow; the faces of the white-bearded, dark-eyed old men in the *Estoire* are the same as those found, with the same high-peaked, broad-brimmed hats of the old men in the Burial of the Virgin in the *Hours*. In both, blue angels, their blue draperies shadowed with gold, are the same; likewise the exuberant flowery borders, with their special use of pansies, which, in the *Estoire*, the artist introduces even into the miniature itself.

The illustrations of the *Estoire* enrich the text with all the accessories of fifteenth-century luxury: the brocades, the great, canopied beds, statues on columns, fireplaces with hooded chimneys. The meeting of a heathen king with the bare-footed Joseph of Arimathea and his followers takes place before a chateau; King Crudens with golden mantle falling over blue brocaded gown, is a magisterial figure, haughty and splendid. (Fig. 290) Nude figures, like those of Evalach dreaming in his great bed (f. 6 v), or of Josephe himself, are anatomically realized. But despite the literalness with which the episodes of Josephe's bleeding nose and his making a cross on the shield (Fig. 291) are painted, the pictures are not overloaded with detail. There is an effect of great clarity in these miniatures, and the imagination of the artist still saw the world as beautiful.

Of about the same period as the *Estoire* but by a very different hand are the miniatures in a bulky *Tristan*, written by that indefatigable scribe Michel Gonnot, who wrote not only this *Tristan* but also later at Tournai an enormous *Lancelot* (Fr. 112). The MS (Fr. 99, Figs. 292–295)[33] was written for Eleanor de Bourbon, the Countess of La Marche, whose arms it bears, and also those of her son, the great collector, Jacques d'Armagnac, Duc de Nemours. In his colophon Gonnot states that the *Tristan* was finished October 8, 1463, by "Micheau Gonnot de la Brouce, prestre, demourant a Crousant" [Crozant, Dép. Creuse]. It was Gonnot we may feel sure, because of the identical writing, who introduced the amusing little caricatures—unique in Arthurian illustration—of figures bearing scrolls which read: (f. 425 v) "cest dinadain le gabaurez tristan"; "This is Dinadan, the mocker of Tristan"; (f. 426) "cest palamedes le bon." (Figs. 293–294)

Some of the illuminations in this *Tristan* of 775 leaves, according to Durrieu,[34] are by the same hand—or, as we believe, hands—that revised the miniatures in Fr. 120. The miniatures of Fr. 99 are commonly admirable in tone and design, especially in such glowing scenes of chivalric life as that of the tourney in which Galahad first proved his prowess. (Fig. 292) The gallery where the king and ladies sit is hung with blue, broidered with Arthur's three golden crowns, and much is made of the shields and horse trappings of Arthurian heraldry. The miniatures above show Galahad being knighted by his father Lancelot, and drawing the sword from the stone before King Arthur, who is here, as again on f. 563, where the coming of the Grail is represented, an ancient bearded king. (Fig. 295) He is singularly reminiscent of the aged Samuel in the upper part of a miniature, ascribed to an immediate precursor of Fouquet, in the *Mer des histoires* (B. N. Lat. 4915, f. 46 v).[35] There is an even more curious resemblance in the harsh faces of the longnosed, dark-eyed men, with accentuated mouth-lines, who sit at the left of the Grail table, to the actual likeness of Louis de Valtan, Archdeacon of Angers, in the miniature showing him offering his *Symbole des apôtres* (Add. 35320, f. 3 v)[36] to Charles VIII. But whatever their models, the best drawn faces in Fr. 99 have that realistic individuality which reflects the contemporary interest in portraiture. Specially to be noted among these more distinctive heads is that of Tristram in the large miniature (f. 1) which shows the birth of the

[32] Reproduction by Bouissounouse, *Jeux et travaux d'après un livre d'heures du XV siècle* (P., 1925); Meurgey, *op. cit.*, p. 97, Pl. LX, LXI. Neither writer refers to Fr. 96.
[33] MS described by Vinaver, *Études sur le Tristan*, p. 38.

[34] Durrieu, *Antiquités judaïques et le peintre Jean Fouquet*, (P., 1908), p. 47, n. 3.
[35] Reproduction by Blum and Lauer, *op. cit.*, Pl. 13.
[36] *Ibid.*, Pl. 83.

hero, his fight with Morhaut, the potion scene, and Tristram's death as he harps before Ysolt. This artist had little skill in rendering light effects, though it is clear in the Grail scene that he was familiar with contemporary renderings of the scene of Pentecost, for here, as in an illuminated *Légende dorée* (Fr. 244, f. 158),[37] the coming of the Divine is represented in similar flakes of fire and golden rays of light. He was better at architecture and painted many a fine castle (f. 673 v); even once picturing (f. 382) an interesting ruined castle behind an encampment. Perhaps it was some conscious feeling for the past or else the influence of some older MS that made him indulge here and there in a bit of archeologizing, as when he introduces ailettes, completely outmoded by 1350, on the shoulders of his heroes (Fig. 292), or elsewhere helmets with nasals or coifs made of chain (f. 165). The fighting scenes in general are best in this MS, which has even less feeling than is usual for the story and even carries realism to the extent of representing seasick folk at sea (f. 115). On the whole, it is, however, a vivid MS, which suffers only from the monotony of its own chivalric scenes.

The arms of Jacques d'Armagnac, which appear on Fr. 99, appear also on the four great volumes of the complete cyclic MS Fr. 113–116. The frontispiece of Fr. 113 was, in Durrieu's opinion,[38] by the same hand that painted the ten small miniatures in the second volume of *Les antiquités judaïques* (Nouv. acq. Fr. 21013). But whether one artist in the employ of the Duke was thus directly under Fouquet's influence or not, a majority of the miniatures show notable similarity to those in another huge cyclic MS. Fr. 112. (Figs. 297–298) This *Lancelot* MS was finished, as we are told on f. 233, by "Micheau Gantelet, prestre, demeurant en la ville de Tournay" on July 4, 1470. Why this Gantelet, who is doubtless the Gonnot of Fr. 99, written in 1463, should have been in Tournai in 1470 we do not know, but that this *Lancelot* (Fr. 112) was in the possession of Jacques d'Armagnac is proved by his arms, partly effaced though they were when the volume was taken from his library after his execution in 1477.[39] Though written in Tournai, the MS must have been soon in the hands of the Duke's own illuminators. Among the illuminators was one of the latest, and in all probability one of the most fatally prolific of all who ever illustrated Arthurian romance. He was the well-known Evrard d'Espingues.

Two Late French Miniaturists
EVRARD D'ESPINGUES AND JEAN COLOMBE

Evrard d'Espingues was born at Cologne but lived in France from 1429–1499. His first patron in Paris was the Duc de Nemours, but after the Duke's tragic downfall, the artist passed into the employment of that Jean du Mas, Seigneur de l'Isle, who seems to have taken over not only some of the finest books from the Duke's library, but also some of his craftsmen. Among these was the scribe Gilles Gassien (Gatien), a native of Poitiers, who wrote and signed the three-volume *Tristan*, now at Chantilly (No. 315–317),[40] which bears the arms of Jean du Mas. In 1479–80 Evrard d'Espingues was at Ahun, near Geret (Creuse), and it was there he illuminated for his second patron not only this enormous *Tristan* but also a *Propriétaire des choses* (Fr. 9140). Guibert has published the documents in which the artist recorded when and what he was paid for these MSS, and the exact costs, amounts, and names of the colors and materials he used. In his itemized list occur *azur, rose de Paris, vermilhon, verte de flambe, verte de montagne, rouge de minium, massicat jaune, noir de fumée et aultre noir*, two kinds of gold—*l'or fin* and *l'or moulu*,—*gomme a destremper toutes les couleurs*. He mentions the specific sums charged for making the big and little letters, *hystoires* and *vignectes* in the different volumes. These methodical details are today one of the most interesting things about this artist, whose heavy-handed, unimaginative style presents Arthurian story at least under the most unalluring aspect. But that in its own time his work was found pleasing is proved by the grants for his services, by his evident popularity among wealthy patrons.[41] The style of Evrard was marked. His figures have large, awkward hands and feet, broad, plain faces, straight hair. He cared little for landscapes, nothing for romantic charm. His taste was for scenes of violence, combats, attempted suicides, murders.[42] He used color thickly and specialized in brown and magenta shades. Stolidly he worked his way through the great volumes, showing at best a certain vigor, but always harsh in effect, both in color and design. Despite the courtly nature of his subject matter, he presented it with a bourgeois element of flat ugliness. His decorative borders on the large miniatures beginning each of the three columns monotonously alternate the arms of Jean du Mas with sections containing flowers or

---

[37] *Ibid.*, Pl. 52.

[38] Durrieu, *op. cit.*, p. 71.

[39] Bradley, *Dictionary of miniaturists and copyists* (L., 1888), II, 52. The old catalog number of Fr. 112 was 6783. On some volumes taken by Jean du Mas, cf. Meurgey, *op. cit.*, p. 111.

[40] For description of the MS see Vinaver, *Études sur le Tristan*, p. 50; Meurgey, *op. cit.*, pp. 115 ff., Pl. LXXV, LXXVI; Blum and Lauer, *op. cit.*, p. 104, Pl. 98 (cited as Chantilly MS. 647).

For the records dating the *Tristan* cf. L. Guibert, *Extrait des Mémoires de la Soc. des Sciences Naturelles et Archéologiques de la Creuse*, 1895, p. 8; Thomas, in *Annales du Midi*, VII (1805), 219 ff.

[41] For Jacques d'Armagnac, Duc de Nemours, Evrard d'Espingues illuminated a *Guiron* formerly at Turin. Cf. Durrieu, in *Rev. archéologique*, Ser. 4, I (1904), 403.

[42] Reproductions by Meurgey, *op. cit.*, Pl. LXXV.

sometimes loveknots intertwining a double I with bourdon and scrip. The large opening miniature of MS. 315[43] shows the author at his double-topped writing desk; at the right, clad in richly chased armor, the heroes of the text, Tristram with *lion d'or* on his shield, Galahad with his red cross, Lancelot with banded shield. The opening miniature of No. 317 (Fig. 296)[44] shows in four compartments scenes from the beginning of the Grail quest: the damsel asking for Lancelot at Arthur's court; Lancelot riding away with her; Galahad being dubbed a knight; the chivalry of the Round Table beholding the Grail.

If this last scene be compared with the late-added miniature introduced by the Duc de Nemours's Reviser B in Fr. 120 (Fig. 287), it will be observed that in both MSS the white-covered, literally round Table and the stalls are related compositions. The table, the shimmering Grail with its supporting angels, the canopied stall of Galahad in Fr. 120 are, moreover, identical with those in the same scene in Fr. 116, f. 610, and in Fr. 112, vol III, f. v,[45] which is the most carefully executed of all. Now if we turn again to the Chantilly *Tristan* we discover in the miniature depicting Ysolt's departure from Ireland[46] that her father is precisely the same figure as the Arthur who looks at Lancelot's paintings in the castle of Morgan le Fay (Fr. 116, f. 667).[47] They wear the same crown, have the same features in profile, the same lank hair, ermine tippet and long gown, the same gesture of the same hand with its stuck-together fingers. Though less precisely, the same figure reappears in Fr. 112 (Fig. 297), where again Arthur studies Lancelot's paintings. The inference is strong that in these MSS, where there are such indisputable identities, and others might be cited, that Evrard d'Espingues was concerned with them all. He was, like the scribe Gonnot, early in the employ of the d'Armagnacs, and it may have been at their command he illuminated in part the huge *Lancelot* Gonnot had finished writing at Tournai in 1470. If the German-French artist worked on all these MSS he must, like his German contemporary Diebolt Lauber of Hagenau,[48] have had numerous men working under his direction. At any rate we meet in these MSS a style that corresponds

to that of Evrard, the same unimaginative and harsh literalness, the same predilection for scenes of horror and violence. The brutal realism of some of the illustrations in these bulkiest of Arthurian texts must, even in the fifteenth century, have required stout nerves to contemplate.

Of far greater import is Jean Colombe, one of the last of our French Arthurian illuminators. In 1467 he was known to the Queen, Charlotte of Savoy, as "ung povre enlumineur a Bourges"; in 1485 he received substantial payment from Duke Charles of Savoy for completing a Book of Hours which has been identified as nothing less than the incomparable *Très riches heures* (Chantilly).[49] It had been left unfinished when Jean Duc de Berry died in 1416, and Jean Colombe was called in sixty-nine years later to complete it. He had already worked on another MS for Duke Charles, the *Apocalypse figurée* (Escorial) in 1482;[50] he was probably already at work in 1485 for Louis de Laval, lord of Chatillon.[51] After the death in 1480-81 of Fouquet, the supreme artist of the school of Touraine, Colombe's work seems to have been in great demand. A number of MSS[52] can be safely assigned to him or to his atelier in Bourges, an atelier scarcely less important, it would seem, in the eyes of contemporaries than that in Tours of his distinguished relative, the sculptor and sometime co-worker with Fouquet, Michel Colombe.[53]

Among the less costly and more hastily executed MSS ascribed to Colombe is an *Estoire del Saint Graal* (Brussels, Bibl. Roy. 9246),[54] the text of which was modernized in October 1480, by Guillaume de la Pierre for Jean Louis of Savoy, Bishop of Geneva. The interesting prologue (f. 1 v) reads:

Lan de grace nostre seigneur mil iiij c iiij^{xx} ou moy de octobre vers la fin ma esté commandé par mon treshault et Redoubté seigneur Jehan loys de Savoie evesque de geneve A moy guillaume de la pierre son treshumble obeissant et petit seruiteur de escripre en la fourme que vous voyes toute listoire de la table Ronde et metre par volupmes autant de liures quy sen pourront trouver touchant Icelle matiere et pource que Ilz sont escrips en langage ancien et le plus en langue picarde ma commandé les metre en francoiz Et poursuiuir toute Icelle matere tant quil sen puise trouuer la fin.

---

[43] Reproduction in catalog of Chantilly, *Le cabinet des livres des manuscrits* (P., 1900), II, Pl. for p. 386.

[44] Reproduced Blum and Lauer, Pl. 98.

[45] Reproduction of Fr. 116, f. 610 b, L. A. Paton, *Lancelot*, p. 348; of Fr. 112, vol. III, f. v, by Lot., *Étude sur le Lancelot*, p. 338.

[46] Reproduction by Meurgey, *op. cit.*, Pl. LXXVI.

[47] Reproduction by L. A. Paton, *Lancelot*, p. 381.

[48] Cf. *infra*, ch. XII. A Lauber miniature such as that in Fig. 382, is not without similarity to Evrard's work, especially in the facial type.

[49] P. Durrieu, *Très Riches Heures de Jean Duc de Berry* (P., 1904), pp. 103-113 (Jean Colombe); Pl. 44-48.

[50] Petit-Delchet, "Visions de S. Jean, Apocalypse de l'Escorial," *Moyen Age*, IX (1905), 68 ff.; J. Guiffrey, "Alcune note

sulle miniature dell'Apocalisse del Escuriale," *L'Arte*, IV (1901), 196 ff.

[51] Chenu, "Note sur un MS (Passages d'outremer, Fr. 5594) dont les illustrations sont attribuées à Jean Colombe," *Soc. des Antiquaires du Centre, Mémoires*, XL (1922), 277 ff. Colombe may have worked on the *Heures de Laval* (Bib. Nat. Lat. 920). Cf. Durrieu, *op. cit.*, p. 1112; Leroquais, *Livres d'Heures*, I, 29.

[52] Durrieu's list, *op. cit.*, p. 112, is incomplete.

[53] P. Vitry, *Michel Colombe et la sculpture française de son temps* (P., 1901), pp. 345, 412.

[54] Alphonse Bayot, "MSS de provenance savoisienne à la bibliothèque de Bourgogne," *Mém. de la Soc. Savoisienne d'Hist. et d'Archéol.*, XLVII (1909), 341-351. M. Bayot alone seems to have noted MS 9246 as work of Colombe.

It is evident from this that the Bishop wished to have a complete Arthurian cycle, but his death in 1482 stopped the project. The text of the *Estoire* alone was completed. It was accompanied by 52 miniatures, all of which survive except the first. That was probably a dedication scene, for the first extant illustration is the one that usually begins the *Estoire* and represents Christ and the gift of the book to the sleeping hermit (Fig. 299), a miniature which, alone in this MS, seems unlike Colombe's handiwork. There are no marginal decorations in this volume, and the illustrations take advantage of even a half line of unwritten space. All the interest is concentrated in the miniatures, which show, like many others of the late fifteenth century, that they were designed by a man who ought to have been a painter of pictures rather than an illustrator of books.

Though the *Estoire* pictures cannot be authenticated by any record, it is not possible to doubt that they emanated from the hand or the atelier of Jean Colombe. His mannerisms are unmistakable. There is a Colombe type of man, for instance, with flattened head, frequently emphasized by a flat cap, a face with heavy features and jowl, a thick bushy beard that yet reveals the wide mouth; the figure is not well proportioned and is commonly clad in long robes of thick falling drapery, hatched with gold; a sash with a single loop, such as the hermit wears, appears frequently. The type is the same whether supposed to represent Josephe in the *Estoire* (Fig. 300) giving to King Mordrain the redcross shield, or St. Joachim in the *Très riches heures* (f. 129 v), or the Numidian king Massinissa in another of the Colombe MSS, the *Romuleon* (Fr. 369, f. 197).[55] Colombe painted, too, a special type of woman, a woman with high rounded forehead, long rippling fair hair, slender figure swaying backward, protuberant stomach. In battle scenes Colombe followed a formula that he made especially his own: as in the miniature in the *Estoire* representing the battle between the Babylonian king Tholomer and the soon-to-be-Christian kings, Evalach and Seraphe (Fig. 301), the foreground is littered with corpses in richly chased gold and silver armor; the surging mass of fighting men is indicated by the tops of hundreds of helms, by a veritable forest of spears and standards. The masses are well balanced, the composition effective. As elsewhere in his work, one or two white horses, charging at full gallop into the conflict, are made focal points of interest. Colombe's colors are always sombre, but in these battle scenes they are not inharmonious. In the furthest background of these strong and only too realistic representations of warfare Colombe commonly introduced a distant landscape of idealized beauty. Like the matchless Fouquet, Colombe loved to picture in what is recognized even by severe critics[56] as one of the best elements in his work, remote and lovely vistas, undulating hills, towers and spires, far shores and silvery waters, soft blue hazes. It is the valley of the Loire he sometimes introduces in the background scenes of the *Estoire*, and sometimes there are Italian suggestions, as in the idyllic shore-line of the picture showing the divine stag leading the holy ones across the sea. (Fig. 302) The *Estoire* displays his fascinated interest in architecture, an interest that made him elsewhere paint the cathedral of Bourges, the Conciergerie, and the Sainte Chapelle in Paris[57] in entirely recognizable forms. The *Estoire* represents the meeting of the Duchess Flegetine with the men of Karabel (Fig. 303) as taking place in a paved castle courtyard; the walls of the chateau behind are many-windowed, and statues stand in niches. A bit of bas-relief—perhaps supposed to be Theseus and the Minotaur—appears on one wall; in the distance beyond is the wooded hill crowned with the three towers built by Flegetine as the "Tombs of Judgment." In interior scenes Colombe's enthusiasm for architectural detail and statuary is exemplified in the already noted Mordrain-Josephe scene (f. 179, Fig. 300). Though the place of their meeting was supposedly an abbey, Colombe depicts it as a great hall divided by dark purplish pillars with many statues against the wall. The incongruous image of a nude woman with shield and spear stands on a pedestal. The same image appears in a lunette in the *Romuleon* (Fr. 348, f. 177), and both alike illustrate the jumble of classical reminiscences and still medieval style which in itself characterizes the transition from the Middle Ages to the Renaissance. Colombe, the last known illuminator in France of an Arthurian MS, (though Jacques de Besançon painted miniatures in incunabula even later, as we shall see in Chapter XIII) exemplifies in the *Estoire* and to a much larger degree in his work as a whole, the transition from one great period to the other. In Colombe's *Estoire*, we realize sharply that the art of illumination which in the beginning had so largely inspired the art of panel painting,[58] has been destroyed by the latter. Colombe's illustrations are pictures which bear no decorative relation to the page of text. Even if the new art of printing and the woodcut had not come to take the place of the hand-written and hand-illuminated book, such a volume as the *Estoire* shows that in a true sense the old art of illumination was already dead.

---

[55] The miniature from the *Très Riches Heures* is reproduced by Meurgey, *op. cit.*, Pl. XLV; that from the *Romuleon* by Blum and Lauer, *Miniature française*, Pl. 24.

[56] D. MacGibbon, *Jean Bourdichon* (privately printed, 1933), 43; Durrieu, *op. cit.*, p. 103.
[57] Blum and Lauer, *op. cit.*, p. 19.
[58] Panofsky, *Lectures on Gothic Illuminated MSS*, p. 92.

A LAST TRISTAN (FR. 103)

But though it was dying, the illuminator's art continued to produce in the late fifteenth and early part of the sixteenth centuries many MSS. With one of these, though its one miniature is not of the finest execution, it is fitting to close this survey of French Arthurian illumination. For the text is a *Prose Tristan* which uniquely reverts to the old poetic ending that told how Tristram died for love, thinking Ysolt was not coming to him, and she, delayed by storm at sea, died of grief on her lover's body. The story had been pictured in the thirteenth century on the Chertsey tiles; but, as was observed in Chapter IV, only two tiles remain (Figs. 58, 59) which are concerned with this tragic conclusion. In French prose and art the displacement of this story by the one telling how Mark assassinated Tristram was apparently complete until, in this one late fifteenth-century manuscript, Fr. 103,[59] the older ending was again revived and again inspired a pictorial rendering. The artist in Fr. 103 (Fig. 304)[60] evidently knew the story as a whole but with fine discrimination touched on only two episodes, both connected with the sea. In the foreground on a green shore that bears in golden letters the word "Yrlande" stand Ysolt's royal father and members of his court. Beyond is a great ship with trumpeters in rose and blue blowing a fanfare on golden trumpets. Puffing sailors raise a bellying white sail and beneath it sit Tristram and Ysolt drinking the love potion. Beside them, as bright letters indicate, sit their friends, "Brangien" and "Gouvernail." The men wear high hats, the women tall peaked hennins with floating veils of the period about 1470. But though in Fr. 103 the elegance and detail of costume are thus emphasized, the miniature is by no means merely a costume piece. Other shores appear in the furthest background,—Brittany and Cornwall with towers and spires. From Brittany another ship departs. Sail and pennant and sailors are all in black; the only touches of color are the blue-covered bier, crossed with gold, where the lovers lie, and beside them a small crimson treasure chest and a gold-handled sword. The whole story is here briefly and poetically envisaged of the love that was death, the love that began on the sea and, in part, was ended by the sea. Beer has compared the miniature unfavorably with a ship scene in another French manuscript, the *Histoire des guerres judaïques* (Vienna, 2538, f. 109),[61] and pointed out the greater delicacy of the latter in execution, its stronger composition, its finer handling of perspective. As a matter of fact the *Tristan* must have been painted by the same not too skilful hand that painted the meeting of Priam and Helen in the *Chronique de Jean de Courcy* (Vienna, 2543, f. 105);[62] the architecture, sea, costumes with large brocaded patterns, high hats, flowered lace veils, turbans, the very face and figure of Tristram and of the young squire in Helen's train, —all these are identical. Both miniatures have obvious faults, but they have, too, indubitable charm. On the *Tristan* page appears some reminiscence of the type of decorative detail, the vine tracery, the patterned strips at the left, the very same initial letter used by Fouquet in the *Antiquités judaïques* (Fr. 247, f. 89).[63] But though the *Tristan* miniature is far from his technical perfection and is, moreover, now badly marred by the flaking away of color it betrays a high quality of pictorial imagination. It is not unworthy, in this, one of the latest of the illuminated prose *Tristans*, of the great love story of the twelfth century poets.

[59] For description of the MS see Vinaver, *Études sur le Tristan*, p. 39. For the text see Bédier, *Romania*, XV (1886), p. 481, "La Mort de Tristan d'après le MS 103." See *infra*, p. 129, n. 50.

[60] For color reproductions see Petit de Julleville, *Hist. de la litt. franç.*, I (1896), 272; F. Ranke, *Tristan und Isold*, Taf. 15.

[61] *Les principaux MSS à peintures de la Bibl. Impériale de Vienne*, SFRMP (Paris, 1912), p. 31, n. 1; Pl. XIX.

[62] Reproduced by Blum and Lauer, *Miniature franç.*, Pl. 46.

[63] Reproduced *ibid.*, Pl. 15.

CHAPTER X

ITALIAN MANUSCRIPTS

TO ITALY Arthurian romance came in the wake of the Breton *conteurs*, the Normans, and the first Crusaders. As we have seen, the Modena archivolt and the Otranto mosaic are possibly the earliest surviving illustrations of Arthurian stories.[1] And the vogue continued. In Pisa there was, even in 1238, an association of militant youths who called themselves the Tavola Ritonda.[2] From the early years of the twelfth century Italians frequently bore Arthurian names;[3] in the latter part of the fourteenth century, it seems to have been an amusingly established custom with the lord of Milan, Bernabo Visconti, to give to his "love" children such engaging names as Palamede, Lancilotto, Sagremoro, Isotta, Ginevra. Allusions to the famous stories appeared constantly in the literature produced in Italy, the story of Tristram being especially beloved by the "scuola siciliana." New versions of Arthurian romance, in French and in Italian, were composed in Italy during both the thirteenth and fourteenth centuries. Among those compiled before the end of the thirteenth century was the *Meliadus* by Rusticiano da Pisa, which we met in Chapter V, probably the earliest Arthurian romance written, though in French, by an Italian; the *Tristano Riccardiano*, the earliest written in Italian; and that "strange medley of historical and apocalyptic prophecies," *Les Prophécies de Merlin*, which Miss Paton has proved to be of Venetian origin.[4] In the fourteenth century was composed the *Tavola Ritonda*, the most important Arthurian romance in Italian, and two romances on the life of Merlin. In his study of *The Arthurian Legend in Italian Literature* Gardner traced through these texts, through the *cantari*, and many allusions in poets of great and small distinction, the amazing vogue of the legend for almost four centuries.

This literary popularity was fostered chiefly by the Italian nobility, who found in the chivalry, the courtly love, the elegance of act and emotion in these French romances, a fascinating picture of life. French books were imported into Italy in great numbers, and among the prized possessions of the princely libraries that began to flourish in the fourteenth century in Italy were the romances of chivalry. Such a treasure

among Arthurian MSS as the late thirteenth-century *Estoire-Merlin*, now known as Fr. 95, was probably imported at this time; it remained in the great Visconti library at Pavia until, at the end of the fifteenth century, it was taken back to France by Louis XII.[5]

The Neapolitan *Meliadus*

Not inconsiderable must have been the influence of such examples of French illumination or of the actual French artists who flocked to Naples and Milan and other courts where princes had a lavish taste for the arts, or of the Italian miniaturists who, like the famous pair mentioned by Dante, acquired honor for their achievements in the art and style recognized by him as originally Parisian.[6] In a French *Meliadus* (Add. 12228), professedly composed by Hélie de Borron and distinct from Rusticiano's *Meliadus*, executed after 1352 for Louis of Taranto, who was crowned King of Naples in that year, and certainly before his death in 1362, the 363 miniatures, by several Neapolitan artists, show some French influence in composition and technique; in a number of the introductory miniatures gold and diaper backgrounds, the panel-like division into separate scenes, even the narrow frames ending at times in an ivy leaf, are all in the French manner. But the illustrators are unmistakably Italian. The church and palace walls of "Kamaalot" on the page showing Arthur riding to mass (Fig. 305), are as Italian as are all the other buildings represented in this manuscript. Italian, too, are the costumes and such figures as winged cupids and servitors blowing long trumpets. The armorial devices are noteworthy. (Fig. 306) The arms of the Kingdom of Naples, dexter, azure, *fleur-de-lys* or with red label; sinister, the arms of Jerusalem, argent a cross with four crosslets or, always distinguish the hero, Meliadus;[7] they appear, for instance, on f. 68 v, on f. 157 (Fig. 307), where, in company with Pellinor and Perceval and their squires, Meliadus is met by a herald in the arms of France. Meliadus bears a crowned helmet, surmounted by two peaks, the dexter side of which displays the *fleur-de-lys* of Naples. The same arms appear occasionally elsewhere, as on Arthur's shield

---

[1] See Ch. III.

[2] F. Novati, *Attraverso il Medio Evo* (Bari, 1905), p. 299, n. 7.

[3] For Italian use of Arthurian names before the 14th century see E. G. Gardner, *Arthurian Legend in Italian Literature* (L., 1930), p. 3. Cf. *supra*, ch. III (Modena).

[4] Lucy A. Paton, *Prophécies de Merlin* (L., N. Y., 1926-27), II, 143-156. The *Prophécies* were written, Miss Paton thinks, between 1272 and 1279.

[5] See Ch. VIII. L. Delisle, *Cabinet des manuscrits* (P., 1868), I, 128. *Infra*, notes 34-36.

[6] Oderisi da Gubbio, Franco Bolognese (*Purgatorio*, XI, 79-

84). Cf. Van Marle, *Schools of Italian Painting* (The Hague, 1924), IV, 293, 397. D'Ancona, *Miniature italienne du X au XVI siècle* (trans. by Poirier, P., 1925), pp. 16-18; Max Dvorak, "Byzantinischer Einfluss auf die italienische Miniaturmalerei des Trecento," in his *Gesammelte Aufsätze zur Kunstgeschichte* (Munich, 1929), pp. 46-47. Toesca, *Storia dell'arte italiana, Il Medioevo* (Turin, 1927), p. 1133, n. 11, for French influence on 13th century Italian illumination.

[7] Described by H. L. D. Ward, *Catalogue of Romances in the British Museum* (L., 1883), I, 364 ff.

and on a royal canopy above him (f. 4). On this leaf and others (f. 150 v, 153 v), the device of a knot recalls that early order of Italian knighthood, the Nodo, which Louis founded.

The sumptuous MS of the Statutes of this Order of the Holy Spirit, of which the triple knot was the emblem, is the manuscript with which parts of the *Meliadus* have the closest affinities. The Statutes (Fr. 4274), long since recognized as one of the most beautiful manuscripts of the Neapolitan school, was decorated between 1353 and 1356 by a Neapolitan master to whose hand or to whose school some seven or eight other manuscripts have been assigned.[8] The book is rich with ornate detail in the borders; its miniatures, by one hand, are perfectly finished and complete, and all the way through them are found the royal arms and the symbolic Nodo; the *Meliadus*, on the contrary, has almost no marginal decoration; its miniatures are incomplete and were done by several hands of very unequal merit. The MS is on many pages badly rubbed and later poor attempts at redrawing and repainting are everywhere apparent. But on some pages clear correspondences with the Statutes can be noted. Practically identical are the king and courtiers of the Statutes with those of the *Meliadus* (Fig. 308), where King Meliadus exhibits the baby Tristram; there are the same heads with straw-colored or chestnut hair, the same mild faces hardly to be differentiated from each other save as some have pointed beards and others none, or as, exceptionally, the single head of an old man is vividly portrayed. There are the same slender figures, the same groups in profile. The same details of costume, the scallop-edged tippets, the close-fitting, long-waisted jupons, the white liripipes worn on the arms, are found throughout the two MSS. On f. 202 v of the *Meliadus* the backgrounds of gold and of gold and blue lozengy, the bright body color, particularly the orange red of the mantle of the old Merlin with a feather in his hat, are precisely in the manner of the Statutes. (Fig. 308) On f. 220 v–221 of the *Meliadus* even King Louis' red tunic and black hose of certain scenes in the Statutes seem specifically imitated.

The *Meliadus*, like the three-volume Vatican Bible (Cod. Lat. 3550),[9] also a product of the same Neapolitan school, seems to have experienced many vicissitudes of production. Both were planned on a lavish scale of illustration, with crowded pictures and a prodigal use of gold and silver. Both exhibit an astonishing incompleteness, a fact which today adds to their interest, as it makes possible the study of different methods[10] and different stages in the completion of MSS by the same atelier. In the *Meliadus* the painted backgrounds give way, even by f. 67 v, to sporadic miniatures having no background at all. On f. 151 v–152 an elaborate tournament with a gallery full of realistically differentiated figures is carefully sketched but has received no touch of color. The use of body color is replaced by light washes, as in the scene where Arthur, on his blue throne, and his courtiers listen to a knight singing to his viol. (Fig. 309) In the beautifully drawn miniature representing the preparations for the tournament of the Pin du Géant (Fig. 310), the figures in the foreground are altogether uncolored, the busy squires carrying treasure chests are done in wash, and only the blue-sleeved squire with the pheasant's feather in his high hat is fully finished in color.

The *Meliadus* also exhibits, not only the formal restraint, in the French style, of miniatures kept within the framework, but the typical Italian tendency to escape such bounds. The pictures, always placed at the bottom of the page, sometimes extend exuberantly across the width of two facing pages as in one of the numerous tournament scenes. (Fig. 311) Here, where the ladies and old men watch excitedly from a wooden gallery, King Mark, on a black horse and bearing the crest of a black dog, with black dog-heads on his green surcoat, seizes *le bon chevalier* by his helmet, and other knights charge on to the right. Such a picture, in its sweep and breadth, was palpably influenced by that art of Italian mural painting, which seems always to have exercised so great an influence on Italian miniatures.[11]

BOLOGNESE MANUSCRIPTS

Another French text, earlier than the *Meliadus*, and probably dating from the first quarter of the fourteenth century is an *Estoire-Merlin* now at Oxford (Douce 178). The numerous small miniatures, mostly contained in initial letters, are undistin-

[8] Fr. 4274 was reproduced, but inaccurately, in color by H. de Viel Castel (Paris, 1853); cf. Erbach von Fürstenau, "Pittura e miniatura a Napoli," *L'Arte*, VIII (1905), 1 ff. Fig. 1; D'Ancona, *La miniature italienne*, p. 46, Pl. XLIII. For other MSS of this school see D'Ancona, pp. 46–47; H. J. Hermann, *Neapolitanische u. Toscanische Handschriften der zweiten Hälfte des XIV Jahrhunderts* in *Beschreibendes Verzeichnis der Illuminierten Handschriften in Oesterreich*, Neue Folge, Bd. V, *Die ital. Handschriften des Dugento u. Trecento* (Leipzig, 1928–30), III, 251; Van Marle, *Italian Schools of Painting*, V, 346–347. Erbach von Fürstenau alone refers (p. 13) to the *Meliadus* and thinks it was in part

executed by one of the artists working on the Vatican Bible (Cod. Lat. 3550).

[9] There is close resemblance between the *Meliadus* (Fig. 313), and that miniature in the Bible where Moses asperges the people bending before him. Cf. Taf. XXII in Stephan Beissel, *Vaticanische Miniaturen* (Freiburg, 1893). The Bible is dated 1362. The meeting of Melchizedek and Abraham (*L'Arte*, VIII, 8, fig. 4) is close to that of Arthur and the Bishop and their trains meeting before Camelot, *Meliadus*. (Fig. 305)

[10] For methods of applying color in the Vatican Bible see Beissel, p. 40.

[11] J. A. Herbert, *Illuminated Manuscripts* (L., 1911), p. 257.

guished copies of French originals, but a few are worthy of note as they are in the distinctive style of the Bolognese school. Particularly is this true of such a miniature as that showing Joseph of Arimathea and his companions. (Fig. 312) The initial letter *A* containing the miniature extends into a lancet or stem-like wand twisting upon itself, curving into leaves foliated on one side, an ornament, in short, which has been noted as one of the most characteristic motifs of north Italian, and particularly Bolognese, decoration in the last half of the thirteenth century and the first half of the fourteenth.[12] Here the long-bodied, hieratic figures, the dark faces with greenish tints and high lights on brow, nose, and cheek, the curious threadlike beards of the old men, the drapery, the architectural framework with inset medallions and slender pillars, are all marked by that Byzantine influence which dominated so much of the painting of this school.[13] In two of the miniatures, one where the five kings who were rulers of Rome after the Crucifixion are represented, and one (Fig. 313), where Vortigern, enthroned, orders the execution of the assassins of the late king, even the jewel-bordered dress of Byzantine emperors is imitated. The probability that some artist of the Bolognese school worked on certain pages in this book is of special interest because, though such great numbers exist of religious, civic, and legal documents decorated by Bolognese miniaturists, many of whose names are known,[14] comparatively few MSS of a more literary character have been identified as belonging to this school.[15] Yet since Bologna, with its cosmopolitan university, was the center of the medieval Italian book trade, since the art of illumination had developed there, first of all in Italy, as a regular industry by lay practitioners, it is hardly to be doubted that many more romances and other secular

narratives were illuminated there or under Bolognese influence than have yet been noted.

An interesting nucleus for such a group might be found in a little known *Mort Artu* now at Chantilly (1111),[16] which bears on its worn first page the characteristic Bolognese lancet ornament with pretzel-like knots, beads and cup-shapes threaded upon it; also some of that deft decorative penwork in which the Italians, no less than the French, delighted. (Fig. 314) On its last page it bears this inscription: "Liber domini Brexiani de Salis. Qui [quem?] scripxit Bo. de Gualandis existens cum eo in regimine mutinensi." Since this Brexianus de Salis was Podesta of Modena only in the last six months of 1288,[17] it is safe to regard this date as approximately that of the MS. Only six of its 71 folios bear any decoration and these have small historiated letters of which we reproduce the following:

Fig. 314. A mounted knight.
Fig. 315. The felon knights enter Guinevere's chamber.
Fig. 316. Guinevere speaks with Modred.
Fig. 317. Arthur returns to Britain.

Though here the earlier and cruder figures lack the Byzantine influence so evident in certain miniatures of Douce 178, a family likeness is evident between these two Arthurian MSS and also a third, a late thirteenth century *Prose Tristan* (Fr. 12599),[18] which is now bound with a fragmentary Italian *Guiron*. They all have similar coloring in prevailing shades of orange, blue, and brown, and they all contain figures curiously akin to those in certain MSS purporting to contain the lives and pictures of the Provençal troubadours. These MSS, Fr. 12473 and Fr. 854, written by Italian scribes in the late thirteenth century,[19] are also closely related, pictorially, to a *Roman de Troie* (Grenoble, Bibl. Pub. 263) which

---

[12] On this motif see Herbert, pp. 171–172; D'Ancona, *La miniature italienne*, p. 14; for illustrations see A. Venturi, *Storia dell'arte italiana* (Milan, 1904), III, figs. 429–437. Erbach von Fürstenau, "La Miniatura Bolognese nel Trecento," *L'Arte*, XIV (1911), 5, fig. 2, gives a miniature from the Vatican Decretals (Pal. lat. 629); cf. also another from Beissel, *op. cit.*, Pl. XXI to which our Fig. 312, (Douce 178 f. 20) is closely akin. See also the Bolognese miniatures reproduced by Mario Salmi, "La Miniatura," in *Tesori delle bibliotheche d'Italia, Emilia e Romagna*, edited by Domenico Fava (Milan, 1932) especially Figs. 134, 143, 152. Cf. Toesca, *Storia dell'arte ital.*, p. 1068, fig. 758, for lancet ornament.

[13] Venturi, III, 472 ff.; Dvorak, *op. cit.*, passim; D'Ancona, p. 14.

[14] On Bolognese miniaturists see D'Ancona, pp. 14–18; F. Malaguzzi-Valeri, "La Miniatura in Bologna," *Archivio storico italiano*, Ser. V, t. XVIII (1896), 244; Van Marle, *op. cit.*, IV (1924), 397–98: Dvorak, p. 64: Salmi, p. 294.

[15] A notable exception would be the *Roman de Troie* (Vienna, Staatsbibl., MS. 2571) with 200 illustrations by an unknown artist of the Trecento whom Hermann assigned to the school of Bologna. Cf. *Beschreibendes Verzeichnis*, Neue Folge, Bd. V, *Oberitalienische Handschriften der Zweiten Hälfte des XIV jahrhunderts*

(Leipzig, 1929), II, 136–152, Taf. LII-LXI. He rejected the opinion of Beer that the Vienna *Roman* was of Tuscan origin. Cf. Beer, *Die Miniaturenausstellung der k. k. Hofbibliothek* in *Kunst. u. Kunstwerk* (Vienna, 1902), V, 462 ff., or *Les principaux manuscrits à peintures de la Bibl. Impériale de Vienne* (Paris) in *Bull.* SFRMP (1912), p. 26.

[16] Miss Fox, *Mort Artu*, p. 14, briefly noted this MS but without observing its important final subscription. Frappier, *Mort Artu* (P., 1936), xxii, quotes the passage but incorrectly and without identification.

[17] Cf. *Monumenti di Storia Patria delle provincie modenesi, Serie delle cronache*, XV (Modena, 1888), p. 82, which quotes from the *Cronaca Bazzano:* "Dominus Ugo de Salo de Brixia Potestas Mutinae in 1288 in ultimis sex mensibus."

[18] Described by Vinaver, *Études sur le Tristan*, p. 45. In this badly mutilated MS the historiated illuminated letters contain chiefly heads or single figures. On f. 320 v there is a dark but unusually effective scene of the lovers at sea.

[19] Jeanroy, *Bibliographie sommaire des chansonniers provençaux* (P., 1916), p. 8. Reproductions of the "portraits" in these MSS are given by Lanson, *Hist. illustrée de la litt. fr.*, I, 65; Bédier et Hazard, *La litt. franç.*, p. 27.

ends with the assertion that it was written in 1298 by a "Johannis de Stennis de Padua."

The business of turning out secular MSS of all sorts was evidently well under way in northern Italy by 1300. Probably there, as in France, certain ateliers made a professional specialty of illustrations for the romances and a few notable MSS still exist which have two hundred or more illustrations.[20]

OTHER LOMBARD MSS

To one rather undistinguished atelier of this type must be assigned the ten or more MSS which contain the earliest transcriptions of Arthurian stories made in Italy in the late thirteenth or early fourteenth century. They present a crude but distinctive type of illustration. In his monumental work on Lombard painting Professor Toesca[21] mentioned by name, as possibly of Lombard origin, two of these manuscripts, both in the library of St. Mark's, a *Guiron le Courtois* (Venice, Fr. IX), and a *Lancelot* (Venice, Fr. XI); and to these may be added five *Tristans*, one in Modena (Estense Bibl. T. S. I), one in the Vatican library (Pal. lat. 1964), one in the British Museum (Harley 4389), one at Aberystwyth (Nat. Libr. of Wales, 446E), one in Paris (B. N., Fr. 760),—a *Meliadus* (Fr. 1463), a *Lancelot* (Fr. 354), and a *Lancelot* in Berlin (Staatsb., Ham. 49). These manuscripts are filled with crude sketches (for they are hardly more than that) which were evidently done by craftsmen of inferior skill, who were, however, attempting a new thing, a quick, roughly effective, relatively inexpensive type of illustration. On the lower margins of the pages usually, but sometimes above, they drew outline sketches of knights, mounted and often in combat, and occasionally figures of ladies. The costumes and caparisons were filled in with dull, dark reds and greens, and only a suggestion of shading. The illustrative detail was of the slightest; trees such as a child might draw, a fountain,[22] or a tent, a ship, as in the *Tristan* scene where the Irish ambassadors come to Mark (Fig. 318), rude benches such as those on which Tristram and Ysolt sit in the assassination scene (Fig. 320), a tomb such as that of Tristram and Ysolt (Fig. 321). Unmistakably in these manuscripts are repeated the same plain faces, often with red dots

on the cheeks, the same oddly elongated bodies; as, for instance, those of the Lady of the Lake and her companions. (Fig. 322) Mark and the ambassadors (Fig. 318) of the *Tristan* (Harl. 4389) are the identical figures of the "Roi de Norgalles" and two knights of the *Meliadus* (Fr. 1463, f. 70). The same horses appear, enormously broad-chested in the frontal position, and always with excessively arched thick necks; likewise the same type of armor, high flat-topped helmets, triangular shields, chain mail except for the greaves; the same flying triangular flap of a knight's surcoat, whether it be that of Palamedes in the Estense MS[23] or of Hector des Mares when he and Marganor encounter Tristram in Harley 4389 (Fig. 319), or of Lancelot riding before Guinevere in the Berlin manuscript.[24] (Fig. 323) This last design of the six or seven women's heads under simple arches is repeated at least seventeen times in the Paris *Tristan* (Fr. 760). The fact may be taken as illustrative of the unimaginative monotony with which the same riding and fighting knights, the same feats and audiences, are used over and over again. It was, indeed, necessary to write the names of the principal personages above their heads in order to differentiate them one from the other. The fact that both Fr. 1463 and Ham. 49 are palimpsests, in which the original writing still shows plainly, is an indication of the commercial haste with which these manuscripts were produced. Both alike illustrate the evils of mass production, even in the Middle Ages.

A richer, more important MS than any of these is the French *Prose Tristan* (Fr. 755), which may be regarded as one of the earliest of the luxury MSS of Arthurian story produced in Italy. It was probably decorated between 1320–1340. At the foot of almost every one of its 161 folios and sometimes spreading across to the opposite leaf, are vigorous illustrations which constantly escape from such slight framework as is given them into the page itself. The decorative effect is enhanced by marginal shields, by bands of gold or color, by medallions, by curving foliated circles, by studs of gold. Though some French influence may be detected, some obvious conventionality in the representation of trees and rocks, in the use of decorative backgrounds and framework, as in the miniature (Fig. 324), where on the right Palamedes

[20] Cf. *Historia Alexandri* (Leipzig, Stadtbibl., MS CCCCXVII); *Roman de Troie*, see *supra*, n. 15. For lists of the romances etc. see those compiled by Toesca in *La pittura e la miniatura nella Lombardia* (Milan, 1912), 384–390, and in his previously cited *Storia dell'arte italiana*, p. 1063, n. 13. For *Huon d'Auvergne* see Olschki, *MSS. franç. d'Allemagne*, p. 38, Pl. XLIV.

[21] Toesca, *La pittura*, pp. 384–385. See also *infra*, n. 40.

[22] The same crude attempt at representing a monumental fountain with stone work and spout in the form of an animal's head appears in Fr. 760, f. 3, where the *Beste Glatissante* is shown drinking from the fountain, and in Fr. 1463, f. 95 v. In this last MS a later hand of about 1360 has introduced the miniatures on

f. 20 v and f. 21. These are done in brown wash. The knights, Lancelot, Tristram, and others, bear palette-shaped shields and have pointed helms.

[23] Reproduced by G. Bertoni, *Poesie, leggende, costumanze del medio evo* (Modena, 1917), p. 234. From the same MS he gives (p. 254) the Death of Tristram, which is practically identical with the one here given from the Paris MS. Fr. 760. (Fig. 320)

[24] Reproduced also by Olschki, *Les manuscrits français à peintures des bibliothèques d'Allemagne* (Geneva, 1932), Pl. XXXIX. He observes (p. 35) that this MS, mentioned neither by Sommer nor in the Marburg edition of the *Lancelot*, deserves to be better known than it is. The MS contains seven miniatures.

rides forth, and on the left Ysolt realistically tends Tristram in Joyous Garde after he has been wounded in the leg, the illustrations on the whole have a lively inventive vigor, freedom from schematic tendencies, in short, a distinctive originality. They are markedly Italian. Though in one miniature the word "Camalot" is written beneath Arthur's throne, an Italian tower rises behind him and he holds court in an open, Giottesque loggia (Fig. 325), just as in another picture Ysolt, her hand in Tristram's, receives two kneeling knights before a many-windowed, golden brown Italian palace. (Fig. 326) The Queen's white-robed figure, here posed against a black and silver broidery, faintly suggests the white figure of Peace painted by Ambrogio Lorenzetti between 1331 and 1349 in the Palazzo Publico of Siena. But the Queen's whole aspect finds its closest parallel in the Madonna di Misericordia[25] of a Bolognese miniature of 1329. The madonna spreads her mantle over religious and lay alike, and again in the faces and costumes of the latter are to be found the closest resemblances to such dark-faced, full-lipped servitors and courtiers, with their coifs and flat projecting hats, as are presented in the *Tristan* in the scene of the washing of hands before a banquet. (Fig. 327)

The miniatures of Fr. 755 have freshness and spontaneity. Entirely on his own initiative the artist introduced this very scene of the ceremonial washing of hands. The text makes mention only of the feast itself, but the illuminator has represented with care and realism the ten servitors who hold bowls and towels and pour water from silver and golden pitchers on the hands of the arriving guests. The scene takes place in Arthur's pavilion; the hangings are green and salmon, criss-crossed with gold. There is a pleasant harmony of color, a skilful grouping of figures, not in themselves any too well drawn. But the outstanding feature is the artist's freedom in reporting an incident from real life. On other pages he represents knights playing chess or checkers (f. 75), a council of kings who sit in elaborate chairs in a wood (f. 76), a crowd looking up eagerly to a trumpeter in a tower (f. 3 v), galleries of lords and another of ladies, (f. 86), stately processions of mounted knights and ladies, the latter with picturesque, wide-brimmed, red hats (ff. 100 v, 120), or of twelve Christian kings, coifed and crowned, marching together (ff. 154 v, 155). He could render vigorous fights, with horses

thrown violently backward (f. 7), but in general his preference was for peaceful scenes and civil rather than military garb. Especially to be contrasted with typical French hunting scenes,[26] in which almost invariably the hunters ride from left to right, is the one depicted on f. 147 and reproduced by Toesca in *La pittura e la miniatura nella Lombardia*, Fig. 108. Four round-topped trees, the fallen stag and the dogs, are in centre of the picture; at the right is a tower on a hill. Beneath it two mounted men charge towards the stag; beside it, on the left, a scarlet-robed Tristram mounted on a white horse blows his horn for the kill. Despite conventional elements, the scene has that quality of improvisation and stylistic freedom which characterizes this artist. He was unrealistic in his use of color, having a special fondness for pink architecture and blue horses, but at his best he achieved a pleasant harmony, as in the pavilion scene. On other pages he used too much ochre and red or pink. Pink is the dominant note, for instance, in the scene where Lancelot arrives at Arthur's court. The courtiers beside the throne wear pink robes; Arthur himself wears a red mantle, and Guinevere, in a pink room, welcomes Lancelot, robed like herself in red and silvery grey. (Fig. 325)

Some years after this *Tristan*, but certainly before 1400, a Lombard artist of ability decorated with 123 miniatures and drawings that MS, the *Queste del SaintGraal* and the *Mort Artu*, which is now in Paris (Fr. 343)[27] and was, like Fr. 755, taken there from Pavia in 1499–1500. The volume bears the signature of Galeazzo Maria Sforza, but it was very probably written and decorated in the time of Gian Galeazzo (1378–1402). It has palpable affinities with Gian Galeazzo's *Hours* (Milan, Bibl. Visconti di Modrone), which Toesca[28] believes was painted before 1395 and was in part at least the work of Giovanni de Grassi. But so close is the relation of Fr. 343 to the interesting Franciscan *Hours* (Paris, B. N., Lat. 757) that Toesca[29] did not hesitate to recognize the hand of one illuminator in both these codices. The St. George of the *Hours* (Toesca, Fig. 219) is but Galahad on his white horse, with the same red cross on the man, the same red trappings on the horse (f. 12, Toesca, Fig. 302); the St. Ursula and her companions of the one (Toesca, Fig. 220) become the maidens of the Castle of Maidens (f. 15 v, Toesca, Fig. 304) of the other; the lion and the dragon attacking St. Anthony

---

[25] Reproduced by Salmi in Fava's *Tesori*, fig. 150, from the inventory of the Societa delle Laudi di Noxadella, Bologna, Bibl. dell'Archiginnasio, n. 52. Toesca, *La pittura*, p. 385, believes this MS represents an early stage in the development of a notable Lombard school of miniaturists.

[26] See *supra* Ch. VIII, Figs. 257–258.

[27] Cf. Paulin Paris, *Catalogue des MSS du Bibl. du Roi*, II, 364.

[28] Toesca, *La Pittura*, pp. 315–316, fig. 238; D'Ancona, *La miniatura ital.*, p. 23, who notes these *Hours* must have been decorated before 1395; Pl. XVIII–XX.

[29] *Ibid.*, pp. 283–294. V. Leroquais, *Les Livres d'Heures manuscrits de la Bibliothèque Nationale* (P., 1927), p. 6, believes this MS was copied about 1380 in the region of Padua. He points out that the sun symbol is introduced several times, but does not note that this was an emblem used by Gian Galeazzo himself. From Lat. 757 Leroquais gives six plates, Pl. VIII–XIII, and seven in his *Les sacramentaires et les missels*, Pl. LXIX–LXXV. Cf. D'Ancona, Pl. XVI (f. 373, St. Ursula; f. 289, St. Anthony); C. Couderc, *Les enlumineurs des MSS du moyen âge* (P., 1927), Pl. XLV, XLVI.

(Toesca, Fig. 221) are the same lion and dragon of the adventure where Perceval saves the one and kills the other (f. 27), or also, it may be added, of his vision wherein he sees ladies representing the New Law and the Old Law riding, respectively, on a lion and a dragon. (Fig. 328) Though the *Hours* have purely decorative backgrounds, though the miniatures are framed and display a much greater interest in elaborate architectural devices, the essential resemblances are not to be mistaken. There are not only likenesses in composition, in the use and juxtaposition of the same colors, in the clothes and figures of men and women, but also in specific and unusual details. The same portrait-like types recur, as of the small pensive doctor beside Perceval's dying sister (Fig. 329) or of the elderly, round-bearded man near the wall in the same scene: these faces have, though less noticeably, the wide dark eyes, the thin nostrils, the poorly designed lips, the fair hair common to these manuscripts. It is, perhaps, worth noting that even the same patterns are repeated in fabrics; the yellowish eye, outlined in black, on the green jupon of the central knight in this last miniature decorates also the jupon of a knight in the *Hours*, f. 72; the symmetrically curved design on the dress of the lady on f. 61 v of the romance recurs on the dress of St. Agnes, f. 291. The triple-pointed, raised vizor of a basinet appears many times in Fr. 343 and is matched precisely, together with all the other realistic details of a knight's accoutrement, in those of the mounted knight in the Crucifixion of the *Hours* (f. 75).[30] In more intangible ways one recognizes throughout the two manuscripts the same tastes, the same habits of observation, even at times the same humor, as in the romance scene noted by Toesca (p. 376, Tav. XXI) where Perceval meets the Fiend who, in the guise of a pretty maiden, is represented as childishly pulling her own long braid of hair, or in the *Hours* where men hold their noses beside the body of Lazarus (f. 311 v), or where one man, overenergetically stoning St. Stephen, bursts the supports of his hose (f. 279 v).

Fr. 343 has not only these close connections with the Franciscan *Hours* and the Paris MS (Lat. Nouv. Acq. 1673) of the *Tacuinum Sanitatis*, which Toesca (p. 377) would assign to the same hand, but similarities also to certain contemporary murals. The two knights before the Virgin in Simone da Corbetta's fresco (Toesca, Fig. 314), painted for a church in Milan about 1382, precisely resemble the men in Fr. 343. (Figs. 330–331) They have hair similarly rolled into a short "bob," and short pointed beards; they wear tight-fitting jupons that emphasize their full chests and slender waists. Their girdles are worn straight across the hips, with the long dagger (misericorde) on the right, the sword on the left side. On their feet are extravagantly long pointed shoes, the mailed *sollerets*, or the long stuffed *poulaines*, for which there was such vogue, not only on the Continent but even in England after the advent of Anne of Bohemia. Similarly the women in Fr. 343 (Figs. 329, 332) in tight-fitting gowns, with long close sleeves overlapping the wrist, and hair worn either in braids about the head or flowing loose on their shoulders, are own sisters, as it were, to the ladies painted in 1368 in the chapel at Lentate for Stefano Porro, a counsellor of Galeazzo Visconti, or to the stately figure of St. Catherine in the oratory of Mocchirolo.[31] As a composition the scene of Arthur's Pentecostal feast (Fig. 330) has several points of likeness to the well-known Last Supper, formerly attributed to Pietro Lorenzetti,[32] which is in the Lower Church at Assisi. In each picture there is an interior room with tesselated floor and curtained wall and corridors at the side, where dogs lurk in the one picture and cats in the other, and where servitors pass. The twelve seats at the Round Table are similarly fashioned and decorated. But the miniature by comparison with the painting is feeble in its attempt to deal with problems of perspective.

Great as is the interest of Fr. 343 for the historically realistic picture it gives of the brilliant seignorial life of Italy late in the fourteenth century, great too as is the interest of its faithful attempt to translate into pictorial form the unearthly adventures of the *Queste*, still the manuscript has manifest flaws. Even with all allowance made for the defacements time has wrought, it is clear that this princely volume, like the Neapolitan *Meliadus*, was never even brought to completion. The very first page is left with the elaborate border design and initial miniature uncolored, as are also the pictures from f. 69 to f. 80, and many others are but partly finished. This is, perhaps, less to be regretted because the artist was more skilful with the pen than with the brush, which he dipped too often in garish red for walls and floors, in hard black for trees, or in startling blue, as in the Pentecostal feast scene, where this light color gives undue emphasis to the legs of the king sitting to the right of the Siege Perilous. Though the manuscript has been described as one of rare beauty,[33] these defects, in common with the artist's

---

[30] Cf. Leroquais, *Livres d'Heures*, Pl. VIII.

[31] Toesca, Fig. 191 and Tav. XII. In addition to his discussion of these frescoes see also Chappée, "Peintres et enlumineurs en Lombardie," *Revue de l'art chrétien*, LXIII (1913), 243 ff. The often reproduced Guinevere of Fr. 343, f. 6 (Toesca, Fig. 297) is particularly close to the ladies of these murals.

[32] E. DeWald, *Pietro Lorenzetti* (Cambridge, Mass., 1930), pp. 23–24, rejects this attribution. Cf. L. H. Loomis, "The Table of the Last Supper in Religious and Secular Iconography," *Art Studies*, V (1927), 73.

[33] D'Ancona, *La miniature ital.*, p. 25.

tendency to overload his pages, to give sometimes an effect of sprawling rather than firm design, the naïveté in his treatment of perspective and landscape, with stylized rocks and most experimental trees, must be acknowledged. Apart from his rendition of the chivalric pageantry of medieval Italian life, notably set forth, for instance, in the Departure of the Knights on the Grail Quest (Fig. 332), where almost every helm bears a fantastic crest, and rich details of costume are realistically presented, some of his most interesting attempts, from the artistic point of view, appear in the fine wrinkled faces of old men, like that of the dying Mordrain (f. 24), or of the suffering Grail king (Fig. 334), and in the drawing of animals, of dogs, of lions (Fig. 328), or the stout Lombard horses he so often and so characteristically introduced. Humorously large-eyed and startled as are the litter-bearing horses in Lancelot's vision of the Grail and the sick knight (Fig. 333), there is charm of line and of feeling in the picture of Lancelot's own horse curving his neck around the tree in order to nuzzle the sleeping hero.

The artistic infelicities of Fr. 343 are replaced in another volume of the same school by a most sensitive and sophisticated use of both color and design. In the illustrations of this fragmentary *Guiron* (Nouv. Acq. Fr. 5243) Toesca (pp. 378–384) finds a perfection which was the logical consequence of the whole development in Lombardy of the work of fresco and miniature painters alike. Imagination, fantasy, acute observation, sensitive feeling, have entered into these renditions, even fuller and richer than in Fr. 343, of the life of the time. If there is a certain monotony, consequent upon the repetitions within the romance itself of the same situations, the artist has at least done his best to individualize the recurrent fights, the eternal *causeries*. Toesca notes with enthusiasm the nocturnal suggestions of the lighted lantern, the burning torch, the candlestick fastened to a pillar in the scene where three knights talk pensively together in a quiet, blue-curtained room (Toesca, Fig. 307), or of the half moon, the dark castle doorway, the fastened horse, in the scene where a noble knight is met by a smiling lady, who leads him gently within her door (Toesca, Tav. XXI). The charm with which this distinguished miniaturist could translate the story into pictures is seen especially in the scene (Fig. 335) where the strange knight, Feramont, arrives at Arthur's court. At the left the dark, rocky shore, the ship with three raised lances and hanging shield, the little mounted dwarf, succeed in giving that effect of strangeness which is the very essence of romance; in the centre is the immobile, powerful figure of Feramont towering on horseback over all others; at the

right is a group of knights who talk among themselves as Arthur listens to the prayer of Blioberis (Blibris), kneeling before him, for permission to accept the stranger's challenge. The strong, slender, graceful figures, the refinement and individuality of feature, the richness of garb, represent chivalry incarnate. The miniature is all the more effective because here and elsewhere the artist has used delicate light washes, thinly transparent colors with soft greenish shadowings, that enhance the suggestion of an atmosphere remote from reality.

The relation of this manuscript to Fr. 343 is much closer than one would at first surmise. The marked dissimilarity in the use and treatment of color is matched by the difference in the treatment of trees and flowery foregrounds, and in the more ideal grace of the figures in the *Guiron*. But there are marked resemblances too. The horses of the one are the horses of the other. The figure of Arthur bidding farewell to the knights going to seek the Grail in the *Queste* (Fig. 332) is only a less fine portrayal than that in the *Guiron* (Fig. 336) where, unarmed, he watches while Gawain catches in his arm the knight who had sought to slay the king. The decorative eyes on Arthur's jupon are the same that, as already noted, occur in both the Franciscan *Hours* and Fr. 343. The fine gesture of the central knight in this same miniature of the *Guiron*, the up-raised right arm with sword swung back behind the knight's head for a slashing blow, is precisely the gesture of a knight in Fr. 343, f. 104 v. The boat with the scallop-like edges of its prow and the two holes for the mooring rope, which appears in scenes connected with Perceval's sister in the *Queste* (Fr. 343, f. 56, 73 v, 75), is the same ship which brings Feramont to land in the *Guiron*. (Fig. 335) The identities of costume and armor are too numerous to note except, perhaps, in the matter of the peculiar half-length leg protector fastened alike to the saddle of a knight of the *Queste* (Fig. 332) and to that of Feramont (Fig. 335). There is no question that the two manuscripts belong to the same period and, after noting these peculiar correspondences, we can hardly doubt that both were the work of the same atelier.

ITALIAN LIBRARIES

The Neapolitan *Meliadus*, the (at least in part) Bolognese *Estoire*, the numerous Lombard MSS which we have been discussing, constitute but a small fraction of the host of Arthurian books in Italy of which in one way or another some record still survives. Through the various catalogues and inventories of the books that once belonged to such great families as the Visconti, the Sforzas,[34] the Estes, the

[34] G. D'Adda, *Indagini storiche, artistiche e bibliografiche sulla Libreria Visconteo-Sforzesca del Castello di Pavia* (Milan, 1875). In the inventory of 1426 are included a *Prophécies* of Merlin in French, no. 213; a *Liber in gallico Regis Artusij*, no. 863; a *Liber de morte Regis Artusij*, no. 916; *unus Tristantis in gallico*, no. 952. On the Visconti MSS now in the Bibliothèque Nationale

Gonzagas, we can trace, from the end of the fourteenth century, all through the fifteenth, the actual presence of these costly MSS in ancient libraries. For instance, among the sixty-seven books in French listed in the catalogue of 1407 for the Archivio Gonzaga twenty are concerned with Arthurian stories;[35] ten Arthurian volumes are listed in the Estense catalogue of 1437,[36] sixteen in that of 1467, and a very large number appear in the collection of Federigo Gonzaga in 1542.[37] Numerous records show that lords and courtiers eagerly read, eagerly borrowed, Arthurian stories. Thus in 1470 Duke Borso of Ferrara, in a letter that warms the heart with its Arthurian enthusiasm, bids Count Ludovico di Cuneo to send back to him his mounted messenger "laden with as many French books as you can, to wit, some of those of the *Tavola Vecchia*, for we shall receive more pleasure and content therefrom than from the acquisition of a city."[38] There are many entries of loans made from the ducal library at Ferrara to courtiers eager for the enjoyment of these beautiful books. Among them we may note one[39] to Francesco Accolti, who received "uno Merlino et uno Meliaduxe—un lanzaloto in gallico—uno libro dito San Gradale," which he kept from March 23, 1460 till August 31, 1461. But the brief records of these volumes, so prized by Italian aristocrats, though they tell of the content and often of the language in which the text was written, tell us usually nothing in regard to their decoration. Still more unfortunately, the rich volumes have for the most part entirely disappeared, and aside from the MSS already discussed, those which do remain and that can be identified with much certainty as artistically of Italian provenance, are of rather undistinguished and unimportant character.[40]

THE VENETIAN COD. PAL. 556

Of considerable interest, however, for Arthurian iconography is the series of 289 pen drawings in Cod. Pal. 556 of the Biblioteca Nazionale of Florence, a Venetian manuscript dated 1446, from which Gardner reproduced sixteen illustrations. The pictures, which illustrate a text closely akin to the *Tavola Ritonda*, range through the adventures of Tristram, Lancelot, Galahad, and various other knights. Our illustrations show Lancelot and Tristram playing chess (Fig. 337), the Maid of Astolat in her barge (Fig. 338), and the passing of Arthur (Fig. 339). The artist has drawn his illustrations with lightness and flowing grace and an evident fondness for picturesque costume, and lively little foreground figures of dogs, waterfowl, and rabbits. In figure style a close analogy to these drawings may be found in the rich decorations on the Taroc cards painted for Filippo Visconti, probably between 1428 and 1447.[41] Alike the figures have the faces and forms of lovely children, an almost excessive delicacy and femininity; the curly-haired men wear short tunics, belted and furred; sometimes a large basket-shaped hat; the ladies have short-waisted, long flowing robes, and their hair piled high in turban-like coiffures. The cards were possibly painted by some member of the Zavattari family,[42] who painted the walls of the Chapel of Teodolinda in the cathedral of Monza. Between the Taroc cards, the Teodolinda frescoes, or those in the Casa Borromeo in Milan, and some of the pen drawings of Codex 556 there is great difference in quality, but unquestionably they all belong to the same period and style. The picture of Tristram and Lancelot playing chess in the house of the Lady of the Lake (Fig. 337), in the representation of graceful female figures especially, reminds one of the drawings of Pisanello.[43]

in Paris see Delisle, *Cabinet des MSS*, I, 130. On Gian Galeazzo's library see C. Magenta, *I Visconti e gli Sforza* (Milan, 1883), I, 226–234.

[35] Braghirolli et Meyer, "Les MSS des Gonzaga," *Romania*, IX (1880), 497–514. The Arthurian items in the inventory of 1407 are a *Merlin*, no. 17; Chrétien de Troyes's *Perceval*, no. 39; redactions of Rusticiano da Pisa, no. 31, 33, 34; *Le Chevalier du Papegai*, no. 36, 37; a *Guiron*, no. 38; a *Lancelot*, no. 32; an *Infantia Lanzalotti*, a *Questa S. Gradalis*, no. 40; several prose *Tristans*, no. 21, 35, 61–67.

[36] Pio Rajna, "Ricordi di codici francesi posseduti dagli Estense nel secolo XV," *Romania*, II (1873), 49–58: *Lancelot*, no. 1; *Tristan*, no. 5, 14, 18, 24; *Guiron*, no. 11, 19, 28, (no. 17, *Guion* for *Guiron*?); *Merlin*, no. 6, 43; *Grail*, no. 20, 30; *Infantiae Lancilotti, Sancti Gradalis et destructionis tabule*, no. 17; *Lanciloti et Sancti Gradalis*, no. 23. Cf. G. Bertoni, *La Biblioteca Estense, 1471–1505* (Turin, 1903), p. 85. In Bertoni's list of Duke Ercole's books in 1495 appear *Meliadus*, no. 119, 211, 320; *Guiron*, no. 199, 214; *Artus*, no. 200, 420; *Merlin*, no. 321, 322, 325; *San*

Graal, no. 445; *Tristano et compagni in francese*, no. 469; *Tristano solo in francese*, no. 470.

[37] F. Novati, *Romania*, XIX (1890), 161–200.

[38] Quoted by Gardner, *op. cit.*, p. 274.

[39] Bertoni, *La Biblioteca Estense*, 62. He records also (p. 77) the entry of Duke Borso: "far alluminare da Gherardo Ghisileri un libro, in vulgare sermone, chiamato Lanzalotum."

[40] Ciampoli, *I codici francesi della R. Bibl. Nazionale di S. Marco in Venezia* (Venice, 1897), lists a *Guiron*, cod. IX; a *Lancelot*, cod. XI; an *Artus*, cod. XV; a *Tristan*, cod. XXIII, a *Merlin*, App. Cod. XXIX. He describes most of the miniatures in these volumes, with the exception of Cod. XV, as being without artistic value. On p. 31 he gives the subject matter of the twenty miniatures in the 14th century *Lancelot* of Cod. XI.

[41] Parravicino, "Three Packs of Tarocco Cards," *Burlington Magazine*, III, 237 ff. Cf. Van Marle, *op. cit.*, VII, 174, and Toesca, *La pittura*, fig. 427, 428, for reproductions.

[42] Suggested by Van Marle, VII, 161.

[43] Cf. G. F. Hill, *Drawings of Pisanello* (P., 1929), Pl. XVI.

CHAPTER XI

MANUSCRIPTS OF THE LOW COUNTRIES

THE EARLY VOGUE

THE ardent dedication to Philip d'Alsace, Count of Flanders, of the *Conte del Graal*[1] by Chrétien de Troyes, leaves no doubt that this Arthurian poem was known in Flanders before Philip's death in 1191. Since Count Philip and his Countess held a court almost as brilliant as those in France and England,[2] the taste of the court for the new romances may be taken for granted. Chrétien's other poems may have followed the *Graal* into Flanders, but there is no specific twelfth century evidence that they did. The celebrated son of the then Flemish city of Lille, the *Doctor Universalis*, Alanus de Insulis, made use between 1174–79, but more probably in Paris than in Lille, of manuscripts of Geoffrey of Monmouth's *Prophetia Merlini* and recorded with amazement the wide-spread celebrity of Arthur the Briton.[3] Geoffrey's *Historia* was also certainly known in Flanders. A copy once belonging to the Abbaye d'Anchin even contains a probably unique illustration in extant twelfth century copies of the *Historia*.[4] The pen drawing (Douai, 880, Fig. 340) shows the Flemish instinct for caricature in presenting the fight of Arthur with the ugly giant of Mont S. Michel.

Though it is thus certain that Arthurian MSS were early in the Low Countries, it is difficult to trace their actual presence. Yet the extent to which they did circulate is shown by the fact that by the end of the thirteenth century no fewer than ten romances[5] had been translated into the native vernacular, and the famous Flemish poet, Jacob van Maerlant (d.c. 1300), who himself in his younger years had turned the French texts into his own *Historie van den Grale* and *Merlijns Boeck*, had some cause for complaint that the imaginary adventures of Tristram and Lancelot, of Perceval and Galahad, could be read by the people, but not the Bible with its teaching of Truth and Justice.[6] As we shall see in connection with the chronicles, his own *Spiegel Historiael* was, however, to be deemed more worthy of artistic concern than were ever his romances. Yet in the first half of the fourteenth century the records concerning romance MSS multiply rapidly and numerous account books and inventories give evidence that the fashionable French-speaking aristocracy, here as elsewhere, liked to own romances. The accounts of Mahaut, Countess of Artois,[7] show that in 1308 her treasurer bought in Arras two romances, a *Histoire de Troye*, and a *Perceval le Gallois*; in 1310 a *Tristan* for seven livres, in 1313 a *Vœux du Paon*. The nineteen books of the Count of Hainaut in 1304 included "uns grans rommans a rouges couvretures ki parolle de Naascien, de Mellin et de Lansclot du Lach," obviously one of the large manuscripts of the *Estoire*, the *Merlin*, and the *Lancelot*. From the great chateau at Hesdin Robert of Artois carried off in 1321 thirteen books, these romances among them, two *Tristans*, a *Roman de la Violette*, an *Enfances Ogier*. Among the twelve books listed in the inventory of 1322 of the possessions at Courtrai of Robert de Béthune, Count of Flanders, were a *Godfrey de Bouillon*, "noef," and a *Merlin*. The inventory at Mons in 1337, lists an *Atis et Porpherias*, a *Vœux du Paon*, and one Arthurian poem, Chrétien's *Cliges*, for this must be the romance carelessly described as of "Aelis et l'empereur et dou roy d'Ingres"; for Alis, the uncle of Cliges, was the Emperor himself, and Count Angres of Windsor was not the king, but King Arthur's faithless regent.

Up to about 1350 it is impossible to speak with certainty of the illumination of these or other secular MSS in the Low Countries. For the most part illuminated secular books were probably French importations. The numerous monasteries of the Low Countries had, of course, produced a long succession of religious works, and certain schools, like that of Maastricht in eastern Belgium, had early attained to fame. The tribute of Wolfram von Eschenbach, who said in his *Parzival* (III, 158, 13–16) that not even the artists of Maastricht[8] or Cologne could represent a more knightly figure than was young Parzival, armed and mounted on the Red Knight's horse, is the earliest known reference to this school at Maastricht. Wolfram's praise, with its hint of the secular in the early Maastricht productions, the

---

[1] Ed. by A. Hilka (Halle, 1932), lines 1–68; for date see p. xxiv.

[2] Cf. Gaston G. Dept, *Les influences anglaise et française dans le comté de Flandre au début du XIII siècle* (Ghent, P., 1928), pp. 21–32.

[3] See *supra*, p. 8. Cf. E. K. Chambers, *Arthur of Britain* (L., 1927), pp. 29, 109–110, for the *Prophecies*. Philippe de Mousket, *Chronique rimée* (Reiffenberg, *Chronique Belge*, XXIV, 627–628, XXV, 201–204) reports the query of the False Baldwin to the crowds about him, c. 1225: "Are ye, then, like the Breton folk, who still look for the coming of Arthur?" Cf. E. Gilliat-Smith, *Bruges* (London, 1909), 115–121.

[4] Geoffrey of Monmouth, *Historia Regum Britanniae*, ed. A.

Griscom (L., N. Y., 1929), pp. 573 ff. lists 48 of these MSS.

[5] J. D. Bruce, *Evolution of Arthurian Romance* (Baltimore, 1923), II, 303–307.

[6] Van Maerlant, *Sinte Franciscus Leven*, v. 31 ff.

[7] The references to Mahaut's books and those that follow are taken in order from C. A. Dehaisnes, *Documents et extraits divers concernant l'histoire de l'art dans la Flandre, l'Artois et le Hainaut* (Lille, 1886), pp. 183, 191, 207, 156, 236, 240, 319.

[8] On the Maasschule cf. Albert Boeckler, "Die buchmalerei des Mittelalters," *Handbuch der Bibliothekswissenschaft* (Leipzig), I (1931), 202 ff.; J. A. Herbert, *Illuminated Manuscripts*, p. 205; Frederik Lyna, *De Vlaamsche Miniatuur van 1200 tot 1530* (Amsterdam, Brussels, 1933), pp. 36 ff.

similarities in figure style, architectural motifs, and drolleries between known Maastricht productions and certain romance manuscripts, lend some color to the suggestion that the latter were likewise produced by the Maastricht school. The manuscripts in question are the *Histoire d'Alexandre*[9] (Brussels, Bibl. Roy., 11040), which was written in 1250, and the richly decorated cyclic Arthurian manuscript in the British Museum now known as Royal 14 E III, with which must also be associated the three large volumes of Additional MSS 10292–94,[10] and the *Lancelot* in Manchester (Rylands, French 1–2). But since proof concerning their specific Maastricht connection is lacking, and since the Arthurian manuscripts are inseparably connected with North-French illumination, they have been discussed in that connection.

It is generally admitted that the art of illumination in the Low Countries, though extensive, shows little independent or distinctive character before 1400, except perhaps in the taste for drolleries.[11] Some fundamental instinct for realism, for the observation of Nature, can be discerned here and there before 1400, but in general the artists were content to imitate the North-French or English style. From the Battle of Bouvines in 1214, which ended with the capture of the Count of Flanders by Philip Augustus and the overthrow of the "English party" and its prestige in Flanders, to 1328 when Philippa of Hainaut was married to Edward III of England, French influence prevailed,[12] no matter how much it was opposed to the native temper and economic interests of the Low Countries. Moreover, from the mid-fourteenth century through the early years of the fifteenth, the best of the native artists, like Jean Bondol of Bruges, Pol de Limbourg, and his brothers, seem often to have flocked to Paris and to the households of the French princes.[13] Those who stayed at home, like Michiel van der Borch, who finished in 1332 his work on Van Maerlant's *Rijmbibel*,[14] produced miniatures that strongly recall the contemporary style in France.

THE *QUESTE* OF PIERART DOU TIELT, DATED 1351

With the exception of the early fourteenth century group of Arthurian MSS sometimes connected with Maastricht, there are only three extant MSS of the cycle which seem to have been decorated at this time by artists of the Netherlands. The first of these is of particular interest because it bears the artist's name and date.

At the end of this MS of the *Queste del Saint Graal* (Arsenal, 5218, f. 91 v), Pierart dou Tielt names himself, states that he finished writing the text on the night of August 15, 1351, and that he illuminated and bound the volume.[15] He was evidently one of those humble craftsmen who did everything necessary for the production of a book. Born in Thielt, he seems to have worked at Tournai, which was a center of French artistic influence; also, it was a place where even the burghers were already aping Arthurian jousts.[16] The *Queste* decorated by Pierart includes a chronicle which stresses local Tournai happenings of the year 1277, and the three miniatures with which Pierart illuminated the text of the *Queste* bear a close family resemblance to those in the works of Gilles le Muisit,[17] the Abbot of St. Martin's at Tournai. The Abbey had been long distinguished for finely written and decorated books, and Pierart may have merely imitated the style of the scribes and illuminators who worked for the Abbot, who, when blindness temporarily befell him, solaced himself with the dictation of various works. Or Pierart may himself have worked on both the *Chronique* of the Abbot and also on the *Queste*, in which case he would afford an interesting instance of a lay scribe and illuminator in ecclesiastical employ.

Only one of the three historiated pages in the *Queste* escapes from the conventional pattern of riding or feasting knights, and that one miniature (Fig. 341) represents the mysteries of the Grail when these

[9] Lyna, *op. cit.*, 38–39; see Pl. II in Eugene Bacha, *Les très belles miniatures de la Bibliothèque Royale de Belgique* (Brussels, 1923).

[10] Georg Graf Vitzthum, *Die Pariser Buchmalerei* (Leipzig, (1907), pp. 133–134: Lyna, *op. cit.*, pp. 37–38. *Supra*, pp. 97 ff.

[11] A. W. Byvanck, G. J. Hoogewerff, *La miniature hollandaise et les MSS illustrés du XIV au XVI siècle* (The Hague, 1926), xvii; Herbert, *op. cit.*, p. 205, and ch. XI, XVIII, passim.

[12] Cf. Dept, *op. cit.*, 133 ff.; H. Pirenne, *Histoire de Belgique— à la mort de Charles le Téméraire* (Brussels, 1908), II, 26 and Index (Edw. III).

[13] The Bible of Charles V, now in The Hague (Mus. Meermanno-Westreenianum 10.B.23), is dated 1371 and names the leading artist, Jean Bondol. The title page shows the scribe Jean de Vaudetar presenting the book to Charles V. On the general movement of native artists to France, see Pirenne, *op. cit.*, 464; Paul Durrieu, *La miniature flamande au temps de la cour de Bourgogne, 1415–1530* (Brussels, 1921), pp. 6–7; Herbert, *op. cit.*, p. 307.

[14] Byvanck and Hoogewerff, *op. cit.*, xvi, I, Pl. I, II, XLI;

also Byvanck, *Les principaux MSS—à la Hague* (Paris, Brussels), SFRMP, 1931, p. 51.

[15] H. Martin, "Un caricaturiste du Roi Jean (Pierart dou Tielt)," *Gaz. des beaux-arts*, CIII (1909), 89–102, p. 90 for colophon. See also F. de Mély, *Les primitifs et leurs signatures* (P., 1913), p. 64.

[16] L. Vanderkindere, *Le siècle des Artevelde* (Brussels, 1879), p. 308. The four dioceses of Arras, Térouanne, Tournai, Cambrai, were included in the archbishopric of Rheims. Moke, *Mœurs, usages, fêtes et solennités des Belges* (Brussels, n.d.), II, 173, notes that the burghers in 1331 represented kings associated with Arthur, "le roy Gallehos, le roi Pellez du Castel-Perilleux," etc.

[17] H. Lemaître, *Chronique et Annales de Gilles le Muisit* (P., 1906); G. Caullet, "Les MSS de Gilles le Muisset et l'art de la miniature au XIV siècle," *Bull. du Cercle hist. et archéol. de Courtrai*, V, 1907–08; Jos. Casier et Paul Bergmans, *L'art ancien dans les Flandres* (Région de l'Escaut), (Brussels, P., 1921), p. 43, Pl. CXXXIV.

were revealed to Galahad, Bors, Perceval, and the chosen knights. They beheld, so the story says, the Bishop Josephe, the angels with tapers, cloth, bleeding lance, and the Christ child in the Grail. The miniature achieves individuality by virtue of Pierart's close following of the text he had copied. It holds little artistic reminiscence of the stately themes of the Divine Liturgy and the Apostolic Communion in Byzantine art,[18] though these pictorial renditions must, in some ancient MS, have inspired the original author of the *Queste*. Pierart puts the knights of the sacred fellowship into the fashionable costume of the mid-fourteenth century, with tippets and buttoned sleeves; to knights and angels alike he gives round, pudgy faces, awkwardly designed. But against the gold background his colors are charming, the standing angels with blue tipped wings, in robes of rose and green, the kneeling angels in white with wings of flame; the Bishop in a robe of green. The picture extends across the top of the page and ivy tendrils leaf out from the frame.

Pierart's chief skill was not as a miniaturist, but, as Martin says, as a caricaturist. With comic gusto and fluent ease he enlivens his pages not only with small human figures in absurd situations but also with fantastic animals, and especially with monkeys, for which he had a special predilection. He represents them in all sorts of enterprises, blowing trumpets, making butter, fighting rams, walking on stilts, juggling, or in the case of a particularly ugly monkey pair, transporting their hideous little offspring, tied up in a sack, in the family wheelbarrow. Pierart jested a little at everything—except the clergy—and in his unpretentious and unmalicious joking lacked neither originality nor wit. The catholicity of medieval taste, however, rarely finds a better example of the incongruities it permitted than the page which presents the mysteries of the Grail above, and below a monkey master and his dancing bear, a drum-playing pig, and a goat with a flute.[19]

DUTCH ROMANCE AND CHRONICLE

The other two MSS of this period to which attention has been called are the only ones of the eleven[20] Dutch versions of Arthurian romance which contain any attempt at illumination at all. The *Ferguut* (Leyden, Rijks-Univ., 191)[21] has only a small faded initial D containing a picture of the hero of the romance, whose identity is established by the white shield he carries. The romance of *Walewein*, composed about 1250, but copied in this manuscript (Leyden, Rijks-Univ., Letterk. 195), according to a statement on f. 182, in the year 1350, has likewise but one illumination, but this is a full size, framed picture (f. 120),[22] covering one page. The parchment is of a different sort from the rest of the MS, and was trimmed to suit the binder. The miniature represents the mounted figure of Gawain in pursuit of the magic black and white chess-board which flies above his head. A red lion's head appears seven times, on Gawain's blue shield, surcoat, and the caparisons of his stiff, dapple-grey horse. On the yellowish earth grow a few tiny red flowers; the foliage of the one large tree and the irregular outline of the mountain suggested at the right, are lightly tinted in green. The background is coral red. Despite a certain firmness of design, the picture offers little of significant interest.

The poverty, both in number and quality, in these Dutch and Flemish illuminations of the Arthurian romances before 1400 suggests what might, in the nature of things, be expected, on both the literary and artistic side. From its first importation, Arthurian romance in the Low Countries remained for the most part a foreign exotic. Before the end of the twelfth century economic and political circumstance had developed within the limited area of Flanders alone numerous rich and busy towns, Ghent, Bruges, Saint-Omer, Douai, Arras, Ypres, Hesdin, Bapaume,[23] and with those towns a practical, hard-headed burgher aristocracy and a bourgeoisie, far more determined and powerful than elsewhere. Feudalism itself was in the Low Countries forever at war with a thriving commercialism, and in that warfare romance, child no less of feudalism than of romantic imagination, was usually worsted. Courtly nobles had their romances, but of popular diffusion or interest there is comparatively little sign. A single instance has been noted of a townswoman owning a romance but that is probably to be explained by some relationship with the professional book maker, Pierart dou Thielt. The instance in question is that of Maignon dou Thielt, living in Tournai, who possessed in 1349–50 three books, among them a *Romaunt dou Cor*,[24] perhaps a text of Biket's *Lai du Cor*.

In the Low Countries romance as romance was in general far less interesting, far less worthy of costly

[18] For the Apostolic Communion cf. C. Diehl, *Manuel d'art byzantin*, Index; G. Millet, *Iconographie de l'Évangile* (P., 1916), p. 286; *Monuments de l'Athos* (Paris, 1927), Index; E. Bertaux, *L'art dans l'Italie méridionale* (1904), I, 122.

[19] Pierart's grotesques are reproduced by Martin, *loc. cit.*, figs. 1–20.

[20] In 1326 Lodewijck van Velthem completed his *Boec van Coninc Artur*. See *supra*, n. 5.

[21] Ed. by J. Verdam, E. Verwijs (Groningen, 1882), XII.

[22] Reproduced in color by Jan ten Brink, *Geschiednis d. Nederlandsche Letterkunde* (Amsterdam, 1897), p. 102; without color, Byvanck and Hoogewerff, *op. cit.*, Pl. XLII; described Byvanck, *Les princ. MSS . . . des Pays-Bas*, p. 93.

[23] Cf. Dept, *op. cit.*, pp. 25–26.

[24] Dehaisnes, *Documents*, I, 369. Practically no use was made in the Low Countries of Arthurian names. A rare exception is the name of Tristram du Four, goldsmith.

rendition in illuminated manuscripts, than when it masqueraded as history. "Mirrors of the World," chronicle histories of all sorts begin to multiply, and from the middle of the fourteenth century form increasingly the most important type of secular illuminated manuscripts in the Low Countries. In them, because Geoffrey of Monmouth's *History* with its account of Arthur's wars and conquests, was accepted as a part of true world history, and as such taken over into Vincent of Beauvais's *Speculum* and other histories, appear some of the best attempts at Arthurian illumination. A good instance of this is the early fourteenth century copy of Jacob van Maerlant's *Spiegel Historiael*.[25] The manuscript contains sixty-eight miniatures, of which four are concerned with Arthur. They picture the High Festival (f. 153 v; f. 154) at Arthur's court, with Arthur himself, four attendant kings with golden swords, the Queen with her maidens, minstrels, etc.; then follows the embassy (f. 154 v) at the court of Lucius, where Gawain kills the man who says the Britons are braggarts; and finally there is a representation of Arthur's last fight with Modred, to which an unique touch is given by the representation of the dying Arthur being carried away in a cart. (Fig. 342)

THE COURT OF BURGUNDY

The accession to her heritage in 1384 of Marguerite, daughter of Louis de Maele, Count of Flanders, and wife of Philip the Bold, Duke of Burgundy, began that fusion of the resources of Burgundy and the Low Countries, which resulted in the magnificent and practically sovereign state ruled over by Philip the Good (1419–67) and his son, Charles the Bold (d. 1477).[26] If in the last decades of the fourteenth century it is difficult to fix any "scientific frontier," from the point of view of art, between France and Flanders, so close and inevitable were their exchanges, so much were both influenced by those international tendencies which, in the decoration of books especially, were affecting the styles of French, Flemish, and Italian illuminators,[27] it is no longer hard, under Philip the Good, to recognize the full emergence, the vital independence, of all that is signified by Flemish art. Whatever Philip did to native institutions, to the spirit of democracy, there is no doubt whatever that this Franco-Flemish Maecenas gave to the arts

all the conditions necessary for a period of richest fruition. No longer did native artists and writers seek patronage in France; rather did they, and foreigners with them, flock to Philip's court; they set up new ateliers on every side, in Bruges and Ghent, in Brussels and Utrecht, for the production of works of art for which there was an apparently inexhaustible demand.

Although the late fourteenth and the fifteenth centuries were eras when book collecting and book decoration were achieved, especially in France and Italy, on a princely scale, still Philip the Good must be remembered as one of the greatest bibliophiles of all time. His library was acclaimed supreme in Europe, and this was probably true, both as to the variety and the value of its contents. In regard to fiction, Doutrepont[28] estimates that Philip had no fewer than eighty-five different romances and *chansons de geste*, some of these in several copies apiece. But in this section of his library, no more than in others, was Philip content merely to own old books, no matter how venerable or how finely illustrated; he wished to have new copies, turned into prose, if the originals had been in verse, or modernized if they had been in prose, embellished by his own illuminators. No less than thirty of these new redactions of epic and chivalric stories were thus made.[29] To the rather few Arthurian romances bequeathed him by his father, Jean, Philip was careful to add several manuscripts, an *Estoire* (*Grand Saint Graal*), two *Lancelots*, one of them the thirteenth century manuscript containing the *Queste* and the *Mort*, now Brussels 9627–28, another *Mort*, three *Tristans* in prose, a *Guiron* in three volumes (Ars. 3477–78), a paper manuscript of *Ysaie le Triste* (Gotha), an early fourteenth century manuscript of *Meraugis de Portlesguez* (Vienna, 2599), with eighteen small miniatures in the French style, and in 1431 he paid a considerable sum to a priest in Brussels to have one of his *Lancelots* rebound.[30] Philip had Chrétien's *Erec* and *Cliges* redacted in prose in a plain paper manuscript, and set his own best copyist, David Aubert, at the task of copying in 1459–60, not any of the finer Arthurian romances, but the almost interminable *Perceforest* (Arsenal 3483–94), which combines the adventures of the heroes of the Quest of the Grail with those of Alexander and his companions, one of whom, Betis, is renamed Perceforest.[31]

---

[25] Until 1933 this MS was in Amsterdam. Cf. M. de Vries and E. Verwijs, *Jacob van Maerlant's Spiegel Historiael* (Leiden, 1863), p. lxxxix ff.; Byvanck, *Les princ. MSS ... des Pays-Bas*, SFRMP, 1931, p. 7. The MS is now (1938) at The Hague.

[26] Cf. Pirenne, *op. cit.*, pp. 188, 234 ff.

[27] See *supra*, Ch. IX. Herbert, *Illum. MSS*, p. 307; J. Mesnil, "Les Origines de l'art des Pays-Bas au XVe Siècle," *Revue d'art*, XXIII (1922), 45.

[28] Georges Doutrepont, *La littérature française à la cour des Ducs de Bourgogne* (P., 1909), p. 484. The library contained, at

Philip's death, almost 900 works. Cf. David Aubert's praise of the library (Doutrepont, p. 17).

[29] Doutrepont, pp. 482–485.

[30] Doutrepont, pp. 17–19. For the *Meraugis*, see Rudolph Beer, *Les princ. MSS ... de Vienne*, SFRMP, 1912, p. 51, Pl. II. For two reproductions from the *Meraugis* see Bella Martens, *Meister Francke*, Abb. 84–85.

[31] Doutrepont, p. 66, for Chrétien's poems; pp. 49–50, for *Perceforest*.

Despite these signs of some Arthurian interest on Philip's part, despite the evidence of Olivier de la Marche[32] as to the delight with which the young Charles the Bold in his boyhood heard of the deeds of Lancelot and Gawain, still it is certain that Arthurian romances did not in number or in decoration compare with the epic legends and chronicle histories which were in the fifteenth century, even more than in the fourteenth, in highest literary and courtly favor in the Low Countries. These were the "anciennes histoires" which every day, according to David Aubert,[33] were read aloud to Philip, and on these were lavished all the resources that wealth and art could provide. They were decorated by such artists as Guillaume Vrelant and Loyset Liedet, both heads of busy ateliers in Bruges, by Jean le Tavernier, by Philippe de Mezerolles, who became a court painter at Bruges in 1467, and by that famous painter and illuminator, Simon Marmion, to say nothing of the distinguished Flemish artists who worked anonymously on various famous MSS of this period.[34]

VRELANT AND THE CHRONIQUES DE HAINAUT

Although the more romantic aspects of Arthurian story were neglected in this history-loving period, the pseudo-historical legend of Arthur himself was revived. Jean Wauquelin of Mons in 1444 translated into French Geoffrey of Monmouth's famous *History of the Kings of Britain*, and drew on this for the second of the three great volumes of the *Chroniques de Hainaut*, which through a long term of years were in course of preparation for Philip the Good.[35] Hainaut was supposed to have been part of Arthur's domains, and the "history" of the legendary conqueror was retold. This Arthurian section in the *Chroniques* was copied by the scribe, Jacotin de Bos, who names

himself and states that he finished the volume on December 8, 1449 (Brussels, Bibl. Roy. 9243, f. 295 v). The volume was not illuminated until almost twenty years later when it was given to Guillaume Vrelant who decorated it with sixty "histoires,"[36] seven of which were concerned with Arthur. In 1468 Vrelant was paid for these sixty pictures, large and small, the total sum of seventy-two livres,[37] and the payment serves to authenticate as Vrelant's the miniatures of this volume. They were evidently accepted as the work of his own hand, or as having been made so directly under his supervision that the work was accepted as his.

Of Vrelant himself not much is known, though a long series of documents, chiefly in connection with the booksellers' and illuminators' Gild of St. John the Evangelist, show that the artist lived in Bruges from 1454 until his death in 1481–82.[38] He was a friend of Hans Memling, who painted on an altar piece now in Turin, but made for Bruges, portraits of the pious artist and his wife.[39] Vrelant's face, reserved, quiet, kindly yet ascetic in expression, accords remarkably with the temperament revealed by the miniatures of a man full of earnest piety, deeply concerned to show religious occasions, baptisms, marriages, preachings, clerical processions, pious deaths, with grave reverence; a man not of imaginative or adventurous mind, but one soberly scrupulous to represent the world about him in clear, exact detail. The gravity of his mind, the definiteness and precision of his artistic methods, must have made him an unusually effective master in that atelier where he trained both men and women to such careful imitation that it is difficult today to differentiate the work of his students and helpers from his own.[40] From his atelier came a large number of religious books—but also, and of supreme interest for comparison with the *Chroniques*, that *Histoire du Bon Roi Alexandre* (Paris, Petit Palais, Dutuit) with 204

[32] *Mémoires*, II, 217.

[33] *Chronique des empereurs* (1462); Doutrepont, p. 467; also pp. 482–485, 490–494, for a general survey of the narratives illuminated at the Burgundian court.

[34] See Friedrich Winkler, *Die flämische Buchmalerei des XV u. XVI Jahrhunderts* (Leipzig, 1925); and the works already cited of Durrieu, Byvanck, Lyna. For Vrelant's work see *infra*. Among the less notable MSS illustrated in Flanders between 1470–80 was the *Tristan* now at Geneva (Fr. 189). For criticism of the 99 miniatures, see H. Aubert, "Les MSS. Petau conservés à la Bibl. de Geneva," *Bibl. de l'École des Chartes*, LXXII (1911) p. 580.

[35] J. van den Gheyn, *Catalogue des MSS de la Bibl. Royale de Belgique* (Brussels, 1909), IX, 215–217; "La Miniature à la Cour de Bourgogne," *Bull. de la Soc. d'histoire et d'archéologie de Gand*, XII (1904); Doutrepont, pp. 414–417; Winkler, *op. cit.*, p. 165.

[36] The name Guillaume (Flemish *Willem*) Vrelant is spelled in a variety of ways, Vreylant, Vredelant, Vreeland. The dedication miniature of vol. II is reproduced by Winkler, *op. cit.*, Taf. 36, and in color, by Leroquais, *Le Bréviaire de Philippe le Bon*

(Brussels, 1909), Pl. 2, who entitles it "Hommage et lecture d'un MS à Philippe le Bon par Guillaume Vrelant."

[37] Laborde, *Les Ducs de Bourgogne* (P., 1849–52), I, 503, no. 1966, pp. lxxxiii–v; Leroquais, *op. cit.*, p. 150.

[38] P. Durrieu, "L'histoire du bon roi Alexandre, MS à miniatures de la collection Dutuit," *Rev. de l'art anc. et moderne*, XIII (1903), 49–64, especially 59 ff.; Weale, *Le Beffroi*, IV, 117, 253.

[39] W. H. James Weale, *Hans Memlinc* (London, 1901), pp. 7, 10, 20. In "Memlinc's Passion Picture in the Turin Gallery," *Burlington Mag.*, XII (1908), 309–311, Weale gives an authoritative history of the picture, and cites a document of 1499 which refers to the portraits of Vrelant and his wife painted on the gild's altarpiece. For reproductions see Weale's *Memlinc*, p. 20; Leroquais, *op. cit.*, Pl. I.

[40] The names of two of his students are known, Elizabeth Scepens and Adrien Raet. Cf. Durrieu, *op. cit.*, p. 59. For Vrelant's students and imitators see Winkler, *op. cit.*, pp. 73–74; Leroquais, *op. cit.*, pp. 172–177.

miniatures, which Durrieu[41] in 1903 was the first to establish as the work of Vrelant.

Although the Abbé Leroquais in his searching analysis of Vrelant's work believes that even in the *Chroniques* a certain mediocrity in some of the miniatures betrays the hand of pupils rather than inept moments on Vrelant's part, the question does not apply to the little group of Arthurian miniatures, which are as characteristic examples of his style, its peculiar faults and virtues, as could be asked. The seven miniatures are concerned with the marriage of Arthur and "Genoivre" (Fig. 343), the meeting of the Saxons and the troops of Arthur (Fig. 344), the single combat of Arthur and "Flolon," the provost of Gaul (Fig. 345), the jousts and sports at the coronation of Arthur (Fig. 346), the combat of Arthur and the giant of Mont S. Michel (Fig. 347), the orations of Arthur and his imperial enemy, Lucius Tiberius of Rome, to their respective armies (Fig. 348), and finally the defeat of the Romans and the death of Lucius.

Altogether characteristic of Vrelant[42] are such architectural settings as that in the Marriage of Arthur (Fig. 343) with its ash grey masonry, pink buttresses, and wide blue arch, with arched, recessed doorways beneath, and traceried windows with leaded panes. Something of Vrelant's favorite device[43] of representing a scene in two parts appears in the way he represents two companies of lords and ladies advancing from the two inner doorways. They are divided by a rose-colored marble pillar, on which stands a miniature image of Moses. Here as elsewhere in his treatment of architectural backgrounds, whether of churches or city walls, Vrelant was unrealistic in color, precise in detail even to an effect of hardness, but fairly skilful in the handling of problems of perspective. His color sense, whether for buildings or costume, was limited, with very little tonality. The colors are invariably bright, clear, metallic, and show a predilection for ultramarine, for reddish carmine, for pea green. In the Marriage scene, over the rich red of Arthur's mantle and of Guinevere's voluminous, ermine-bordered skirt, is the shimmer of innumerable fine gold lines. The Bishop is in grey and white with a black stole adorned with gold crosses; the courtiers are in blue, green, and red. The light is hard and dry as it is in the landscapes, for which, when he introduced them at all, he used very pale greens for earth and trees, pale

blues for skies and for the seas, which he made yet more faint by a trick of pointing the waves with delicate white lines. In that most characteristic picture, the battle of Arthur with the giant of Mont S. Michel (Fig. 347), the light fades, as so often in Vrelant's miniatures, from an azure band of sky at the top of the picture, into a kind of milky whiteness on the far horizon. The rounded yet crag-like rocks with their curious volcanic shapes are of a kind which especially distinguish the work of Vrelant and his school.

Vrelant's pages are crowded with figures, for he was rarely content to paint a picture in which a large number of people did not appear. These he was apt to represent with more skill in the compositional scheme than with variety of human types. The artist had but one type of woman; the slender, fair-haired Guinevere is typical, with her pretty rather than beautiful, oval face, her sweet, inexpressive aspect. Other women are to be distinguished only by their costume, or even more by their headgear, by the golden or jewelled cauls, the horned headdress or else the hennins or those tall steeple shapes, from which hung those diaphanous floating veils which it was the delight of Flemish painters to depict, if only as proof of their skill. Among Vrelant's men there is more differentiation than among the women. There are some fine faces of older men, like that of the Bishop in the Marriage of Arthur, but in general not much emotion, and less of character, is conveyed by the faces in Vrelant's miniatures. Gestures have to tell the story. Sometimes, but not often, he escapes from convention and introduces an appealing bit of simple, homely detail, as when he represents the sorrowful old nurse on Mont S. Michel drawing up her skirts and warming her feet before the fire of faggots (Fig. 347), or when he represents the armorers at work on their benches furbishing pieces of plate. (Fig. 348) In scenes of combat he knew how to balance the massed groups, but not how to escape a static effect. His horses do not move, and his men are in attitudes of conversation rather than combat.

Despite its palpable limitations, Vrelant's work as a whole has a notable dignity and competence. To be sure, Winkler considers that Vrelant's painting, especially in the many devotional books which issued from his atelier, attained a higher level of excellence than that which is found in the secular manuscripts.

[41] *Rev. de l'art anc. et moderne*, XIII, 49 ff., where he attributed 8 works to Vrelant. In 1915 Winkler, *Jahrb. der kunsthist. Samml.*, XXXII, 294–299, added 8 more, and in 1925, *Die flämische Buchmalerei*, p. 71, listed 33 instances. These are considered, but some with scepticism, by Leroquais, *op. cit.*, pp. 153–172.

[42] For comments on Vrelant's work see Durrieu, *op. cit.; La miniature flamande, 1415–1530* (P., Brussels, 1921), pp. 17–18; Winkler, *op. cit.*; Leroquais, *op. cit.*, pp. 151–153; Eugene Bacha,

Les très belles miniatures de la Bibl. Royale de Belgique (Brussels, 1913), p. v; Herbert, *op. cit.*, pp. 311–312. None of these critics mention the Arthurian illustrations.

[43] The Marriage scene, the only indoor scene among the Arthurian illustrations, does not represent Vrelant's frequent device of placing before a threshold a semi-circular slab of stone, or of dividing the two parts of his scene by a partly opened doorway. Cf. Leroquais, p. 151, and plates.

But this is a judgment which does not, perhaps, take fully into account the influence on Vrelant of that traditional religious iconography to which he owed so much, nor do justice to the intelligence and patient, meticulous care with which he transcribed in the terms of contemporary life the fictions he was called upon to decorate. Certainly the seven Arthurian miniatures have little of the "factory made" quality; they are vivid and vigorous; they have an originality of their own, a quality of freshness and interest. They help to justify the conclusion that Vrelant was one of the best of the illustrators who worked for the Dukes of Burgundy.[44]

THE *ST. ALBANS CHRONICLE*

After 1468 when Marguerite of York, sister of King Edward IV of England, was married to Charles the Bold, a new taste developed among the English nobility for manuscripts decorated by Flemish, not French, artists.[45] In consequence a new trade developed, new at least in its extensiveness, for the ateliers of Bruges and Ghent, in the decoration of manuscripts destined for export to England. English texts were imported to be recopied and decorated in Flemish ateliers. Definitely of this sort is the *St. Albans Chronicle* (Lambeth Palace Libr., No. 6).[46] It is written in English but in a Flemish hand and decorated by a far less conscientious but not less recognizably Flemish artist than Vrelant. The text was composed after 1436, since it makes mention of the Siege of Calais in that year, and the style of the miniatures, with conventional flower, fruit, and leaf borders, with no attempt at shadow effects, suggest a date about 1470, shortly after Vrelant's miniatures in the *Chroniques*. The nineteen large and fifty-one small miniatures, these last without borders, seem to have been done by two artists, but were planned by the head of the atelier, who left notes that are still visible on the lower margins of the pages, a fact which Mr. Millar considers the most interesting thing about this manuscript. In the Arthurian section, which extends from f. 37 v to 66 v and includes nine miniatures, one such note occurs in connection with the death of Arthur. It reads:

bataille ou le Roy arthur transperce oultre en oultre le corps de sa lance son adversaire, ne pas ung roy, mais pourtrait en homme darmes, lequel aussi transperce et navre arthur, et est homme [sic] le dit homme darmes modred.

The nine miniatures picture the battle with the Saxons (f. 37 v), the meeting of Vortigern and Hen-

gist with their troops (f. 40), the fight of the red and white dragons (Fig. 349), the death of King "Aurelambros" (f. 49 v), Merlin advising King "Uthred" (f. 52), the crowning of King Arthur (Fig. 350), the killing of the Giant of Mont S. Michel (f. 62 v), Arthur's victorious cavalcade approaching Rome and carrying on a sword the Emperor "Lucy's" head (f. 63 v), and the final combat between Arthur and Modred. (Fig. 351) The figures are frequently disproportionate to their surroundings and lack finesse, especially in the representation of faces and hands; the coloring lacks charm through excessive use of yellow, brown, grey, and a harsh blue black. But the pictures, though undistinguished, are by no means devoid of animation and picturesque detail. There are pleasant bits of landscape, as in the scene of Arthur's crowning, or in the fight of the dragons. In this last, always a difficult scene for illustrators to portray, there is a good deal of originality and concreteness. The bushy bearded Vortigern, known by his ermine-bordered, yellow-brown robe, stands with the eager, youthful Merlin beside a strange pit. Realistic are the piled up mounds of earth from the excavation, the wattled fence, the strong stakes and boarding to keep the pit sides secure, the pale blue of the pool, and the lithe powerful bodies of the red and white dragons, which come far nearer to resembling modern conceptions of prehistoric monsters than do most medieval imaginings. Despite the grotesque central hill in the miniature representing Arthur's last combat, there is vigor in the charging white and brown horses, and the line of Arthur's body with the stiffened, outstretched leg and down-pointing spurred foot, aptly suggests the shock of a sudden blow.

THE DOUCE *GUIRON*

In addition to the MSS designed for export to England, the ateliers of Bruges and Ghent were busy in the last decades of the fifteenth century and the first years of the sixteenth, despite the waning commercial prosperity of Bruges, with the execution of a large number of secular manuscripts of a particularly luxurious type. Many of these were designed for members of the Toison d'Or, that brilliant order, chivalric, religious, and political, which was founded in 1430 by Philip and carried on, with undiminished splendor, by his son, and by his son's successor, Maximilian of Austria. This institution gave rise to the making not only of magnificent tapestries and mural paintings, but to new literary redactions of the legend of Jason and the Golden Fleece, to poems

[44] Durrieu, *Revue de l'art anc. et mod.*, XIII, 58; Leroquais, p. 177.
[45] Herbert, *op. cit.*, p. 313.
[46] For full description see Montague R. James, *A Descriptive Catalogue of the MSS in Lambeth Palace* (Cambridge, 1930), pp.

15–18; Eric Millar, *Les princ. MSS à peintures du Lambeth Palace à Londres*, SFRMP, 1925, pp. 15–19. P. W. Kershaw, *Art Treasures of the Lambeth Library* (London, 1873), pp. 59–61, gives two plates with drawings of f. 122 and f. 251.

and histories of the Order itself,[47] and above all to richly decorated copies of the Statutes of the Order, some of them, like the Vienna copy (Stadtsbibl. 2606),[48] veritable masterpieces of color, of portraiture, and of decorative design. Simon Bening himself received payment for no fewer than four of these manuscripts,[49] which regularly included not only portraits of the heads of the Order, but the individual arms of all the members. These arms, thus fully documented in the Statutes, provide an invaluable clue to the identification of other manuscripts commissioned by members of the Order, members who, like the Dukes, Philip and Charles, like Anton de Bourgogne, "le grand Bâtard," or the famous Louis de Gruthuyse of Bruges,[50] were also great collectors of illuminated manuscripts.

A specific instance of one of these late luxury manuscripts, all the more interesting because of the comparative rarity at this period of newly decorated Arthurian manuscripts, is the Oxford *Guiron* (Douce, 383, Figs. 352–353). Of this once large illuminated manuscript there are now but seventeen folios, cut out by some vandal hand for the sake of the illustrations. But the original destination of the manuscript is still indicated on the present fols. 1 and 17, which bear the insignia of a knight of the Toison d'Or. The arms can be identified by reference to the *Statutes* (Vienna, 2606, f. 94 v), as those of Engelbert, Count of Nassau and Vianden, who died in 1504, and are presented in the *Statutes* and the romance in the same way, the arms surrounded by the collar with its pendant fleece, and surmounted by a winged helmet against a background of long swirling, slender leaves. This precise similarity, together with the marked resemblance in the treatment of the borders and occasionally even of initial letters—the same gracefully twisting, elongated leaves on sturdy, symmetrically curving, root-like branches—the similar use too of the new style of border treatment in vogue from about 1475, strongly suggests that the *Guiron* must have been made in the same atelier which produced not only the Vienna Statutes but also the finest of the late Flemish manuscripts of the *Roman de la Rose* (Brit. Mus., Harley 4425).

The *Guiron*, like these other manuscripts, has borders of a marvelous technical virtuosity, even though the final effect has something of what Herbert[51] has called a glorified "seedman's catalogue." Here, on yellowish backgrounds, are the short sprays of flowers, clove pinks, tiny pansies or heart's-ease, forget-me-nots, strawberry blossoms and fruit, peascods, butterflies, insects, small crested birds, peacocks with splendid tails, all done with inimitable skill, and with shadow effects which greatly enhance the illusion of reality. Too many Flemish illuminators excelled in producing this type of border decoration for it to lead, apart from the treatment of the leaves and insignia noted above, to any identification of artist or school. But fortunately the illustrator who did the miniatures of the *Guiron* had such outstanding peculiarities that he can be identified with the artist of several other important manuscripts. Two of these seem to have been made for no less a member of the Toison d'Or than Charles the Bold.

These manuscripts were alike French translations made by the Portuguese scholar and courtier, Vasque de Lucene, who was drawn to Flanders after the marriage of Isabel of Portugal to Philip the Good. After the latter's death, Vasque de Lucene, sensitive to Duke Charles' special preference for ancient history, translated the Latin history of Quintus Curtius Rufus into the *Faictz et gestes d'Alexandre le Grand* (1468), and, also, from a Latin version, turned Xenophon's account of Cyrus into the *Cyropédie*.[52] Two manuscripts of these works, the *Alexandre* now in Geneva (Univ. Bibl. Fr. 76)[53] and the *Cyropédie* now in Brussels (Bibl. Roy. 11703),[54] seem once to have borne the arms of Duke Charles. Both were alike illustrated in large part by the same artist. Because of this man's predilection for old men, which went so far as to make him represent even the hero Alexander, who died at thirty-three, in the guise of a bearded, elderly man, Aubert has termed the artist "le peintre aux vieillards." To this same illustrator of the *Cyropédie*, Winkler assigns a number of other works and terms this artist of about 1479 the Master of Edward IV.

The characteristics which mark the artist's work elsewhere are amply illustrated in the *Guiron*. On the present f. 1 (Fig. 353), once the beginning of the fourth volume of the *Guiron*, the large miniature represents the arrival of a maiden messenger at Arthur's court. Arthur sits at table beneath a canopy, and both he and the courtier standing in the right

[47] Doutrepont, *op. cit.*, pp. 147–171; and Index.

[48] Cf. Hans Gerstinger, *Le livre de l'Ordre de la Toison d'Or* (Vienna, 1934), with 196 plates, 14 in color, and a valuable bibliographical note, pp. 65–66, on MSS of the Toison d'Or.

[49] Gerstinger, p. 43.

[50] Doutrepont, *op. cit.*, Index; also *Inventaire de la 'librarie' de Philippe le Bon, 1420* (Brussels, 1906); A. Boinet, *Un bibliophile du XV siècle, Le Grand Bâtard de Bourgogne, Bibl. de l'École des Chartes* (Paris, 1906), pp. 255–269. Anton's library included no Arthurian MS. The famous library at Bruges of Louis de Gruthuyse included a number. Cf. Van Praet, *Recherches sur Louis de*

Bruges (1881). Among his MSS illuminated by Flemish artists late in the 15th century was a *Lancelot* (now Paris, Fr. 121) which has one large miniature. The *Tristan* (Fr. 103, Fig. 304) may have belonged to Gruthuyse (Van Praet, No. lxviii). *Supra*, p. 113.

[51] *Illuminated Manuscripts*, p. 315.

[52] Doutrepont, *La litt. franç.*, pp. 178, 182. For the translation of Curtius Rufus see F. Magoun, *Gests of King Alexander* (Cambridge, Mass., 1929), p. 22, n. 1.

[53] Hippolyte Aubert, *Les princ. MSS . . . de la Bibl. Publique et Universitaire de Genève*, SFRMP, 1912, pp. 97–101, Pl. XLV.

[54] Winkler, *Die fläm. Buchmalerei*, p. 137, Taf. 79.

foreground, are alike the unmistakable "vieillards" of the other manuscripts. They have the same thick scrubby grey beards and hair, the wide thick-lipped mouths, the cavernous, darkly encircled eyes, the heavy figures clad in the cumbersome *houppelande* with deep, furred collars. The same aged Arthur appears in the tourney scene (Fig. 354); he sits in the middle of a gallery hung with orange-colored cloths, resting his arms on a green cushion. He wears a blue cap and is robed in red. The artist who thus transformed the heroic figure of romance into one heavy and gross with age, was evidently an individualist, insistent on his own conception, careless of its allurement to others. And this appears also in his technique, in his habit of shading by means of minute brush strokes and not by dark color.[55] Golden lights accentuate the folds in the brown robe, the blue

[55] Winkler, p. 79; Aubert, p. 98. Neither writer refers to the Oxford *Guiron* miniatures.

scarf of the beautifully painted figure of the old courtier in the scene on f. 8, where Lancelot and his friend, Galehaut, the High Prince, talk together in the Chateau de l'Isle Perdue. The artist avoided brilliance, using instead a sober but harmonious color scheme in which grey blue, olive green, and neutral tints generally predominate. His naturalistic backgrounds, as in Fig. 352, with a green meadow, trees and rocks bathed by the slow current of the river, have at once the realistic power observed in his human figures, and also something of idyllic mood. The frank domesticity which so often in Flemish art reinforces the appeal of its realistic skill, is illustrated by the little background scene in Arthur's feast, where an aproned cook hands out food to the waiting servitors.

This *Guiron* was one of the latest, and, to judge from what is left, one of the most richly illustrated and decorated Arthurian manuscripts produced in Flanders in the late fifteenth century.

CHAPTER XII

GERMAN AND ENGLISH MANUSCRIPTS

THE wave of enthusiasm for chivalric romance swept into Germany well before the end of the twelfth century. German chivalry, German poetry, alike, at the turn of the century, were at their period of most brilliant medieval fruition. French Arthurian legends were seized upon with avidity for independent adaptation into German verse. About 1170 Eilhart von Oberg composed his *Tristrant*, about 1194 Ulrich von Zatzikhoven his *Lanzelet*, and between 1189 and 1220 Hartmann von Aue his redactions of Chrétien de Troyes's *Erec* and *Ivain*. Before 1210 had been completed those masterpieces, the richly human *Parzival* of Wolfram von Eschenbach, the luminous *Tristan* of Gottfried von Strassburg. Numerous lesser poets contributed to the celebration of Arthurian heroes so that before the end of the thirteenth century no fewer than twenty-three original German versions of Arthurian poems were in existence.[1]

Though the illustrations of secular books had been begun in Germany before 1200, as Pfaffe Konrad's *Ruolandsliet* (Heidelberg Univ. Pal. germ. 112) and the *Eneide* (Berlin, Staatsb. Germ. 282) of Heinrich von Veldeke bear witness,[2] only two of the extant illustrated Arthurian MSS may be dated before or about 1300. Despite the zeal of German poets, despite the fame of Wolfram's *Parzival* and Gottfried's *Tristan* and the many copies made of these romances, no first rate artist worked on any of the extant MSS. As a matter of fact, few German Arthurian texts, even including those of the fifteenth century, have illustrations; five or six *Parzivals*, four *Tristans*, a remarkable fourteenth-century copy at Leyden of *Wigalois*, a fifteenth-century copy at Donaueschingen, two copies of *Lanzelet*, a fourteenth-century copy of Der Stricker's *Daniel von dem Blühenden Tal*, and the list is approximately complete. Unimpressive as it is, both in numbers and in actual artistic importance, in comparison with the grander achievements of German miniature painting, still these Arthurian illustrations have their special significance. From first to last they exhibit, even if sometimes very crudely, the German instinct for linearism; they pre-

sent a variety of styles of almost as much interest as the changing representations of armor and costume; they become successively more German, and even the earliest seem comparatively unaffected by French influences. Like other secular manuscripts contemporary with them, they exhibit the liveliest romantic zest in picturing chivalric life and in elucidating the narrative by vivid if naïve pictorial means.[3]

The two oldest German Arthurian MSS with illustrations are now in Munich. Originally both texts were copied in the same workshop, presumably in Strasbourg, about 1240. The copy of Wolfram's *Parzival* (Staatsbibl. Cgm. 19) and that of Gottfried's *Tristan* (Staatsbibl. Cgm. 51)[4] were subsequently adorned by the insertion of separate leaves, those in the *Parzival* apparently antedating those in the *Tristan*.

THE MUNICH *PARZIVAL*

The twelve *Parzival* illustrations are to be found on two leaves painted back and front with three pictures on each side. The scenes represent episodes from Books XIII–XV and seem to have been chosen somewhat casually, for they do not by any means represent the most dramatic moments of even these later, less impressive books. No doubt the two leaves are but a fragment of a whole original series. On the first leaf (Fig. 355) are scenes which succeed those stitched on the Brunswick embroidery described in Ch. VI and are concerned with the reconciliation of Gawain and King Gramoflanz. In the top section Arthur and his queen, and Gramoflanz are in their respective tents; in the second the kings approach each other on horseback, accompanied by armed knights; in the third Gramoflanz, in the presence of Arthur, Gawain, and courtiers, gives the kiss of peace to Orgeluse. On the reverse side (Fig. 356) the top section shows the wedding feast of Gramoflanz to Gawain's young sister, Itonje, with Arthur in the center of the long, elaborately set, straight table, and Parzival beyond the wedded pair; the second miniature shows the combat of Parzival and his half-

---

[1] Bruce, *Evolution of Arthurian Romance*, II, 295–300.

[2] For the *Ruolandsliet* see A. von Oechelhauser, *Die Miniaturen der Univ.-Bibl. zu Heidelberg* (Heidelberg, 1887), p. 56, Taf. 10; for the *Eneid*, see Margareta Hudig-Frey, *Die älteste Illustration der Eneide des Heinrich von Veldeke* (Strassburg, 1921); also Hans Wegener, *Beschreibendes Verzeichnis der Miniaturen ... in den deut. Hss—bis 1500* (Leipzig, 1928), pp. 1 ff. He dates the *Eneide* MS early in the thirteenth century. For even earlier *Ruolandsliet* illustrations cf. Schilter, *Thesaurus* (Ulm, 1727), II.

[3] Cf. the MSS cited by M. Bernath, *Malerei des Mittelalters* (Leipzig, 1916), pp. 177 ff.; Haseloff in Michel, *Hist. de l'art*, II, 368 ff., especially the late 13th century *Sächsische Chronik* (Gotha,

Cod. I, 90); the 1334 *Wilhelm von Oranse* (Cassel, Landesbibl. MSS poet.); the account of the Roman journey of Emperor Henry VII, illustrated after 1308 for his brother, Archbishop Baldwin of Trier (Koblenz, Cod. Baldwini); the famous early fourteenth century Manesse MS of the minnesingers (Heidelberg, Pal. germ. 848, reproduced Insel-Verlag, 1926–29); cf. *Apollo*, XI (1930), 286 f.

[4] Cf. Erich Petzet, *Die deut. Pergament-Handschriften, 1–100, der Staatsbibl. in München* (Munich, 1920), pp. 33 ff. for *Parzival*; 84 ff. for *Tristan*, with full descriptions of the MSS and bibliographies, including lists of reproductions to 1920. The miniatures in the two MSS have been variously dated from 1235 to 1300.

brother, Feirefis; the third their recognition of each other and reconciliation, the broken sword between them that had saved Parzival from killing his brother. On f. 50 (Fig. 357) in the first row Parzival and Feirefis are welcomed to Arthur's camp; in the second, at the feast of the knights of the Round Table, Kundrie, the Loathly Lady, her fang-like teeth apparent, abjectly kisses the foot of Parzival in her plea for pardon; in the third Kundrie, Parzival, and Feirefis ride toward the Grail Castle. On the reverse side (Fig. 358) the Grail feast is presented, with five diminutive damsels serving on the forward side of the table; in the second Parzival rides joyously to seek his wife, even as Kondwiramur, holding her two children on horseback, rides to find him; the third, and one of the best, shows the baptism of Feirefis the Saracen. His love, the beautiful Grail Queen, Repanse de Schoye, stands beside the font at the left; at the right, with covered hands, she holds up the Grail to Feirefis, who reaches out his arm to indicate that he now beholds what formerly was hidden from him.[5]

The recurrence and the similarity of the feast scenes and the singularly repetitious plan of the three arrival scenes on f. 49 render it evident that the draftsman was not of very original temper. The influence of religious iconography is plain both in the Magdalen-like attitude of Kundrie at the feet of Parzival, and in the baptismal scene of Feirefis, but Kundrie's fangs in the first, the large yellow hat of the knight at the Grail feast in the second alike indicate the ways in which the illustrator sought both to depict the special features of the story, and to present them in up-to-date fashion. He had the usual German passion for scrolls, though several of these are left unlettered despite the necessity for identifying names when figures are so little differentiated and heads so ill-drawn. The illustrator was more facile than skilful; his fighting heroes, Parzival and Feirefis, leaping from their horses, seem to dangle in mid-air. Yet they and their horses have animation, and a homely but engagingly domestic air is given to the scene representing the brothers in converse, each one sitting on a little hillock, or to that of Kondwiramur precariously holding her children.

The story-telling in these *Parzival* illustrations is more significant than their artistic technique. Yet they have a real if somewhat stiff compositional sense, and place groups not ineffectively together.

The miniatures resemble the Schmalkalden frescoes (*supra*, p. 77) in point of armor and costume, but Weber[6] thinks the miniatures of superior merit. The *Parzival* illustrator bound his pictures together by framing them in brownish strips with horizontal mid-bands of red, but differentiated the three pictures on each leaf by giving to each row a different yet harmonious background, of olive-green, or light or dark blue, or, as in the banquet scenes, of gold. He used color altogether unrealistically, making his horses orange or purplish brown at will. Olive-green, shades of blue, brown, straw-yellow, were his favorite colors, though here and there, as for the tepee-like tents, he used a pale pink wash with patterned figures of red. Red dots appear on the cheeks of some of the figures; the familiar three-dot pattern in white on several of the costumes; gold or silver on the crowns, swords, helmets. The black pen outlines are occasionally reinforced by a broad brush stroke. Different colors are used for shading, as in the black, acute-angled folds of the orange-colored table cloth of the marriage feast. Despite the flat, archaic effect of these miniatures, it is doubtful if they are to be dated before 1250.[7] Like the MS itself, they came presumably from the same Strasbourg workshop.

THE MUNICH *TRISTAN*

Far more profusely illustrated than the Munich *Parzival* is the copy of Gottfried von Strassburg's *Tristan* (Cgm. 51). This manuscript contains the continuation composed about 1236 by Ulrich von Türheim, and is now thought to have been copied in Strasbourg under the auspices of the distinguished notary, Meister Hesse von Strassburg (1230–40). The writing throughout is by the same hand as that which wrote the first part of the Munich *Parzival*. Though this *Tristan* is the oldest of the eleven MSS of Gottfried's whole poem, it is not a close transcript, but a copy of the so-called "improved" version, perhaps the work of Meister Hesse himself, which changed and shortened the original text.[8] The fact is not without significance for the illustrations, which seem to be of considerably later date than the text.

The artistic interest of this *Tristan* lies, like that of the *Parzival*, in the fifteen separate leaves, painted on both sides and here scattered through the text. Altogether there are eighty-four pictures, regularly arranged in rows of three on each side, though on

[5] Cf. Karl Benziger, *Parzival in der deut. Handschriften-Illustration des Mittelalters* (Strassburg, 1914), pp. 23 ff., Taf. 28–31. Benziger confused the order of the miniatures and wrongly identified as Gawain's meeting with the Princess Obie and Obilot (an episode belonging to Bk. VII) the representation of Parzival and Kondwiramur on f. 50 v. For a colored reproduction of f. 49 v. see Fr. Vogt, Max Koch, *Gesch. d. deut. Lit.* (Leipzig, 1919), I, 122, Taf.

[6] "Die Iwein-bilder . . . zu Schmalkalden," *Zeitschrift für*

bildende Kunst, XII (1901), 119.

[7] Without any decisive evidence Franz Jacobi, *Die deut. Buchmalerei* (Munich, 1923), p. 34, dates the *Parzival* c. 1235, the *Tristan* c. 1240; Alfred Stange, *Deutsche Malerei der Gotik* (Berlin, 1934), I, 2–3, dates them both c. 1240, and strangely considers the *Parzival* a retrogression from the *Tristan*.

[8] F. Ranke, "Die Uberlieferung von Gottfrieds Tristan," *Zts. f. deut. Altertum*, LV (1914), 405–417; also *Tristan u. Isold* (Munich, 1925), pp. 250, 275.

f. 7, 10, 11, only two rows appear. Many of the miniatures are now much rubbed.

The first three leaves are devoted to the courtship of the hero's young parents. King Mark's May-time court is happily presented by youths in one miniature, by maidens in the others, who alike appear beneath the swirl of light canopies. The worn but often reproduced first miniature[9] shows Mark sitting at the right, legs most royally crossed; Rivalon, his guest, at the left; a graceful group of courtiers between. In a vigorous tourney on f. 10 (Fig. 359) Rivalon receives the impact of a hostile spear on his blue shield; beneath the picture Blanchefleur hears from her "Meisterin" of his supposedly fatal wound, and at the right throws herself into her lover's arms, while the pretty "Meisterin," whose fluted cap is her chief sign of maturity, weeps with distress beside the lovers. On f. 11 (Fig. 360) in the first row the lovers are in flight; within a crowded boat sit the helmsman with his paddle, a lady, unmentioned in the poem, and in the bow Rivalon, with Blanchefleur kneeling, her upraised arms about him, and her eyes fixed languishingly on his; at the right, arrived in Brittany, the two, standing hand in hand, one slightly behind the other, meet the faithful Roald. In the second row they are married by a tonsured priest, and Blanchefleur rides away in care of Roald, the "Foitenant," to find safe shelter during her husband's war with the usurper, Morgan. The reverse side of f. 11 (Fig. 361) shows above, Duke Morgan, mounted, striking down the mortally wounded Rivalon; below, in the presence of clerics and weeping women, the body of Rivalon is lifted from a stretcher to his stone coffin, in what is for romance illustration an unusual and impressive scene.

The adventures of the true hero begin on f. 15. After three scenes devoted to the sad circumstances of his birth, f. 15 (Fig. 362) shows us Roald's wife, the supposed mother of the newborn child, carrying him to church and baptism; then his subsequent youthful training in various accomplishments; he learns to read, and the boy's hand seems to pluck at the letters, *Beatus Vir, Deus, Veni sancte Spiritus*, of the huge book supported on a three-legged stand. With slim boyish grace he puts the stone, an accomplishment unmentioned by the courtly Gottfried; he plays a harp. In the third row he is seated, hawk on wrist in the ship of the Norse merchants who were to abduct him, but who here hold the birds they wish to sell. One foster brother is shown just leaving the ship; another, and his foster father, stand on land; Governal (Kurwenal), his tutor, remains in the ship. Six scenes are devoted to Tristram's arrival at

Mark's court (f. 30 r, v), and six to his return to Brittany and his victory over Morgan (f. 37). On f. 46 is shown Tristram's famous combat with Morhaut, and on f. 46 v his departure to seek healing in Ireland for his own poisonous wound. With special vigor are the events depicted after his second return to Ireland. On f. 67 (Fig. 363) he cuts out the dragon's tongue; the false seneschal finds the dragon, and takes back the head of the blandly smiling "Sarphant" to town. The reverse of this leaf pictures the young Ysolt and her mother first finding the headless dragon, then the wounded Tristram, and in the last row shows the Princess, after she has discovered his identity, attempting to slay him. Despite an apparent difference in style, the dragon episodes are all by the same hand as the first miniatures, as the forms of the horses, the women, and the armed knights show.

It is indicative of the growing haste with which this last picture and the ones subsequent to it were completed, that no illustration was contrived for Gottfried's supremely beautiful account of the drinking of the Love Potion. The adventures of the lovers begin with the episode of the Chips on the Stream— the chips used by Tristram as a signal to Ysolt (f. 76).[10] The style becomes notably more coarse with f. 82 (Fig. 364), where Mark talks to Ysolt, who lies in bed; where Mark tells his suspicions of Ysolt to lords and prelates; where the Queen herself makes her vow to Mark to undergo the ordeal of the hot iron. This coarser style pervades the scenes representing the ordeal (f. 82 v) and those showing Tristram's winning and sending to Ysolt the fairy dog, Petit-Criu, who here becomes an ungainly creature (f. 86 v). Not more carefully executed but more vivaciously conceived are the illustrations (f. 90, Fig. 365) showing Mark sending the lovers into exile, lovers who step off, lightly as to a dance, to their forest life; then of their sleep in the grotto, the sword between them, and Mark and his horse outside; and finally of their virtuous return, in company with Governal, who holds up an admonitory finger to warn Mark against again suspecting Ysolt, who stands before him, a model of innocence. The barren representation of the grotto was, as Ranke[11] points out, no doubt due to the fact that the illustrator had before him the "improved" version, which omitted the rich details of Gottfried's original poem.

The picturing on f. 90 of episodes connected with the Flour on the Floor and Tristram's leap to Ysolt's bed are by the same hand as the first miniatures. But with those on f. 104 (Fig. 366) another illustrator sets forth with neat deftness Tristram's escape in

[9] For reproductions since 1920 see Anselm Salzer, *Illust. Gesch. d. deut. Lit.* (Regensburg, 1926), p. 270; Ranke, *Tristan u. Isolde*, p. 176; Stange, *Deut. Malerei*, Abb. 2.

[10] Reproduced by Erich Petzet and Otto Glauning, *Deut.. Schrifttafeln des IX bis XVI Jhds.* (Munich, 1912), Taf. xxxii. Different, later hands have written in the inscriptions.

[11] Ranke, *Tristan u. Isold*, p. 281.

the garb of a fool, when he clubbed his way from Ysolt's room,—his encounters with Mark and Pleherin, whom, in the third row, he strikes down with the club, and with the same club paddles away.[12] The illustrations for Ulrich's continuation of Gottfried's poem begin on f. 101.

This whole pictorial rendition of the *Tristan* is a vivacious, if often sentimentalized, commentary on the story itself. Without power to suggest the radiance and depth of the poem, the earlier miniatures in particular, by their rhythmical grace of line, by their soft, rounded contours, their refinements in gesture and the swirl of drapery, do suggest, more characteristically than most medieval miniatures, something of the special lyrical quality of the text they illustrate.

The miniatures throughout are divided from each other by one or two colored strips, as in the *Parzival*. The backgrounds are more heavily painted than the figures, which are lightly tinted. The outlines are much more lightly drawn before the coarser style begins. Throughout the drapery falls in swirling, incomprehensible folds about the feet, but in the first miniatures, this swirling is notably accentuated. The earlier figures are slender and svelte, unusually well-modeled, with but a hint of that emphasis on the hip curve, the long waist, which gradually become dominant features. Some of these earlier, gracefully plastic figures might, indeed, be compared with the lovely statues of Ecclesia and Synagoga of Strasbourg Cathedral, but the broad, smiling facial type corresponds better with the later figures of the same church, the Wise and Foolish Virgins.[13] There is, as Stange[14] has pointed out, unquestionable relationship between the Strasbourg statues and the Strasbourg miniatures, but the miniatures are later. The gradual "modernizings" by the same illustrator of figure style and costume point to a date about 1300. Particularly to be noted are the long, false mantle sleeves, the tight-buttoned dress sleeves, the little round fluted caps of the women of a style precisely analogous to that seen in the famous Manesse MS of the early fourteenth century. The progressive coarsening of the first illustrator's style can be easily observed. He worked more and more rapidly, with increasing resort to the one- or two-figure type of scene, and in the figures themselves, increasingly

careless of modeling or proportions, he continued to accent, almost to the point of caricature, the backward slant of the body, the fashionable protuberant stomach. In the simplified figures of the prelates on f. 82 (Fig. 364) and the crudity of the architectural details, it would be natural to surmise the influence of some earlier model, but the drapery, the figure of Mark, the drawing of hair, hands, and wrists, seem merely careless modifications of the first illustrations. At least two men must have been employed on the decoration of this, the oldest and most important of the four illustrated German *Tristans*.[15]

WIGALOIS

After the Munich *Tristan* comparatively little illustration of Arthurian stories seems to have been undertaken in the fourteenth century in Germany, though there were numerous and fertile schools of illumination. But, as in the Low Countries at this time, illustrated chivalric romances were evidently in less demand in Germany, than were the more serious chronicles and legends on which the most profuse illustration was lavished. From the fourteenth century only one illuminated Arthurian MS of any significance has survived. It contains the Austrian romance *Wigalois* of Wirnt von Gravenberg.[16]

This manuscript, now in Leyden (Bibl. der Ryks-Univ. No. 537),[17] is remarkable in several ways. Not only does it reveal stylistic likeness to the Tristram and Gawain embroideries of Wienhausen and Brunswick noted in Chapters IV and VI, but the copyist and illuminator has given us the date of its completion, his own name and that of his patron, and even a portrait of himself. He was "Jan von Brunswik," a brother of the Cistercian monastery of Amelungsborn; his patron was Duke Albrecht von Braunschweig-Grubenhagen (1361–84); the date was 1372. On the last page (Fig. 374) he represents himself in a grey and white habit standing at a writing desk, with a page before him on which the word *Tode* is inscribed. Above his desk is a bird, possibly reminiscent of the talking parrot of the story; also a rayed, round ornament. At the right is a tree with a dog beneath it; above are two heraldic devices separated by a small knight standing with lance erect. At the

---

[12] Reproduced in color, *ibid.*, Taf. 8.

[13] For the Strasbourg figures see Erwin Panofsky, *Die deut. Plastik des elften bis dreizehn. Jhds.* (Munich, 1924), Abb. 112–113, 120; pp. 163 ff. (bibliography, p. 169). He dates Ecclesia, Synagoga, c. 1230–35; the Foolish Virgins, c. 1280.

[14] Stange, *Deut. Malerei*, pp. 2–3, gives the earlier dating for all the Strasbourg statues.

[15] The Munich *Tristan*; the Cologne *Tristan* (Hist. Archiv. 88), dated 1323, which contains seven miniatures; the two *Tristans* of the fifteenth century: Heidelberg, Pal. germ. 346; Brussels, Bibl. Roy. 14697. For the two last, see *infra*. Cf. Gott-

fried von Strassburg, *Tristan*, ed. K. Marold (Leipzig, 1906), pp. viii f.

[16] See *supra*, pp. 79 f. Besides the illustrated Leyden MS of *Wigalois* there is one at Donaueschingen (71), decorated in the workshop of Diebolt Lauber with twenty-six large colored pen drawings. Cf. J. M. Kapteyn, *Wigalois* (Bonn, 1926), p. 61. See *infra*, note 25.

[17] The MS is described by Kapteyn, *ibid.*, pp. 29–31; and by A. Byvanck, *Les princ. MSS à Peintures des Pays-Bas*, Bull. SFRMP (Paris, 1931), p. 96; Pl. xxxi (f. 53 v, 72 v). *Supra*, p. 81.

left is a small shield with two golden lions surmounted by a helmet with two curved horns; at the right a defaced shield is surmounted by a helmet bearing the device of a white horse.

The fact that the illuminator knew his text intimately enabled him to draw upon its bizarre contents for specific and unusual details, to which he sometimes added touches of his own. His forty-seven miniatures illustrate *Wigalois* with an unusual and entertaining precision and in a way that is altogether peculiar to Jan von Brunswik himself. Besides Jan's portrait, seven of these little known miniatures have been chosen for reproduction.

(Fig. 367) On a full page ten figures, including Arthur and Guinevere, most of them clad in red and white, sit at the Round Table, waiting for an adventure to happen. Five maidens, four with large gold cups in hand, wait upon the others. The emphasis on the presence of the women is perhaps designed to illustrate the poet's remark that Arthur's palace was full of "richer vrouwen." The table is set with cups, dishes, large red-handled, silver-bladed knives, a large mounted horn of gold. The absence of the faintest suggestion of space or perspective is noteworthy.

(Fig. 368) Wigalois in fashionable court dress accompanies Queen Elamie of Tyre to the tent of the Red Knight, who had reft from her by force the horse and parrot that had been awarded her as the most beautiful of women. Against a dark blue background hangs the golden cage that cost, according to the poet, over a thousand pounds, and within is the talking parrot, whose exclamation is reported on a ribbon-like inscription:

> Willekome, leue vrowe min,
> ich solde iuwer diu rehte sin!
>
> O welcome, dear lady mine;
> I should of right be thine!

Below on a chequered wine-and-lilac-colored quilted couch rest the Red Knight, Hojir, and his *amie*. She is shown in the act, unmentioned by the poet, of combing Hojir's red hair.

(Fig. 369) Wigalois and the Red Knight meet in combat. Their squires stand by, holding the many spears that were used in the fight.

(Fig. 370) In the attempt to avenge the murdered king of Korntin, Wigalois follows his spirit, which appears in the form of a crowned black beast, into a marvelous castle.

(Fig. 371) Wigalois encounters the unhappy lady Beleare, whose husband has been attacked by the dragon Pfetan. The poet has much to say of the lady's frenzied grief, her torn clothes, her disheveled hair, details which are faithfully reproduced in the miniature. The inscription above her head repeats her cry in the poem: "Owe, lieber herre, owe owe!"

(Fig. 372) Wigalois, stripped of his armor by fisherfolk as he lay unconscious after a fight with the monster Pfetan, takes refuge in a cave. He sits with an air of alarmed vigilance while outside the grateful lady Beleare, whose husband he has rescued, and her attendant make proffer of Beleare's furred mantle.

(Fig. 373) The lower miniature shows one of the last and greatest exploits of Wigalois, his encounter with the enchanter Roaz. It is supposed to take place in Roaz's own castle of Glois, where only women dwell. In the upper miniature Roaz's wife, Japhite, accompanied by attendant maidens bearing candles, watches the teriffic nocturnal combat.

The miniatures of *Wigalois* are unusual in their coloring. The backgrounds are blue, lilac, purple brown, olive green, ochre; shades of red, cerise, pink, are frequently used in combination with black and gold. The artist was consciously striving for ornate effects, as can be seen especially in the Round Table scene and in the combat with Roaz. The Queen is pictured in grey, her throne is patterned in red and adorned with gold; her maidens wear costumes of black, red, and pink, flecked with gold and silver; Wigalois wears a jupon of white, blue, and gold. Roaz is in white, pink, and gold. Jan was meticulous about fashionable details of costume and recorded faithfully the liripipes on the women's arms, the elaborate helmets of the men, their thigh-length, tight-fitting jupons of the mode prevalent in the last half of the fourteenth century.

But the feature which most distinguishes Jan von Brunswik's painting is his palpable imitation of embroidery technique. It is surely no accident that the monastery of Amelungsborn lies in the same district as the nunneries of Wienhausen and of Brunswick, from which in all probability came the Tristram and Gawain embroideries. The very framework of many of the miniatures, the representation of castle walls, of throne and spear shafts, no less than of textiles, is made up of little rectangles enclosing a rosette or a four-leaf pattern. Jan scattered rosettes and stars over his backgrounds, and introduced stiffly conventional foliage designs in a way to suggest appliqué work, an effect enhanced by fine black edging lines that look like stitches. Whether Jan was a monk who designed embroidery patterns for clever-fingered nuns to copy, or whether he was himself copying some actual *Wigalois* embroidery, it is certain that his sense of design was based on and proper to textile work rather than painting. Whatever the love of ornament in Lower Saxony in the fourteenth century, it could not by itself account, as Habicht[18] suggests, for the wholly exceptional performance of Jan von Brunswik.

---

[18] Cf. V. C. Habicht, "Zu den Miniaturen der Leidener Wigalois Handschrift," *Cicerone*, XIV (1922), 471, Abb. 1–3; also *Die mittelalterliche Malerei Niedersachsens ... bis 1450* (Strasbourg, 1919), p. 70.

Fifteenth Century German MSS

The fifteenth century produced in Germany a number of illuminated Arthurian books of no great distinction in themselves, but of interest as presenting a popular, national type of illustration. The type is related, in certain MSS, to the new art of woodcuts, and illustrates, though sometimes crudely, the German taste for linearism. None of these volumes were of the luxury type produced at this time in France and Flanders; they give the impression of having been made mostly for the trade, though some seem to have been ordered, and many to have passed promptly into the possession of the Counts of the Palatinate and other noble families of the time.[19] The MSS were turned out chiefly from Swiss and South German workshops, such as those in Constance, Strasbourg, Stuttgart, and Hagenau; and all have an essentially popular character.[20] They show no connections with contemporary painting, no finesse in design, but have the practical and practised economy, the deliberate simplifications, enforced upon workmen who had to work rapidly and with but slight knowledge, either from life or literature, of the courtly scenes for which the text called.

In the fairly large collection of MSS of this type now preserved in the library of the University of Heidelberg,[21] are four fifteenth-century Arthurian books: two *Lanzelots*, a *Tristan*, and a *Parzival;* the earliest of these is an Alsatian manuscript dated 1420 by its colophon, "finitus est iste liber in vigilis purificacionis marie virginis anno domini MCCCCXX jor." In this German *Lanzelot* (Pal. germ. 371) on f. 1 Lancelot rides beside a tower, and on f. 2 a robust, spectacled scribe is at work.[22] (Fig. 375) The brightly colored pen sketches, without hatching, show an early stage in a technique that became as popular in use as it was altogether "popular" and non-aristocratic in effect. The *Tristan* (Pal. germ. 346) is a version of Eilhart von Oberg's lost twelfth-century poem. The volume was once owned, Wegener believes, by Margaret of Savoy, who in 1433 married Ulrich V of Wurtemberg; it was apparently copied

from an earlier fifteenth-century MS since it bears on f. 174, in the pictured inscription of Tristram's tomb, the date MCCCCIII.[23] Both the dialect of the text and the style of the thirty-nine miniatures alike suggest that the extant copy was made about 1460 in the region of Lake Constance. Though the illustrator was as unimaginative in his conventional representation of the scenes of the story as his figures are expressionless, he worked with some care, especially on the first three pictures. He used his pen not only for outlines but also for hatchings in the angular folds of drapery. He was uncertain about proportions and perspective but factual in conception, as is seen in his representation of Tristram playing at dice for money with the king and queen. (Fig. 376) He was archaic and meagre, as were most of the designers of these late German miniatures, in the treatment of Nature, of background, of accessories. All his miniatures are framed in red or green bands, into which the design sometimes extends. The figures, if several are presented, are massed together in head groups, and are commonly placed, as was the favorite practice with these contemporary illustrators, on a flat, thin, slab-like base with sharply cut edge.

The fourth Arthurian MS at Heidelberg is a copy of Wolfram von Eschenbach's *Parzival* (Pal. germ. 339).[24] It came from the busy workshop of Diebolt Lauber[25] in the little Alsatian city of Hagenau, which seems to have been the center of a lively booktrade. Lauber employed no fewer than sixteen designers,[26] of whom the best known is Hans Schilling. Lauber himself was both scribe and illustrator, and the thirty-eight or thirty-nine manuscripts that have been attributed to his workshop have a strong family resemblance, though they are of various degrees of skill. Records still survive of the orders that came to Lauber; the Heidelberg *Parzival* with its sixty-four illustrations, being the one ordered by Palsgrave Ruprecht von Simmern in 1440, as was also a lost *Kunig Artus*.[27] Other Arthurian manuscripts ascribed to Lauber's workshops are: the *Parzival* now in Dresden (M. 66), which was done by one of Lauber's

[19] Cf. K. Burdach, "Die pfälzischen Wittelsbacher u. die altdeut. Handschriften der Palatina," *Centralblatt f. Bibliothekswesen* (1883), 3.

[20] In addition to the MSS described below, we may note that Der Stricker's *Daniel von dem Blühenden Tal*, composed early in the 13th century, has 46 illustrations in the Berlin MS (Germ. quart. 1340). This MS is a Middle-Rhenish production of about 1410–30, according to Hans Wegener, *Beschreibendes Verzeichnis der Miniaturen . . . in den deut. Hss. bis 1500* (Leipzig, 1928), p. 27, Abb. 24–26.

[21] Cf. Hans Wegener, *Beschreibendes Verzeichnis der deut. Bilder-Hss. des späten Mittelalters in der Heidelberger Universitäts-Bibliothek* (Leipzig, 1927).

[22] Wegener, *ibid.*, p. 18, Abb. 18. He describes (p. 57) the second *Lanzelot* (Pal. germ. 147) as a mid-fifteenth century "Mitteldeutsche HS" showing a strong Bohemian influence in its il-

luminated letters. He ascribes (p. 83, Abb. 74–75) a *Lohengrin* (Pal. germ. 345), dated 1475, to the workshop of Ludwig Henneflin in Stuttgart.

[23] Wegener, *ibid.*, p. vii, 62, Abb. 55, 56. For three other miniatures from this MS see R. Forrer, "Tristan et Yseult sur un coffret inédit du XII siècle." (Strasbourg, 1933), figs. 36–37, 52 (the tomb).

[24] Wegener, *ibid.*, p. 46; Benziger, *Parzival*, p. 30.

[25] Wegener, *ibid.*, pp. 34–48; also R. Kautzsch, "Diebolt Lauber u. seine Werkstatt in Hagenau," *Centralblatt f. Bibliothekswesen*, XII (1895), 1–32, 57, 113; also *Archiv f. Buchgewerbe u. Gebrauchsgraphik*, Sonderheft Ludwig Volkmann (Leipzig, 1926).

[26] Kautzsch, in *Centralbl. f. Bibliotheksw.*, XII, 18.

[27] Wegener, *Bilder HSS. in Heidelberg*, p. vii; Benziger, *Parzival*, p. 31.

best workmen, called Meister A by Kautzsch; the Vienna *Parzival* (2914); the Brussels copy of Gottfried von Strassburg's *Tristan* (Bibl. Roy. 14697),[28] which was written by the same hand as the Heidelberg *Parzival*; and the Donaueschingen *Wigalois*.[29] The Dresden manuscript with its forty-six extant miniatures (about fifteen have been lost), and the Vienna *Parzival* with its twenty-five, have many practically identical rubrics, and closely related though not identical scenes.[30] Both make the amusing mistake of representing Perceval finding Sigune sitting in a tree, not under it, both bear the rubric: "Wie parcifal Sigunen vff einer linden vant."[31] The Meister A had a somewhat more finished style, a lighter, surer, if less pronounced, pen stroke, a different use of colors, from his fellow workmen; a trick of representing rather more details, especially in matters of costume, where he regularly introduced wide sleeves and wide-bordered garments. He had a lively contemporary sense in illustration, as in the picture where he represents Perceval releasing two prisoners from the stocks (Dresden M. 66, Fig. 378).[32] But he, like others of the Lauber group, made the heads of his figures too large, gave their broad, oval, sometimes peevish-looking faces no individuality, endowed them all with the same dark, staring eyes, always turned sidewise, the same short curly hair, the refined, gesticulating hands, for by hand gestures alone, in all these illustrations, is any dramatic sense of the scene conveyed. The rapid illustrators of all these volumes specialized in easy combats and dialogues, and were apt to use two figures only. They omitted nearly all landscape features except for an occasional tree of more or less archaic type; their architecture was crude; they used almost no backgrounds; suggested no interiors except by a bed or a table, and usually placed their figures on a flat green or yellow base. A penchant for feathered headdresses is to be noted in the Heidelberg *Parzival*, as in the miniature representing the young Moorish queen entertaining Gamuret (Fig. 377), or in that in the Vienna MS (2914, Fig. 379) showing the early morning visit of the fair maid Bené to the couch of Gawain.[33] Plumes and gesticulating hands alone give interest to the representation in the Heidelberg MS of Perceval's final asking of the question that healed the Grail King. That poignant scene is unimagina-

tively rendered as merely a dialogue between two standing figures.[34]

The three fifteenth-century *Parzivals* already noted and another now at Berne (Stadtbibl. AA 91) make up, in addition to the thirteenth-century Munich *Parzival*, the group of five MSS which alone, of the seventy-four whole or fragmentary MSS of Wolfram's poem, contain illustrations. To Benziger, who made a special study of these five books, the one at Berne[35] seemed at once the most original, the most independent, in its illustrations of the text. It is dated 1467 by the colophon of its one scribe, "Joh. Stemhein de Constanica," and the inscription of its first owner, "Dis buch ist Jorg Friburgers von Bern 1467." The well-preserved volume, made from paper bearing the Berne watermark, contains twenty-eight drawings, eleven occupying the whole page. They are framed on three sides, but not always on the fourth side, by a single black line. The vigorous pen-drawn outlines are filled in with fresh colors, and the effect is that of colored woodcuts of a more pleasing type than most of those in the fifteenth-century *Parzivals*. The designer may have been following some earlier model, for he is notably archaistic in representing tree and plant forms, which alike are given conventionalized heart or trefoil or maple-shaped leaves. His compositions, like those of the other illustrators already noticed, are as simplified as possible. His slender figures, far more carefully executed than anything else, and set in symmetrically balanced groups, are not individualized except by some external detail, such as the flying scarf by which Perceval is distinguished (Fig. 381) after he has ceased to wear the literal fool's costume, tight-fitting and topped with donkey-ears, in which he is represented for several scenes, as in those when he kills and puts on the armor of the Red Knight. (Fig. 380) The same literalness is to be observed in the representation (Fig. 382) of Gawain's adventure (Book XI) with the Perilous Bed, a scene often represented on the ivory caskets discussed in Chapter VI. In the miniature the bed's rollers are shown, the falling stones and arrows from crossbows, Gawain himself as he leapt upon the swiftly moving bed, the peasant with his club who threatened the hero; but the designer did not try to represent the peasant's otter-hide covering or his broad hose, as Wolfram described

[28] Cf. Karl Marold, *Tristan*, p. xlviii; Kautzsch, *Centralbl.* XII, 74.

[29] See *supra*, notes 16, 25.

[30] Benziger, *Parzival*, describes these MSS and gives a complete list of the rubrics accompanying the miniatures. For the Dresden MS see pp. 33–37, 54–57, Taf. 32–34; for the Vienna MS, pp. 37–40, 58–60, Taf. 35–41. See also for the Vienna MS Rudolph Beer, *Les princ. MSS à peintures de la Bibl. Impériale de Vienne*, Bull. SFRMP (Paris, 1913), I, 14, 54, Pl. XXIII (Parzival killing the birds).

[31] Cf. Benziger, Abb. 39 (Vienna, f. 160).

[32] Reproduced from Robert Bruck, *Die Malereien in den Hss. des Königreichs Sachsen* (Dresden, 1906), Abb. 197.

[33] This episode begins Bk. XI of Wolfram's poem and is the preface to Gawain's adventures in what is called *Schactell Marferlie* (Chateau Merveil).

[34] Reproduced by C. Busse, *Gesch. d. Weltlit.* (Leipzig, 1910), Abb. 149.

[35] Benziger, *Parzival*, pp. 7–22; rubrics, pp. 44–47; reproductions of all but five of the miniatures, Abb. 1–23. See Figs. 380–383, reproduced from Benziger.

them. The whole scene has a curious stage-like setting within the broad arch of castle towers that are themselves set on the usual sharp-edged base of contemporary illustrations. The illustrator's realistic originality is amusingly indicated in the picture of the old Queen Arnive reviving Gawain, after his combat with a ferocious lion, by sprinkling the hero's face with water from a feather; his literalness by his representation, half-black, half-white, of the "piebald" face of Perceval's Moorish half-brother, Feirefis. Somewhat more elaborately than was usual with him, the illustrator set forth the later adventures of Gawain (Fig. 383), when at the wish of his lady, Orgeluse, the hero went beyond the river to pluck the forbidden branch from the tree guarded by King Gramoflanz (Bk. XII). This well-balanced picture conveys some idea of distance, of grassy heights, as well as the specialist's sense of armor and costume, which were characteristic of the fifteenth century. Benziger assigns all these illustrations of the Berne manuscript to the region of Lake Constance. They may be taken as offering, perhaps, the best Arthurian examples of that stage when the old art of miniature painting with its primary insistence on color was in the process of being displaced by the new art of the woodcut with its primary interest in line and its greater suitability to the art of the printed page.

English Manuscripts

A small group of English MSS may, finally, be noted here, though rather for the sake of convenience than of any consistent relation with German MSS. With special recognition of the irony of "survivals," we recall how little medieval England, homeland though it was of some of the finest versions of Arthurian story, contributes to the history of Arthurian iconography. The Chertsey tiles, a few wood-sculptures of the Tryst beneath the Tree and of Ivain, and two stained-glass portraits of Arthur, are the only extant examples in the decorative arts. English MSS offer so scanty and so undistinguished a group of miniatures that they have not seemed worthy of a chapter to themselves and are here treated cursorily.[36] The best of them is the earliest (1250-1270), a graceful tinted drawing of the youthful Merlin before King Vortigern from MS. Cotton Claud. B VII (Fig. 384), the elongated figure of the King and the "flying fold" of the prophet's garment being much in the English style. The text is Geoffrey's *Prophetia Merlini*. An early fourteenth-century copy of Peter de Langtoft's *Chronicle*, which runs to the

year 1307, in MS Royal 20 A II has some interesting pictures of the early British kings, among them Vortigern taking counsel with his nobles; Votigern burning to death in his tower (Fig. 385); Arthur armed, carrying his red shield blazoned with the Virgin and Child, the crowns of thirty kingdoms beneath his feet. (Fig. 386) These tinted drawings give the impression of being copied from murals. To the middle of the fourteenth century belong the illustrations in an abridgement of Wace's *Brut* (Egerton 3028). The subjects are listed in the *Catalogue of Additions to the MSS in the British Museum*, 1926–30 (L., 1933, p. 240). Of particular interest are the dragons fighting erectly on their tails near Vortigern's falling tower (Fig. 387), and the curious attempt to depict the building of Stonehenge (Fig. 388), perhaps the earliest and least recognizable effort to depict that mighty monument.

The nadir of English illustrative art is found in the caricatures which accompany the unique MS of *Gawain and the Green Knight*, Cotton Nero A X. It is ironic that one of the most exquisite and technically the most finished of medieval English poems should be illustrated by infantile daubs. There are four full-page pictures, of which three, sketching dramatic moments in the story, are here reproduced.[37] The first (Fig. 389) shows the startling moment when the Green Knight holds up his severed head before the court of Arthur; the second (Fig. 390) shows Gawain in bed visited by his host's wife. The lady's reticulated headdress and high-collared gown place the work close to the year 1400, as does Gawain's armor in the next miniature.[38] In the picture of Gawain's arrival at the barrow to receive the return stroke from the Green Knight's ax (Fig. 391) the illustrator's incompetence is displayed in the oval daub indicating the cave, the rocking horse which Gawain bestrides, the normal coloring of the Green Knight's face and hair instead of an abnormal, gruesome green.

Though these pictures could hardly be worse, the painter was not a crude child playing with a pot of colors; he had at least seen and was copying from afar the English miniaturists of his age. The Lydgate *Troy Book* at the Rylands Library, Manchester (Crawford English 1), for instance, shows similar mannerisms; flowering plants rendered by bunched lines with white dots at the top; wooden horses; shores indicated by dark green banks, cut by sharp brown gashes. Likewise a miniature[39] in a MS of Gower's *Confessio Amantis* (B. M. Harley 3869) depicts a recumbent figure and a bed with curtains and

---

[36] For doubtful ascriptions of certain MSS to English illustrators see *supra*, ch. VII, n. 8 and 28.

[37] The subjects are taken from vv. 430–456, 1178–494, 2170–238, 2489–94. There are many modernizations and summaries of this famous romance. A facsimile of the MS was published by

the Early English Text Society in 1923.

[38] Druitt, *Manual of Costume on Brasses* (L., 1906), pp. 252 f. Enlart, *Manuel d'archéologie*, III (P., 1916), fig. 438 f.

[39] Garnett and Gosse, *Illustrated History of English Literature*, I, 183.

drapery very like those in the temptation of Gawain scene of the Cotton MS. The influence of the art of the Upper Rhine on English miniature of this period, to which Mr. Millar and Miss Saunders have drawn attention,[40] seems to account for the curious analogies between the crude daubs of the Cotton MS and certain German MS illustrations of the fifteenth century. There is a marked resemblance between the temptation of Gawain as treated by the Englishman and the visit of Bené to Gawain's bedside as treated by the member of Lauber's Alsatian workshop in the Vienna *Parzival* (Fig. 379), even though there is possibly an interval of fifty years or more between.

Moreover, a MS of the Upper Rhine region now at Bâle, dated about 1400, represents a Daniel on his couch according to the same pattern; and the stream portrayed by wavy lines of wash and the vision of an angel beyond the stream suggest comparison with the visionary stream and the damsel beyond it which illustrate the *Pearl*, a poem also contained in the Cotton MS.[41] Though the illustrator of this MS could not have seen either the English or the Rhenish miniatures specified—MS chronology, in fact, eliminates the possibility—we may urge that he, if no craftsman, had learned something from the practices of his contemporaries in England and on the Upper Rhine.

[40] E. G. Millar, *English Illuminated MSS of the XIV and XV Centuries* (P., Brussels, 1928), pp. 29–31. O. Saunders, *English Illumination* (1928), I, 112–114.

[41] K. Escher, *Miniaturen in den Basler Bibliotheken, Museen und Archiven* (Basel, 1917), Pl. XXXIII, p. 107. Garnett and Gosse, *op. cit.*, I, 123.

CHAPTER XIII

WOODCUTS AND INCUNABULA

THOUGH woodblock printing had been used in Europe in the latter part of the fourteenth century, as the Venetian cloth stamped with designs from the Œdipus legend and the Protat block showing a fragment of the Crucifixion[1] prove, yet no portrayal of the redoubted Arthur appeared in this medium until, about 1465, there developed a demand for woodcut sheets of the Nine Worthies.[2] Apart from the German copper engraving by the "Meister mit den Bandrollen," dated 1464, at the British Museum,[3] we have five more or less complete sets of woodcuts of the subject. The sets at Metz and Brussels are fragmentary,[4] but the remaining three deserve notice. The first consists of three sheets, each with its triad of Worthies, which were bound in a MS in the handwriting of Gilles le Bouvier, herald at arms to the ingrate Charles VII. Both the MS and the cuts are in the Bibliothèque Nationale. Since Gilles died in 1458, it used to be held that the cuts must be earlier; but authorities are now inclined to a later date. The style of the armor and the fact that Hector seems to be a portrait of the young Charles the Bold combine to place the cuts between 1465 and 1470.[5] This connection with the heir to Flanders and the signs of Flemish influence noted by Mr. Hind offer a clue as to provenance. All the Worthies are depicted monotonously on horseback in much the same attitude, with little to differentiate them but the faces, horse-trappings, helmets, heraldry, and the rimes below. (Fig. 392) That beneath Arthur reads:

Je fu roy de bretaigne descoche et dengleterre
Maint roialme Ie vos *par* ma force conquerre
le grand gaiant rusto fis morir & deffaire
Sus le mont saint miciel .j. aul*tre* en alai q*u*erre
Je vis le sang greal mes la mort me fist g*er*re
Qui mochit v° a*n*s puis q*ue* dieu*s* vi*n*t sus terre.[6]

The printed outlines are filled here and there with a wash of water color. Arthur bears a red shield with yellow crowns; orange, straw, brown, and green are applied to his collar and horse-trappings, and the modeling of the animal is crudely indicated by broad brush-strokes in dark brown.

The Worthies are found also on nine prints from a MS chronicle written at Königsfelden in 1479, and now in the Stadtbibliothek at Berne.[7] Though it is obvious that the date must be close to that of the Bibliothèque Nationale set and much the same technique of water color is used, yet there are marked differences. All the warriors are afoot; both the identifying scroll and the lines below are in German, and it is therefore inferred that the work is Swiss or Upper Rhenish.[8] The inscription under Arthur (Fig. 393) is a fairly close translation of the lines under the Bibliothèque Nationale Arthur, but just as in one case the Saint Graal has been misunderstood as "Sang Greal," so here we have in the fifth line: "Ich gesach das heilig grab, darin god geleit ward"; "I saw the holy grave, wherein God was brought." The shield has the same tinctures as those on the Paris cut. The ground on which Arthur walks is painted green; there is pink on his face, shoes, and swordhilt, and elsewhere cream color and a light brown.

Such awkward and childish prints are far surpassed by a set in the Kunsthalle at Hamburg, which Hind attributes to the Low Countries and would date about 1490.[9] Not only is there greater variety, greater craftsmanship, greater strength in the standing figures, but the designer has obviously attempted to suggest, despite the modernity of much of his costuming, an exotic or antique air. Arthur, in particular (Fig. 394), bears a shield of obsolete form and a helmet adorned with strange and superfluous appendages; his chin is covered with mail specially shaped to accommodate his forked beard.

Lancelot, together with Hogier, Rolant, and Valéry, appears as a knave in a set of playing cards printed in Provence about 1440; and at the end of the century Arthur is introduced into this frivolous company.[10]

The great giant Rusto I caused to die and perish.
On Mont S. Michel I went to seek another.
I saw the gladdening blood, but Death made war on me,
Who slew me five hundred years after God came on earth.
Cf. the similar lines under the La Manta paintings, *supra* p. 39.

[1] R. Forrer, *Zeugdrücke* (Strasbourg, 1894), pp. 26 f. *Mittheilungen d. antiquarischen Gesellschaft in Zürich*, XI (1857), p. 139. A. Michel, *Histoire de l'art*, III, 1, 331–333.

[2] On Nine Worthies cf. *supra* pp. 37 ff., 48.

[3] W. H. Willshire, *Catalogue of Early Prints in the Brit. Mus., German and Flemish Schools* (L., 1883), II, 150–153.

[4] A. M. Hind, *Introd. to History of Woodcut* (L., 1935), I, 157, n. 2.

[5] A. Blum, *Origins and Early History of Engraving in France* (N. Y., Frankfort, 1930), p. 54. P. A. Lemoisne, *Les xylographies du XIV et du XV siècle au Cabinet des Estampes* (P., Brussels, 1930), II, 30. Cf. pl. LXXIV.

[6] I was king of Britain, Scotland, and England.
Many realms I wished to conquer by my might.

[7] C. Benziger, *Holzschnitte des XV Jahrhunderts in der Stadtbibliothek zu Bern* (Strasbourg, 1911).

[8] Hind, *op. cit.*, I, 157, n. 2.

[9] *Ibid.* W. L. Schreiber, *Manuel de l'amateur de la gravure au bois*, VI (Berlin, 1893), pl. XVIa.

[10] C. P. Hargrave, *Hist. of Playing Cards* (Boston, 1930), colored frontispiece; p. 43. H. R. d'Allemagne, *Cartes à jouer du XIV au XIX siècle* (P., 1906), I, 83.

SORG'S *TRISTAN*, 1484

Meantime the illustration of printed books by means of woodcuts had been rapidly capturing the imagination and the market, and Germany seems to have been the first to exploit the possibilities. Naturally, then, the first Arthurian romance to be printed and illustrated by the new process was German, but its quality reflects little credit on the compatriots of Dürer who contributed to it. Obviously it was aimed at a public with little money or taste. It was entitled the *Historie von Tristan und Isolde*, and was printed at Augsburg in 1484, the year before Caxton published his unillustrated Malory. The printer, Anton Sorg, did a flourishing business, issuing more than a hundred books between 1475 and 1493.[11] The text is a faithful prose version of Eilhart von Oberg's poem of some three hundred years earlier, a version destined to be often reprinted during the next two hundred years and to maintain the popularity of the old romance in Germany,[12] as shown for instance by the Schwartzenberg tapestry of 1539 in the Kunstgewerbemuseum, Leipzig.[13]

The fifty-nine small woodcuts have all been reproduced by Schramm,[14] and of these we reproduce nine from near the end of the romance. English and American readers may follow the incidents conveniently in Miss Schoepperle's summary (*Tristan and Isolt*, I, 52 ff.) of Eilhart.

1. (Fig. 395) Mark chases a hart; Ysolt diverts attention from Tristram's hiding place.
2. (Fig. 396) Tristram, disguised as a pilgrim, puts the stone further than any of Mark's men.
3. (Fig. 397) Kaherdin speaks with "Kunigin Gardeloye."
4. (Fig. 398) Andret casts a spear at Tristram and Governal disguised as minstrels.
5. (Fig. 399) Ysolt gives clothes and caps to the minstrels, Haupt and Plot.
6. (Fig. 400) Tristram disguised as a jester offers the Queen some cheese.
7. (Fig. 401) While Kaherdin visits Gardeloye, Tristram displays to the ladies his skill in shooting twigs.
8. (Fig. 402) Pursued by Gardeloye's husband, Kaherdin is killed and Tristram wounded.
9. (Fig. 403) Ysolt sails with the messenger to Brittany.

DUPRÉ'S *LANCELOT*, 1488

Four years later, in 1488, the first illustrated Arthurian romance to be printed in France was issued by Jean Dupré, and though the cuts are few they are vastly superior to those employed by Sorg.

Dupré had begun his printing of illustrated books with a missal in 1481.[15] His romance of 1488 was entitled "Le livre des vertueux faix de plusiers nobles chevaliers, specialement du chevalier Lancelot du Lac,"[16] and was in fact a *Vulgate Lancelot, Queste* and *Mort Artu*. It is remarkable that the second volume, of which there is a copy in the Newberry Library, Chicago, was issued from Dupré's shop in Paris on September 16, while the first volume came out over two months later, November 24, from the printing establishment of Jean le Bourgeois at Rouen.[17] But Paris supplied the type and the woodblocks of the first volume, for a glance at the opening illustrations of the two volumes is enough to prove that the same atelier, if not the same engraver, has been at work.

The first volume has a full-page illustration of Arthur holding high feast at the Round Table. (Fig. 404) At his right is "messire Gauvain," at his left "le siege perilleux," and beyond it Lancelot, while the Queen looks down from a gallery. The second volume opens with a half-page picture of the occupation of the Siege Perilous by Galahad (Fig. 405), the same subject as that found in numerous miniatures (cf. Figs. 287, 295, 296, 330), but here far more realistically suggested. The Holy Grail in the form of a chalice stands prosaically among the rolls and the four platters of chicken. The words "galaat" and "le s gra" have been written in red in the appropriate scrolls; the initial *L* below is illuminated by hand in blue and red. Several features are almost identical with those in the first volume: the servitor (lower left), the seated knight with a collar (lower right). The Lancelot of the first volume betrays a family likeness to his son Galahad in the second. One of the important modifications in the cut which introduces the second volume is the insertion of several scenes anticipatory of the entrance of Galahad at Arthur's court. To the left of the royal canopy is the maiden messenger leading Lancelot to the nunnery. In the upper left corner is Lancelot knighting his son; immediately below, Galahad rides to Arthur's court escorted by an old man in religious habit. In the upper right corner Galahad kneels before the Grail.

ANTOINE VÉRARD

This particular woodcut the thrifty Paris printer Vérard utilized incongruously in his *Tristan* of 1508.[18] In fact, it is one of the blemishes of early printing that blocks were often used again and again without much regard to the text they were supposed to illustrate. Not infrequently the same cut is repeated in

[11] Hind, *op. cit.*, II, 295.
[12] F. Ranke, *Tristan u. Isold* (Munich, 1925), pp. 254 ff.
[13] *Germania*, XXVIII, 1.
[14] A. Schramm, *Bilderschmuck der Frühdrucke*, IV (Leipzig, 1921), Taf. 300–03.
[15] Hind, *op. cit.*, II, 628.

[16] *Ibid.*, 624.
[17] A. Claudin, *Histoire de l'imprimerie en France au XV et XVI siècle* (P., 1900), I, 273. On the Newberry copy cf. *Mod. Phil.*, XXX (1932), 2.
[18] Hind, *op. cit.*, II, 665.

one book more than once. A purchaser of Vérard's *Merlin* of 1498 must have felt some annoyance when he came on the same design for the twentieth time.[19]

Vérard had been a professional calligrapher and miniaturist, and had the energy and shrewdness to ride the wave of printed books instead of being drowned by it. Not only did he become the chief printer of vernacular books between 1485 and 1512, but also printed special copies on vellum, had them illuminated in the latest style for royal patrons. Until 1492 he used such woodblocks as he could buy or borrow from various quarters and there is a great variety of hands and styles to be noted in the books which he published. But after 1492, there is a marked uniformity, as if Vérard had found the designer he liked and retained him in his employ.[20] As early as 1489 Vérard had printed at Rouen a *Prose Tristan* without cuts.[21] In 1494 he produced at Paris another *Tristan* and a *Vulgate Lancelot*, both illustrated. In 1497 there was the *Prophecies de Merlin*, known only from a mention, and in 1498 the *Vulgate Merlin* already referred to. 1499 saw the publication of an inferior *Tristan*, 1504, a smaller *Lancelot*, wrongly dated 1494. About 1504 appeared a *Guiron*, and another *Tristan* about 1506.

The *Lancelot* of 1494, of which a copy is in the Morgan Library, New York, exemplifies Vérard's methods. It was issued in three handsome volumes, and for the first, most of the cuts were specially designed to fit the text; but in the other volumes it is obvious that old blocks that could do duty in any romance were thrust in. The frauds of salesmanship are not new. Two cuts from the first volume, however, provide specimens of the honest work of Vérard's chief illustrator.[22] The lines are rather thick; the perspective is usually good; and as in contemporary miniatures there is a predilection for remote distances with towered hilltops cutting the sky. There is, however, not a single attractive face to be seen; only globular heads, projecting noses, mouths grinning slightly. And no brocaded robes can atone for the posture of the ladies.

On the verso of the second folio marked liii (there are two folios with the same number) we see Lancelot before the Dolorous Garde (cf. H. O. Sommer, *Vulgate Version*, III, 144 f.). (Fig. 406) He has already unhorsed two knights of the castle and is presumably encountering the third. In the courtyard behind are gathered the ten defenders of the first gate and the defenders of the second gate. Above the gateway on the right is the image thus described: "a knight of copper on a horse, well fashioned, armed at all points. He held in his hand a great ax, and he was set up

there by enchantment." Except that in the illustration the copper knight is not mounted on a steed, the artist has given a faithful and ingenious picture of a complicated situation. This block was used again in the *Tristan* of 1506, where it is quite irrelevant.

On folio ccxxxii we see the surrender of the keys of the Dolorous Tower (not the Dolorous Garde) to King Arthur (cf. Sommer, *op. cit.*, IV, 138). (Fig. 408) On the left are the tents and pavilions of Arthur's host and two up-to-date siege guns; on the right is the Dolorous Tower. "Lancelot came forth he and his companions and the damsel with the folk of the castle, who bore the keys to king Arthur, and Lancelot bears the head of Caradoc, which was right large." Strange to say, Vérard used this same cut to illustrate his Boethius of the same year.[23]

The one-volume *Tristan*, which belongs to 1494 or 95, employs woodcuts which seem to have little or no relation to the text. An instance is the picture in part two, f. lxxxii verso (Fig. 407), which is supposed to illustrate the tedious tourney at Louzeph (cf. Malory, Bk. X, ch. 68; Löseth, *Tristan en prose*, 272 ff.). Exactly the same cut had already been used in the *Lancelot* (vol. I, f. i), and in neither case is there real correspondence with the text. Unsatisfactory as illustration, this design is also blundering as art. The spectators' stand projects from behind a battlemented building a mile away, yet the occupants are drawn on as large a scale as the king in the foreground.

Despite his scanting practices, Vérard enjoyed marked success with royalty itself. On f. ii of the *Lancelot* there is a scene in which the publisher presents a copy to Charles VIII. And for this monarch and for Henry VII of England he prepared special copies of many works, printed on vellum and illuminated by various hands.[24] There are three such volumes of the *Lancelot* of 1494 at the Bibliothèque Nationale (vélin 614–616), once owned by Charles VIII. In the same library is the first volume of the *Tristan*, destined for Charles d'Angoulême (vélin 623), and the second volume of the 1498 *Merlin* (vélin 1123). In the British Museum there are two volumes of the same *Merlin* made for the first Tudor king (North Library, C. 22.c.6, C. 22.c.7).

These books are all profusely adorned with miniatures; some covering but following closely the lines of the woodcut; others replacing the woodcut entirely; still others—the small ones—being introduced in blank spaces. The first volume of the *Lancelot* contains 13 large and 140 small miniatures, most if not all of them recognized by Durrieu as the work of Jacques de Besançon.[25] Miss Eleanor Spencer has

[19] J. Macfarlane, *Antoine Vérard* (L., 1900), p. xix.
[20] Hind, *op. cit.*, II, 654.
[21] Macfarlane, *op. cit.*, p. 5. For dates of other books of Vérard cf. Macfarlane.
[22] Cf. the style in Hind, *op. cit.*, II, Fig. 405.

[23] Macfarlane, *op. cit.*, p. xxix.
[24] Claudin, *op. cit.*, II, 468 f.
[25] P. Durrieu, *Un grand enlumineur Parisien, Jacques de Besançon* (P., 1892), p. 98.

traced the career of this artist,[26] who rose to be the chief assistant in the atelier of Maître François at Paris, carried on the business after the master's death, but was forced by the conditions of the book market to enter the employ of Vérard in 1492 and to remain in it till 1497 or 98. Jacques de Besançon was the painter of the first three large miniatures, reproduced by Claudin in color with fidelity if not exactitude,[27] depicting a tourney, a battle, and the knights of the Round Table respectively. A good example of his craft is to be seen in Fig. 409, a miniature covering over the woodcut of Lancelot with the head of Caradoc of the Dolorous Tower, reproduced in Fig. 408. Jacques has retained the short and ungainly figures of his original, but has rejected the angular facial contours, and has modified though without improvement the tents, the architecture, and the landscape. His treatment of grass and remote hillsides is much like that of Jean Colombe in Figs. 301, 302; and like most of his contemporaries he relies heavily on gold streaking in his draperies for an effect of luxury.

The small miniatures in this volume and the *Tristan* seem to be the work of the same artist. We see knights playing chess in the Val sans Retour (Fig. 411), Ysolt's discovery of Tristram as he sits luxuriously feasting in a bathtub in the fifteenth century manner (Fig. 413), and the shepherds at the Fountain of Morois. (Fig. 414) It is apparently a much cruder hand, however, which painted Bors riding with a hermit in the third volume of the *Lancelot* (Fig. 412); the drawing of horse and chapel is botched, and the knight wears a clumsy suit of pseudo-Roman armor. Even more marked is the incompetence in the opening scene of the same volume. The woodcut (Fig. 410) below the paint, though supposed to illustrate Lancelot taking his grandfather's head from the boiling spring, actually depicted Judith with the head of Holofernes! The miniaturist has at least read his text and tried to follow it, but the ridiculous bleeding lions in the foreground, the preposterous attitude of Lancelot, the diminutive head of his ancestor, the confused juxtaposition of tomb, well-heads, and horse reveal the depths to which cheap labor had carried a glorious art. If our final remarks on Vérard's illustrators are derogatory, they are justified surely by the crass commercialism displayed here.

THE *MORTE D'ARTHUR*, 1498

In the closing decades of the fifteenth century English printing and woodcut developed, as is well known, under the strong influence of Flanders. Though Vérard printed a book in English and supplied de luxe editions to Henry VII,[28] the most significant fact in connection with the early English press is the alliance by marriage of Margaret, sister of Edward IV, with Charles the Bold and the encouragement which she gave to Caxton.[29] At Bruges he began the translation of the *Recuyell of Troye* and collaborated in the printing of this and another English book, before he moved to Westminster. His foreman, Wynkyn de Worde, from Worth in Alsace, succeeded to the press in 1491, and in 1498 published the illustrated Malory, of which the only known copy is in the Rylands Library. A new edition in 1529 contains many of the same cuts, differentiated only by worm-holes.

The cutter of the designs which headed each of Malory's books in the edition of 1498 may have been an Englishman, but the conventions of his art were naturally Flemish. Dr. Hodnett, after noting that the man's first work appears in the *Cronycle of Englonde* of 1497–98, goes on to say:[30]

Of all the hands that come under our eyes in English books the Arthur cutter [designer?] is the most markedly individual and most amusing. His heavy "mourning" borders, his diving black birds, the heavy-lidded eyes of his narrow-chested women and long-legged men, and particularly his heavy outlines and habitual use of white line in fur, hair, foliage and in the patchy, enlarged thumbprint shading trimmed at the edges as though by shears —his idiosyncrasies are as good as a signature. Crude and careless as his cutting is, it is not the wretched hacking of the *Vitas patrum*, and apart from the excessive width of the borders, his two-column cuts at the beginning of each book consort with the robust type-pages of the *Morte d'Arthur* without friction. They effect a more significant harmony with the subject matter—or at least with the "fantastickalness" which charms the unscholarly reader of Malory.

The illustrator likes to place indoor scenes in a romantic landscape, as when (Fig. 415) Balin (Bk. II, ch. 2) draws the sword which the damsel has brought to Arthur's court. He may include more than one scene in one frame, as in Fig. 419, where the crazed Lancelot first draws the sword from its sheath and lashes at the shield (Bk. XII, ch. 1), then dances in maniac frenzy, then crushes a knight to earth; or as in Fig. 418 Queen Elizabeth is shown the new-born Tristram and then lies in *rigor mortis* (Bk. VIII, ch. 1).

But there is more than mannerism in this artist's work; there is a certain power. He suggests well the weight of young Gareth as he enters leaning on his

[26] Eleanor P. Spencer, *The Maître François and His Atelier* (unpublished dissertation, Radcliffe College Library, Cambridge, Mass.), ch. IV.

[27] Claudin, *op. cit.*, II, 462, 466, 468. Here the order of the second and third miniatures has been reversed.

[28] Hind, *op. cit.*, II, 666, n. 1. Claudin, *op. cit.*, II, 468.

[29] N. S. Aurner, *Caxton, Mirrour of XV Century Letters* (Boston, 1926), pp. 26 ff.

[30] Edward Hodnett, *English Woodcuts, 1480–1535* (L., 1935), p. 14.

servants (Bk. VII, ch. 1). (Fig. 416) The enchantment of Merlin by Nyneve (Bk. IV, ch. 1) (reproduced in Fig. 417 from the 1529 edition at the British Museum) shows not only technical skill in the rhythm of the lines, but also feeling in the hesitant approach of the wizard toward the rocks that fatefully overhang him. Perhaps it is not inappropriate that this survey of the art of the Middle Ages concerned with the Arthurian cycle should close with this symbolic figure of the great enchanter losing his sway, ceasing to be a force in the affairs of men, passing into oblivion. For that was to be the slow doom of the magic tales of that goodly fellowship of the Table Round— until with the Romantic Movement Arthur and Merlin heard the magic horn pealing through Fairyland and returned once more to the fellowship of men.

INDEX

INDEX

The Index gives an alphabetical list of Arthurian *objets d'art* cited both by place and by kind; of the Arthurian characters and certain motifs represented in medieval art; of the illuminated manuscripts, Arthurian and non-Arthurian, mentioned in the discussion and here listed by subject title. Under *Manuscripts* the Arthurian manuscripts are also listed by place and catalog number. The illustrations are cited by Figure number under objects and manuscripts.

ILLUSTRATIONS

3

4

5

6

3. Capital, Perros. St. Efflam and Arthur (?).   4. Detail, Modena Cathedral. Galvariun.
5. Detail, Modena Cathedral. Isdernus.   6. Detail, Modena Cathedral. Galvaginus.

TWELFTH CENTURY SCULPTURES.

7. Arthur, Gawain, and Other Knights Rescue Winlogee.
ARCHIVOLT, MODENA CATHEDRAL. EARLY XII CENTURY.

8. Winlogee and Mardoc.
DETAIL, MODENA ARCHIVOLT. EARLY XII CENTURY.

REX
AR TV
R VS

ABEL

9

REX
ARTv
R VS

9a

ARTVSES

10

9. Mosaic Pavement, Otranto Cathedral. 1165. Arthur Riding Goat.

9a. Otranto Pavement before Restoration.
After Millin.

10. Mural, Constance. C.1300.
Guinevere and Arthur.

11. Charlemagne and Arthur.
STATUES, HANSASAAL, COLOGNE. *C.*1325.

12

13

12. Tapestry, Metropolitan Museum. *C.*1400. Parisian Work. Arthur.
13. MS Bib. Nat. Fr. 12559, f. 125. *C.*1390. The Nine Worthies.

14. Judas Maccabeus, Arthur, Charlemagne.
MURAL, LA MANTA. *C.* 1430.

16. Glass, Coventry. C.1450. Arthur.

15. Tapestry, Historisches Museum, Bale. C.1475. The Three Christian Worthies.

17

18

17. Mural, Sion, Switzerland. *C.*1490. The Three Christian Worthies. After Klinka.
18. Round Table, Winchester. First Painted 1486 (?).

19   20

21

22   23

19. Tristram Fights Morhaut.   20. Mark and Ysolt.
        21. Bringvain Brings Potion to Mark and Ysolt.
22. Tristram and Ysolt.   23. The Harp and the Rote.
            IVORY CASKET, COLOGNE WORK. *C.*1200.
                    Coll. R. Forrer, Strasbourg.

25

26

28

24. Clerics; Tristram and Ysolt.
IVORY, COLOGNE WORK. C.1200.
Formerly Baslini Collection.

25. Rivalon Receives Letter (?).
26. Tristram Learns Archery (?).
28. Huntsman.
CHERTSEY TILES. C.1270.

27

29

30

31

27. Tristram Plays Chess.
30. Tristram Harps before Mark.

29. Tristram Brought before Mark.
31. Porter Opens to Roald (?)

CHERTSEY TILES. *C.*1270.

32

33

34

35

32. Mark Gives Tristram Arms (?).
34. Tristram.

33. Tristram Receives Homage.
35. Duke Morgan.

CHERTSEY TILES. *C.*1270.

36

37

38

39

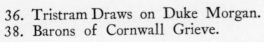

36. Tristram Draws on Duke Morgan.
38. Barons of Cornwall Grieve.

37. Tristram Slays Duke Morgan.
39. Barons Implore Mercy.

CHERTSEY TILES. *C*.1270.

40

41

42

43

40. Tristram Challenges Morhaut (?).
42. Barons Embrace Tristram.

41. Mark Kisses Tristram.
43. Morhaut Wounds Tristram.

CHERTSEY TILES. *C.*1270.

44

45

46

47

44. Tristram Kills Morhaut.
46. Gormon Runs to See Morhaut's Body (?).

45. Morhaut Is Carried from Field.
47. Mark Visits Wounded Tristram.

CHERTSEY TILES. *C.*1270.

48

49

50

51

48. Tristram Drifts in Boat.
50. Tristram Returns to Cornwall (?).

49. Tristram Teaches Ysolt to Harp.
51. Tristram Rides to Tintagel.

CHERTSEY TILES. *C*.1270.

52. Tristram Rides.

53. The Dragon.

55a. Detail of 55.

54. Tristram Gives His Gage.

55. King Gormon Receives Gage (?).

CHERTSEY TILES. *C*.1270.

56

57

58

59

56. Tristram Offers Potion.
58. Ysolt Voyages to Heal Tristram.

57. Ysolt Signals to Tristram.
59. Tristram on His Bier.

CHERTSEY TILES. *C*.1270.

60

61

60. The Three Christian Worthies.
61. Perceval, Gawain, Ivain.
MURALS, RUNKELSTEIN. *C.*1400.

62

63

62. Three Famous Pairs of Lovers; Tristram and Ysolt in Middle.
63. Riel and Two Other Famous Giantesses.
MURALS, RUNKELSTEIN. *C.*1400.

64. MURAL, RUNKELSTEIN. C.1400. TRISTRAM SLAYS MORHAUT; HE SAILS TO IRELAND.

65. MURAL, RUNKELSTEIN. C.1400. TRISTRAM'S VOYAGES TO IRELAND.

66. MURAL, RUNKELSTEIN. C.1400. TRISTRAM CUTS OUT DRAGON'S TONGUE.

67. MURAL, RUNKELSTEIN. *C*.1400. YSOLT REVIVES TRISTRAM.

68. MURAL, RUNKELSTEIN. *C.*1400. YSOLT THREATENS TRISTRAM.

69

70

69. MURAL, RUNKELSTEIN. *C.*1400. THE POTION.
70. DRAWINGS OF FIGS. 67, 68, 69 BY SEELOS.

71. MURAL, RUNKELSTEIN. *C.*1400. MARK WEDS YSOLT.

72a. DRAWING OF 72 BY SEELOS.

72. MURAL, RUNKELSTEIN. C.1400.
The Attempted Murder of Bringvain.

73

74

73. Mariodoc Spies on the Lovers; The Tryst beneath the Tree; The Leap. (From Copy)
74. The Leap to Ysolt's Bed; Mark and Dwarf Go to Chapel.
MURALS, RUNKELSTEIN. *C.*1400.

75. MURAL, RUNKELSTEIN. *C.*1400. TRISTRAM CARRIES YSOLT ASHORE; THE AMBIGUOUS OATH.

76. WIENHAUSEN EMBROIDERY I. (LEFT HALF)
*C.*1310. TRISTRAM SCENES.

77. WIENHAUSEN EMBROIDERY I. (RIGHT HALF)
*C.*1310. TRISTRAM SCENES.

78. WIENHAUSEN EMBROIDERY II. *C.*1325. TRISTRAM SCENES.

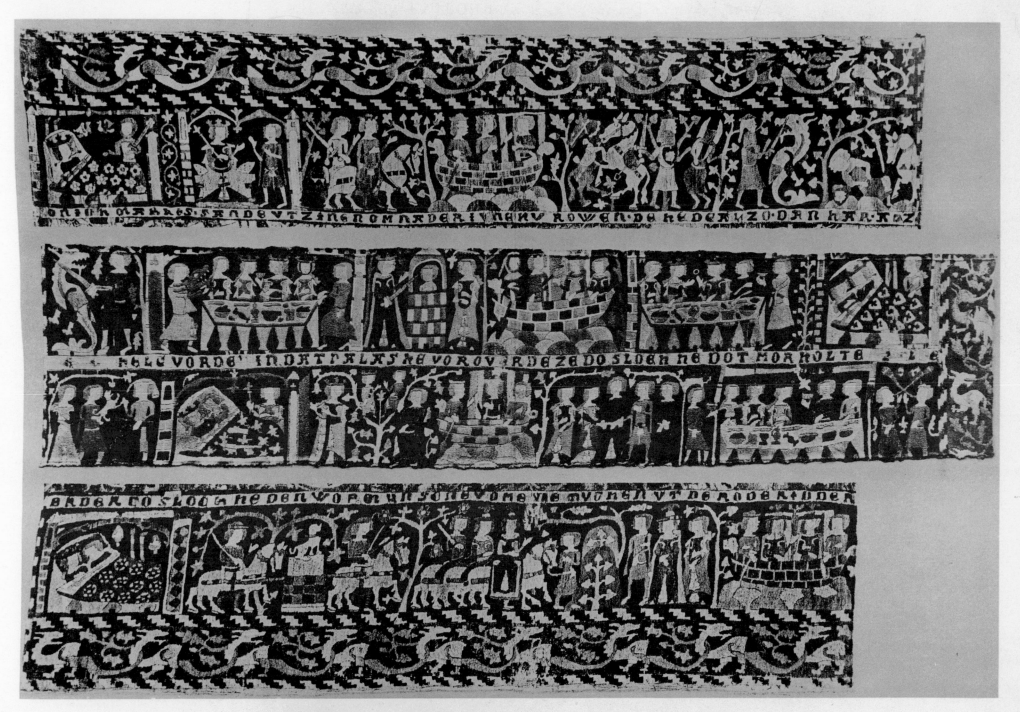

79. WIENHAUSEN EMBROIDERY III. *C*.1340. TRISTRAM SCENES.

80. Tristram Recognized in Bath.　　　81. The Lovers' Tryst.　　　82. Entire Fragment.

EMBROIDERY, MUSEUM, LUENEBURG. *C*.1300.

83. TABLE-CLOTH, ERFURT CATHEDRAL. *C.*1370. TRISTRAM SCENES.

84. TABLE-CLOTH, ERFURT CATHEDRAL. *C.*1370. TRISTRAM SCENES.

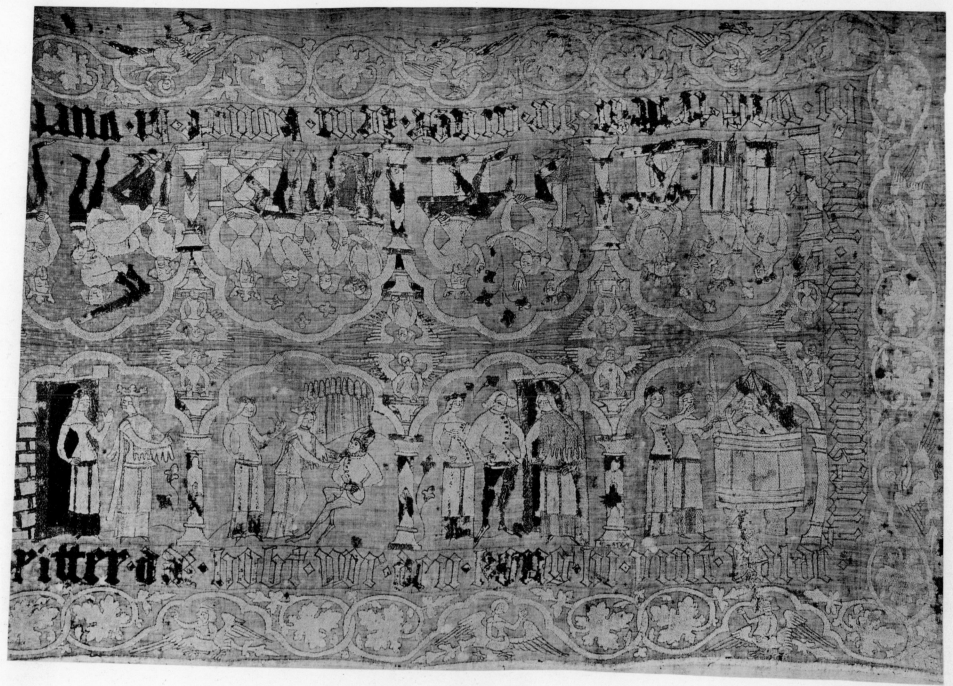

85. TABLE-CLOTH, ERFURT CATHEDRAL. *C.*1370. TRISTRAM SCENES.

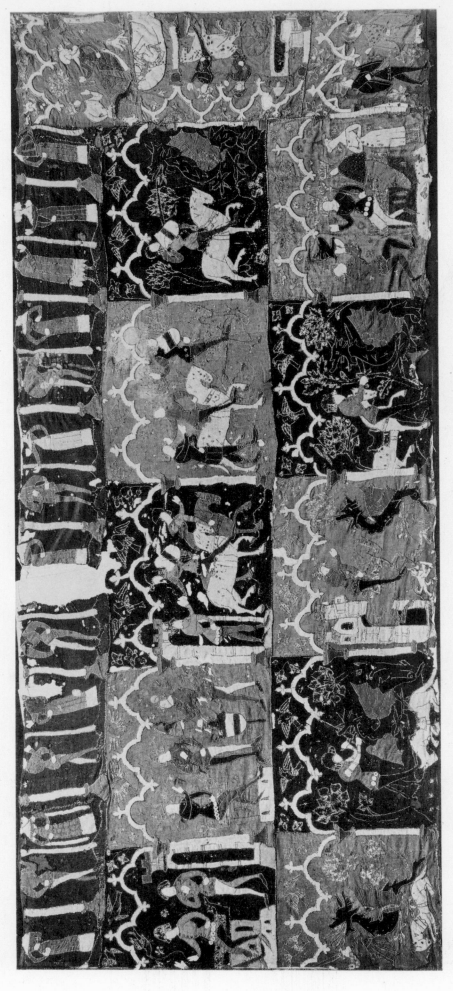

86. GERMAN EMBROIDERY, SOUTH KENSINGTON MUSEUM. C.1370. TRISTRAM SCENES.

87

88

89

90

87. The Potion; the Embrace; Ysolt Welcomed by Mark.
89. Tristram and Ysolt; Ysolt Carried to Shore; The Ambiguous Oath.

88. Bringvain in Mark's Bed.
90. Ysolt Puts Ring in Tristram's Bowl.

HERMITAGE IVORY CASKET I. PARISIAN WORK. *C.*1325.

91

92a

92

91. Hermitage Ivory Casket II. *C*.1325. The Tryst and the *Folie Tristan*.
92a. Racinet's Lithograph of Fig. 92.
92. Mural, S. Floret. *C*.1350. Branor Engages Foes of the Countess.

93a

93

93a. Gélis-Didot's Free Reconstruction of Fig. 93.
93. Branor Slays Caracados.
MURAL, S. FLORET. *C*.1350.

94a

94

94a. Racinet's Lithograph of Fig. 94.
94. Branor Rescues a Captive Knight.
MURAL, S. FLORET. *C.*1350.

95. MURAL, S. FLORET. *C.*1350. QUEEN GUINEVERE AND DAMSELS.

97

96. Tristram.   97. Mark's Head.

MURALS, S. FLORET. *C.*1350. THE TRYST BENEATH THE TREE.

98. Ysolt.

MURAL, S. FLORET. *C.*1350. THE TRYST BENEATH THE TREE.

100. Palamedes Overhears Tristram's Complaint.

99. Tristram Sleeps in Adventurous Forest.

MURALS, S. FLORET. C. 1350.

101a

101

101a. Racinet's Lithograph of Fig. 101.
101. Palamedes Delivers Tristram from Execution.

MURAL, S. FLORET, *C*.1350.

102. Galahad.   103. Tristram and Palamedes.

MURALS, S. FLORET. *C.*1350. GALAHAD ENCOUNTERS TRISTRAM.

104a

104

105

104a. Racinet's Lithograph of Fig. 104.   104. The *Chevalier à l'Escu Vermeil*.   105. Tristram.

MURALS, S. FLORET. *C.*1350. TRISTRAM AND OTHERS ROUT ENEMIES.

106

107

108

106. Tristram and Ysolt Disembark at Tintagel.
107. King Mark Welcomes Ysolt as His Bride.
108. Ysolt Places Wreath on Tristram's Head.

CEILING PAINTINGS, PALERMO. 1377-1380.

109

110

111

112

109. Tristram and Ysolt in the Forest of Morrois.
110. The Lovers Are Welcomed by a Cornish Knight.
111. A Love Scene.   112. Ysolt Welcomes Tristram.
CEILING PAINTINGS, PALERMO. 1377-1380.

113

115

114

116

113. Love Scene. 114, 115. Tristram Plays Chess with Ysolt. 116. The Tryst beneath the Tree. CEILING PAINTINGS, PALERMO. 1377-1380.

117. Morhaut's Embassy and Combat with Tristram.
SICILIAN QUILT, SOUTH KENSINGTON MUSEUM. *C.*1395.

118. Morhaut's Embassy and Combat with Tristram.
SICILIAN QUILT, BARGELLO, FLORENCE. *C.*1395.

119. Tristram and Ysolt; Allegorical Figures.
SICILIAN QUILT, MARCHESI PIANETTI. *C.*1395.

iicii cii moy ⁊ moiit moiiſtre bii giaf

120

121

122

123

124

125

120. Miniature, MS Chantilly, 1078-9.
121. Ivory Casket, British Museum.
122. Ivory Casket, Metropolitan Museum.
123. Mirror Case, Vatican Library.
124. Mirror Case, Musée de Cluny.
125. Hair Parter, Turin.

THE TRYST BENEATH THE TREE. NORTH FRENCH. 1325-1340.

126

127

126. Enameled Goblet Base, Poldi Pezzoli Museum, Milan.
127. Leather Case, Museum, Namur.
THE TRYST BENEATH THE TREE.
NORTH FRENCH, 1325-1340.

128

129

128. Detail, Embroidery. Rathaus, Ratisbon. Bavarian. *C.*1370.
129. Wooden Casket, South Kensington Museum. English. *C.*1350.
THE TRYST BENEATH THE TREE.

130

131

132

130. Corbel. Gruthuyse Museum, Bruges. 1376-1387.
131. Misericord, Chester Cathedral. 132. Misericord, Lincoln Cathedral.
THE TRYST BENEATH THE TREE. *C.*1380.

133

134

133. Wooden Comb, Bamberg. Rhenish. *C.*1410.
134. Corbel, House of Jacques Cœur, Bourges. 1443-1450.
THE TRYST BENEATH THE TREE.

135. Tristram, Lancelot, and Other Devotees of Venus.
TRAY, LOUVRE. NORTH ITALIAN. *C.*1400.

136

137

136. Ivory Casket, British Museum. Parisian. C.1325.
137. Ivory Casket, Metropolitan Museum. Parisian. C.1325.

GAWAIN FIGHTS LION; LANCELOT ON SWORD-BRIDGE; GAWAIN ON PERILOUS BED.

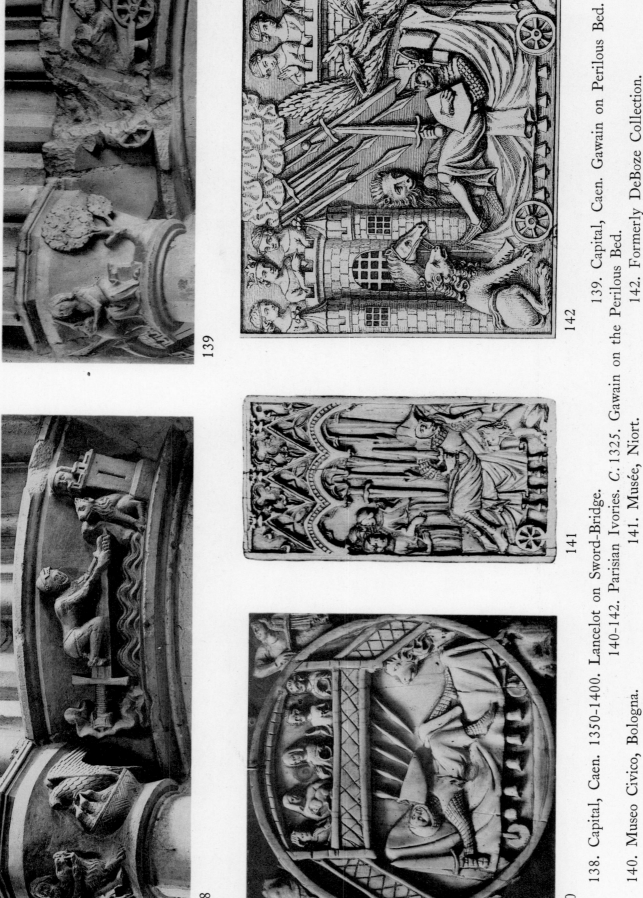

138

139

140

141

142

138. Capital, Caen. 1350-1400. Lancelot on Sword-Bridge.

139. Capital, Caen. Gawain on Perilous Bed.

140-142. Parisian Ivories. *C.* 1325. Gawain on the Perilous Bed.

140. Museo Civico, Bologna.

141. Musée, Niort.

142. Formerly DeBoze Collection.

143. Adventures of Gawain from Wolfram's *Parzival*.
EMBROIDERY, LANDESMUSEUM, BRUNSWICK. C.1330.

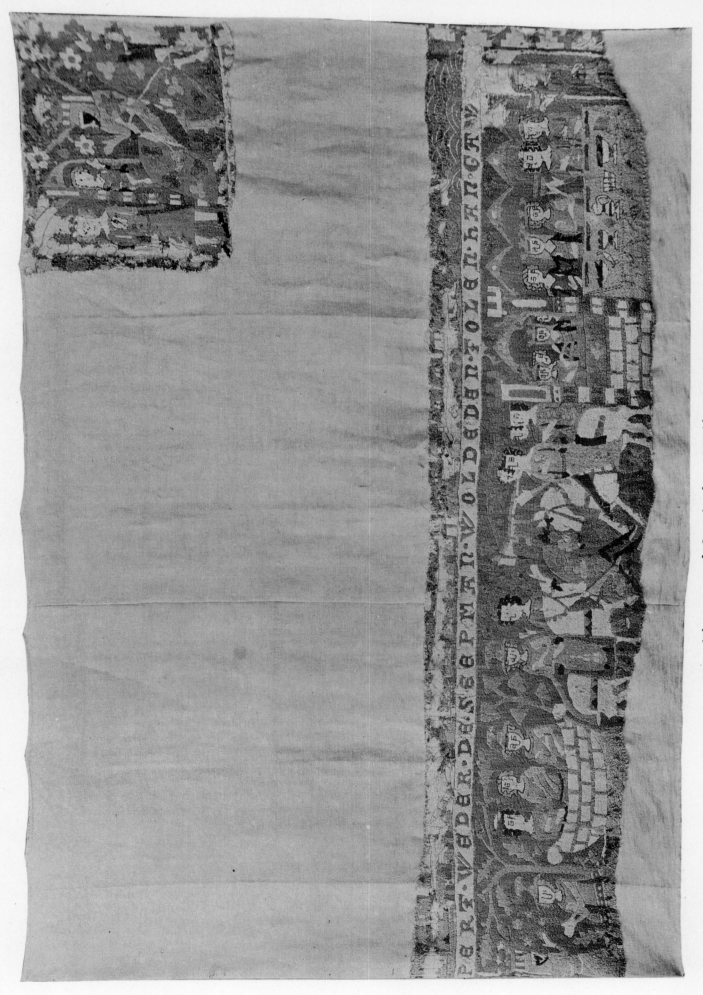

144. Adventures of Gawain from Wolfram's *Parzival*.
EMBROIDERY, LANDESMUSEUM, BRUNSWICK. C.1330.

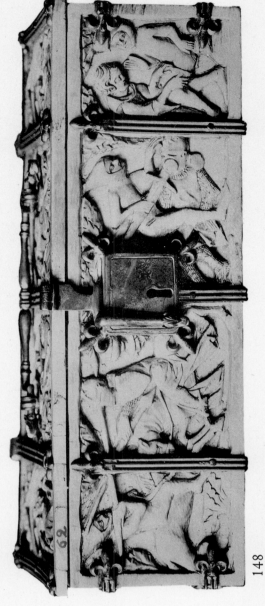

145

146

147

148

145. Perceval Meets Arthur's Knights.	146. Perceval Leaves His Mother and Kisses Damsel in Tent.
147. Perceval in Arthur's Hall.	148. Perceval Slays Red Knight and Is Clad in His Armor.

IVORY CASKET, LOUVRE. PARISIAN. C.1325.

149

150

149. Mural, Constance. *C.*1300. From Copy. Perceval and a Lady.
150. Mural, Lübeck. *C.*1330. After Boht. Perceval and Mother. Perceval Hunting.

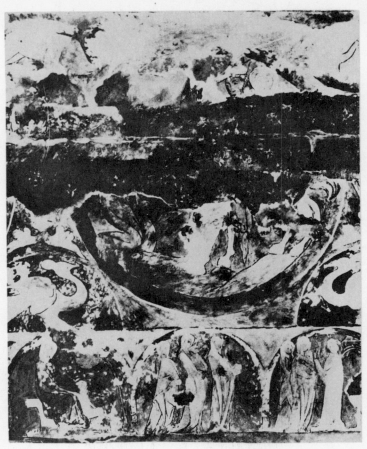

151

152

151. Perceval Meets Arthur's Knights.
152. Perceval Leaves Mother; Perceval Kisses Damsel in Tent.
MURALS, LUEBECK. *C.*1330. AFTER BOHT.

153

154

153. Perceval Meets Fisherman; Perceval Rides into Arthur's Hall.
154. Perceval and Feirefis (?); Perceval and the Grail.

MURALS, LUEBECK. *C.*1330. AFTER BOHT.

156

158

155

157

159

160

159. Laudine Proclaims Ivain Her Destined Husband.
160. Wedding Feast of Ivain and Laudine.
MURALS, SCHMALKALDEN. *C*.1250.

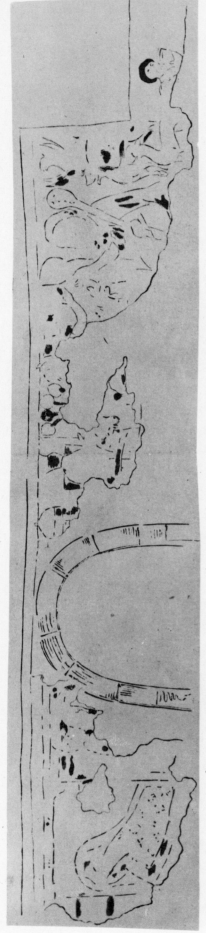

161

162

163

IVAIN PAINTINGS, SCHMALKALDEN. C.1250. AFTER WEBER.

164

165

166

IVAIN PAINTINGS, SCHMALKALDEN. C.1250. AFTER WEBER.

167. Ivain Slays Ascalon; Ivain Presented to Laudine.
EMBROIDERY, MUSEUM, FREIBURG. C.1325.

168

169

170

168. Lincoln Cathedral. *C.*1380.   169. Boston. *C.*1385.   170. New College, Oxford. *C.*1480.

MISERICORDS. PORTCULLIS DROPS ON IVAIN'S HORSE.

171

173

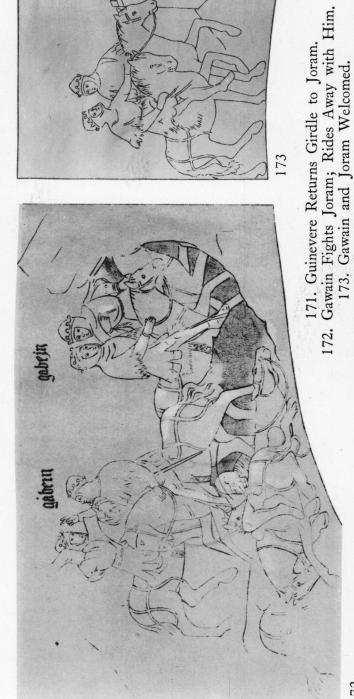

172

171. Guinevere Returns Girdle to Joram.
172. Gawain Fights Joram; Rides Away with Him.
173. Gawain and Joram Welcomed.
MURALS, RUNKELSTEIN. C.1400. AFTER WALDSTEIN.

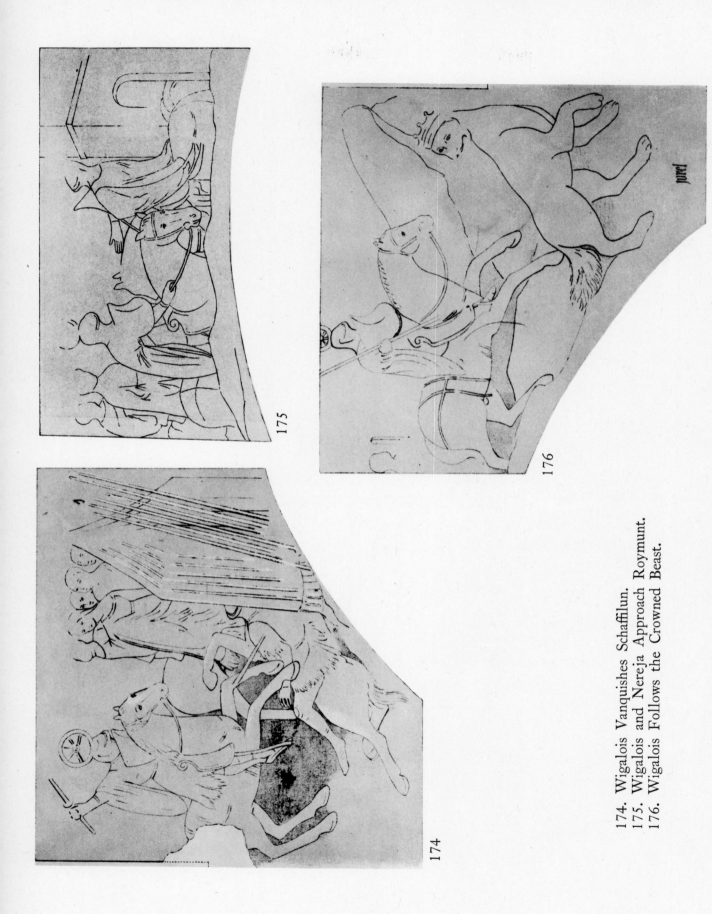

175

176

174

174. Wigalois Vanquishes Schaffilun.
175. Wigalois and Nereja Approach Roymunt.
176. Wigalois Follows the Crowned Beast.

MURALS, RUNKELSTEIN. C.1400. AFTER WALDSTEIN.

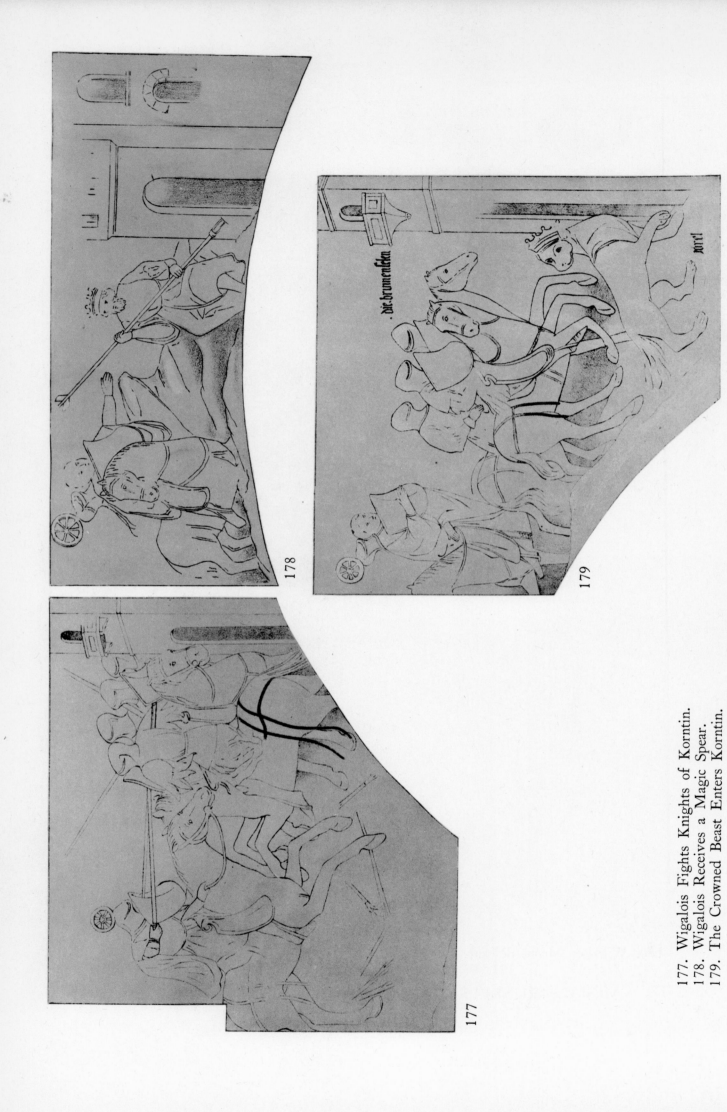

177. Wigalois Fights Knights of Korntin.
178. Wigalois Receives a Magic Spear.
179. The Crowned Beast Enters Korntin.

MURALS, RUNKELSTEIN. C.1400. AFTER WALDSTEIN.

180

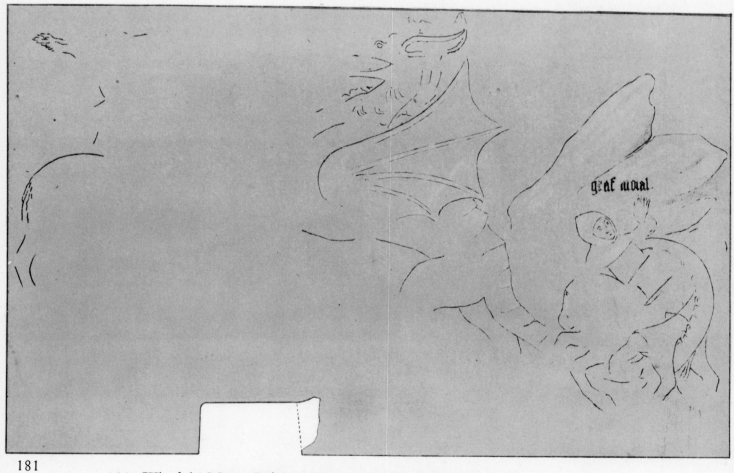

181

180. Wigalois Meets Belekar, Whose Husband Has Been Slain by a Dragon.
181. Wigalois Encounters Dragon.

MURALS, RUNKELSTEIN. *C.*1400. AFTER WALDSTEIN.

182

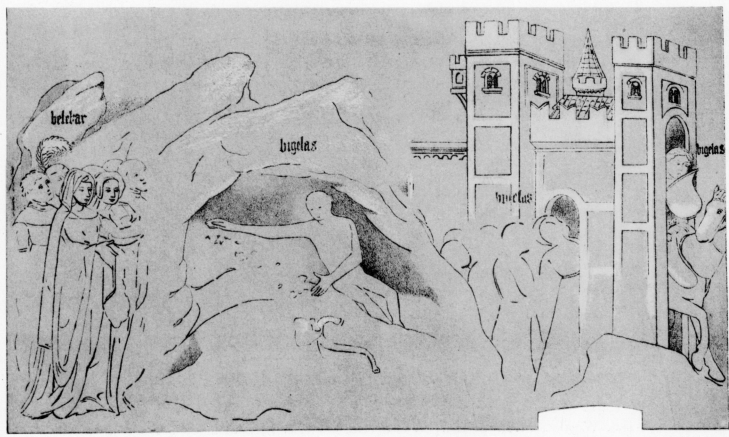

183

182. Wigalois Is Stripped by Fisherman and His Wife.
183. Wigalois Is Discovered and Entertained by Belekar.

MURALS, RUNKELSTEIN. *C.*1400. AFTER WALDSTEIN.

184. GARELSAAL, RUNKELSTEIN.

186. Karabin Comes before Arthur.

185. Arthur Points at Meleagant and Guinevere.

MURALS, RUNKELSTEIN. C.1400.

188. Garel Unhorses Gerhart.

187. Garel Follows Karabin to Merkanie.

MURALS, RUNKELSTEIN. *C*.1400.

189

190

191

192

189. Garel and the Dwarf King.
191. Duzabel Welcomed by Her Father.

190. Duzabel Thanks Garel.
192. Garel Fights Vulgan.

MURALS, RUNKELSTEIN. *C.*1400. COPIES BY SEELOS.

193

194

195

193. Garel Welcomed by Laudamie.   194. Garel Receives Homage.
195. Garel Takes Hand of Malseron.
MURALS, RUNKELSTEIN. *C.*1400. AFTER SEELOS.

196. Giants and Tjofrit before Tent of Ekunaver.
MURAL, RUNKELSTEIN. *C.*1400.

197. MURAL, RUNKELSTEIN. *C.*1400. BATTLE BETWEEN GAREL AND EKUNAVER.

198. MURAL, RUNKELSTEIN. *C.*1400. GAREL DEFEATS KAY. AFTER SEELOS.

199. MURAL, RUNKELSTEIN. *C.*1400. GAREL WELCOMED BY ARTHUR.

200. MURAL, RUNKELSTEIN. *C.*1400. GAREL AT ARTHUR'S ROUND TABLE.

201. MURAL, RUNKELSTEIN. *C.* 1400. GAREL'S RETURN.

203. f. 5ᵛ. Tristram and Ysolt. The Love Grotto.

202. f. 3ᵛ. Cliges and Fenice. The Doctors.
FR. 2186. *ROMAN DE LA POIRE*. C.1260. N.FRENCH SCHOOL.

204. Fr. 12576, f. 261. *Conte del Gral. C.*1250.   206-207. Brussels, 9627, f. 139ᵛ, f. 140. *Mort Artu.*

205. Fr. 110, f. 405. Galahad Comes to Arthur's Court. He Draws the Sword.

FLEMISH OR N. FRENCH SCHOOL. *C.*1250-1280.

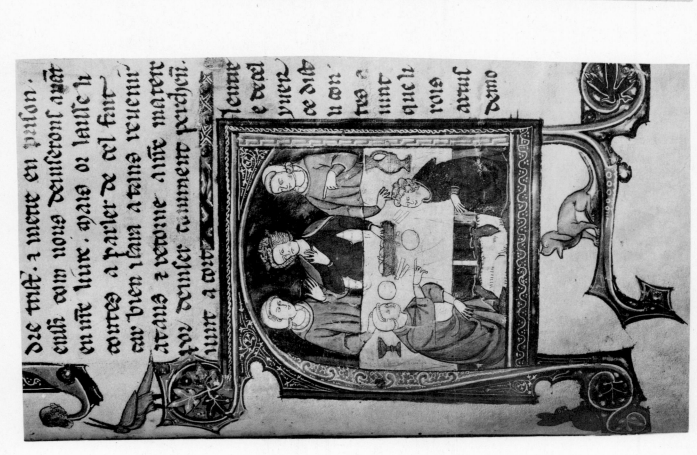

209. f. 271ᵛ. Dinadan's Harper Before Mark.

208. f. 231. Arthur Awaits an Adventure.

FR. 776. TRISTAN. C.1280. FLEMISH OR N.FRENCH SCHOOL.

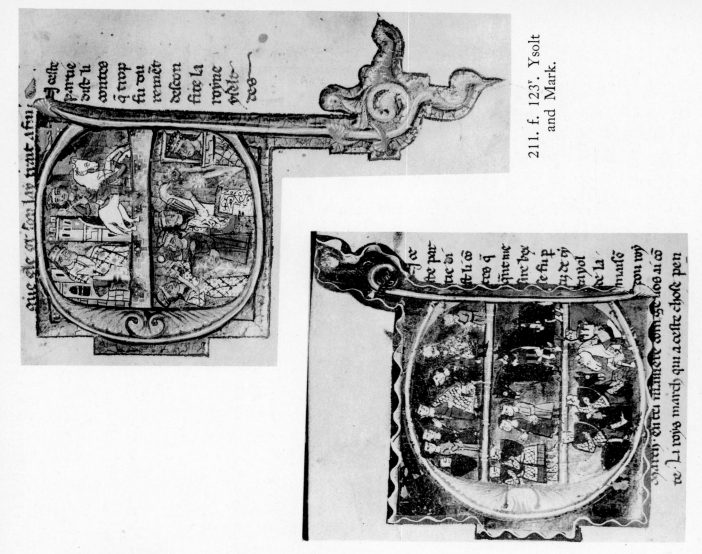

211. f. 123ᵛ. Ysolt and Mark.

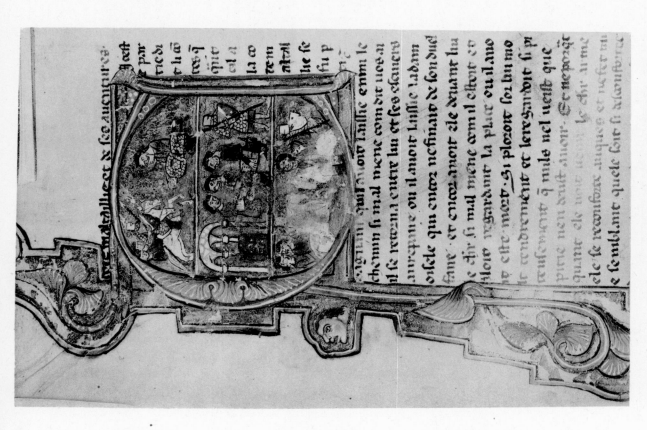

212. f. 287ᵛ. Mark and Andred.

210. f. 42ᵛ. Chevalier à la Cote Mal Taillée and the Body of Lyas.

FR. 750. TRISTAN. DATED 1278. SPANISH SCHOOL.

213

A' biaus sire der le ces souies
uous gars su'. ne demou
va gaires que il sen dort. Et qn't
li sains uaissiaus or grant piece de

maint en autun grant pechiet dont
il onqes ne se sist conses dot il est par
auenture coupaulet enus nostre seig
nour. si que il ne li plaist mie que il

214

Percheuaus regarde le lit et
auise. tant que il set bien q
il git dedens v hom v feme.
mais il ne set li ques. car il ot couuert
le tus dune touaile blanche. z delise

car il uent agist mierueille ceste cose
z uoit quant la messe su cantee que
li prestres prist entre ses mais corpu
domini z le porta a celui ki gisoit el
lit. z li douna aster z maintenant q

213. f. 77. Lancelot's Vision of the Sick Knight. 214. f. 84ᵛ. Perceval and the Maimed King.
FR. 342. DATED 1274. N. FRENCH SCHOOL.

ors regardent entraus qui
elr il sont · et truevent kil
sont xxxij par conte · cascus
monte sor son ceval · 7 puis prendet

si mal atorne kil na mestier de mu...
car il est navres amort · 7 li aut...
ki apres venoient · se fierent ent...
les autres · si en abatent pte · Et

215

pres cou q̃ maistres gautiers map
or portraite des aventures del
graal asses soufisaument si cõ il

il auoit les proeces ramenteues ·
en son liure · et pote recomencha
il ceste dairaine prtie · Et quãt

216

215. f. 186. Lancelot Rescues Guinevere.   216. f. 150. Return of Bors. King Henry and Map.
FR. 342. DATED 1274. N. FRENCH SCHOOL.

217. BONN, 526, f. 1. SCENES FROM THE *ESTOIRE*. DATED 1286. N. FRENCH SCHOOL.

218. f. 57ᵛ. Alain Heals the Leprous King.
220. f. 211ᵛ. Lancelot Fights the Copper Men.
222. f. 415ᵛ. Lancelot Insane.

219. f. 306. Lancelot Tourneys.
221. f. 400. Bors in the Palace Adventurous.
223. f. 483. Guinevere Seeks Refuge.

BONN, 526. DATED 1286. N. FRENCH SCHOOL.

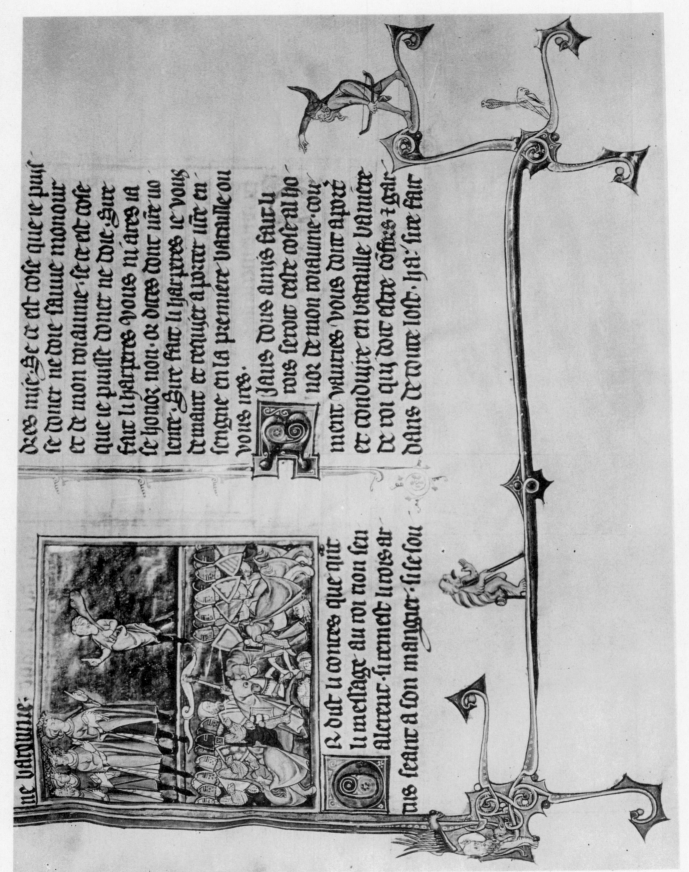

224. f. 327ᵛ. Merlin as a Boy. Merlin Carries the Pendragon.
FR. 95. *ESTOIRE, MERLIN.* C.1290. N.FRENCH SCHOOL.

227

228

225

226

225. f. 6. Descent from Cross. Christ's Burial.
226. f. 223. Merlin Dictates to Blaise.

227. f. 4ᵛ. The Hermit and the Beast.
The Man Possessed.
228. f. 59. Celidoine and the Lion Set Adrift.

FR. 95. ESTOIRE, MERLIN. C.1290. N.FRENCH SCHOOL.

229

230

231

232

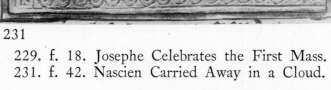

229. f. 18. Josephe Celebrates the First Mass.
231. f. 42. Nascien Carried Away in a Cloud.

230. f. 99ᵛ. Chanaan Kills His Brothers.
232. f. 100. Symeu. Chanaan Buried Alive.

FR. 95. *ESTOIRE, MERLIN. C.*1290. N.FRENCH SCHOOL.

233

234

235

236

233. f. 113ᵛ. Council of Demons. Conception of Merlin.   235. f. 159ᵛ. Arthur Draws the Sword. Coronation.
234. f. 138ᵛ. The Triple Death.   236. f. 173ᵛ. Arthur in Battle.

FR. 95. *ESTOIRE, MERLIN. C.*1290. N.FRENCH SCHOOL.

237

238

239

237-238. Rylands, Fr. 1, f. 114ᵛ. The Knights Tell of Their Quests.
f. 77. Lancelot with His Ancestor's Head. C. 1316.
239. Fr. 95, f. 291. Arthur and Ban Plan a Tourney. C. 1290.
N. FRENCH SCHOOL.

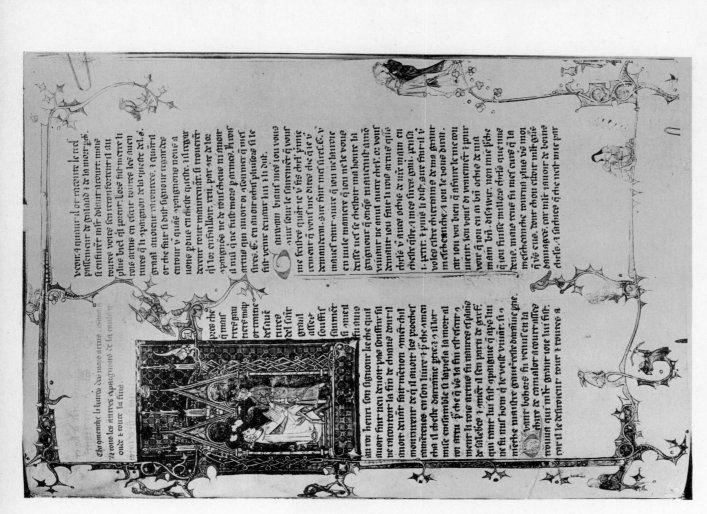

240. Rylands, Fr. 2, f. 212. King Henry and Map. 241. Royal 14 E III, f. 140. King Henry and Map.

N. FRENCH SCHOOL. C.1316.

243

244

245

la ueille de la pentecou
ste q̃nt tout li compaig
non de la table ronde fu
rent uenu a camaelot τ il oient
on le seruice il fisent mettre les ta

242. Royal 14 E III, f. 89. Arthur's Feast.
243-244. Royal 14 E III, f. 125. Solomon's Ship. f. 78ᵛ. The Divine Stag.
245. Add. 10294, f. 89. Arthur on the Wheel of Fortune.

N. FRENCH SCHOOL. *C.*1316.

246

247

248

249

246. Royal 14 E III, f. 153ᵛ. Maid of Astolat.
248. Add. 10292, f. 55ᵛ· The Duchess Flegetine
Orders Three Tombs. Tomb Dated 1316.

247. Add. 10294, f. 65ᵛ· The Maid of Astolat.
249. Add. 10294, f. 94. Excalibur.

N. FRENCH SCHOOL. *C.* 1316.

250

251

250. f. 161ᵛ. Lancelot Opens Ancestor's Tomb.   251. f. 158. Lancelot Rides in the Cart.
FORMER YATES THOMPSON MS. *LANCELOT.* C.1300–1320. N.FRENCH SCHOOL.

252. f. 166. Lancelot on the Sword Bridge.   253. f. 207. Gawain and Hector in the Perilous Cemetery.
FORMER YATES THOMPSON MS. *LANCELOT.* C.1300-1320. N.FRENCH SCHOOL.

252

253

254

255

256

257

258

254. f. 123ᵛ. Balin and the Damsel.   255. f. 97ᵛ. Arthur Sets the Children Adrift.

256. f. 185. Merlin and His Love.

257. f. 193. Arthur Hunting a Stag.   258. Fr. 24403, f. 119. *Erec.* The White Hart.

254-257. HUTH *MERLIN*. ADD. 38117. *C.*1300-1325. N.FRENCH SCHOOL.

259

260

259. f. 60. A Wedding.   260. f. 67ᵛ. Ivain and the Hospitable Host.
FR. 1433. *L'ATRE PERILLEUX, IVAIN*. *C*.1300-1325. FRENCH SCHOOL.

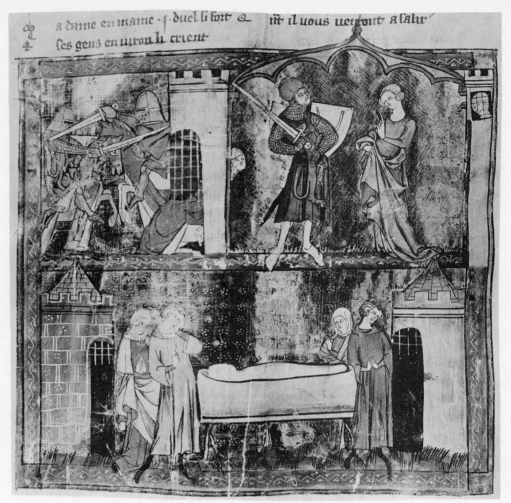

261

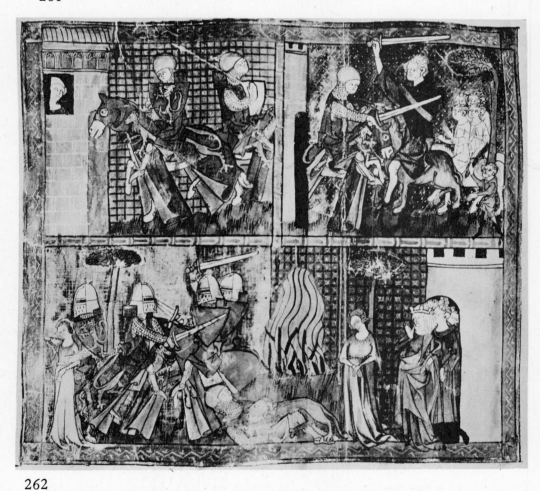

262

261. f. 69ᵛ. Ivain Kills Esclados. Lunete. Funeral of Esclados.
262. f. 90. Lunete in Prison. Ivain Vanquishes the Giant. Rescue of Lunete.
FR. 1433. *IVAIN*. C.1300-1325. FRENCH SCHOOL.

L comment te romuans de per
aucntures qui tuaindrent. &c co

ceual le galois. or deuse de moule de
ment il conquesta les armes vmeilles

263. f. 1. Perceval Meets Arthur's Knights. He Leaves His Mother. He Kills the Red Knight.
FR. 12577. *CONTE DEL GRAAL.* C.1330. FRENCH SCHOOL.

264

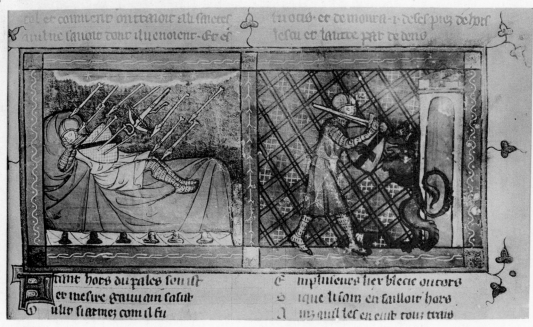

265

266

264. f. 18ᵛ. Perceval at the Grail Castle. 265. f. 45. Gawain on the Perilous Bed. A Lion.
266. f. 169. Perceval and His Sister. Perceval Confesses to a Hermit.
FR. 12577. *CONTE DEL GRAAL.* C.1330. FRENCH SCHOOL.

267. f. 1. Lancelot on the Sword-Bridge. He fights with Meleagant.
FR. 122. *LANCELOT.* DATED 1344. FRENCH SCHOOL.

268. f. 137ᵛ. Lancelot Releases the Prisoners from the Magic Carole.
FR. 122. *LANCELOT*. DATED 1344. FRENCH SCHOOL.

270

271

272

269. f. 50. Tristram's Life Saved by Irish King.
271. f. 71. The Departure from Ireland.

270. f. 85. The Questing Beast.
272. f. 95ᵛ. Mark Receives the Horn of Chastity.

FR. 100. *TRISTAN. C.*1402. FRENCH SCHOOL.

273

275

274

276

273. Fr. 100, f. 242. The Castle of Morgan le Fay.
274. Fr. 101, f. 43ᵛ. Perceval at Galehaut's Tomb.

275. Fr. 101, f. 307ᵛ. Perceval and the Recluse.
276. Fr. 101, f. 383ᵛ. Mark Slays Tristram.

FR. 100-101. *TRISTAN*. C.1402. FRENCH SCHOOL.

sub le col de son cheual z lemporta Siuarto

F Sist le conte que qit le roi marc out mengie z ceulo de son hostel · Jls sen aletent la

277

Il dit quil a a nom Galaad.

Pchaz ment aemourt lenfant entre lba

279

278

277. Fr. 335, f. 57. Blyoberis Overthrows Segurades.   279. Ars. 3480, f. 360. Bors Sees the Child Galahad.
278. Fr. 335, f. 1. Luce de Gast and His Book. *Tristan.* Dated 1399.
FRENCH SCHOOL. *C.*1399-1420.

282

283

280

281

280. Fr. 120. f. 520. The Crucifixion and Joseph of Arimathea (?).
281. Ars. 3480. p. 508. Galahad at the Castle of Maidens.
282. Ars. 3480. p. 508. Galahad Overthrows Seven Knights.
283. Ars. 3480. p. 525. Perceval Slays a Dragon.

FRENCH SCHOOL, c. 1400-1420.

284

la fece sur la sur et cecor sue trune z moustresaue

Cheualiere du monde. si lest fist autout entout

285

La bille de la pontheon se quant les cheualiers de la

286

E meseur lanc et gauuian le cheuer de lat gaune.

R duk haultes quequant hups auns or us auaur la cucegau

285. Ars. 3480, p. 490. A Damsel Asks for Lancelot.   284. Ars. 3480, p. 377. Lancelot in Combat.
286. Fr. 120, f. 590v. Combat of Lancelot and Gawain.
Repainted, c.1460.

FRENCH SCHOOL. C.1400-1460.

287

288

287. Fr. 120, f. 524ᵛ. Galahad in the Siege Perilous. Repainted *c.*1460.
288. Fr. 357, f. 241, *Guiron*. Meliadus Meets the King of Scotland. *C.*1410-1430.

FRENCH SCHOOL.

289. f. 1. Christ Gives the *Estoire* to the Hermit.
FR. 96. *ESTOIRE. C.*1460. FRENCH SCHOOL.

291. f. 58. Joseph Crosses the Shield with His Blood.

290. f. 47. King Crudens and Joseph of Arimathea.

FR. 96. *ESTOIRE. C.1460.* FRENCH SCHOOL.

292. f. 561. Galahad Knighted. Galahad Achieves His Sword. A Royal Tourney.
FR. 99. *TRISTAN.* DATED 1463. FRENCH SCHOOL.

293

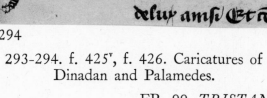

294

295

293-294. f. 425ᵛ, f. 426. Caricatures of Dinadan and Palamedes.

295. f. 563. Galahad in the Siege Perilous.

FR. 99. *TRISTAN.* DATED 1463. FRENCH SCHOOL.

296. f. 1. King Arthur. Lancelot and the Damsel. Galahad Knighted. Galahad in Siege Perilous.
CHANTILLY 317. *TRISTAN*. 1479-1480. FRENCH SCHOOL.

297

298

299

297. Fr. 112, vol. III, f. 193ᵛ. Arthur Beholds Lancelot's Paintings. Dated 1470. 298. Fr. 112, vol. I, f. 239. Tristram and Ysolt Drink the Potion. Dated 1470. 299. Brussels, 9246, f. 2. The *Estoire* Given to the Hermit. Dated 1480.

FRENCH SCHOOL.

300

301

300. f. 179. Joseph and Mordrain's Shield. 301. f. 37ᵛ. The Battle of Evalach.
BRUSSELS, 9246. *ESTOIRE*. DATED 1480. FRENCH SCHOOL.

302

303

302. f. 164. The Divine Stag.   303. f. 137. The Duchess Flegetine and the Men of Karabel.
BRUSSELS, 9246. *ESTOIRE*. DATED 1480. FRENCH SCHOOL.

304. f. 1. The Love Potion and the Return of the Bodies of the Lovers.
FR. 103. *TRISTAN. C.*1470. FRENCH SCHOOL.

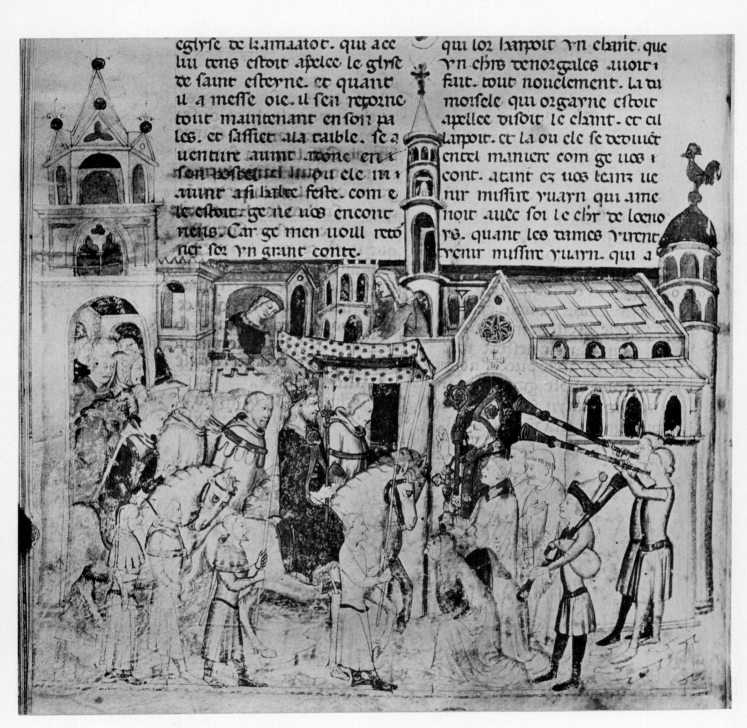

305. f. 221ᵛ. Arthur in Camelot.

ADD. 12228. *MELIADUS*. 1352-1362. ITALIAN SCHOOL.

306

307

308

306. f. 213. A Tourney.   307. f. 157. Meliadus and the King of Estrangore.
408. f. 202ᵛ. Meliadus with the Child Tristram. Merlin.

ADD. 12228. *MELIADUS*. 1352-1362. ITALIAN SCHOOL.

309

310

311

309. f. 223. A Knight of Meliadus Sings to Arthur.   310. f. 150. Preparations for a Tourney.

311. f. 187ᵛ. Meliadus and Mark in a Tournament.

ADD. 12228. *MELIADUS*. 1352-1362. ITALIAN SCHOOL.

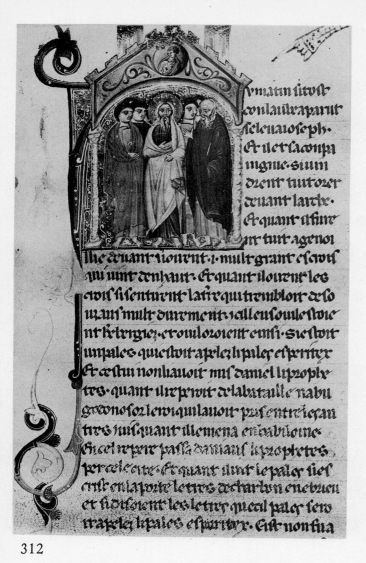

312

313

312-313. Douce 178, f. 20. Joseph of Arimathea.
f. 156ᵛ. King Vortigern. 1300-1325.

314. Chantilly 1111, f. 1. *Mort Artu.* C.1288.

ITALIAN SCHOOL.

315 316 317

318

319

315-317. Chantilly 1111, f. 33ᵛ, f. 51, f. 63ᵛ. Scenes from *Mort Artu.* C.1288.
318-319. Harl. 4389, f. 17, f. 42ᵛ. Scenes from *Tristan.* C.1300.
ITALIAN SCHOOL.

323

322

320

321

320. Fr. 760, f. 121. Mark Slays Tristram. *Tristram. C.1300.*   323. Berlin, Ham. 49, f. 19ᵛ. Lancelot Tourneys. *Lancelot. C.1300.*
321. Fr. 1463, f. 104. Tombs of the Lovers. *Tristan. C.1300.*   322. Berlin, Ham. 49, f. 3. Arthur and the Lady of the Lake.

ITALIAN SCHOOL.

324

325

324. f. 148. Ysolt Nurses Tristram.
325. f. 2ᵛ. Arthur Enthroned. Lancelot
and Guinevere.
FR. 755. *TRISTAN. C.*1330-1350. ITALIAN SCHOOL.

il noient la roine il sa genoille
tenant li. et se humilient tant co
il puent. et dient qil sont so chr.
en totes les choses qil porroient
faire a honor deli. et ele les en m

pam en tel maniere qe ie ñar
se le plus i int et tot le peior p
tie. et selone le mien senz di ge
dame qe a son ami doit len
doner vamor et a son ami por

326

d trop grant amor ne qil fust
ia loing de moi. fors qy sor moi
uenoit souent. et se ie eusse sa

faure siroit in cabut. tant ia des
autres meillors qy len ne me doit
metre en contre. vos aues en uue

ysenc.   royart.   pal. lañe.t.   arh. dv.un

327

326. f. 46ᵛ. Ysolt Receives Gaheris and Dinadan.
327. f. 115. Arthur's Pavilion.
FR. 755. *TRISTAN. C.*1330-1350. ITALIAN SCHOOL.

328. f. 28ᵛ. Perceval's Vision of the New Law and the Old Law.

FR. 343. *QUESTE.* C.1380-1400. ITALIAN SCHOOL.

329. f. 59ᵛ. The Death of Perceval's Sister.
FR. 343. QUESTE. C.1380-1400. ITALIAN SCHOOL.

330. f. 3. Galahad Comes to the Siege Perilous.
FR. 343. *QUESTE. C.*1380-1400. ITALIAN SCHOOL.

qui la uoulliseut lesser en uelle men
cit cet il nia pith que fest pruuie;
et ce seroit trop giunt dessoulautez qi
te ce les uouldroit requeir par soi ser
luois ge soi bien qe nos dites uoir.
ores li gnint amors qe ge auoie auoc
et as autiters me uoueues dire. Et
nefust inchaenable chose ne se auz
qe le uoulisse bien. Car trop me grena
li de partiment: de uos uouz. et des autre
epiguuous

Int ont pule entrauz. qe li toz fu
leuz a esclaus alisolauz or la auqs
abitue la rosee. et li palez comeu acu
plir des barons del rriaunnes. Et la rate
qi si fu leuee. et uint la ou li rois estoit
et dit sur cil. chez. nos atauder leauz
por aler ou messe. Atant se leua li rois.
li esinese; tans poroe qe cil qe leue
ront ne sachient le wel qil ot mene
Et mesite. Sau comade. qe len li aport
ses armes. et ausi fist lancelot. Et quit
il sunt arme. deleur armes senz des escu
et senz des haumes. se uient el palez.
a inouriert lor epiguuos qil estoient a
apuellie por aler ale glesse

Vant il furent uenu au mostier. et
il orent oi le suise tot. si arme ai
il estoient. et il furent retorne el palez
si salerent aseoir li uns de les autre. cil
qi compiguuos estoiet de la queste. Si
ur serlurois. Batemaguu au roi artu.
puis qe cest aferes est enpus si fiere
mat. qi ne puet mes estre leisiez. ielo
ezoie qe li sant fuissant apo te si uue
ront le seuremat ausi com cil font qi
enqiste touent entre. Ge le uoil bien
puis qil uos plest fer li rois. puis qil
ne puet estre. autremat.

Des furet as clere de leen: les sa
int apo tier. sor coi en fesoit le seu
mant de la cort. et qint il furent apo
te deuat le matir uouz. si apella li rois
mon seigneur. Sau. et ludit uos esine
ustes pmieremat ceste queste. Venez
auant et si ferez le seiremat qe cil
teuoient fere. qi en ceste queste uot

331. f. 7. The Knights Swear the Quest for the Grail.
FR. 343. *QUESTE. C.* 1380-1400. ITALIAN SCHOOL.

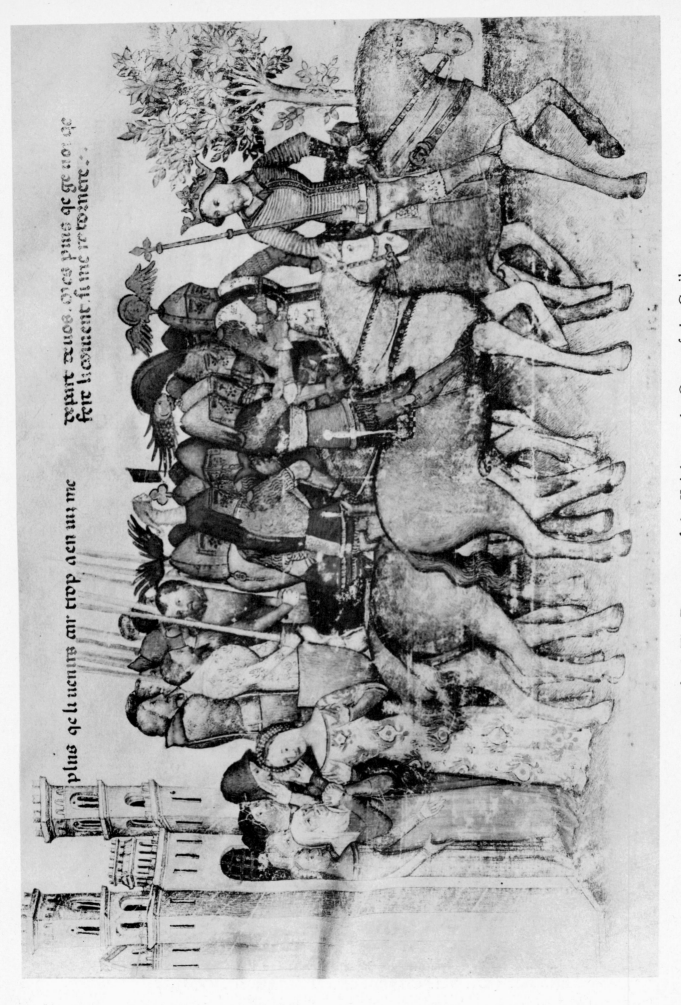

332. f. 8ᵛ. The Departure of the Knights on the Quest of the Grail.
FR. 343. *QUESTE.* C.1380-1400. ITALIAN SCHOOL.

333

334

333. f. 18. Lancelot's Vision of the
Sick Knight.
334. f. 103. The Maimed King Healed.
FR. 343. *QUESTE. C.*1380-1400. ITALIAN SCHOOL.

335. f. 2ᵛ. Arthur Receives Feramont and his Dwarf.

NOUV. ACQ. FR. 5243 *GUIRON*. C.1380-1400. ITALIAN SCHOOL.

336. f. 7. Gawain Saves Arthur's Life.

NOUV. ACQ. FR. 5243 *GUIRON*. C.1380-1400. ITALIAN SCHOOL.

337

illa sancti inchestri cosi como loro pero cherieso digna etitte queste cosse stameno apsso & ley alora litri

338

339

337. The Lady of the Lake.   338. The Maid of Astolat.   339. The Passing of Arthur.
FLORENCE, PAL. 556. DATED 1446. ITALIAN SCHOOL.

342

340

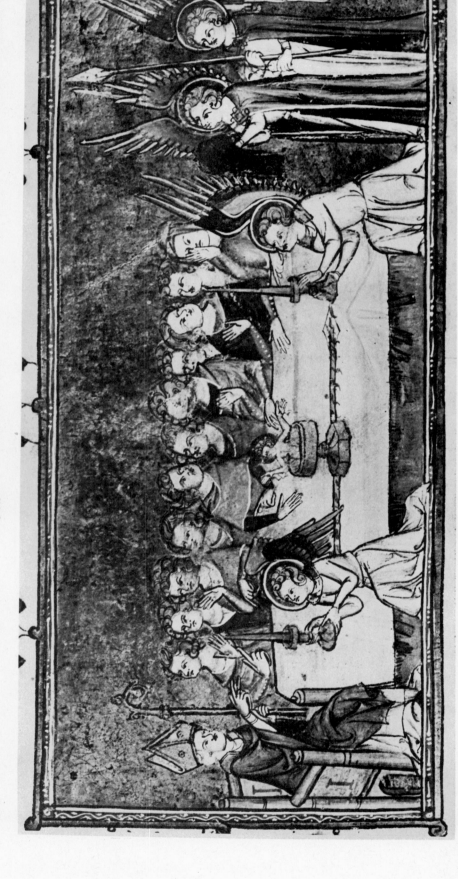

341

340. Douai, 880, f. 66ᵛ. *Hist. Reg. Brit.* Arthur and the Giant. Late XII Century.
341. Ars. 5218, f. 88. *Queste.* The Mysteries of the Grail. Dated 1351.
342. The Hague, MS XX, f. 163ᵛ. *Spiegel Historiael.* Arthur's Last Fight. Early XIV Century.

FLEMISH AND DUTCH SCHOOLS.

343

344

343. f. 39ᵛ. Marriage of Arthur. 344. f. 36ᵛ. Arthur's Army and the Saxons.
BRUSSELS, 9243. *CHRONIQUES DE HAINAUT*. DATED 1468. FLEMISH.

345

346

345. f. 42. Arthur Fights Frollo.
346. f. 45. Sports at Caerleon.
BRUSSELS, 9243. *CHRONIQUES DE HAINAUT*. DATED 1468. FLEMISH.

347

348

347. f. 49ᵛ. Arthur and the Giant of
Mont S. Michel.
348. f. 55ᵛ. Arthur's Army and the Romans.
BRUSSELS, 9243. *CHRONIQUES DE HAINAUT*. DATED 1468. FLEMISH.

349

351

350

349. f. 43ᵛ. The Red and White Dragons.   351. f. 66ᵛ. Arthur's Fight with Modred.

350. f. 54ᵛ. Coronation of Arthur.

LAMBETH 6. *ST. ALBAN'S CHRONICLE.* C.1470. FLEMISH SCHOOL.

352. Knights at the Chateau de l'Isle Perdue.
DOUCE 383. *GUIRON. C.*1480–1500. FLEMISH SCHOOL.

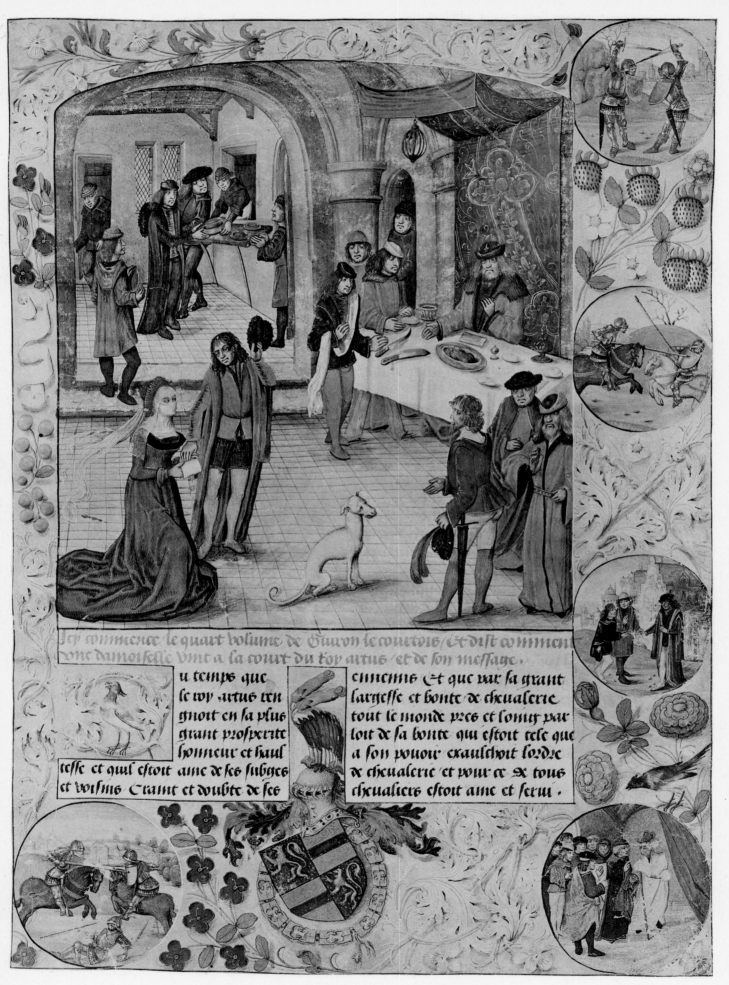

Iey commence le quart volume de Guiron le courtois / et dist comment
one damoiselle vint a la court du roy artus / et de son messaige.

u temps que
se roy artus ten
gnoit en sa plus
grant prosperite
honneur et haul
tesse et quil estoit ame de ses subgies
et voisins craint et doubte de ses

ennemis Et que par sa grant
largesse et bonte & cheualerie
tout le monde pres et lomg par
loit de sa bonte qui estoit tele que
a son pouoir exaulchoit lordre
& cheualerie et pour ce & tous
cheualiers estoit ame et serui .

353. A Damsel Comes to Arthur's Court.
DOUCE 383. *GUIRON. C.*1480-1500. FLEMISH SCHOOL.

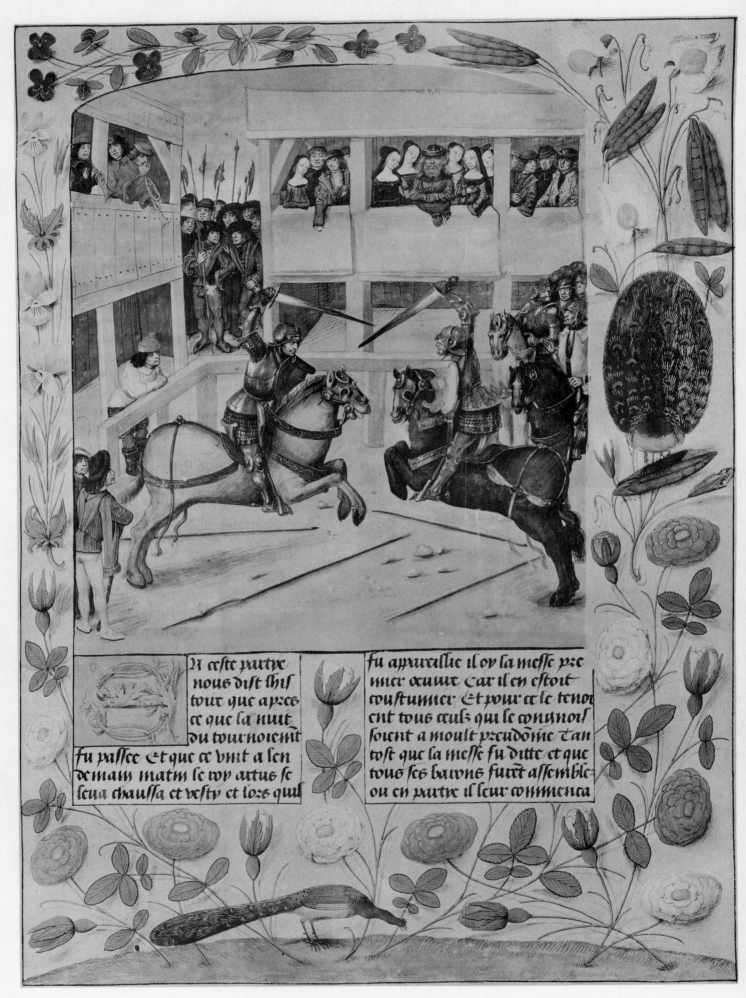

A ceste partie
nous dist lhis
toir que apres
ce que la nuit
du tournoiemt
fu passee Et que ce vmt a sen
demam matm le roy artus se
leua chaussa et vestu et loes quil

fu appareillie il oy la messe pre
mier oeuure Car il en estoit
coustumier Et pour ce le tenoi
ent tous ceulx qui se congnoif
soient a moult preudome tan
tost que la messe fu ditte et que
tous ses barons furet assemble
ou en partie il seur commenca

354. A Tournament before Arthur.
DOUCE 383. *GUIRON*. *C*.1480-1500. FLEMISH SCHOOL.

355. f. 49. Reconciliation of Gawain and Gramoflanz. 356. f. 49v. Wedding Feast. Perceval and Feirefis.

MUNICH, CGM. 19. *PARZIVAL. C.1250. GERMAN SCHOOL.*

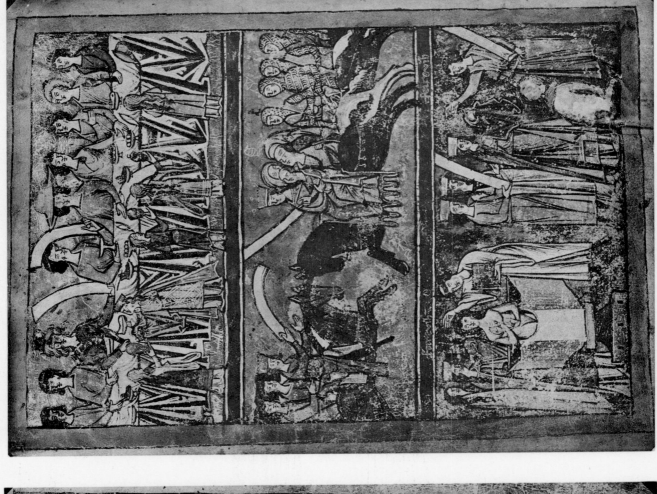

358. f. 50ᵛ. The Grail Feast. Perceval and Kondwiramur.
Feirefis Baptized.

357. f. 50. Perceval and Kundrie.

MUNICH, CGM. 19. *PARZIVAL. C.*1250. GERMAN SCHOOL.

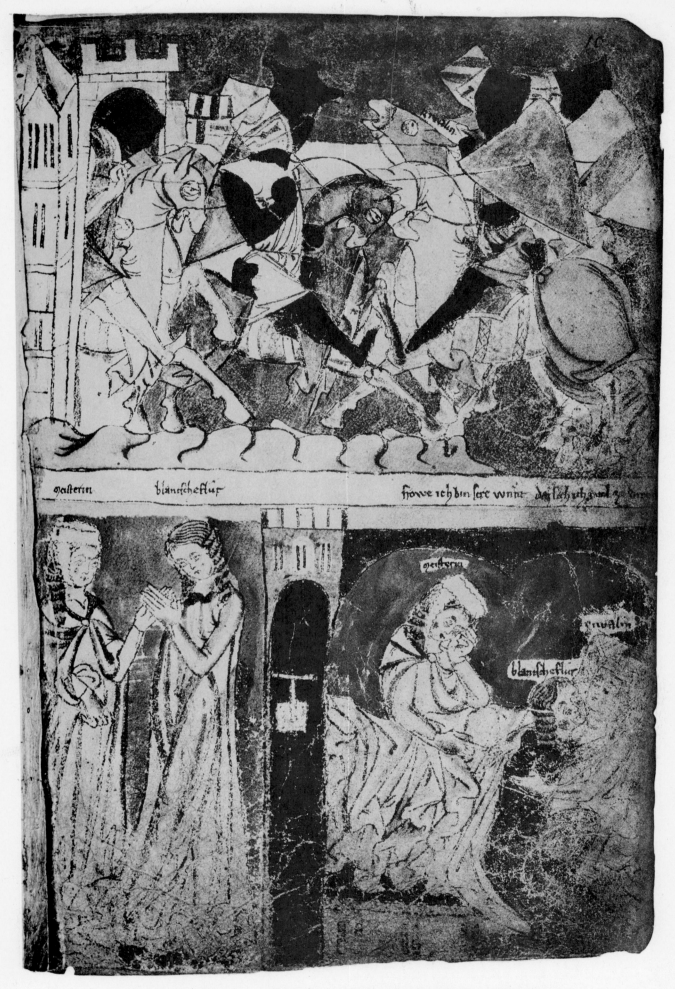

359. f. 10. Rivalon in a Tourney. Blanchefleur and her *Meisterin*.
MUNICH, CGM. 51. *TRISTAN*. C.1300. GERMAN SCHOOL.

360. f. 11. Rivalon and Blanchefleur Return to Brittany.
MUNICH, CGM. 51. *TRISTAN. C.*1300. GERMAN SCHOOL.

362. f. 15ᵛ. Scenes from the Youth of Tristram.

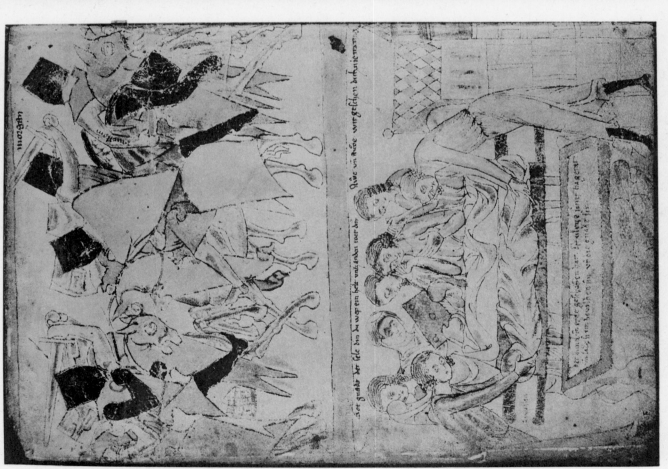

361. f. 11ᵛ. Rivalon's Death and Burial.

MUNICH, CGM. 51. *TRISTAN.* C.1300. GERMAN SCHOOL.

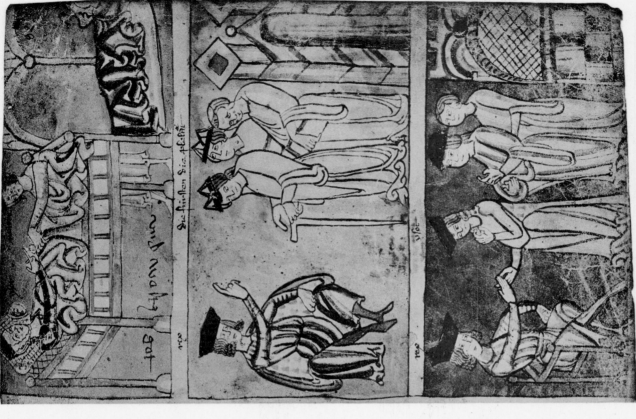

364. f. 82. Mark and Ysolt. The Prelates. Ysolt's Oath Concerning the Ordeal.

363. f. 67. Tristram, the Dragon, and the False Seneschal.

MUNICH, CGM. 51. *TRISTAN. C.*1300. GERMAN SCHOOL.

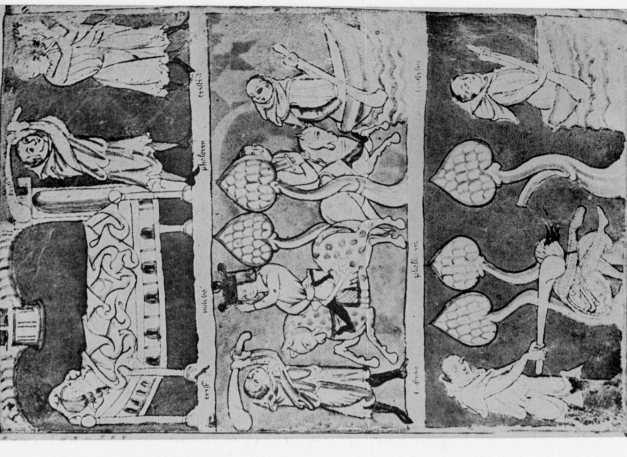

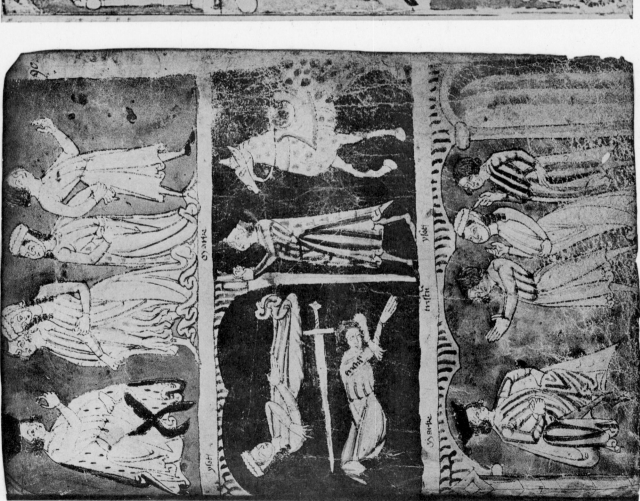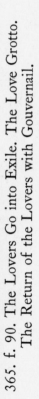

365. f. 90. The Lovers Go into Exile. The Love Grotto.
The Return of the Lovers with Gouvernail.

366. f. 104. Tristram's Deeds as a Fool.

MUNICH, CGM. 51. *TRISTAN. C.1300.* GERMAN SCHOOL.

368. f. 28ᵛ. Wigalois Visits the Tent of the Red Knight.
LEYDEN, 537. *WIGALOIS.* DATED 1372. GERMAN SCHOOL.

367. f. 1. Arthur's Round Table.

Pes en wartt in micht kern   Von den luiten uber al
Wan li lin selle her gedacht   Wart da eyn peinlich schal
Do wurden lie zu lamene bracht   Sie clageten alle des ritters val

369

370

369. f. 36ᵛ. Wigalois Fights the Red Knight.
370. f. 47ᵛ. Wigalois and the Crowned Beast.
LEYDEN, 537. *WIGALOIS.* DATED 1372. GERMAN SCHOOL.

371

372

371. f. 51ʳ. Wigalois Comforts Beleare.
372. f. 64. Wigalois Hides in a Cave.
LEYDEN, 537. *WIGALOIS*. DATED 1372. GERMAN SCHOOL.

373. f. 79. The Wife of Roaz the Enchanter.
The Combat of Wigalois and Roaz.

374. f. 118. The Scribe, Jan van Brunswik.

LEYDEN, 537. *WIGALOIS*. DATED 1372. GERMAN SCHOOL.

375

376

378

377

379

375. Pal. germ. 371, f. 2. *Lanzelot*. Dated 1420.
376. Pal. germ. 346, f. 118. *Tristan*. C.1460.
377. Pal. germ. 339, f. 27. *Parzival*. 1440-1450.

378. Dresden, M66, f. 146. *Parzival*. 1440-1450.
379. Vienna, 2914, f. 359. *Parzival*. 1440-1450.

GERMAN SCHOOL.

381. f. 56. Perceval Overthrows Kay.
Perceval's Love Trance.

380. f. 29ᵛ. Perceval Kills the Red Knight and
Puts on His Armor.

BERNE, AA. 91. *PARZIVAL.* DATED 1467. GERMAN SCHOOL.

382. f. 118. Gawain on the Perilous Bed.　　383. f. 126. Gawain Plucks the Forbidden Branch.

BERNE, AA. 91. *PARZIVAL.* DATED 1467. GERMAN SCHOOL.

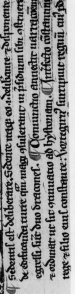

384. Cotton Claud. B VII, f. 224. *Prophetia Merlini.*   385. Royal 20 A II, f. 3. Langtoft's Chronicle.   386. Royal 20 A II, f. 3ᵛ.
Late XIII Century. Merlin and Vortigern.   1307–1330. Vortigern's Court. His Death.   King Arthur.

ENGLISH SCHOOL.

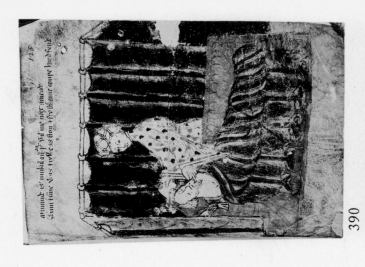

390

391

389

387-388. Egerton 3028. *Brut. C.*1350.
387. f. 25. The White and Red Dragons.
388. f. 25. The Building of Stonehenge.
389-391. Cotton Nero A X. 1390-1400.
389. f. 94ᵛ. The Decapitated Green Knight.
390. f. 129. Gawain Visited by His Host's Wife.
391. f. 129ᵛ. Gawain at the Green Chapel.

ENGLISH SCHOOL.

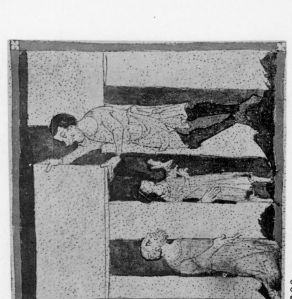

387

388

392. Pasted in MS. Fr. 4985. *C*.1470.   393. Stadtbibliothek, Berne, S 1947 m. *C*.1475.

WOODCUTS OF ARTHUR, NINE WORTHIES SERIES.

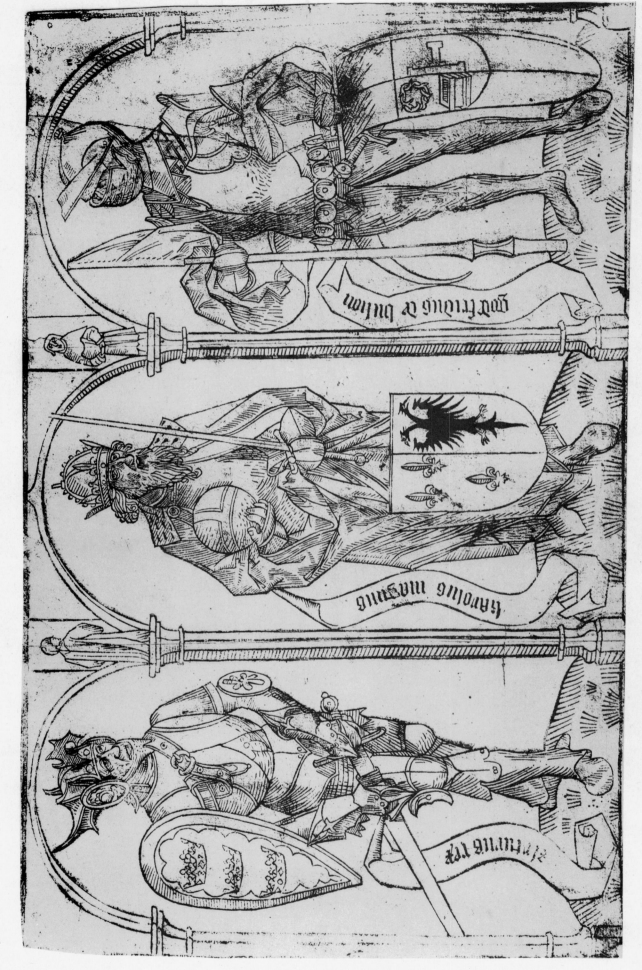

394. WOODCUT, KUNSTHALLE, HAMBURG. C.1490. THE THREE CHRISTIAN WORTHIES.

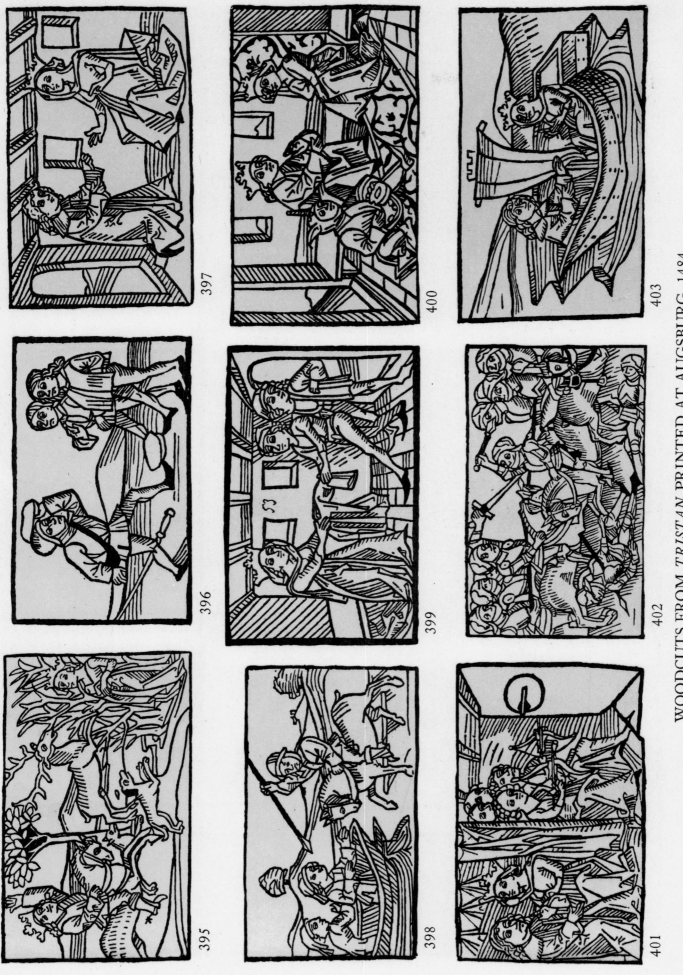

395 396 397 398 399 400 401 402 403

WOODCUTS FROM *TRISTAN* PRINTED AT AUGSBURG, 1484.

404. WOODCUT FROM DUPRÉ'S *LANCELOT*, ROUEN, 1488. THE ROUND TABLE.

A Beille de sa pen
thecouste que les
compaignons de
sa table ronde su
rent venus a ka
masot a ilz eurêt
ouy se seruice. Ai
si que on boufoit
mettre les tables a heure de nonne: entra en sa
court Bne moult belle damoiselle a cheual q̃
moult fort se stoit hastee a bien y apparoit / car
son palefroy estoit tout tressuant. Elle descê

dit: puis mõta en sa sale ou estoit le roy a tous
les compaignons. Si Bint deuât le roy a le
salua / a le roy sui rendit son salut moult cour
toisemêt. Sire pour dieu sist elle dictes moy
se lancelot est ceans. Oup certes damoiselle
veez le sa. Si sui monstra / a elle asa inconti
nent celle part ou il estoit / puis sui dist. Lan
celot ie Bous dy de par le roy perles que Bous
Biengniez auec moy iusques a celle forest. Et
il sui demanda a qui elle estoit. Je suis sist el
le a celui de qui ie Bous parse. Et quel besoig
dist il auez Bous de moy / ce Berrez Bous Bien

405. WOODCUT FROM VÉRARD'S *LANCELOT*, PARIS, 1494. THE SIEGE PERILOUS.

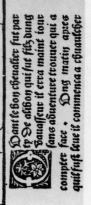

407. *Tristan*, 1494-1495. The Tourney of Louzeph.

406. *Lancelot*, 1494. Conquest of the Dolorous Garde.

WOODCUTS FROM VÉRARD'S INCUNABULA.

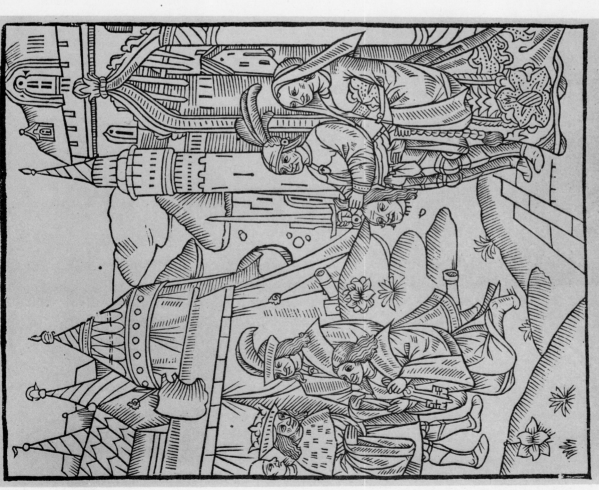

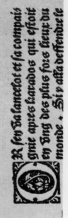

409. Jacques de Besançon's Miniature over Fig. 408.

WOODCUT AND PAINTED WOODCUT.

408. Lancelot, 1494. Arthur Receives Keys of Dolorous Tower.

411

410. Lancelot and the Head of His Grandfather. 411. The *Val sans Retour.* 412. Bors and Hermit.
MINIATURES IN VELLUM COPY OF VÉRARD'S *LANCELOT.* 1494.

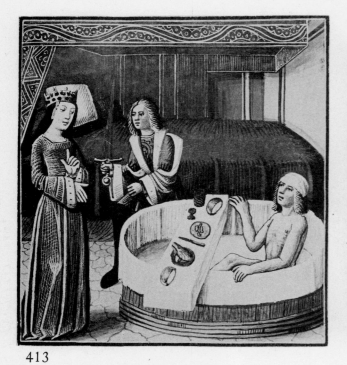

413

415

414

416

Miniatures. Vél. 623. *Tristan*. 1494-1495.
413. f. 37. Tristram in the Bath.
414. f. 136. Shepherds at Fountain.

Woodcuts, *Morte d'Arthur*. 1498.
415. Balin Draws Sword.
416. Gareth Enters Arthur's Hall.

LATE XV CENTURY BOOK ILLUSTRATION.

417

419

418

420

417. Nineve Enchants Merlin.
418. The Birth of Tristram.

419. The Madness of Lancelot.
420. Lancelot in the Cart.

WOODCUTS, WYNKYN DE WORDE'S *MORTE D'ARTHUR*. 1498.